TY

P9-DMI-018

PERFECTING PREGNANCY

Prenatal and preimplantation testing technologies have offered unprecedented access to information about the genetic and congenital makeup of our prospective progeny. Future developments such as preconception testing, noninvasive prenatal testing, and more extensive preimplantation testing promise to increase that access further still. The result may be greater reproductive choice, but it also increases the burden on women and men to avail themselves of these technologies in order to avoid having a child who has a disability. The overwhelming question for legislators has been whether and, if so, how to regulate the use of these technologies in the face of compelling but seemingly contradictory claims about the advancement of reproductive choice and the dangers of eugenic or discriminatory effects. This book examines the evolution of this legislative oversight across a number of jurisdictions and explores the tensions and ambiguities that inform these laws.

Isabel Karpin is a Professor in the Faculty of Law, University of Technology, Sydney.

Kristin Savell is an Associate Professor in the Faculty of Law, University of Sydney.

Cambridge Disability Law and Policy Series

The Disability Law and Policy series examines these topics in interdisciplinary and comparative terms. The books in the series reflect the diversity of definitions, causes, and consequences of discrimination against persons with disabilities while illuminating fundamental themes that unite countries in their pursuit of human rights laws and policies to improve the social and economic status of persons with disabilities. The series contains historical, contemporary, and comparative scholarship crucial to identifying individual, organizational, cultural, attitudinal, and legal themes necessary for the advancement of disability law and policy.

The book topics covered in the series also are reflective of the new moral and political commitment by countries throughout the world toward equal opportunity for persons with disabilities in such areas as employment, housing, transportation, rehabilitation, and individual human rights. The series will thus play a significant role in informing policy makers, researchers, and citizens of issues central to disability rights and disability antidiscrimination policies. The series grounds the future of disability law and policy as a vehicle for ensuring that those living with disabilities participate as equal citizens of the world.

Books in the Series

Ruth Colker, *When Is Separate Unequal? A Disability Perspective*, 2009

Larry M. Logue and Peter Blanck, *Race, Ethnicity, and Disability: Veterans and Benefits in Post–Civil War America*, 2010

Lisa Vanhala, *Making Rights a Reality? Disability Rights Activists and Legal Mobilization*, 2010

Alicia Ouellette, *Bioethics and Disability: Toward a Disability-Conscious Bioethics*, 2011

Eilionoir Flynn, *From Rhetoric to Action: Implementing the UN Convention on the Rights of Persons with Disabilities*, 2011

Isabel Karpin and Kristin Savell, *Perfecting Pregnancy: Law, Disability, and the Future of Reproduction*, 2012

PERFECTING PREGNANCY

Law, Disability, and the Future of Reproduction

Isabel Karpin

University of Technology, Sydney

Kristin Savell

University of Sydney

CAMBRIDGE UNIVERSITY PRESS
Cambridge, New York, Melbourne, Madrid, Cape Town,
Singapore, São Paulo, Delhi, Mexico City

Cambridge University Press
32 Avenue of the Americas, New York, NY 10013-2473, USA

www.cambridge.org
Information on this title: www.cambridge.org/9780521765206

© Isabel Karpin and Kristin Savell 2012

This publication is in copyright. Subject to statutory exception
and to the provisions of relevant collective licensing agreements,
no reproduction of any part may take place without the written
permission of Cambridge University Press.

First published 2012

Printed in the United States of America

A catalog record for this publication is available from the British Library.

Library of Congress Cataloging in Publication data
Karpin, Isabel.
    Perfecting pregnancy : law, disability, and the future of reproduction / Isabel Karpin,
    Kristin Savell.
       p.   cm. – (Cambridge disability law and policy series)
    Includes bibliographical references and index.
    ISBN 978-0-521-76520-6 (hardback) – ISBN 978-0-521-75839-0 (paperback)
    1. Human reproduction – Law and legislation   2. Pregnancy – Law and legislation.
    3. Pregnant women – Legal status, laws, etc.   I. Savell, Kristin, 1968–   II. Title.
    K3611.A77K37   2012
    344.04'19–dc23   2011050126

ISBN 978-0-521-76520-6 Hardback

Cambridge University Press has no responsibility for the persistence or accuracy of URLs
for external or third-party Internet Web sites referred to in this publication and does not
guarantee that any content on such Web sites is, or will remain, accurate or appropriate.

Contents

Acknowledgments

We share responsibility for this book as a whole as each chapter is the collaborative effort of both authors. However, Kristin took primary responsibility for writing Chapters 1, 3, and 5 while Isabel took primary responsibility for writing Chapters 2, 4, and 6.

Our very special thanks must go to Laura Crommelin, Andrew Dyer, Claire Deakin, Lauren Hustler, and Eloise Chandler, who worked as our research assistants during the development and writing of this book. We are immensely grateful for their patience and commitment. Thanks also to the clinicians and regulators who gave up their valuable time to speak with us so candidly about their experiences with the law and testing technologies. They gave us special insights that would not otherwise have been accessible.

The research for this book was supported by an Australian Research Council Discovery Grant (DP0988103), and we would especially like to thank Janice Mountford and Terry Carney for assisting us with the preparation of the grant application. It should also be noted that the views expressed herein are those of the authors and are not necessarily those of the Australian Research Council.

We would also like to thank a number of our colleagues past and present who have provided a nurturing intellectual environment and the space to undertake this task. Jointly we thank Belinda Bennett, Marie Fox, and Emily Jackson for their intellectual generosity and Karen O'Connell for being a great friend and sounding board.

Acknowledgments

Kristin would like to thank other friends and colleagues at Sydney University – especially Cameron Stewart, Roger Magnusson, and David Rolph, who have all shown great enthusiasm for the project – and Mark Findlay and Terry Carney for sharing their wisdom and experience at critical times. She would also like to express gratitude to her students in the Masters of Health Law program at Sydney University, who have debated and challenged her on many of the issues raised here, and past mentors Carl Elliott, Shauna Van Praagh, Rene Provost, and Jeremy Webber for getting her started on the intellectual journey that led to this point.

Isabel would like to thank overseas friends and colleagues; Martha Fineman, an untiring mentor and inspirational feminist legal scholar who set her on an academic path; Roxanne Mykitiuk, a longtime collaborator, who first drew her attention to many of the issues raised in this book; and Sarah Franklin, Rosemary Hunter, Jeff Nisker, and Sally Sheldon for their exchange of ideas and intellectual support. Closer to home she would especially like to thank Jenni Millbank, collaborator, colleague, and friend across two universities (Sydney and UTS), and other UTS colleagues Anita Stuhmcke, Jill McKeough, Lesley Hitchens, and Laurie Berg, who provide support and encouragement on a daily basis. She would also like to express her gratitude to former Sydney University colleagues Reg Graycar, Julie Stubbs (now UNSW), and Helen Irving.

These friends, colleagues, and mentors have all, in various ways, supported and fostered our academic careers, and, without their support, we would not have been able to write this book. Our thanks too must go to our editor, John Berger, and the team at Cambridge University Press for their expertise in shepherding the manuscript through the editorial process. Finally, the authors would like to thank each other for a stimulating, productive, and richly rewarding collaboration.

On a personal note we must, of course thank each of our loving friends and family who have supported us both through thick and thin:

Acknowledgments

For Isabel: special thanks to Alwyn, Phyllis, Max, Angela, Zoe, Alex, Matthew, and especially my beloved David Ellison (with whom I have had the great privilege to write) and our darling children, Zach and Ondine.

For Kristin: special thanks to Margaret, Terry, Katrina, and Gemma. My deepest gratitude is to my partner, David, and our beautiful girls, Tara and Remy, for their unqualified love and support.

Introduction

WHY PERFECTING PREGNANCY?

Over the last twenty years there has been a proliferation of diagnostic technologies aimed at identifying and eliminating potential abnormalities in future children.[1] Alongside this rapid development in diagnostic technologies we can chart an equally rapid development in the technologies of "reproductive management." These include new tertiary degrees in genetic and prenatal counseling;[2] the new centrality of the role of the clinical geneticist;[3] the inclusion in laws, ethical guidelines,

[1] Prenatal testing technologies have expanded so that we now have on the horizon the potential to take a simple blood test to test for a number of disabilities including Down syndrome: see I. Sample, "Simple Blood Test for Down's Syndrome Is on Its Way, Say Scientists" *Guardian*, 6 March 2011: see http://www.guardian.co.uk/science/2011/mar/06/downs-syndrome-simple-test-in-pregnancy (accessed on 27 June 2011). Preimplantation Genetic Diagnosis (PGD) can now test for more than 150 different disorders: "PGD Conditions Listed by the HFEA": see http://www.hfea.gov.uk/cps/hfea/gen/pgd-screening.htm (accessed on 27 June 2011). Preconception testing is now able to identify more than 400 recessive genes for severe childhood disorders: National Health Service, "Gene Test 'Predicts 448 Child Diseases'": see http://www.nhs.uk/news/2011/01January/Pages/dna-gentic-test-for-parents-before-pregnancy.aspx (accessed on 27 June 2011).

[2] See the Human Genetics Society of Australasia, "Guidelines for Training and Certification in Genetic Counselling" 2010 GL/01, 20 February 2010 at 8.

[3] See, for instance, the Human Genetics Society of Australasia, "Guidance: Clinical Geneticist's Role" 2010 GD01, August 2010, which states: "Clinical

1

and clinical best practice notes of a requirement for genetic counseling; and a proliferation of online fact sheets and decisional aids. We have also seen a burgeoning of informal networks of information exchange via the Internet, parenting magazines, disability support groups, and the media more broadly. At the same time that this has been happening there has been vigorous public debate in countries all over the world about the broader social implications of these diagnostic technologies. A significant portion of this debate is *not* concerned with the moral or legal status of the fetus or embryo per se but, rather, with the use of these technologies for eugenic and discriminatory purposes.[4] These debates around new prenatal diagnostic technologies often focus on the question of whether it is *right* to *choose* "better," "unaffected," "nondisabled" children.[5] While this is a concern of our book, too, our focus is different. We called this book "Perfecting Pregnancy," rather than "Perfecting Progeny," for example, because our focus is on the way that these discourses regulate and influence the behavior of people who are already in the world. One of our primary goals in writing this

geneticists see referred patients for diagnosis, management, genetic testing and genetic counselling."

[4] The critical literature on this point is expanding: see, for example, E. Parens and A. Asch, "The Disability Rights Critique of Prenatal Genetic Testing: Reflections and Recommendations" (1999) 29(5) Special Supplement *Hastings Center Report* S1; J. Gillott, "Screening for Disability: A Eugenic Pursuit?" (2001) 27 *Journal of Medical Ethics*, Suppl II: ii21.

[5] R. Scott, *Choosing between Possible Lives: Law and Ethics of Prenatal and Preimplantation Genetic Diagnosis* (Oxford: Hart Publishing, 2007); S. Wilkinson, *Choosing Tomorrow's Children: The Ethics of Selective Reproduction* (Oxford: Oxford University Press, 2010); J. Glover, *Choosing Children: Genes, Disability and Design* (Oxford: Clarendon Press, 2007); L. Skene and J. Thompson (eds.), *The Sorting Society: The Ethics of Genetic Screening and Therapy* (New York: Cambridge University Press, 2008); R.M. Green, *Babies by Design: The Ethics of Genetic Choice* (New Haven, Conn.: Yale University Press, 2008); A.R. Chapman and M.S. Frankel, *Designing Our Descendants: The Promises and Perils of Genetic Modifications* (Baltimore: Johns Hopkins University Press, 2003); M. Sandel, *The Case against Perfection: Ethics in the Age of Genetic Engineering* (Cambridge, Mass.: Harvard University Press, 2009).

book was, therefore, to find out just who *is* making the decisions about the way in which we (society, women, mothers) manage the potential for disability in our reproductive futures.

In order to answer this question we begin by unpacking some fundamental assumptions about the "badness" of disability and the "realness" of reproductive choice.[6] Some scholars have argued, for example, that prenatal testing and abortion and/or selective embryo implantation using PGD express a discriminatory or negative attitude toward people who have the disability for which such testing is offered. Concerns have also been raised about whether "disability" has been, or may be, given too broad a construction in these contexts. This theme is a major consideration of our book. Second, others, including us, have written about the pressure on women – from medicine, law, and society – to manage their pregnancies and potential pregnancies to ensure the "best" possible opportunity for a "good," "healthy," "normal" outcome, even if this may require the abandonment of the process altogether. Thus we find that women in contemporary Western society are encouraged to imagine their pregnancies as processes that can be perfected, indeed that they have a responsibility to perfect.

In order to understand how this kind of framing of reproductive options is instantiated, we chart the regulatory history of abortion, prenatal testing, and preimplantation genetic diagnosis in a number of jurisdictions including Australia, the United Kingdom, the United States, Canada, and some European countries. We examine how law has regulated, and continues to regulate, these fields but also, perhaps more important, how it *does not*. What we discover is that medical

---

[6] See, for example: T. Shakespeare, "Debating Disability" (2008) 34 *Journal of Medical Ethics* 11; S. Edwards, "The Impairment/Disability Distinction: A Response to Shakespeare" (2008) 34 *Journal of Medical Ethics* 26; T. Koch, "Is Tom Shakespeare Disabled?" (2008) 34 *Journal of Medical Ethics* 18; R. Gillon, "Is there a 'New Ethics of Abortion'?" (2001) 27 *Journal of Medical Ethics* 5; J. Savulescu, "Is Current Practice around the Termination of Pregnancy Eugenic and Discriminatory?" (2001) 27 *Journal of Medical Ethics* 165.

professionals play a critical role in determining what kind of diagnostic testing is made available, who may have access to it, and the reasons that will justify the grant of such access. This is despite the fact that many countries (Australia, the United Kingdom, New Zealand, and a number of European countries) have responded to innovations in diagnostic technologies in the area of reproduction with a period of intense regulatory activity.

Toward the end of our study we begin to chart the potential impact of new technologies that are being developed, including inheritable genetic modification techniques and – perhaps most important – the proliferation of preconception technologies that, paradoxically, push our reproductive futures backward to an earlier point in time so that actions taken yesterday and today are conflated with the child possibly conceived tomorrow.

In the face of these novel technologies, the overwhelming question for regulators has been whether and, if so, how to limit reproductive decision making. One particularly popular strategy worldwide has been to limit the use of such technologies to those circumstances where the aim is to avoid "serious disability." However, while concepts of seriousness, disability, and of course normality are currently used to frame legislative limits, they are, more often than not, left undefined.

In *Perfecting Pregnancy* we examine this use of "serious disability" as a tipping point in the regulation of prenatal testing (PNT) and abortion and preimplantation genetic diagnosis (PGD). We ask whether this concept can, or should, do the work required of it by legal and ethical regulatory frameworks.

APPROACH AND ANALYSIS

A crucial dimension to our approach is our exploration of the meaning of "serious disability" as a legal concept compared with a medical concept. By drawing upon legal texts, policy documents, and the growing empirical literature about the attitudes and experiences of those engaged or potentially engaged by these reproductive technologies and their understandings of disability, we examine whether there is a shared normative framework that grounds legal conceptualizations. In this book we focus on the attitudes of regulators as well as those of health care professionals, including genetic counselors, clinical geneticists, in vitro fertilization (IVF) practitioners, and others who work in the industry. However, we are also engaged in an ongoing study that explores the attitudes of women and patients to these technologies and the conceptualization of disability. The material from that research will be the subject of subsequent publications.

In this book we have drawn heavily on existing empirical literature and draw fresh insights from our own empirical research, in which we interviewed Australian regulators and clinicians. These interviews are part of an ongoing qualitative study of expert accounts of the use of preimplantation genetic diagnosis and prenatal testing technologies in Australia.[7] Given the small number of participants, we include these excerpts for their anecdotal value. They offer individual insights that may not otherwise have been accessible. Participants so far included have been from the federal sphere and the states of New South Wales, Victoria, South Australia, and Western Australia. We have included excerpts from 12 interviews conducted between June 2010 and October 2011 in this book. The interviewees include regulators, clinical geneticists and genetic counselors. In each case the experts were selected because they were known to be key actors in the field. The broad intention of our interviews was to elicit participants' views on how the meaning of "serious disability" is determined in different clinical and regulatory contexts and by whom. We also wanted to find out what role the law plays in shaping this meaning.

[7] This work has been undertaken as part of Australian Research Council Grant DP0988103, "The Legal Function of Serious Disability in Prenatal and Neonatal Healthcare Settings." Ethics approval was obtained from the Sydney University Ethics Committee and the University of Technology, Sydney, Ethics Committee.

Consequently our research approach was intended to open a space for discussion and to allow for the flexibility to adapt the interview depending on the direction the interviewee's response dictated. It was specifically intended to be iterative. Thus, as will be seen in our discussion of these interviews in later chapters, we adopted a "narrative-based" research methodology. Our interviews were conducted as "guided conversations."[8] Open-ended questions were used with a set of prompts so that all participants were asked a select set of common questions. All expert participants were contacted by letter/ email and asked whether they would be interested in providing their views. Each participant was then interviewed in person for 45 minutes to an hour. The interview was recorded and transcribed, and participants were given the opportunity to review the transcripts and amend them where they felt necessary. All contributions were provided on condition of anonymity and interviewees have been given numbers. Clinicians are represented by a *C* and regulators by an *R*. Chapters 2, 4, and 5 contain excerpts from these interviews.

THE STRUCTURE OF THE BOOK

Framing Concepts – Disability and Risk

Disability and its avoidance is a concept that frames clinical approaches to the routine management of pregnancy, public health prenatal screening programs, the development of new advanced techniques such as PGD, women's experiences of pregnancy, and legal and regulatory efforts to delimit the range of appropriate responses to prenatal testing and diagnoses. Chapter 1 examines the use of disability as a framing concept for

---

[8] J. Lofland and L.H. Lofland, *Analyzing Social Settings: A Guide to Qualitative Observation and Analysis* (Belmont, Calif.: Wadsworth, 1984); K. Ehrich, C. Williams, and B. Farsides, "The Embryo as Moral Work Object: PGD/IVF Staff Views and Experiences" (2008) 30(5) *Sociology of Health & Illness* 772.

reproductive decision making and asks: "What does disability mean?" "is it always bad?" "how is it understood and by whom?" and "what are its particular dimensions in the context of prenatal screening and selection practices?" We begin the chapter by noting that, despite the heavy reliance on the concept of disability to frame both legal and medical responses to diagnostic testing technologies, disability remains a somewhat enigmatic concept. We follow this observation with a thorough interrogation of the varied and rich scholarship exploring the question of what disability is and how it should be understood. We consider a number of significant debates concerning the way in which disability is constructed in contemporary society, and we unpack some of the key insights produced by the disability studies movement. In the context of prenatal testing we note the argument sometimes made by disability rights scholars that once an abnormality is detected, women do not have a true choice about whether to continue the pregnancy because a diagnosis of disability is portrayed unfavorably. At the same time, however, it is recognized that women do want to be informed and to be able to make choices freely about whom and how they reproduce. In addition to this, we note that there is a strong feminist concern that prenatal testing is presented to women as being something they have a responsibility to undergo. Although the literature provided to pregnant women about prenatal testing is at pains to present as *genuine* the choice confronting women about whether to (a) accept the offer of testing and (b) have an abortion for an abnormality if identified (or in the case of PGD to select against disability), in fact it sometimes creates an environment in which pressure is placed on women to make particular decisions to reproduce "responsibly."

In Chapter 2 we turn to a discussion of how the debate about the construction of disability is informed by (and/or informs) the discourse of risk management that pervades prenatal screening and testing. We explore how risk, as a conceptual apparatus, is deployed in legal and biomedical discourses, government and policy discourses, cultural and media discourses, and, of course, the minds and bodies of individuals. Chapter 2 enlarges upon the idea that social attitudes and pressures limit women's freedom to make reproductive decisions for themselves. The argument here is that we live in a "risk culture": that is, a culture in which the concept of risk has become a pervasive conceptual tool driving regulatory responses and disciplining pregnant women. As feminist legal theorists, in this chapter, we explore the way risk discourse gives rise to both legal and nonlegal forms of regulation enacted on and through the bodies of pregnant and potentially pregnant women. This is done while recognizing the tension between the opportunities risk discourse offers for informed reproductive decision making and the burdens it imposes.

A Genealogy of "Serious Disability" as a Regulatory Concept

Although concepts of disability and normality are currently used to frame legislative limits, they are, more often than not, left undefined. In Chapters 3 and 4 we argue that in order to understand how this regulatory approach has evolved, it is important to consider the context. Early regulation of PNT and abortion was shaped by the background events of the rubella/thalidomide outbreaks while regulation of PGD took place in the context of the project to map the entire human genome and the developments in cloning technology. In Chapter 3 we trace the development of abortion law reform in Australia and the United Kingdom over the period of the last 50 years, paying particular attention to the way in which abortion to avoid "serious handicap" emerged in law as a distinct category of legal abortion. Although this reform has not been uniformly enacted, it nevertheless provides a conceptual apparatus that takes on a wider relevance. In jurisdictions that do not have such a provision in law, decisions about late termination are nonetheless made by reference to this concept by clinicians acting within their professional guidelines. Furthermore, "serious disability" laid the conceptual foundation for legislative intervention into the field of PGD. Thus, in Chapter 4 we examine the history of regulation of preimplantation genetic diagnosis over the last 20 years in Australia and the United Kingdom. In both chapters, we also map out the contemporary legal terrain in Australia, the United Kingdom, Canada, the United States, and a number of European countries. In both the PGD and PNT contexts, most of the legislatures discussed have ultimately devolved responsibility for determining when disability avoidance technologies can be used to licensing bodies or to the clinicians themselves. Where clinicians must seek approval from a licensing body that has been given the responsibility of making such determinations, more often than not that body draws on clinicians' expert guidance to assess whether treatment meets the relevant criteria. In the absence of a licensing body and any other decisive legislative guidance, the decision lies in the hands of the individuals seeking treatment, with the medical profession acting as a "gatekeeper." Despite there being some concern about the appropriateness of reposing in the medical profession this gatekeeping function, as we see in Chapters 3 and 4, the overall pattern of regulation has nonetheless been to favor this approach. In both the abortion and PGD contexts, the principal legislative means to restrict the medical profession's discretion has been by inserting the qualifying term "serious" (or some version thereof) to limit the kinds of disabilities these techniques can be used to avoid. In Chapter 4 we draw on interviews with regulators who discuss whether the absence of a legislative or regulatory definition for this qualifying term is appropriate. They consider whether it is meaningful as a legal restriction on medical decisionmaking insofar as it creates a framework for decisionmaking that requires, at the very least, discussion and forethought before a determination is made.

The Future for Existing and Emerging Technologies for Avoiding Serious Disability

Although legislators have resisted providing a definition of "serious" handicap, disability, or condition, it remains the case that the term must be given meaning in order for the law to function. In the context of prenatal testing and abortion, the available evidence suggests that doctors in Australia and the United Kingdom hold quite divergent views about which conditions are seriously disabling. In Chapter 5, we provide a closer examination of the various strategies – both substantive and procedural – that have been used to structure or guide the decisionmaking of individual clinicians as they interpret the meaning of "serious disability" in the abortion context, and we compare these with regulatory approaches to the meaning of disability and serious disability in the field of PGD.

We then turn to the question of how decisions about "serious disability" are made by women, their partners, and clinicians through an analysis of the available empirical research and our discussions with relevant clinicians. We observe that often decisions about whether a disability is "serious" are complex and contextual. Accordingly, the question of what constitutes a seriously disabling condition cannot be answered simply by focusing on the potential child's prognosis. Although the perceived seriousness of the condition in question is an important consideration, a number of other factors and pressures bear upon decision making across these two fields. These include the attitudes, experiences, and resources of the family into which the child would be born; the capacity of technology to detect abnormalities in utero or in vitro; the professional regulation of clinician discretion within clinics and hospitals; and the moral and social status of embryos and fetuses.

A key point to emerge from our analysis is that the interpretation of "serious disability" is informed by social and moral perceptions of the avoidance strategy in question. We therefore consider what the implications might be for law and clinical practice. If there are material differences in the perception of moral or social risk associated with abortion compared with PGD, a further question that arises is whether alignment of the interpretation of "serious disability" in the two fields will be sustainable into the future. We begin an exploration of this important question through our interviews with clinicians involved in the provision of PGD and prenatal testing services.

In Chapter 6 we explore technologies that are currently under development that may create new dilemmas for legislatures and ethicists. While the federal and state governments discussed in this book seem to be ambivalent about imposing constraints on reproductive decision making to avoid disabilities (however they may be defined) through PGD and selection or PND and termination, there have been limits placed on other kinds of reproductive technologies such as cloning and inheritable genetic modification. Here we take an extended look at some new technologies that are likely to be made available for clinical use in the near future, and we ask whether they pose new or different regulatory questions. We begin by exploring recent developments in prenatal testing that have led to the creation of noninvasive blood tests early in pregnancy for a range of congenital disorders previously only diagnosable at the 15- to 20-week stage by chorionic villus sampling (CVS) or amniocentesis. This new simpler and faster test may eventually allow clinicians to do a full fetal deoxyribonucleic acid (DNA) scan. Once this is possible we may find that the range of what constitutes a normal unaffected embryo is narrowed. Consequently this technology has the potential to change our understanding of disability, pregnancy, and normalcy.

In the second half of the chapter we examine the potential for disability avoidance using gene manipulation therapies. Gene therapy has been argued by some to be the next obvious stage in disability avoidance technology. When conducted on an embryo, gene therapy can lead to an inheritable modification. Inheritable genetic modification is illegal in almost all of the jurisdictions that we examine in this book, and yet it offers the possibility of treating rather than avoiding disability. In other words, the affected embryo or fetus (or gamete) can continue to develop after the particular abnormality or defect has been treated. It does not, however, resolve concerns about eugenic impulses. Genetic modification inevitably involves a preference for some traits and the rejection of others. We focus on one genetic manipulation therapy in particular – that used to avoid mitochondrial disease. Chapter 6 concludes with a brief examination of advances in preconception testing technology aimed at identifying carrier status for severe childhood disorders in adults. We consider the implications of this kind of testing, which occurs prior to the existence of even a conceptus, and speculate on how it constitutes the ultimate demand for responsible reproduction toward a perfected pregnancy.

We conclude the book by answering a series of questions that we have considered throughout. First, how do we understand the concepts of "disability" and "normality" when used as threshold categories for framing regulation? Second, can we offer a feminist reading of the critical disability studies critique of PND and PGD without ceding that these two positions are incompatible with one another? Third, drawing on the burgeoning field of empirical texts that examine attitudes and responses to both disability and prenatal and preimplantation testing technologies, we ask how the concepts disability and seriousness are understood both within and without the law. Finally, we combine these empirical and theoretical elements to develop a framework, from a legal/regulatory perspective, for thinking through the challenges of disability avoidance technologies and the pursuit of perfection on and through the bodies of women.

1

Disability

For most parents, the news that an abnormality has been identified in their unborn baby is completely unexpected. A problem or abnormality identified in the developing baby generally comes as a shock.... In the light of the technologies available to monitor pregnancy, more and more abnormalities are also being identified through "routine" examinations such as ultrasound. Often the parents of babies identified in this way have never given consideration to the possibility that such a routine test would find something wrong with their unborn baby.[1]

The increasing sophistication of diagnostic testing would suggest that more rather than fewer abnormalities will be diagnosed prenatally and yet, as the preceding quote suggests, these diagnoses remain unexpected for many prospective parents.[2] There may be a range of reasons for this common reaction – because prospective parents undertake testing in ignorance of its potential implications, or because they expect

---

[1] NSW Health, "Prenatal Testing: Special Tests for Your Baby during Pregnancy" (8 August 2007), at 5.

[2] It is important to note that while it might be that for some couples the prospect of having a disabled child might occupy a mere shadowy presence at the edges of the expectation of a perfect pregnancy, for others this prospect will be front and center. This may be because they are or a family member is affected by a genetic condition, or because they have a child who has such a condition. These couples will have different expectations and may – or may not – take particular steps to select against known traits in their children.

13

that testing will provide reassurance. There may even be an expectation of a "perfect" pregnancy. If such an expectation or ideal does exist for some or even many prospective parents, where does this come from? What shape does it take? Can we be more precise about the kinds of expectations or ideals that prenatal diagnoses of abnormality might challenge? Do they relate to the health, well-being, or the capacity for self-sufficiency, educational attainment, longevity, success, and/or prosperity of the prospective child? Are they expectations relating to parental capacities to adapt to the needs of the child?

Understanding what lies behind responses to prenatal diagnoses of abnormality is a necessary step to thinking carefully about the meaning or meanings given to disability in the context of reproductive decision making. Disability is a concept that now frames clinical approaches to the routine management of pregnancy, public health prenatal screening programs, the development of new advanced techniques such as PGD, women's experiences of pregnancy, and legal and regulatory efforts to delimit the range of appropriate responses to prenatal testing and diagnoses. Thus, the clinical contexts in which pregnancy is managed are important sites for the generation of our understandings about the meaning of disability. But, despite its crucial role in framing these public and private efforts to expand reproductive choices, disability remains a somewhat enigmatic concept. Its meaning, causes, and effects are highly contested. In this chapter, we seek to interrogate disability as a concept. We set the scene for this analysis by first considering some of the debates around the construction of disability. We then turn to some of the key critical insights produced by the disability studies movement in response to selective termination and implantation after prenatal testing and diagnosis, and we consider the norms that inform and constrain the manner in which prenatal tests are made available and are acted upon. We examine this material from a feminist perspective, drawing upon critical feminist responses to prenatal testing and diagnosis and biopolitical accounts of the body. We close this chapter with the observation that the prenatal testing technologies and their attendant practices are crucial to the way in which concepts such as disability and normalcy are defined and understood. We suggest that disability is to some extent an artificial construct of these technologies but, more importantly, that our understanding of disability as a concept is embedded in the social, political, clinical, and legal contexts in which it operates.

1 WHAT IS DISABILITY?

The search for a coherent conception of disability has occupied philosophers, bioethicists, disability scholars, and others for well over two decades.[3] During this time, scholars have debated the merits of understanding disability as an inherent biological condition (sometimes referred to as the "medical model of disability") or as the product of a discriminatory or oppressive social and/or political

---

[3] For a selection of the considerable literature on this topic see: M. Oliver, *The Politics of Disablement* (London: MacMillan Education, 1990); T. Shakespeare, *Disability Rights and Wrongs* (London: Routledge, 2006); J. Harris, "Is There a Coherent Social Conception of Disability?" (2000) 26(2) *Journal of Medical Ethics* 95; S. M. Reindal, "Disability, Gene Therapy and Eugenics – a Challenge to John Harris" (2000) 26 *Journal of Medical Ethics* 89; T. Koch, "Disability and Difference: Balancing Social and Physical Constructions" (2001) 27 *Journal of Medical Ethics* 370; T. Koch, "One Principle and Three Fallacies of Disability Studies" (2002) 28 *Journal of Medical Ethics* 203; T. Koch, "The Difference That Difference Makes: Bioethics and the Challenge of 'Disability'" (2004) 29(6) *Journal of Medicine and Philosophy* 697; T. Koch, "Is Tom Shakespeare Disabled?" (2008) 34 *Journal of Medical Ethics* 18; A. Silvers, "On the Possibility and Desirability of Constructing a Neutral Conception of Disability" (2003) 24 *Theoretical Medicine* 471; R. Amundson, "Against Normal Function" (2000) 31(1) *Studies in History and Philosophy of Biological and Biomedical Sciences* 33; R. Amundson and S. Tresky, "On a Bioethical Challenge to Disability Rights" (2007) 32 *Journal of Medicine and Philosophy* 541; R. Amundson and S. Tresky, "Bioethics and Disability Rights: Conflicting Values and Perspectives" (2008) 5 *Bioethical Inquiry* 111; L. Davis (ed.), *The Disability Studies Reader* (2nd edition) (New York: Routledge, 2006); and M. Shildrick, "The Disabled Body, Genealogy and Undecidability" (2005) 19(6) *Cultural Studies* 755, at 756–7.

environment (referred to as the "social model of disability"). More recently, the debate has taken a postmodern turn, with critical scholars reflecting on the limitations of the social model of disability and critically interrogating the categories of impairment and disability. In the particular context of prenatal testing technologies, feminist scholars too have provided key insights into the meaning of disability, suggesting that it is highly contingent on context. Our primary concern in this chapter is to consider and critique the meanings given to disability in the context of prenatal selection practices and reproductive autonomy. However, in order to give appropriate context to the discussion, it is worthwhile canvassing, albeit briefly, the models of disability and some of the insights that have emerged from this important debate.

1.1 Modeling Disability

As Silvers points out, the use of "disability" as a term collectively to describe people "lacking normal powers of body or mind" is of relatively recent origin and can be traced to the early twentieth century.[4] Prior to this, understandings of disability were less generalized and more confined to specific impairments with designated causes.[5] However, from around the start of the twentieth century, disability came to be understood as a "reference to natural limitations imposed by illness or accident" and emerged as an umbrella term to "collect individuals with different kinds and degrees of corporeal and cognitive limitation under a single label."[6]

---

[4] A. Silvers, "On the Possibility and Desirability of Constructing a Neutral Conception of Disability" (2003) 24 *Theoretical Medicine* 471, at 471.

[5] A. Silvers, "On the Possibility and Desirability of Constructing a Neutral Conception of Disability" (2003) 24 *Theoretical Medicine* 471, at 471.

[6] A. Silvers, "On the Possibility and Desirability of Constructing a Neutral Conception of Disability" (2003) 24 *Theoretical Medicine* 471, at 472.

This shift toward understanding disability as a largely natural or biological phenomenon remains the dominant mode of thinking about what constitutes disability. Koch describes the "medical model of disability" as a framework of understanding that designates disability as "the presence of a physical or cognitive difference that deviates negatively from a 'mundane' norm."[7] The mundane norm is commonly delineated by reference to "species-typical functioning."[8] Thus, a "condition of a part or process in an organism is pathological when the ability of the part or process to perform one or more of its species-typical biological functions falls below some central range of the statistical distribution for that ability."[9] Locating this analysis within medical practice, "normality refers to a certain distribution of the population around an average measure for a particular trait. Individuals ordinarily are considered normal in regards to a specific trait if they are no more than two standard deviations from the mean of the population for that trait."[10] Within this framework, it is thought that deviations from species-typical functioning constitute disabilities "because there are important options and experiences that are foreclosed" by these deviations.[11]

This way of understanding disability has been challenged by the theorists who have conceptualized disability as contextual rather than

---

[7] T. Koch, "Disability and Difference: Balancing Social and Physical Constructions" (2001) 27 *Journal of Medical Ethics* 370, at 370.

[8] A. Asch, "Prenatal Diagnosis and Selective Abortion: A Challenge to Practice and Policy" (1999) 89 *American Journal of Public Health* 1649, at 1650.

[9] C. Boorse, "Concepts of Health" in D. Van de Veer and T. Regan (eds.), *Health Care Ethics* (Philadelphia: Temple University Press, 1987), 359–93, as cited in A. Asch, "Prenatal Diagnosis and Selective Abortion: A Challenge to Practice and Policy" (1999) 89 *American Journal of Public Health* 1649, at 1650.

[10] A. Silvers, "On the Possibility and Desirability of Constructing a Neutral Conception of Disability" (2003) 24 *Theoretical Medicine* 471, at 484, referring to the work of Maxwell Mehlman.

[11] J. Harris, "Is There a Coherent Social Conception of Disability?" (2000) 26 *Journal of Medical Ethics* 95, at 98.

inherent, thus calling attention to the contribution of the social and political environment to disability. The "social model of disability" contends that disability is the product of an individual's interaction with social and political environments. This is not to say that physical or cognitive differences (impairments) do not exist but, rather, to question whether such differences necessarily entail disability. To borrow from Iris Marion Young, "moving on wheels is a disadvantage only in a world full of stairs."[12] By seeking to distinguish impairment from disability, the "social model of disability" argues that "the importance of a physical difference lies ... in discriminatory social reactions to or ignorance of the effects of that difference. It is the reaction to these conditions, not the inherent limits that they impose that are their signal features."[13] On this view, disability can be seen as a form of oppression, an artifact of cultural or sociopolitical arrangements that disvalue and exclude individuals with impairments.[14]

The "social model of disability" seeks to advance our understanding by challenging the "naturalness" of disability, thereby creating opportunities to think differently about justice and inclusion for people with disabilities. Nevertheless, the question remains: Is it possible to understand disability as an exclusively social phenomenon? Some scholars have expressed concern that the social model "diverts attention

[12] I. M. Young, "Foreword" in M. Corker and T. Shakespeare (eds.), *Disability/Postmodernity: Embodying Disability Theory* (London: Continuum, 2002), at xii.

[13] T. Koch, "Disability and Difference: Balancing Social and Physical Constructions" (2001) 27 *Journal of Medical Ethics* 370, at 370.

[14] As Jackie Leach Scully explains, "social models of disability redirect the analytic gaze away from the pathologised individual and towards social practices. The strong social model attempts to sever the link between embodiment and disability by arguing that disability is not about the individual impaired body, but about a stigmatised group being oppressed within a disabling society." J. Leach Scully, "Disability and the Thinking Body" in K. Kristiansen, S. Vehmas, and T. Shakespeare (eds.), *Arguing about Disability – Philosophical Perspectives* (Oxford: Routledge, 2010) 57, at 59.

from the body of the person and fosters a gaze that becomes locked onto the social environment."[15] This approach illogically assumes, in Shakespeare's words, "that a focus on social barriers necessitates a neglect of medical interventions."[16] Such criticisms have led to further refinements in the model. For instance, Amundson and Tresky distinguish between "conditional disadvantages of impairment" (CDIs) and "unconditional disadvantages of impairment" (UDIs).[17] The first category covers those disabilities that are caused by the social context in which an impaired person lives, while the second covers disadvantages that are inherent to the person's particular impairment. Thus, while Amundson and Tresky consider most disabilities to fall into the first category, this approach acknowledges that some disabilities are inherent.[18]

The social model of disability has also been criticized for assuming that impairment is "that fixed point on which disability as a disadvantage is socially constituted."[19] Tremain puts this point slightly differently when she claims that the social model contends that impairment is a necessary but not sufficient condition for disability.[20] In this sense, neither the medical nor the social model challenges the assumption that impairment or biological difference is a natural given. According to Hughes and Paterson, however, this "leaves the impaired body in

---

[15] S. D. Edwards, "Book Review: Disability Rights and Wrongs" 34 *Journal of Medical Ethics* 222, at 222.

[16] T. Shakespeare, *Disability Rights and Wrongs* (London: Routledge, 2006), at 32.

[17] R. Amundson and S. Tresky, "On a Bioethical Challenge to Disability Rights" (2007) 32 *Journal of Medicine and Philosophy* 541, at 544.

[18] R. Amundson and S. Tresky, "On a Bioethical Challenge to Disability Rights" (2007) 32 *Journal of Medicine and Philosophy* 541, at 544.

[19] L. Carlson, *The Faces of Intellectual Disability: Philosophical Reflections* (Bloomington: Indiana University Press, 2010), at 8.

[20] S. Tremain, "On the Government of Disability: Foucault, Power and the Subject of Impairment" in L. Davis (ed.), *The Disability Studies Reader* (2nd edition) (New York: Routledge, 2006), at 191.

the exclusive jurisdiction of medical hermeneutics,"[21] a result that is ultimately unlikely to favor the transformative political ends sought by disability activists.[22] Tremain observes that "the identity of the subject of the social model ('people with impairments') is actually formed in large measure by the political arrangements that the model was designed to contest."[23] She writes: "Consider that if the identity of the subject of the social model is actually produced in accordance with those political arrangements, then a social movement that grounds its claims to entitlement in that identity will inadvertently *extend* those arrangements."[24] In response to concerns like these, disability scholars working with postmodern theoretical approaches have attempted to disrupt further the category of disability by challenging an understanding of impairment as fixed and determinate.[25] Carlson refers to this body of work as the "postmodern model of disability," which she characterizes as approaches that "expose the dynamic and constructed nature of impaired bodies and minds in order to adequately capture the way in which disabilities and disabled identities are

[21] B. Hughes and K. Paterson, "The Social Model of Disability and the Disappearing Body: Towards a Sociology of Impairment" (1997) 12(3) *Disability and Society* 325, at 330.

[22] Note that the social and postmodern models do share some common ground – they both attempt to disrupt mainstream conceptualizations of disability as inherent to the individual. Iris Marion Young suggests that postmodern approaches should be seen as complementary, rather than antagonistic to social model approaches, especially those rooted in political activism. However, some social model theorists reject postmodern approaches. See I. M. Young, "Foreword" in M. Corker and T. Shakespeare (eds.), *Disability/Postmodernity: Embodying Disability Theory* (London: Continuum, 2002), at xiv.

[23] S. Tremain, "On the Government of Disability: Foucault, Power and the Subject of Impairment" in L. Davis (ed.), *The Disability Studies Reader* (2nd edition) (New York: Routledge, 2006), at 192.

[24] S. Tremain, "On the Government of Disability: Foucault, Power and the Subject of Impairment" in L. Davis (ed), *The Disability Studies Reader* (2nd edition) (New York: Routledge, 2006), 192.

[25] L. Carlson, *The Faces of Intellectual Disability: Philosophical Reflections* (Bloomington: Indiana University Press, 2010), 8.

created."[26] An example of this approach can be found in the work of Tremain, who argues that

> the materiality of "the body" cannot be dissociated from the historically contingent practices that bring it into being, that is, bring it into being as that sort of thing. Indeed, it seems politically naïve to suggest that the term "impairment" is value-neutral, that is "merely descriptive" as if there could ever be a description that was not also a *prescription* for the formulation of the object (person, practice, or thing) to which it is claimed to innocently refer. Truth-discourses that purport to describe phenomena contribute to the construction of their objects.[27]

This approach to disability is useful for thinking through certain issues that are central to our concerns in this book, in particular, the structuring of reproductive choices (to have or not to have a child with a particular condition) in response to prenatal testing. Tremain's approach prompts us to consider that prenatal testing practices may themselves play a role in the constitution of the identity about which the choice is being made. This in turn highlights the way in which normalcy is also a construct.

1.2 Is Disability Necessarily Negative?

Medicalized understandings of disability tend to assume that disability is not only objectively ascertainable (species atypicality) but also inherently negative. For instance, Harris argues that a disability is necessarily negative because it is "a physical or mental condition we have a strong [rational] preference not to be in."[28] Harris calls this a

---

[26] L. Carlson, *The Faces of Intellectual Disability: Philosophical Reflections* (Bloomington: Indiana University Press, 2010), 8.

[27] S. Tremain, "On the Government of Disability: Foucault, Power and the Subject of Impairment" in L. Davis (ed.), *The Disability Studies Reader* (2nd edition) (New York: Routledge, 2006), 187.

[28] J. Harris, "Is There a Coherent Social Conception of Disability?" (2000) 26 *Journal of Medical Ethics* 95, at 97.

"harmed condition" because certain opportunities are foreclosed by the disabling trait.[29] He argues further that without the medical model, "it is impossible to give an account of the wrong that one might do in disabling someone or failing to cure a disability."[30]

Some disability scholars do not necessarily disagree that "disability puts some limits on the 'open future'" of children with disabilities,[31] but nor do they assume that this is always harmful. Silvers argues that "impairments are anomalous in that they differ from what is typical, but anomalies are not necessarily harmful, disadvantageous or otherwise bad."[32] She observes further that

> [i]n conceptualising disability, we too easily slide down a slippery slope from attributions of anomalies to verdicts of badness. To characterise an anomaly as a weakness or loss improperly closes by definition what should be an open process of weighing value, for whether a particular physical or cognitive difference is unfavourable should be an open empirical question not one closed by social convention.[33]

Disability scholars have offered a number of reasons for attempting to disentangle disability from badness and for embracing a more open process of weighing value. It has been argued, for instance, that the focus on the "opportunities foreclosed" by disabling traits fails to capture the ways in which accommodations to the social environment could ameliorate the impact of those traits. Thus, Asch has noted

---

[29] J. Harris, "Is There a Coherent Social Conception of Disability?" (2000) 26 *Journal of Medical Ethics* 95, at 97.

[30] J. Harris, "Is There a Coherent Social Conception of Disability?" (2000) 26 *Journal of Medical Ethics* 95, at 99.

[31] E. Parens and A. Asch, "Disability Rights Critique of Prenatal Genetic Testing: Reflections and Recommendations" (2003) 9 *Mental Retardations and Developmental Disabilities Research Reviews* 40, at 44.

[32] A. Silvers, "On the Possibility and Desirability of Constructing a Neutral Conception of Disability" (2003) 24 *Theoretical Medicine* 471, at 479.

[33] A. Silvers, "On the Possibility and Desirability of Constructing a Neutral Conception of Disability" (2003) 24 *Theoretical Medicine* 471, at 479.

that the inclusion and accommodation of children with disabilities in institutions such as child-care centers, schools, even children's literature and media might themselves reduce "the anguish and isolation that have marred life for generations of disabled children."[34] Further, Parens and Asch urge consideration of the ways that might be found to enable people with disabilities to enjoy alternative modes of the activities in which they cannot participate.[35]

The focus on the "opportunities foreclosed" has also been criticized on the basis that this inhibits a full appreciation of the satisfying lives and possibilities still open to many people with disabilities. Silvers points out that many of our abilities (e.g., talking, walking, seeing) are so commonplace, "we imagine that the sheer exercise of the faculties that support them necessarily gratifies us"[36] with the result that the absence of these faculties must be bad. But she goes on to examine this assumption more carefully:

> [I]t sometimes is argued that not being able to hear music or look at paintings is intrinsically bad. Yet no one questions the quality of life of the many nondisabled people who could enjoy these pleasures but pass them up. It seems biased to say foregoing these pleasures is deleterious to those who cannot experience them but indifferent to those who can but don't experience them.[37]

Further, the emphasis on "opportunities foreclosed" is itself a reflection of the priority given to certain functions and abilities. As Koch points out, "the medical model assumes ... that autonomy and

---

[34] A. Asch, "Prenatal Diagnosis and Selective Abortion: A Challenge to Practice and Policy" (1999) 89 *American Journal of Public Health* 1649, at 1653.

[35] E. Parens and A. Asch, "Disability Rights Critique of Prenatal Genetic Testing: Reflections and Recommendations" (2003) 9 *Mental Retardations and Developmental Disabilities Research Reviews* 40, at 44.

[36] A. Silvers, "On the Possibility and Desirability of Constructing a Neutral Conception of Disability" (2003) 24 *Theoretical Medicine* 471, at 479.

[37] A. Silvers, "On the Possibility and Desirability of Constructing a Neutral Conception of Disability" (2003) 24 *Theoretical Medicine* 471, at 479–480.

self-sufficiency are defining elements of the 'normal' human condition. It is the standard against which the lives of those with limiting conditions are typically measured."[38] However, some have argued that the "assumption of independence and self-sufficiency as a norm is itself reflective of prejudice rather than reality."[39] According to Koch, Nussbaum makes this point well when she observes that "the relative independence many of us enjoy looks more and more like a temporary condition, a phase of life that we move into gradually, and which we all too quickly begin to leave."[40] In light of this, it may be preferable to accept the ubiquitous nature of impairment and to shift our emphasis from the things that people with disabilities cannot do to the "nearly infinite range of remaining opportunities."[41]

A closely related set of challenges emerges from the empirical evidence that people with disabilities, even severe disabilities, do not rate their quality of life as poor and that people without disabilities

---

[38] T. Koch, "Disability and Difference: Balancing Social and Physical Constructions" (2001) 27 *Journal of Medical Ethics* 370, at 371.

[39] T. Koch, "Disability and Difference: Balancing Social and Physical Constructions" (2001) 27 *Journal of Medical Ethics* 370, at 371.

[40] M. Nussbaum, "Disabled Lives: Who Cares?" (2001) *New York Review of Books* as cited in T. Koch, "Disability and Difference: Balancing Social and Physical Constructions" (2001) 27 *Journal of Medical Ethics* 370, at 371.

[41] E. Parens and A. Asch, "Disability Rights Critique of Prenatal Genetic Testing: Reflections and Recommendations" (2003) 9 *Mental Retardations and Developmental Disabilities Research Reviews* 40, at 44. In a similar vein, feminist legal theorists have argued for the incorporation of vulnerability into legal and political theorizing about the subject. Martha Fineman, for example, writes: "What should be the political and legal implications of the fact that we are born, live, and die within a fragile materiality that renders all of us constantly susceptible to destructive external forces and internal disintegration? Bodily needs and the messy dependency they carry cannot be ignored in life, nor should they be absent in our theories about society, politics and law." M. Fineman, "The Vulnerable Subject: Anchoring Equality in the Human Condition" (2008) 20 *Yale Journal of Law and Feminism* 1, 12. See also I. Karpin and R. Mykitiuk, "Feminist Legal Theory as Embodied Justice" in M. Fineman (ed.), *Transcending the Boundaries of the Law: Generations of Feminism and Legal Theory* (New York: Routledge, 2011), 115.

frequently overestimate the impact of impairment.[42] In one such study, Albrecht and Devlieger found that 54.3 percent of participants with serious disabilities "reported that they had an excellent or good quality of life".[43] This is not to say that impairments do not cause difficulties for people with disabilities and that these do not impact adversely on quality of life. The study found that those respondents who reported a poor quality of life suffered from pain, or unpredictable pain, which in turn adversely impacted on their sense of control over their bodies and lives.[44]

However, for a majority of respondents, their impairments did not foreclose important sources of life satisfaction, such as "doing a good job with" their lives and overcoming challenges posed by their impairments and the environments within which they live.[45] Other reported sources of life satisfaction derived from a sense of spirituality and purpose and/or assisting others. The authors observed:

> While disability was a resource that stimulated value clarification and goal orientation for some, for others it provided an impetus for psychological growth. Some people said that helping and giving to others improved their quality of life. Where it might be expected that people with disabilities should take from others, they also have a deep need to give to and help others.[46]

---

[42] G. L. Albrecht and P. J. Devlieger, "The Disability Paradox: High Quality of Life against All Odds" (1999) 48 *Social Science and Medicine* 977, 978–79; T. Koch, "Disability and Difference: Balancing Social and Physical Constructions" (2001) 27 *Journal of Medical Ethics* 370, at 371.

[43] G. L. Albrecht and P. J. Devlieger, "The Disability Paradox: High Quality of Life against All Odds" (1999) 48 *Social Science and Medicine* 977, at 981.

[44] G. L. Albrecht and P. J. Devlieger, "The Disability Paradox: High Quality of Life against All Odds" (1999) 48 *Social Science and Medicine* 977, at 984.

[45] G. L. Albrecht and P. J. Devlieger, "The Disability Paradox: High Quality of Life against All Odds" (1999) 48 *Social Science and Medicine* 977, at 983.

[46] G. L. Albrecht and P. J. Devlieger, "The Disability Paradox: High Quality of Life against All Odds" (1999) 48 *Social Science and Medicine* 977, at 983.

This subjective emphasis on factors such as "doing a good job with one's life"[47] and helping others may signify a departure from the sorts of abilities and goods that typically figure in conventional understandings of life's quality, such as the accumulation of material wealth, ability to perform in highly competitive work environments, or holding positions of power and influence. As we have already seen, employing these goods as a measure of quality of life already limits the definitional field. Goering's analysis sheds further light on this point. She argues that bioethicists tend to unfairly discount people with disabilities' claims to a satisfying life on the grounds that they are "emotional and therefore lacking validity."[48] They do this, she argues, in two ways: via accusations of denial and lowered expectations. In the former case, bioethicists assume that people with disabilities who insist that they are satisfied with life must be in denial about what they prefer. This approach relies on the problematic view that individuals can be ranked according to the quality of their life and, as such, a life that lacks certain ability, opportunities, and options is always worse than a "normal life." As Goering notes, this erroneously implies that quality of life is necessarily reliant on the body's condition:

> what matters to people when thinking about how to improve their quality of life is not only or even primarily the state of their bodies, but rather their opportunity for achieving self-determination, building community, and participating in work and social life.[49]

---

[47] G. L. Albrecht and P. J. Devlieger, "The Disability Paradox: High Quality of Life against All Odds" (1999) 48 *Social Science and Medicine* 977, at 983.

[48] S. Goering, "'You Say You're Happy, but...': Contested Quality of Life Judgments in Bioethics and Disability Studies" (2008) 5 *Bioethical Inquiry* 125, at 126, quoting L. Crow, "Including All of Our Lives: Renewing the Social Model of Disability" in J. Morris (ed.), *Encounters with Strangers: Feminism and Disability* (London: Women's Press, 1996), at 215.

[49] S. Goering, "'You Say You're Happy, but...': Contested Quality of Life Judgments in Bioethics and Disability Studies" (2008) 5 *Bioethical Inquiry* 125, at 129.

The second device for marginalizing the claims made by people with disabilities is to suggest that they are a product of lowered expectations. Here the argument is that while we "may recognize an individual's sincerity of belief about quality of life with an impairment ... any preferences for this way of living are likely the result of lowered expectations given the limited opportunities inherent in living with an impairment."[50] In other words, the "subjective satisfaction" cannot be taken at face value and "should be tempered by more objective measurements of quality of life, in which impairment is presumed to be negatively correlated with quality of life because of its ties to limited opportunity."[51]

Goering's analysis suggests that the negative correlation between quality of life and disability is so entrenched in the cultural imagination that even the contradictory views of people with disabilities are insufficient to challenge it seriously. This accords with Albrecht's and Devlieger's conclusions that "[t]he able-bodied public and even health care and social service workers" tend to focus on "the organic, functional and rational aspects of the conditions and problems" and as a result "grossly under-estimat[e] ... the importance of the mental, spiritual, emotional and social components that contribute to the persons with disabilities' quality of life."[52] They call this the "disability paradox," which they explain in the following way:

> [T]he disability paradox exists in two forms: first, people with disabilities report that they have serious limitations in activities of daily living, problems in performing their social roles and experience persistent discrimination yet they say that they have an excellent

[50] S. Goering, "'You Say You're Happy, but ...': Contested Quality of Life Judgments in Bioethics and Disability Studies" (2008) 5 *Bioethical Inquiry* 125, at 126.

[51] S. Goering, "'You Say You're Happy, but ...': Contested Quality of Life Judgments in Bioethics and Disability Studies" (2008) 5 *Bioethical Inquiry* 125, at 126.

[52] G. L. Albrecht and P. J. Devlieger, "The Disability Paradox: High Quality of Life against All Odds" (1999) 48 *Social Science and Medicine* 977, at 987.

or good quality of life; and, second, the general public, physicians and other health care workers perceive that persons with disabilities have an unsatisfying quality of life despite the fact that over 50% of these people report an excellent or good quality of life.[53]

The disabled respondents in Albrecht's and Devlieger's study pose two related challenges: first, to normative understandings of the impact of disability on life satisfaction and, second, to normative understandings of what goods make up a life of quality. Thus, if we take the disability paradox together with Goering's analysis, we can see multiple but related contradictions at work. Nondisabled views about the impact of disability on quality of life both inform and are informed by the "goods" against which quality of life is conventionally judged. Because self-sufficiency, competitiveness, and autonomy are conventionally seen as the primary goods that make life full, the authenticity of the subject that locates life's quality elsewhere (empathetic connection, helping others, doing a good job despite limitations) is questioned. At the very least, the disabled subject who claims to have a good quality of life seems difficult for the nondisabled majority to comprehend.

1.3 Is Disability Benign Bodily Difference?

As one challenge to this way of thinking about the relationship between disability and quality of life, disability scholars have criticized the "acute care paradigm of medicine"[54] in characterizing impairment. Asch, for example, has argued that medical understandings of the impact of disability on life tend to assume erroneously "that the life of a person with a chronic illness or disability is forever disrupted, as one's life might

---

[53] G. L. Albrecht and P. J. Devlieger, "The Disability Paradox: High Quality of Life against All Odds" (1999) 48 *Social Science and Medicine* 977, at 982.

[54] A. Silvers, "On the Possibility and Desirability of Constructing a Neutral Conception of Disability" (2003) 24 *Theoretical Medicine* 471, at 474.

be temporarily disrupted as a result of a back spasm."[55] The difficulty with this thinking, according to Asch, is that many "disabilities" are not experienced as illness or ill health, with the result that the comparison to sudden illness is misguided. As she goes on to explain, "[m]ost people with conditions such as spina bifida, achondroplasia, Down Syndrome and many other mobility and sensory impairments perceive themselves as healthy, not sick, and describe their conditions as givens of their lives – the equipment with which they meet the world."[56] This conceptualization of disability as a distinct way of being in the world, rather than a diminished state of being, is a shift that opens up new possibilities for thinking about impaired embodiment. It also raises myriad theoretical questions, as Jackie Leach Scully points out:

> If disability is a form of being rather than a medical condition, what form of being is it? ... What relationship does disability have to other social or ontological categories, such as gender, ethnicity or class? Is disability a genuine ontological category ... ? And if it *is* an identity, can it ever be anything other than a spoilt one ... that we are morally obliged to restore to normality if we can, or prevent happening if we can't?[57]

The idea that disability is or might be an identity thus has the potential to place disability on a similar footing to other embodied differences (sex, race, sexual orientation). This seems to have particular resonance in the context of prenatal diagnosis, where matters of identity (parental as well as prospective child) seem central to the decision to select against disability and, for some, the broader social implications of these decisions. However, these are highly contested positions.

---

[55] A. Asch, "Prenatal Diagnosis and Selective Abortion: A Challenge to Practice and Policy" (1999) 89 *American Journal of Public Health* 1649, at 1650.

[56] A. Asch, "Prenatal Diagnosis and Selective Abortion: A Challenge to Practice and Policy" (1999) 89 *American Journal of Public Health* 1649, at 1651.

[57] J. Leach Scully, "Disability and the Thinking Body" in K. Kristiansen, S. Vehmas and T. Shakespeare (eds.), *Arguing about Disability – Philosophical Perspectives* (Oxford: Routledge, 2010), 57 at 58.

Buchanan et al, for instance, argue for a distinction between the disability rights movement and other civil rights movements on the grounds that, unlike the sexual or racial minorities, the able-bodied majority have a "morally legitimate interest" in "avoiding the costs of changing society" to better accommodate people with disabilities.[58] In other words, disability is essentially different from other aspects of identity (sex, ethnicity, etc.) with respect to claims for social inclusion. Buchanan et al. argue that whereas the costs of changing society to include sexual or racial minorities is of "no moral weight because no one can have a morally legitimate interest in preserving unjust arrangements,"[59] there is a countervailing moral claim in the case of changing society to include people with disabilities. This countervailing claim is the majority's interest in "having access to a cooperative scheme that is the most productive and rewarding form of interaction in which he or she can participate effectively."[60] According to Buchanan et al., then, the minority's legitimate interest in inclusion must be balanced against the also legitimate majority interest in avoiding the costs associated with inclusion.[61]

Does this mean that it is not possible to have a conception of disability that is not value laden? Recently, Silvers has asked whether "disability can be other than an essentially contested concept."[62] An essentially contested concept, she explains, is one whose definition is

---

[58] A. Buchanan, D. Brock, N. Daniels, and D. Wikler, *From Chance to Choice: Genetics and Justice* (Cambridge: Cambridge University Press, 2000), 284.

[59] A. Buchanan, D. Brock, N. Daniels, and D. Wikler, *From Chance to Choice: Genetics and Justice* (Cambridge: Cambridge University Press, 2000), 284.

[60] A. Buchanan, D. Brock, N. Daniels, and D. Wikler, *From Chance to Choice: Genetics and Justice* (Cambridge: Cambridge University Press, 2000), 284.

[61] A. Buchanan, D. Brock, N. Daniels, and D. Wikler,, *From Chance to Choice: Genetics and Justice* (Cambridge: Cambridge University Press, 2000), 294. For a critique of this position, see R. Amundson and S. Tresky, "Bioethics and Disability: Conflicting Values and Perspectives" (2008) 5 *Bioethical Inquiry* 111.

[62] A. Silvers, "On the Possibility and Desirability of Constructing a Neutral Conception of Disability" (2003) 24 *Theoretical Medicine* 471, at 473.

"underspecified" with the result that "people with different beliefs" can "flesh [it] out in different ways."[63] The problem with ceding the definitional field to essential contestation, according to Silvers, is that "interlocutors load the term variously with their assumptions about value with no mutual method of resolving differences."[64] Silvers argues for a suspension of "dogmatically held normative convictions about disability"[65] (including the assumption that disability is intrinsically bad *as well as* the categorical insistence that "life with a disability always is worth living")[66] and argues instead for a neutral conception of disability. Silvers's suggestion that we create a neutral conceptual space around disability requires a nuanced approach that will accept that some impairments can be inherently bad (e.g., those associated with uncontrollable pain)[67] without conceding that all impairments are necessarily bad.

2 RESPONDING TO DISABILITY IN THE CONTEXT OF PRENATAL SCREENING AND SELECTION PRACTICES

The crafting of appropriate responses to disability is tied to conceptions of disability. Therefore, it is not surprising that there is disagreement about this issue also. There is an ongoing and lively debate about whether disability avoidance strategies constitute or contribute

[63] A. Silvers, "On the Possibility and Desirability of Constructing a Neutral Conception of Disability" (2003) 24 *Theoretical Medicine* 471, at 473.
[64] A. Silvers, "On the Possibility and Desirability of Constructing a Neutral Conception of Disability" (2003) 24 *Theoretical Medicine* 471, at 474.
[65] A. Silvers, "On the Possibility and Desirability of Constructing a Neutral Conception of Disability" (2003) 24 *Theoretical Medicine* 471, at 475.
[66] A. Silvers, "On the Possibility and Desirability of Constructing a Neutral Conception of Disability" (2003) 24 *Theoretical Medicine* 471, at 476.
[67] A. Silvers, "On the Possibility and Desirability of Constructing a Neutral Conception of Disability" (2003) 24 *Theoretical Medicine* 471, at 477.

to discrimination against people with disabilities. This debate wrestles with a range of tensions and oppositions, for example, between individual choice and social justice, harm and difference, and actions characterized as avoiding suffering, on the hand, and seeking perfection, on the other.

2.1 Eugenics, Discrimination, and the Expressivist Objection

If disability is a biological condition that is inherently bad, then it is possible to argue for the eradication of disability where this is possible. The means to ensure this may range from improving the health of the population through public health strategies, to curing the sick, remediating disabling conditions, and using the technologies available to prevent the births of people with (serious) disabilities. Within the medical model framework, all of these measures are taken to be socially useful and may even be morally required. Harris, for instance, argues that because disability is a harmed condition, it is morally permissible (or even morally preferable) to take steps to prevent it, including preventing the births of people who we know in advance will have disabling traits.[68]

If, on the other hand, disability is conceptualized in contextual or relational terms, then these remedial efforts might be cast in a different light. A familiar concern about prenatal selection practices is that they are a form of eugenics. Abby Lippman argues that the existence of screening programs "necessarily reflects the state-sponsored use of some genetic variation alone to value one group more than another."[69] Popular accounts also occasionally cast prenatal screening

[68] J. Harris, "Is There a Coherent Social Conception of Disability?" (2000) 26(2) *Journal of Medical Ethics* 95 at 99.

[69] A. Lippman, "Letter: Eugenics and Public Health" (2003) 93(1) *American Journal of Public Health* 11.

in this light. To take one example, a 2006 newspaper article on the rising incidence of abortions in Britain for Down syndrome observes that "[t]he NHS National Down Syndrome Cytogenic Register shows that there were 657 live births and an estimated 937 abortions in 2004 – the highest number of terminations for the condition on record, representing a three-fold increase over the past 15 years."[70] The article claims that when the national Down syndrome screening program was launched in 2003, there "were fears that it would be used to 'weed out' less than perfect babies, with parents pressured into having abortions.... Those fears now appear to have become a disturbing reality."[71]

The claim that antenatal screening programs are eugenic pursuits has, however, been criticized on the grounds that decisions to end pregnancies are made by individuals and not the state.[72] This criticism implies a more complex relationship between genetic intervention and social justice. Buchanan, for instance, has argued that the use of genetic technologies to reduce disabilities is appropriately framed as an attempt to improve people's lives, rather than a "commitment to *perfectionism*."[73] While this may be true, it is not clear that the individual pursuit of better lives can provide a decisive separation between past eugenics and contemporary selection practices. As Shildrick observes, "contemporary 'biomedical' decisions as to which disabilities are intolerable and should be eliminated at a genetic level, or foetal stage, or

---

[70] *Telegraph*, "Harrison's Parents Chose His Name When He Was a 35-week Foetus – Then They Were Offered a Termination" (21 May 2006), available online at http://www.telegraph.co.uk/news/uknews/1518952/Harrisons-parents-chose-his-name-when-he-was-a-35-week-foetus-then-they-were-offered-a-termination.html.

[71] *Telegraph*, "Harrison's Parents Chose His Name When He Was a 35-week Foetus – Then They Were Offered a Termination" (21 May 2006), available online at http://www.telegraph.co.uk/news/uknews/1518952/Harrisons-parents-chose-his-name-when-he-was-a-35-week-foetus-then-they-were-offered-a-termination.html.

[72] N. Rose, "The Politics of Life Itself" (2001) 18 *Theory, Culture & Society* 1, at 5.

[73] A. Buchanan, "Choosing Who Will Be Disabled: Genetic Intervention and the Morality of Inclusion" (1996) 13 *Social Philosophy and Policy* 18 at 46.

which should be subjected to interventionary procedures are no less likely made on the basis of cultural values."[74]

Another objection, often referred to as the expressivist objection, holds that medical interventions aimed at eliminating disabilities express a bias or constitute discrimination against people with those disabilities. Moreover, the drive toward normalcy exposes people with disabilities to risky and possibly unnecessary medical procedures.[75] In the sphere of remedial medical treatment, however, this objection has been criticized as lacking coherence. Silvers notes that

> whoever objects on the basis of principle to medical interventions aimed at avoiding disability must for consistency's sake eschew prophylactic medical treatment for all disabling conditions, both for themselves and their children. Yet there is no evidence that even the most ardent disability advocates are prepared to do so.[76]

More relevantly for our purposes, another form of the expressivist objection relates to the effects of prenatal and preimplantation selection practices. In this form, the argument is that selection practices such as termination of pregnancy "express a hurtful attitude about and send a hurtful message to people who live with those same traits."[77]

---

[74] M. Shildrick, "The Disabled Body, Genealogy and Undecidability" (2005) 19 *Cultural Studies* 755 at 763.

[75] A. Silvers, "On the Possibility and Desirability of Constructing a Neutral Conception of Disability" (2003) 24 *Theoretical Medicine* 471, at 476.

[76] A. Silvers, "On the Possibility and Desirability of Constructing a Neutral Conception of Disability" (2003) 24 *Theoretical Medicine* 471, at 476.

[77] E. Parens and A. Asch, "Disability Rights Critique of Prenatal Genetic Testing: Reflections and Recommendations" (2003) 9 *Mental Retardations and Developmental Disabilities Research Reviews* 40, at 42. The validity of the claim has been widely debated in the medical ethics literature: see, e.g., T. Shakespeare, "Debating Disability" (2008) 34 *Journal of Medical Ethics* 11; S. Edwards, "The Impairment/Disability Distinction: A Response to Shakespeare" (2008) 34 *Journal of Medical Ethics* 26; T. Koch, "Is Tom Shakespeare Disabled?" (2008) 34 *Journal of Medical Ethics* 18; R. Gillon, "Is There a 'New Ethics of Abortion'?" (2001) 27 *Journal of Medical Ethics* 5; J. Savulescu, "Is Current Practice around the Termination of Pregnancy Eugenic and Discriminatory?" (2001) 27 *Journal of Medical Ethics* 165.

Lippman highlights the impact of negative connotations stemming from prenatal genetic testing: "having a prenatal screening test specifically orientated to detect a particular condition – and Down syndrome provides a compelling example – expresses a social statement about the quality or the value of fetuses and children based solely on their genetic or chromosomal material."[78]

This objection has been criticized on a number of grounds: first, that fetuses and embryos do not have the moral status of persons, and, thus, actions taken in relation to these entities do not bear any relation to actual persons, who, by contrast, do have a moral status; [79] and, second, that no particular message can be conveyed by prenatal diagnosis and termination or embryo selection because the reasons behind these decisions are individual and justifiable. Gillot, for instance, argues that reproductive decisions are "framed by attitudes towards illness and not unreasonable expectations about the impact of such genetic disorders on their own and their children's lives."[80] Parents are merely making "a judgment about impairment ... and a guess about the life they, and a child with the particular condition, would have."[81] Harris also rejects the suggestion that "attempts to remove or pre-empt dysfunction or disability constitute discrimination against the disabled as a group, any more than medical treatment of a disease discriminates against the sick as a group."[82] He suggests that "we must separate the

---

[78] A. Lippman, "The Genetic Construction of Prenatal Testing: Choice, Consent or Conformity for Women?" in K. H. Rothenberg and E. J. Thomson (eds.), *Women and Prenatal Testing: Facing the Challenges of Genetic Technology* (Columbus: Ohio State University Press, 1994), at 17.

[79] J. Gillott, "Screening for Disability: A Eugenic Pursuit?" (2001) 27 *Journal of Medical Ethics* ii21–ii23, at ii22.

[80] J. Gillott, "Screening for Disability: A Eugenic Pursuit?" (2001) 27 *Journal of Medical Ethics* ii21–ii23, at ii22.

[81] J. Gillott, "Screening for Disability: A Eugenic Pursuit?" (2001) 27 *Journal of Medical Ethics* ii21–ii23, at ii22.

[82] J. Harris, "Is There a Coherent Social Conception of Disability?" (2000) 26 *Journal of Medical Ethics* 95, at 96.

question what is of use to existing disabled people from the question of what constitutes disability and the ethics of minimising its occurrence in the future."[83] Thus, Harris accepts on social justice grounds that efforts should be made to improve the lives of people with disabilities, but he rejects the suggestion that efforts to prevent the births of people with disabilities constitute discrimination of any kind.

2.2 Identity, Discrimination, and Autonomy

Nevertheless, disability scholars have questioned whether preventing the births of people with traits that are perceived as disabling goes beyond the scope of "preventing disability" to preventing people with disabilities from existing.[84] This is an important distinction to maintain, they argue, for without it we are in danger of allowing disability to overwhelm personhood. Parens and Asch claim that the tendency to conflate a single trait with the whole person is discriminatory:

> With both discrimination and prenatal diagnosis, nobody finds out about the rest. The tests send the message that there's no need to find out about the rest. Prenatal testing seems to be more of the discriminatory same: knowledge of the single trait is enough to warrant the abortion of an otherwise wanted fetus.[85]

---

[83] J. Harris, "Is There a Coherent Social Conception of Disability?" (2000) 26 *Journal of Medical Ethics* 95, at 99.

[84] For instance, see A. Asch, "Disability, Equality and Prenatal Testing: Contradictory or Compatible?" (2003) 30 *Florida State University Law Review* 315; E. Parens and A. Asch, "Disability Rights Critique of Prenatal Genetic Testing: Reflections and Recommendations" (2003) 9 *Mental Retardations and Developmental Disabilities Research Reviews* 40; A. Asch, "Prenatal Diagnosis and Selective Abortion: A Challenge to Practice and Policy" (1999) 89(11) *American Journal of Public Health* 1649.

[85] E. Parens and A. Asch, "Disability Rights Critique of Prenatal Genetic Testing: Reflections and Recommendations" (2003) 9 *Mental Retardations and Developmental Disabilities Research Reviews* 40, at 42.

In such a scenario, a "single trait stands in for the whole, the trait obliterates the whole."[86] We make a similar mistake, Asch argues, when we regard prenatal tests as a pathway to enhance the liberty of women:

> The tests do nothing to promote the health of the developing fetus or the health of the pregnant woman. Rather, they are offered so that people may decide against becoming a parent of a child with a particular characteristic that clinicians and policy makers understand to be detrimental to a satisfying life for the child or the family or that may require outlays of societal resources.[87]

There is, however, debate about whether this constitutes a form of discrimination. Sheldon and Wilkinson argue that the question of whether or not a decision to prevent the birth of a child with a disability is discriminatory depends on the nature of the harm being avoided. They argue that it is not discriminatory to select against impairments that are inherently seriously harmful. On the other hand, selections that seek to avoid impairments that are relatively minor, but that attract social stigma, might constitute a form of discrimination or at the very least collusion.[88] Of course, drawing distinctions between "serious" and "not serious" can be a challenging task, as we will see in Chapters 3, 4, and 5.

Holm also argues for a refinement of the notion of discrimination by distinguishing between actions that are "discriminatory" and those that are merely expressive of a "negative attitude."[89] He regards

---

[86] E. Parens and A. Asch, "Disability Rights Critique of Prenatal Genetic Testing: Reflections and Recommendations" (2003) 9 *Mental Retardations and Developmental Disabilities Research Reviews* 40, at 42.

[87] A. Asch, "Disability Equality and Prenatal Testing: Contradictory or Compatible?" (2003) 30 *Florida State University Law Review* 315, at 337.

[88] S. Sheldon and S. Wilkinson, "Termination of Pregnancy for Reason of Fetal Disability: Are There Grounds for a Special Exception in Law?" (2001) 9 *Medical Law Review* 85 at 104–5.

[89] S. Holm, "The Expressivist Objection to Prenatal Diagnosis: Can It Be Laid to Rest?" (2008) 34 *Journal of Medical Ethics* 24, at 24.

prenatal diagnosis as expressing the latter but not necessarily the former. Thus:

> If having a particular disability is an essential part of my personal identity, part of what I am, the mere fact that I know or have reasonable reasons to believe ... that others evaluate that disability negatively may affect my sense of identity and social standing negatively. And I may justifiably feel that way even if the negative evaluation does not lead to any actual discrimination.[90]

Holm reasons that, at the very least, when parents decide to terminate an otherwise wanted pregnancy they are expressing a negative attitude toward disability.[91] He reasons, "they are choosing between a world with the disabled child and another without it, and this must, in some cases at least, entail that they value (the particular) disability so negatively that they think the world without the disabled child is preferable simply because it does not contain that child."[92]

Parens and Asch argue that the fact that "prospective parents do not intend to send a hurtful message does not speak to the fact that many people with disabilities receive such a message and are pained by it."[93] However, it is also important to observe that the way in which parents respond to a prenatal test result is highly contingent and can conceivably range from negative or discriminatory attitudes toward disability, to concern about the impact that a child with extra needs may have on their life (either emotionally or financially), to fear about the grief, loss, and suffering that passing on a trait with which they

---

[90] S. Holm, "The Expressivist Objection to Prenatal Diagnosis: Can It Be Laid to Rest?" (2008) 34 *Journal of Medical Ethics* 24, at 24.

[91] S. Holm, "The Expressivist Objection to Prenatal Diagnosis: Can It Be Laid to Rest?" (2008) 34 *Journal of Medical Ethics* 24, at 24.

[92] S. Holm, "The Expressivist Objection to Prenatal Diagnosis: Can It Be Laid to Rest?" (2008) 34 *Journal of Medical Ethics* 24, at 24.

[93] E. Parens and A. Asch, "Disability Rights Critique of Prenatal Genetic Testing: Reflections and Recommendations" (2003) 9 *Mental Retardations and Developmental Disabilities Research Reviews* 40, at 42.

have personal experience (either as an affected person or as the parent or relative of an affected person) will entail.[94] Indeed, Parens and Asch concede that "the meaning of prenatal testing for would-be parents is not clear or singular."[95] Moreover, Murphy suggests that even if selecting against disability expresses a hurtful attitude toward disability, this alone does not settle the question of whether limits should be placed on such practices. He argues that reproductive autonomy can be defended in this context even if selection practices do express a hurtful attitude toward disability.[96]

We can see that this debate reflects and extends many of the themes explored in our discussion of the construction of disability. The arguments against the contention that selection practices are discriminatory approach this question with an understanding that at least some forms of impairment are inherently bad or constitute a cause of suffering that can be ameliorated quite legitimately – on either individual or distributive justice grounds – by preventing the births of children

[94] E. Parens and A. Asch, "Disability Rights Critique of Prenatal Genetic Testing: Reflections and Recommendations" (2003) 9 *Mental Retardations and Developmental Disabilities Research Reviews* 40, at 42. For the argument that selection decisions in the context of pregnancy do not necessarily imply a negation of people with those disabilities see also J. Nelson, "The Meaning of the Act: Reflections on the Expressive Force of Reproductive Decision-making Policies" (1998) 8 *Kennedy Institute of Ethics Journal* 165; J. Malek, "Deciding against Disability: Does the Use of Reproductive Genetic Technologies Express a Disvalue for People with Disabilities?" (2010) 36 *Journal of Medical Ethics* 217.

[95] E. Parens and A. Asch, "Disability Rights Critique of Prenatal Genetic Testing: Reflections and Recommendations" (2003) 9 *Mental Retardations and Developmental Disabilities Research Reviews* 40, at 42.

[96] T. Murphy, "When Choosing the Traits of Children Is Hurtful to Others" (2011) 37 *Journal of Medical Ethics* 105. There is in addition a considerable feminist literature that explores and defends women's reproductive autonomy to select against disability. See, for example, B. Bennett, "Prenatal Diagnosis, Genetics and Reproductive Decision-making" (2001) 9 *Journal of Law and Medicine* 28–40; B. Steinbock, *Disability, Prenatal Testing and Selective Abortion* (Washington, DC: Georgetown University Press, 2002); E. Jackson, "Abortion, Autonomy and Prenatal Diagnosis" (2000) 9 *Social and Legal Studies* 467.

that would have those impairments. Disability scholars have countered that selection practices have broader social impacts: They prevent the births of people with disability and they contribute to cultures of social exclusion for people with disabilities (who in turn interpret selection practices as personal affronts). Importantly, this debate is overlain by a vigorous sociocultural commitment to the value of individual autonomy, which feeds into these characterizations of selection practices and further complicates matters. Thus, even those who would argue that selection practices are discriminatory or at least express a negative attitude toward disability have found it difficult to answer persuasively the objection that prenatal selection practices are a matter of reproductive choice that parents are entitled to exercise. Nonetheless, it is questionable whether a simple appeal to individual autonomy can provide any sort of final resolution to this debate. Reproductive decisions and selections do not take place apart from cultural understandings of and commitments to supporting people with disabilities, and so there appears to be some circularity in these debates about disability and reproductive choice. This is an issue to which we now turn.

3 HOW DOES THE DISABILITY CRITIQUE RELATE TO REPRODUCTIVE CHOICE?

Prenatal tests are often presented as having the neutral purpose of conveying information to prospective parents to facilitate an "informed choice" about their pregnancies rather than predetermining any particular outcome. As Lippman has observed, "choice has been a cardinal theme"[97] in the field of prenatal testing. The emphasis on "choice" has the dual effect of foregrounding the individual autonomy of women and simultaneously distancing prenatal screening and diagnosis from

---

[97] A. Lippman, "Choice as a Risk to Women's Health" 1 *Health, Risk and Society* 281, at 281.

the eugenics of the recent past. Consequently, many feminists have supported prenatal testing technologies as a means of enhancing reproductive freedom by enabling women to make individual assessments about the limits of maternity from their own perspectives.[98] However, "choices" are necessarily dependent on the availability of at least two courses of action that are reasonably open to the decision maker and both critical feminist and disability scholars have questioned whether this is an accurate description of social reality for many women. Lippman, for instance, asks, "is continuing a pregnancy after testing suggests the baby to be born will have Down's syndrome a real choice when society does not accept children with disabilities or provide assistance for their sustenance?"[99]

As examined previously, the disability critique has questioned negative assumptions about disability, and these arguments have particular relevance to our understanding of the social context in which reproductive choices are being made. Feminist scholars have added texture to this critique by critically examining the complex sociopolitical environment that informs and shapes women's responses to offers of testing.[100] Rapp, for instance, has provided rich accounts of the multiple

[98] See, for example, B. Bennett, "Prenatal Diagnosis, Genetics and Reproductive Decision-making" (2001) 9 *Journal of Law and Medicine* 28–40; B. Steinbock, *Disability, Prenatal Testing and Selective Abortion* (Washington, DC: Georgetown University Press, 2002); E. Jackson, "Abortion, Autonomy and Prenatal Diagnosis" (2000) 9 *Social and Legal Studies* 467. For an argument that the feminist and disability rights approaches are fundamentally irreconcilable with respect to selective abortion see S. Sharp and S. Earle, "Feminism, Abortion and Disability: Irreconcilable Differences?" (2002) 17 *Disability and Society* 137.

[99] A. Lippman, "Choice as a Risk to Women's Health" 1 *Health, Risk and Society* 281, at 283.

[100] See R. Rapp, "Women's Responses to Prenatal Diagnosis: A Sociocultural Perspective on Diversity" in K. Rothenberg and E. Thomson (eds.), *Women and Prenatal Testing: Facing the Challenges of Genetic Technology* (Columbus: Ohio State University Press, 1994), 219; A. Lippman, "Embodied Knowledge and Making Sense of Prenatal Diagnosis" (1999) 8 *Journal of Genetic Counseling* 255; A. Lippman, "The Genetic Construction of Prenatal Testing: Choice, Consent, or Conformity for Women?"

ways in which individual, familial, and community histories intersect to generate the beliefs about disability and reproductive responsibility that women deploy in their decision making. Further building on these analyses, some feminists have emphasized the interdependence of individual testing choices and the social contexts within which these choices are embedded, arguing that "political systems, cultural beliefs and complex patterns of human relationships overlap, alter and are altered by the application of screening."[101]

The multiplicity of feminist responses to prenatal testing technologies reflects the fact that these technologies are, to borrow from Rapp, "always potentially both" "liberatory [and] socially controlling … depending on the weight various social and individual experiences hold in a particular woman's life."[102] This suggests that a uniform feminist response to prenatal testing technologies may be neither possible nor desirable. However, the critiques of prenatal testing persuade us that we ought to be circumspect about overly simplistic assurances that "choice" always governs decision making in these contexts. From this perspective, it seems important to maintain a focus on whether, and if so how, the full range of reproductive choices are being enabled or constrained. In this section, therefore, we focus on two of the key decision points that arise during the prenatal testing process: the decision

in K. Rothenberg and E. Thomson, (eds.) *Women and Prenatal Testing: Facing the Challenges of Genetic Technology* (Columbus: Ohio State University Press, 1994), 9. For criticism of some of the feminist critiques of testing technologies see: D. Wertz and J. Fletcher, "A Critique of Some Feminist Challenges to Prenatal Diagnosis" (1993) 2 *Journal of Women's Health* 173.

[101] A. Lippman, "The Genetic Construction of Prenatal Testing: Choice, Consent or Conformity for Women?" in K. Rothenberg and E. Thomson (eds.), *Women and Prenatal Testing: Facing the Challenges of Genetic Technology* (Columbus: Ohio State University Press, 1994) 9, at 30.

[102] R. Rapp, "Women's Responses to Prenatal Diagnosis: A Sociocultural Perspective on Diversity" in K. Rothenberg and E. Thomson (eds.), *Women and Prenatal Testing: Facing the Challenges of Genetic Technology* (Columbus: Ohio State University Press, 1994), 219, 229.

whether to accept prenatal testing and the decision of how to respond to the testing results. Our principal focus concerns how disability is presented in these decisions, but we also want to consider how testing may shape both the idea and possibility of authentic choice, and how individuals' reproductive choices in turn construct cultural understandings of disability. Finally, as disability and risk are both concepts that have been deployed in the exercise of reproductive choice, we touch lightly on risk in the following analysis. However, this will be the subject of more extensive interrogation in Chapter 2.

3.1 Constructing the Choice to Accept Testing

A good place to begin this analysis is to ask: How is disability presented to women in the context of testing? What reasons are offered for testing for the particular disability in question? A NSW Health pamphlet entitled "Special Tests for Your Baby during Pregnancy" describes the purpose of prenatal testing as follows:

> A prenatal test is usually done to determine if your baby is developing in the usual way or if it could be at risk of or affected by a specific condition.[103]

However, it is important to notice that the choice about testing is simultaneously framed by a set of normative propositions about what prospective parents want. Thus, the pamphlet also states that

> every couple wants to have a healthy baby. However, there are some couples whose baby may have or will develop a serious physical and/ or intellectual condition.[104]

---

[103] NSW Health, "Prenatal Testing: Special Tests for Your Baby during Pregnancy" (8 August 2007), at 3.

[104] NSW Health, "Prenatal Testing: Special Tests for Your Baby during Pregnancy" (8 August 2007), at 2.

We can see a number of key ideas deployed in this advice to prospective parents – reproductive ideals ("everyone wants a healthy baby"), the prospect of having reassurance that the baby is "developing in the usual way," and an awareness of the risk that the baby may "have or will develop a serious condition." Together these ideas comprise a complex set of norms and associations – among health, abnormality, and reproductive norms – that prospective parents must negotiate in order to make their choice about whether to accept testing. On closer examination, it can be seen that a number of messages are conveyed: first, that prenatal tests detect problems that will adversely affect the health of a prospective child; second, that the meaning of "health" is self-evident; third, that testing will uncover risks of "serious" conditions (and that what is "serious" is self-evident), and, finally, that testing can fulfill the prospective parents' desire to be reassured that their baby is healthy.

While all of these messages may be true for some cases, they do not provide a complete account of the possibilities raised by prenatal testing. Testing may, for instance, detect anomalies that may not seriously affect health – either because the health effects associated with the detected anomaly will be only mild or because there is not necessarily an association between the anomaly detected and "unhealthiness" as it is commonly perceived (for example, is a child who has Down syndrome, dwarfism, or a cleft palate necessarily "unhealthy"?). Conversely, they may not detect other anomalies that *will* seriously affect health. Although the disability studies critique has opened a small space to allow these distinctions to be made and interrogated, there remains minimal social acceptance of the idea that it is reasonable for parents to accept the birth of an "unhealthy" child or, more radically, to challenge the claim that a child with that condition is in fact unhealthy. Thus, there is a danger that the articulation of the ideal ("everyone wants a healthy baby") as the implicit goal of testing, combined with the caution that "some babies will have a serious condition," constrains the possibility of genuine choice. In a social context in which health is highly valued, the conflation of abnormality with ill health in effect expands our sense of what ill health means to encompass the full range of detectable differences. This feeds into and encourages a moral logic in which parents who reject testing have knowingly imposed a negative "health" outcome on their child, if the tested-for condition materializes.

In addition to this, the use of the concept of a "serious condition" to frame the offer of testing may itself exert a subtle form of pressure to accept the offer. "Serious" suggests an abnormality that is inherently bad. This in turn carries the implication that these are the sorts of risks that responsible parents will wish to guard against. Silvers observes that after a diagnosis has been confirmed, "prospective parents [are placed] on the defensive if they do not display reservations about having such a child."[105] Indeed, by framing the offer of testing with the claim that "every couple wants a healthy baby," there is a clear implication that the failure to take up the offer of testing is not only risky, but also reckless in the absence of some compelling justification for it. Silvers argues then that there is a conceptual pressure brought to bear on prospective parents to justify their reproductive decisions. She goes on to say:

> They are expected to justify continuing "risky" pregnancies that may result in children with disabilities, but the discourse does not equally require them to defend pregnancies with no such prognosis. In other words, the discourse exerts conceptual pressure by putting parents on the defensive if they do not exclude the option of living with (a child who has a) disability.[106]

The claim that reproductive decisions require, either implicitly or explicitly, some form of justification at the very least complicates the idea that testing is freely chosen. Shakespeare has argued that

> there is evidence that the choice to have ante-natal tests, and the freedom to decide whether or not to proceed with pregnancy, is not

---

[105] A. Silvers, "On the Possibility and Desirability of Constructing a Neutral Conception of Disability" (2003) 24 *Theoretical Medicine* 471, at 480.
[106] A. Silvers, "On the Possibility and Desirability of Constructing a Neutral Conception of Disability" (2003) 24 *Theoretical Medicine* 471, at 480.

as free and open as the medical establishment would suggest.... The very existence of a test for foetal abnormality can create pressures to use the technology. Therefore, it is naive to say that technology is neutral, because the possibility of obtaining prenatal genetic information inevitably creates new problems and dilemmas which were not previously available, and the implication is that testing and selection is a desirable outcome.[107]

To illustrate this same point neatly, Barbara Katz Rothman compares the assimilation of testing into everyday prenatal management with the advent of the motorcar and asks, "is there any meaningful way one could now choose horses over cars as a means of transportation?"[108]

The decisional aid produced by the Murdoch Children's Research Institute (MCRI) provides an opportunity to explore these concerns in more depth. This is an online resource that has been developed to assist women with the decision of whether to undergo testing.[109] The resource explains the various tests available, how they work, and the conditions they are designed to identify. After this, the aid canvasses, using a simple narrative structure, four women who made "different decisions [about prenatal testing] based on their views on accuracy, safety and timing of the tests." Wendy, a twenty-four-year-old woman having her first baby, decided to have the screening test because "[s]he wants as much information as possible on her pregnancy." Tania is a twenty-eight-year-old woman who "has decided not to have any prenatal testing because she thinks that the risk of women her age is low for Down syndrome." Rebecca, a thirty-seven-year-old having her third baby, wants to have "definite information" about her pregnancy

---

[107] T. Shakespeare, "Choices and Rights: Eugenics, Genetics and Disability Equality" (1998) 13(5) *Disability and Society* 665, at 675–6.

[108] B. Katz Rothman, "The Products of Conception: The Social Context of Reproductive Choices" (1985) 11 *Journal of Medical Ethics* 188, at 192.

[109] Murdoch Children's Research Institute, "Your Choice: Screening and Diagnostic Tests in Pregnancy" (2004) available at http://www.mcri.edu.au/Downloads/Prenatal TestingDecisionAid.pdf. The women's stories (discussed below) appear at 15–16.

so has decided to have a diagnostic test rather than screening tests. Finally, Sue is "a 40 year old woman who is pregnant for the first time after trying to have a baby for years." Being aware of "the increased risk of women her age for chromosomal abnormalities like Down syndrome," she has decided to have screening because she wants to avoid the risk of miscarriage. The attitudes of these women toward abortion for abnormality are also canvassed in their stories, and here too a range of opinions is represented. Thus, "Wendy doesn't think she would terminate the pregnancy. However, she thinks knowing about an abnormality before her baby is born would be helpful to her." Tania, who did not accept testing, also did not express a view on abortion, while Rebecca "doesn't think she would continue" with her pregnancy, and Sue does not know what she would do.

The vignettes canvass a range of possible approaches that might be taken, as a means to help women to clarify their own values and needs with respect to prenatal testing and thus reach their decision. Importantly, the aid does not construct the decision to accept testing as necessarily "selecting against disability" (though it may of course lead to that result) but rather as "being informed" rather than not being informed. While this undoubtedly is a more balanced approach, this opportunity to gather information about the pregnancy may be difficult to resist, especially in a social environment that values information and understands "being informed" as central to self-determination. Lippman, for instance, argues that the emphasis on measures that are meant to foster some degree of competence and control over pregnancy frequently translates "into a 'need' for testing." This perspective also suggests that undertaking testing is rather more complex than a straightforward expression of choice would suggest. Lippman continues:

> Evidence that the fetus is developing as expected may provide some women with a sense that all is under control … Personal experience is set aside in favor of external and measured evidence. Moreover, given that a pregnant woman is more and more frequently reduced

to a "uterine environment" and looked upon as herself presenting dangers to the fetus,... being tested becomes an early warning system to identify whether this "environment" is adequate.[110]

The MCRI aid states that women may decide not to have any testing. Nevertheless, three of the four women represented in the vignettes accepted some form of testing, and the woman who did not, declined, not because she was comfortable with the idea of having a child with Down syndrome but because she rated her risk of having a baby with Down syndrome as low. The aid does not include a scenario in which a woman declines testing because she *does not wish to make any choice* about whether to continue her pregnancy based on prenatal diagnostic or screening information. A difficulty with this is that without the inclusion of this response to testing, users of the decisional aid are primed to consider the reasons for not accepting testing in terms of their perceptions of risk – either of disability or of miscarriage. These then become the main reasons for refusing testing. In other words, the aid acknowledges that testing may be refused according to subjective perceptions of risk, but offers limited space for refusing testing simply because one does not want to know or one does not accept the premise of the test: that is, that it may identify a "disabling" condition. This implies that being "informed" about risk is the norm for women's reproductive behavior, and this may be so even when a woman would not terminate the pregnancy.

This raises a more general question about how risk information is presented as this will inevitably influence women's own perceptions of risk. The *type of risk information* on which perceptions of risk are based is an issue taken up in Chapter 2 where we argue that the growing perception that all pregnancies are presumptively at risk results in such information, perhaps unwittingly, adding to a panoply of forces that

[110] A. Lippman, "Prenatal Genetic Testing and Screening: Constructing Needs and Reinforcing Inequities" (1991) 17 *American Journal of Law and Medicine* 15, at 29.

helps to create an environment in which there is pressure on women to undergo testing.

Interestingly, one of the four women, Wendy, does not think that a finding of abnormality would disrupt her plans to continue the pregnancy, but, crucially, she accepts testing because "she thinks knowing about an abnormality before her baby is born would be helpful to her." Thus, the choice to continue with an abnormal pregnancy is acknowledged as a possible outcome of the testing process, where it is made with full knowledge. Accordingly, the aid elaborates on the nature of the information that is provided to women such as Wendy with a view to arming them with knowledge about an abnormality.

While some hospital policies and patient guides on prenatal testing acknowledge the possibility of not wanting to participate in testing at all, these statements are nonetheless made within a context that emphasizes the importance and benefits of "informed choice."[111] Where more information is constructed as a good thing, the choice "not to know" or to make an "uninformed" choice by deciding not to

[111] See, for example, the NSW Health policy entitled "Prenatal Testing/Screening for Down Syndrome and Other Chromosomal Abnormalities" (8 August 2007), which states that "offers of screening need to be accompanied by sufficient information and counselling, with professional interpreter services if necessary, to *help women choose screening* on an informed basis" (at 3 – our emphasis) and "[i]t is recognised that not all women will want to use prenatal screening or diagnostic tests. Any test undertaken should be consented to on the basis of provision of full relevant information. It is important that women/couples considering prenatal screening or diagnostic testing make an informed choice appropriate to them and free from coercion" (at 5). For another example, see the Queensland Health brochure "Screening for Down Syndrome in Pregnancy," which suggests all women should consider having testing because "[e]ven if you don't want to know [the risk of your baby having Down syndrome], ... a nuchal translucency scan can give you other important information about your pregnancy such as whether you are having twins." For an example of one pamphlet that better balances the right to know with the right not to know, see the Victorian Government 3 Centres pamphlet "A Guide to Tests and Investigations for Uncomplicated Pregnancies," which notes (at 14) that testing may make women anxious, and that "[j]ust because we have a test available doesn't automatically mean you should be tested."

have prenatal testing may be constructed as an abnormal, and potentially even irresponsible, path for prospective parents to take.[112] In this context, it is clear that – despite what may be legitimate efforts by health care providers to portray testing in a neutral way – this may be difficult to achieve under current social conditions.

3.2 Selecting against Disability

While taking up the offer of testing is one decision that would-be parents can make, an adverse outcome to the testing will necessarily throw up other more distressing decisions. As we have seen, in accepting the offer of testing, women necessarily surrender the option not to make a decision about continuing their pregnancy based on the detection of a disabling trait. A woman may theoretically choose to accept or reject the option of continuing with the pregnancy, but the option to do neither – simply to avoid making a decision altogether – has been foreclosed by the test result. Katz Rothman sounded a note of concern about this almost 15 years ago:

> In gaining the choice to control the quality of our children, we may rapidly lose the choice not to control the quality, the choice to accept them as they are. The new reproductive technology is offered to us in terms of expanding choices. But it is always true that while new reproductive technology opens up some choices, it closes down others.[113]

---

[112] Indeed, the information that is presented to women about prenatal testing has to be seen in a broader societal context: that is, a societal context in which the need for "responsible reproduction" is emphasized strongly. Even before conception, women are confronted by messages that stress the importance of maintaining optimal health so as to enable the birth of a "healthy" baby. This is discussed at length in Chapter 2.

[113] B. Katz Rothman, *The Tentative Pregnancy: Prenatal Diagnosis and the Future of Motherhood* (New York: Viking, 1986), at 11.

Although many prospective parents might be grateful for the opportunity to choose to abandon an affected pregnancy, the fact that a conscious decision must be made might itself be a distressing or painful realization for parents, as the following passage extracted from a NSW Health publication suggests:

> The "pain" felt was I think, often caused, not because of the emotions felt e.g. anger, fear etc but because of there not being any clear and definite "right" decision to make, too many options and yet not enough information about the available resources.[114]

In addition to the pain and distress of having to make a decision that may otherwise have remained unmade, parents who find themselves in this position are given a strong message that the decision facing them is a terrible one. The adverse result transforms the parents from being in the positive and valued position of "being able to make an informed choice" to being told that prenatal diagnosis of abnormality is necessarily a negative event. This construction of the diagnosis of abnormality is captured in another NSW Health brochure, "Diagnosis of Abnormality in an Unborn Baby: The Impact, Options and Afterwards."[115] This brochure describes the identification of an abnormality prenatally as "often the beginning of a very difficult, perhaps devastating sequence of events."[116] The characterization of the "sequence of events" following diagnosis as devastating conveys a cluster of ideas about a prenatal finding of abnormality, including the result's unexpected nature, the difficulty of reaching the decision to

---

[114] NSW Health (Support after Fetal Diagnosis for Abnormality), "Diagnosis of Abnormality in an Unborn Baby: The Impact, Options and Afterwards" (August 2006), at 5.

[115] NSW Health (Support after Fetal Diagnosis for Abnormality), "Diagnosis of Abnormality in an Unborn Baby: The Impact, Options and Afterwards" (August 2006).

[116] NSW Health (Support after Fetal Diagnosis for Abnormality), "Diagnosis of Abnormality in an Unborn Baby: The Impact, Options and Afterwards" (August 2006), at 4.

terminate a previously wanted pregnancy, the difficulty of continuing with a pregnancy in the face of a positive diagnosis, and perhaps grief for what has been lost. Indeed, the pamphlet goes on to articulate many of these ideas specifically. Thus, the reader is informed that "parents say that learning that their unborn baby has serious problems means the end of all their hopes and dreams about having a healthy, normal baby"[117] and that "finding out your unborn baby has an abnormality is one of life's most unjust events and it is very difficult to accept."[118] The overall message is that prenatal diagnosis of abnormality will, at least initially, evoke fear, grief, and possibly anger. We can see then that this literature is working from the premise that prenatal diagnosis of abnormality will necessarily elicit a negative response.

In addition to the prenatal diagnosis of abnormality's being constructed as a negative experience, prospective parents in this situation must also confront the implicit expectation that their decision will be to select against disability. Once again this expectation or norm emerges despite attempts to construct a "neutral" space for parents making this choice. For example, the same NSW Health publication explains that if a baby has a problem:

> you and your partner will be given as much information as possible about the condition. This includes the implications it might have for the future health or development of the baby. You will be given time to make an informed choice about whether or not you would like to continue the pregnancy.[119]

---

[117] NSW Health (Support after Fetal Diagnosis for Abnormality), "Diagnosis of Abnormality in an Unborn Baby: The Impact, Options and Afterwards" (August 2006), at 6.

[118] NSW Health (Support after Fetal Diagnosis for Abnormality), "Diagnosis of Abnormality in an Unborn Baby: The Impact, Options and Afterwards" (August 2006), at 6.

[119] NSW Health (Support after Fetal Diagnosis for Abnormality), "Diagnosis of Abnormality in an Unborn Baby: The Impact, Options and Afterwards" (August 2006), at 19.

While this seems to present a rational, neutral approach to decision making Bauer, drawing on her experiences as the mother of a daughter with Down syndrome, provides an illustration of how in reality, these "neutral spaces" may be reshaped by a social world in which the presence of children like her daughter seem to require an explanation:

> Many young women, upon meeting us, have asked whether I had "the test." I interpret the question as a get-home-free card. If I say no, they figure, that means I'm a victim of circumstance, and therefore not implicitly repudiating the decision they may make to abort if they think there are disabilities involved. If yes, then it means I'm a right-wing antiabortion nut whose choices aren't relevant to their lives. Either way, they win.[120]

To pose the question "did you have the test?" implies that something about the presence of a child who has Down syndrome is unexpected. In this respect, Down syndrome may be a special case: Affected individuals are quite recognizable, the condition is widely understood to be detectable prenatally, and, indeed, screening programs have been established to do just that. Nevertheless, the question "did you have the test?" seems to invite some explanation for the child's presence in the world. That this should be so really only makes sense if the birth of the child signals a departure from some imagined "normal" course of events. In this way, the "neutral space" discussed is shown to be an illusion, the norm of selecting against disability is instantiated, and the possible reasons for continuing with the pregnancy are narrowed to prenatal ignorance of the diagnosis (victim of circumstance) or willful maternal resistance (religious objection) to the norm.

The notion that the reproductive norm is to select against disability is also evident in other literature disseminated to women after an adverse result. Although such literature maintains the position that

---

[120] P. Bauer, "The Abortion Debate No One Wants to Have: Prenatal Testing Is Making Your Right to Abort a Disabled Child More like 'your Duty' to Abort a Disabled Child" *Washington Post* (18 October 2005), available online at http://www.washingtonpost.com/wp-dyn/content/article/2005/10/17/AR2005101701311.html.

women have two available paths, the social pressure to select against disability is clearly recognized:

> You may not have met with much encouragement to continue your pregnancy. Sometimes doctors, radiologists or your family can be critical of this decision and may try to discourage you from giving birth to a baby with a medical problem. To make a decision in the face of opposition is a very difficult and courageous thing to do.[121]

Lippman wonders whether women feel able to refuse prenatal testing when it is offered to them because they harbor fears about whether "there will be support, acceptance, and appreciation for a child predicted to have some disability if that child is brought into the world."[122] This too is canvassed in the other NSW Health brochure, which notes that "[s]ome people may not understand why you have chosen to continue a pregnancy when you know there is a diagnosed problem. They may feel that you somehow asked for all the trauma and difficulties when you made the decision you did."[123] These responses demonstrate how the norm of selecting against disability has become so well established that not only are parents who decide to continue with an affected pregnancy acting outside standard behaviors, they have gone so far beyond the norm that it is acceptable to position them as solely responsible for the repercussions of that decision.[124] Thus we see that "informed choice" has a downside, especially where choice entails personal responsibility for the outcome. Where the choice is to continue

---

[121] NSW Health, "When Your Unborn Baby Has a Problem: How to Manage the Weeks Ahead (a Book for Families)" (March 2006), at 7.

[122] A. Lippman, "Letter: Eugenics and Public Health" (2003) 93(1) *American Journal of Public Health* 11, 11.

[123] NSW Health , "When your Baby has a Problem: How to Manage the Weeks Ahead (a Book for Families)" (March 2006), at 14.

[124] For an extended discussion of how the choice to test has the potential to reframe our understandings of responsibility, see A. Lippman, "Choice as a Risk to Women's Health" (1999) 1 *Health, Risk and Society* 281, at 288.

with an affected pregnancy, this might include responsibility for any suffering the child may experience, for any difficulties the parents may experience in raising the child, or for any additional "costs" to society associated with the child's disability. For many parents, this responsibility may seem too heavy a burden to bear alone. As a result, this transfer of responsibility from society to the individual in turn further strengthens the norm of selecting against disability, as the specter of sole responsibility seems likely to influence more and more parents to terminate affected pregnancies so as to avoid this burden.

3.3 Do Prenatal Tests Overdetermine Disability?

In light of the preceding analysis, we might ask: To what extent does the availability of prenatal testing influence our understanding of what counts as a disability? This question seems to have a persistent, nagging presence in media reports about prenatal testing technologies despite the fact that prenatal diagnostic technologies are predominantly presented as socially beneficial. To take one example, Alasdair Palmer, writing for the London-based *Telegraph* newspaper, responds cautiously to the news that a new noninvasive test is being developed that will enable parents to discover any genetic "disorders" in a fetus at six to seven weeks gestation. He writes:

> There is ... a downside in that the test may also eventually make it possible for parents to obtain a complete genetic profile of the foetus they have conceived. This raises the spectre of an enormous proliferation of abortions, as parents decide to get rid of unborn babies not just because of genetic illnesses such as spinal muscular atrophy or Huntington's disease, but also because the foetus's DNA profile suggests the child will be born with a cleft palate or with below average intelligence.[125]

[125] A. Palmer, "Genetic Tests Could Prevent Those like Me Being Born at All" *Telegraph* (11 December 2010), available online at http://www.telegraph.co.uk/comment/

Palmer is troubled by the prospect that "any genetic defect" will result in termination, though he seems supportive of that outcome if the genetic defect is serious enough. This bifurcation of "serious" and "other" defects is the very thing that seems threatened by this new development in prenatal testing. For some people, it raises troubling questions: When all genetic variation can be discovered at a very early stage in pregnancy, will parents refuse to accept "any" genetic defect? In other words, will disability be increasingly understood as "any" genetic variation? Will parents increasingly expect to be able to "perfect" their pregnancies?

Further, we might ask: To what extent does the availability of a test prescribe, or at least contribute to the perception that, the trait is a disabling one? Silvers argues that it is "unlikely that medical procedures themselves are the cause of disregard for disability. A more plausible analysis understands medicine to be influenced by, and the instrument of, broader societal attitudes."[126] This leads her to the conclusion that selective termination "which harms the yet-to-be-born … can be traced to a prior underlying cause, namely societal antipathy against the disabled."[127] However, it seems unclear to us that definitive claims about cause can be made in any straightforward way. No doubt there is a background of societal antipathy toward people with disabilities, but there is also a sense in which disability is constructed by the technologies that test for it. Thus, it seems to us that the anxiety expressed in the media report quoted previously stems from a recognition that what amounts to "disability" is, at least at some level, constructed by prenatal detection technologies and the myriad ways in which they are or might be used. In that case, this recognition seems to have triggered a

---

columnists/alasdair-palmer/8196287/Genetic-tests-could-prevent-those-like-me-being-born-at-all.html. We consider these technologies in detail in Chapter 6.

[126] A. Silvers, "On the Possibility and Desirability of Constructing a Neutral Conception of Disability" (2003) 24 *Theoretical Medicine* 471, at 476.

[127] A. Silvers, "On the Possibility and Desirability of Constructing a Neutral Conception of Disability" (2003) 24 *Theoretical Medicine* 471, at 476–7.

fear that if there is testing for what might be considered to be a "trivial" condition such as cleft palate, this may in turn lead to the characterization of this condition as a "disability" and, after this, an "enormous proliferation of abortions." The media report seems to suggest that while women should be able to choose to have an abortion for some conditions, abortion for trivial conditions would amount to *too much* reproductive choice.

One solution to this concern is to limit the use of abortion or PGD to the avoidance of "serious" conditions. In many jurisdictions, this is the approach taken by law. Thus, in Chapters 3 and 4, the legal requirement that a disability be "serious" will be examined in considerable depth, and in Chapter 5 we will consider how decisions about which conditions are "serious" are being made in practice. Throughout these chapters we will be examining the meaning of seriousness and in particular the question of whether this term has a singular or agreed meaning or whether its meaning is shifting and highly contested. We also wish to consider whether the seriousness limit can provide an effective threshold for constraining reproductive decision making, and, in addressing this task, we will be especially concerned to reflect back on some of the key themes of this chapter, such as whether this restriction is an affront to reproductive choice and/or whether it risks sending an unfavorable message to people who have "serious" disabilities.

4 CONCLUSION

Whatever else one can say about the conceptualization of disability, we argue that "disability" is given meaning each time those who are called upon to make determinations in the context of reproductive decisions do so. It is difficult to see how these determinations could be other than plural and shifting. Would-be parents very likely make their determinations according to a multiplicity of factors that might include negative attitudes toward disability, the impact of the diagnosis on their plans as parents, their future child's life prospects, personal or familial experience (or lack of) with the diagnosed condition, available resources, fear of social rejection, and emotional support, and the list goes on. But one of the factors that must influence their decisions is the health literature discussed in this chapter, which arguably reinforces the need to undergo screening tests and – in the event that these screening tests reveal fetal abnormality – the desirability of having an abortion for that abnormality or of selecting an unaffected embryo in the case of PGD. In Chapter 2, we will discuss the messages that prospective parents are given about the risks involved in pregnancy and will show how they both inhibit genuine reproductive choice and create a milieu in which being at risk is itself a problem/pathological state.

2

Risk

> Risk is the chance that any activity or action could happen and harm you. Almost everything we do has an associated risk. Living is a risky business. People will generally take risks if they feel that there is an advantage or benefit. We need to look at risks and benefits together. Normally the benefits of an action should outweigh the risks. There is no such thing as a zero risk.
>
> (Advice to patients from the Royal College of Obstetricians and Gynaecologists in "Understanding how Risk Is Discussed in Healthcare")[1]

Prenatal testing[2] is all about calculating risks. However, the idea of "risk" is contested. Calculating prenatal risk presupposes the problem (as the preceding quote suggests, – "there is no such thing as a zero risk") and predetermines the solution – you can either take the risk or avoid it. At the same time as women are informed about potential risks to their future progeny, they are also given advice about the range of possible solutions – termination, preimplantation selection of embryos, use of donor sperm or eggs, adoption, surrogacy, and, of course, *taking the risk*. Furthermore, the subject of risk calculation in prenatal testing –potential disease, genetic defect, disability, or impairment – is also controversial. As we argued in Chapter 1, disability and its

---

[1] February, 2010. Available for download from http://www.rcog.org.uk/understanding-how-risk-is-discussed-healthcare (last reviewed 19 January 2011).

[2] Prenatal testing includes both preimplantation testing and testing during pregnancy.

correlates are constructed socially, politically, historically, scientifically, and legally.

As feminist legal theorists, in this chapter, we are interested in exploring the way risk discourse gives rise to both legal and nonlegal forms of regulation enacted on and through the bodies of pregnant and potentially pregnant women. We do so while foregrounding the tension between the opportunities risk discourse offers for informed reproductive decision making and the burdens it imposes.[3]

In the first chapter we outlined some of the theoretical debates around the construction and conceptualization of disability. We also argued that, although the literature provided to pregnant women about prenatal testing is at pains to present as *genuine* the choice confronting women about whether to (a) accept the offer of testing and (b) have an abortion or selectively transfer an unaffected embryo if an abnormality is identified, it in fact creates an environment where in some circumstances pressure is placed on women to make particular decisions to reproduce "responsibly." We now turn to a discussion of how the debate about the construction of disability is informed by

---

[3] The focus of this chapter is biomedical uses of risk discourse. However, our analysis of their viability steps off from the work of a number of influential theorists including scholars such as Mary Douglas, who developed a cultural theory of risk exploring the way in which risk perception is constituted and reinforced by the social and political frames within which it operates – see M. Douglas, *Risk Acceptability According to the Social Sciences* (New York: Russell Sage Foundation, 1985). Ulrich Beck, too, is particularly influential in debates about risk and what he calls the risk society. Tied to his concept of reflexive modernity, Beck defines risk as a kind of "virtual reality" born of the consequences of rapid modernization. Rather than relying on the postmodern paradigm, Beck's reflexive modernity emphasizes the role of institutional reorganization and reform. See U. Beck, "Risk Society Revisited: Theory, Politics and Research Programmes" in B. Adam, U. Beck, and J. Van Loon (eds.), *The Risk Society and Beyond: Critical Issues for Social Theory* (London: Sage, 2000), 214. See also A. Giddens, *Modernity and Self-identity: Self and Society in the Late Modern Age* (Stanford, Calif.: Stanford University Press, 1991); Z. Bauman, *Modernity and Ambivalence* (Cambridge: Polity Press, 1991), and Z. Bauman, *Postmodernism and Its Discontents* (Cambridge: Polity Press, 1997), for other accounts.

(and/or informs) the discourse of risk management that pervades prenatal screening and testing. We explore how risk, as a conceptual apparatus, is deployed in legal and biomedical discourses, government and policy discourses, cultural and media discourses, and, of course, the minds and bodies of individuals.

As we work our way through this highly complex and often scientistic field, one of the central questions is, what is the norm against which everything else is being measured? The provision of prenatal tests, for an ever-increasing array of conditions, occurs in a sociocultural climate of shifting normative ideals. This makes the basis of risk calculation in prenatal testing inherently unstable. There cannot be, if there ever was, a fixed or self-evident state of normalcy against which risk is measured. As Abby Lippman has argued, "where the conditions for which testing is done to identify risks keep increasing; the range of normal keeps decreasing..."[4] In recent months, there has been news of the potential for detailed microarray testing of both preimplantation embryos[5] and, via chorionic villus sampling (CVS) and amniotic fluid analysis, fetuses of pregnant women. These tests may offer the possibility of whole genome scans to detect a larger range of potential abnormalities that, by extension (per Lippman), will further narrow the field of what constitutes a normal embryo/fetus.[6] The net effect is

[4] A. Lippman, "Choice as a Risk to Women's Health" (1999) 1(3) *Health, Risk & Society* 281, at 284.

[5] See Jill Stark, "New IVF Technique Set to Lift Birth Rates" *Age* (24 October 2010), http://www.theage.com.au/national/new-ivf-technique-set-to-lift-birth-rates-20101023–16yn2.html, accessed 14 January 2010.

[6] See Murdoch Institute, http://www.mcri.edu.au/pages/research/research-group. asp?P=projects&G=41, accessed 17 February 2011, who explain the process as follows: "There are two new technologies being considered for prenatal testing: non-invasive prenatal diagnosis (NIPD) using free fetal DNA or RNA from maternal blood, for determining a specific fetal gene status; and more detailed microarray testing on CVS and amniotic fluid. NIPD promises to offer all women a safe, reliable prenatal test for abnormalities such as Down syndrome, whilst microarrays are a whole genome scan, able to detect a larger range of abnormalities than the current karyotyping. However, as NIPD is likely to replace current Down syndrome screening, there

to broaden the scope of risk calculation to include a range of abnormalities not previously considered. Given that most embryos/fetuses will carry some genetic anomalies it will also raise questions about which mutations, abnormalities, defects, or conditions should be identified and which should not.[7] In Chapter 6 we examine the implications of these new technologies in detail.

We begin this chapter, however, with an examination of how risk is currently constituted through available prenatal and preimplantation testing and how it is measured against statistical norms. In the second part, we examine the role of risk in framing (and institutionalizing) ideas of the normal. In the final part, we look at some broad based prenatal and preconception risk aversion strategies implemented by governments and regulatory bodies in a number of jurisdictions across the world. By doing this we begin to understand the way in which risk has become a pervasive conceptual tool driving regulatory responses and variously disciplining and assisting pregnant women.

will inevitably be changed testing pathways for women resulting in some chromosome abnormalities not being detected. This contrasts with the ability to detect new microdeletion and duplication syndromes using microarrays on invasive specimens. We will be surveying pregnant women to determine how they would decide between choosing a non-invasive test that is limited in its ability to detect abnormalities and an invasive test that may detect a larger range." For a discussion of NIPD and other new technologies on the horizon see Chapter 6.

[7] See K. E. Lohmueller, "Proportionally More Deleterious Genetic Variation in European Than in African Populations" (21 February 2008) 451 *Nature* 994; N.E. Morton, J.F. Crow, and H.J. Muller, "An Estimate of the Mutations Damage in Man from Data on Consanguineous Marriages" (1956) 42 *Proceedings of the National Academy of Sciences of the United States of America* 855–63, and A.S. Kondrashov, "Contamination of the Genome by Very Slightly Deleterious Mutations: Why Have We Not Died 100 Times Over?" (1995) 175 *Journal of Theoretical Biology* 583–94. It is also worth noting new advances in carrier testing technology that are likely to lead to preconception carrier screening for more than 448 "severe recessive childhood diseases": see C. J. Bell et al., "Carrier Testing for Severe Childhood Recessive Diseases by Next-Generation Sequencing" (2011) 3 *Science Translational Medicine* 1.

1 CONSTITUTING, MANAGING, AND MEASURING RISK IN PRENATAL AND PREIMPLANTATION TESTING

In the context of prenatal testing it seems clear that contemporary best practice starts from the position that all pregnancies are presumptively at risk. As we shall see later, standard clinical practice in prenatal testing in Australia, the United Kingdom, the United States, Canada, and Europe is based on the premise that all women should be offered the opportunity to undergo prenatal testing for certain known anomalies. These anomalies are a presumptive concern of all women by constituting the woman's risk status as either "low risk," "increased risk," or "high risk."[8] Importantly, there is no such thing as a "no risk" pregnancy.[9]

As we will see in the second section of part 1 of this chapter in the assisted reproductive technology (ART) context, testing involving preimplantation genetic diagnosis of embryos created by using in vitro fertilization (IVF) is generally only made available to those who present with a genetic history of some kind of abnormality. There are some moves to make PGD more widely available in some jurisdictions; however, currently in the majority of cases the request for this kind of diagnostic testing will be initiated by the patient. IVF patients (and

---

[8] The language used to describe a relevant risk varies. For instance, the Royal College of Obstetricians and Gynaecologists describes a risk of Down syndrome that is more than 1 in 250 as a "high risk" (see RCOG, "Understanding How Risk Is Discussed in Healthcare" February 2010, http://www.rcog.org.uk/understanding-how-risk-is-discussed-healthcare), whereas the Royal Australian and New Zealand College of Obstetricians and Gynaecologists describes a 1 in 250 or greater risk of Down syndrome as an "increased risk" (see RANZCOG College Statement, "Prenatal Screening Tests for Trisomy 21 (Down Syndrome), Trisomy 18 (Edwards Syndrome) and Neural Tube Defects" (statement no. C-Obs 4 July 2007), http://www.ranzcog.edu.au/publications/statements/C-obs4.pdf).

[9] See RCOG "Understanding how Risk is Discussed in Healthcare," February, 2010 Available for download from http://www.rcog.org.uk/understanding-how-risk-is-discussed-healthcare (last reviewed 19 January 2011).

those utilizing other ART services), however, will encounter the usual prenatal testing regimes recommended for non-ART pregnancies once they have an established pregnancy. Indeed even those people who have used PGD will still be considered as presumptively at risk (a) because PGD is not 100 percent accurate and (b) because PGD will only rule out a particular tested abnormality.

Having established the way in which risk is foregrounded in the prenatal and preimplantation contexts, we go on in the last section of Part 1 to interrogate risk management and measurement as a practice.

1.1 Prenatal Testing

For pregnant women in Australia, in most jurisdictions, best practice – as determined by the Royal Australian and New Zealand College of Obstetricians and Gynaecologists (RANZCOG) – requires that all women be offered a detailed fetal morphology ultrasound at approximately eighteen weeks gestation. The aim of this scan is to screen for structural anomalies and to check "pregnancy wellbeing."[10] In addition, in most jurisdictions pregnant women will be made aware of the availability of first trimester screening tests for three specific abnormalities – trisomy 21, trisomy 18, and neural tube defects. RANZCOG recommends that "[a]ll pregnant women should be advised of the availability of prenatal screening as early as possible in pregnancy to allow time to discuss the options available and facilitate an *informed choice* [our emphasis]."[11] Screening tests (usually blood tests or ultrasounds,

[10] RANZCOG College Statement, "Prenatal Screening Tests for Trisomy 21 (Down Syndrome), Trisomy 18 (Edwards Syndrome) and Neural Tube Defects," (Statement no. C-Obs 4 July 2007), 5.

[11] RANZCOG, "Prenatal Screening Tests for Trisomy 21 (Down Syndrome), Trisomy 18 (Edwards Syndrome) and Neural Tube Defects," (Statement no. C-Obs 4 July 2007), 1. We will return to the issue of informed choice later. See also our earlier discussion of this in Chapter 1.

including nuchal translucency scans) provide information regarding the risk that one of these disorders is present. They do not offer a definitive diagnosis. Diagnostic tests (usually CVS or amniocentesis) identify the presence of a "disorder." They do not generally, however, provide information about the severity of the condition in the particular fetus tested.

For some time it has been standard practice to offer screening tests (and/or invasive diagnostic tests such as CVS and amniocentesis) for these disorders to women older than thirty-five in most jurisdictions in Australia. More recently it has become routine to ensure these screening tests are made available to *all* pregnant women, not just those identified as at increased risk.[12]

Similarly, in the United Kingdom, the National Institute for Health and Clinical Excellence (NICE) clinical guideline 62 (*Routine Care*

[12] In Australia the changing rates of testing facilitated by the introduction of screening tests are demonstrated in a study by Cheffins et al. They note that "[t]he introduction of maternal serum screening in South Australia has resulted in increased use of prenatal testing for Down's syndrome from about 7% (mainly older women having amniocentesis and chorionic villus sampling) to 84% of women (about 8% having direct amniocentesis or chorionic villus sampling and 76% having maternal serum screening first)." See T. Cheffins et al., "The Impact of Maternal Serum Screening on the Birth Prevalence of Down's Syndrome and the Use of Amniocentesis and Chorionic Villus Sampling in South Australia" (2000) 107 *British Journal of Obstetrics and Gynaecology* 1453, at 1453. For more information on testing across Australia, see P. O'Leary et al., "Regional Variations in Prenatal Screening across Australia: Stepping towards a National Policy Framework" (2006) 46 *Australian and New Zealand Journal of Obstetrics and Gynaecology* 427. It should be noted, however, that in Australia, the Medicare rebate (introduced in 1993) has at various times covered only the blood test component of the combined first trimester test with the nuchal translucency scan (ultrasound) being eligible for a rebate only in the event a high risk indication exists (advanced maternal age or other risk factor for fetal abnormality) – see for eg. http://www.ncrad.com/patients/nuchal-translucency-medicare-rebate/ (accessed on 16 January 2012) and http://www.hunterimaging.com.au/site/index.cfm?display=112593; but cf. http://www.cmmi.svhm.org.au/downloads/news-letters/cmmi_0406.pdf (accessed 16 January 2012). As noted previously, new testing technology that makes screening for Down syndrome and other childhood illnesses a very simple matter is likely to be available in the near future. This may change the rates of uptake significantly. See also Chapter 6.

for the Healthy Pregnant Woman) provides that ultrasound screening for fetal anomalies should be routinely offered (1.7.1) and that all pregnant women should be offered screening for Down syndrome (1.7.2).[13] Accordingly, most pregnant women in England are now offered both a screening test for Down syndrome and a midpregnancy ultrasound scan for other fetal anomalies including Edward's syndrome and Patau's syndrome.[14] Where there is a positive screening test result for Down syndrome, a diagnostic test will be also be offered.[15] The *Down's Policy Recommendations* are currently under review, however, there appears to be little doubt that they will continue to provide for routine screening and, where such screening test results are positive, confirmatory diagnostic testing.[16]

In the United States, the American College of Obstetricians and Gynecologists (ACOG) published a Practice Bulletin in January 2007 containing the guidelines *Screening for Fetal Chromosomal Abnormalities*. These provide that *both* screening and "invasive diagnostic testing for aneuploidy"[17] should be available to all women who seek prenatal

---

[13] March, 2008 http://www.nice.org.uk/nicemedia/pdf/CG062NICEguideline.pdf. Note also that Recommendation 3 of the NHS Fetal Anomaly Screening Programme – Screening for Down's Syndrome: UK NSC Policy Recommendations 2007–2010: Model of Best Practice [Down's Policy Recommendations] at http://fetalanomaly.screening.nhs.uk/getdata.php?id=10938 provides that "all women should be offered [Down syndrome] screening with a screen positive rate (SPR) of 3% and a detection rate (DR) of more than 75%" (see also Recommendations 9–19 for recommended screening strategies).

[14] NHS Fetal Anomaly Screening Programme, "Screening Tests for You and Your Baby" http://fetalanomaly.screening.nhs.uk/getdata.php?id=11279, 17–41.

[15] Human Genetic Commission, Advisory Committee on Genetic Testing, *Prenatal Genetic Testing, Report for Consultation*, February 2000, at 1.1 and 6.3; and the *Down's Policy Recommendations*, at 22.

[16] NHS Fetal Anomaly Screening Programme Review of the Model of Best Practice 2008: Down's Syndrome Screening for England at http://fetalanomaly.screening.nhs.uk/getdata.php?id=11297.

[17] An aneuploidy is an abnormality involving a chromosome number that is not an exact multiple of the haploid number (i.e., one chromosome set is incomplete).

care before twenty weeks of gestation. Under this model, the decision whether to undergo diagnostic testing is left to the patient: the woman may decide to bypass screening and proceed straight to diagnostic testing should she consider the risk to her pregnancy to justify such a course.[18]

In Canada, the Society of Obstetricians and Gynaecologists of Canada (SOGC) Practice Guideline *Prenatal Screening for Fetal Aneuploidy* (February 2007) recommends that "[a]ll pregnant women in Canada, regardless of age, should be offered, through an informed consent process, a prenatal screening test for the most common clinically significant foetal aneuploidies in addition to a second trimester ultrasound for dating, growth and anomalies." Recommendation 2 provides that maternal age should be removed as an indication for invasive testing for women younger than age forty and that for these women amniocentesis/CVS should be performed if there have been

---

[18] It should be noted that each state has its own regime, and the particulars of the state system will vary. For example, in New York, the Medicaid Prenatal Care Standards follow the ACOG recommendations. They state that prenatal care providers shall offer all pregnant women screening tests to identify birth defects at specific times throughout the prenatal period based on ACOG and American Academy of Paediatrics Guidelines: see H. 7 (a). Invasive diagnostic testing for aneuploidy should be available to all women regardless of maternal age, although amniocentesis should not be performed before 15 weeks gestation (see H. 7 (b)). New York State Department of Health, "Medicaid Prenatal Care Standards," http://www.health.ny.gov/health_care/medicaid/standards/prenatal_care/ (accessed on 17 January 2012) In California, the position is different. Whereas three types of screening are offered to women (at a cost of $162, which is covered by most prepaid health plans, insurance companies, and Medi-Cal), it is only in the case that these tests reveal that the woman is at high risk that diagnostic testing will occur. This further testing is conducted free of charge: see http://www.cdph.ca.gov/programs/pns/Documents/Easy%20To%20Read%202009.pdf (accessed 16 January 2011) and http://www.cdph.ca.gov/programs/pns/pages/default.aspx (accessed 16 January2011). In Iowa, screening is available to all women during pregnancy. As in California, if the screen produces a positive result, the woman will be offered a diagnostic test such as amniocentesis to determine whether the fetus has a chromosome abnormality or birth defect: see http://www.healthcare.uiowa.edu/programs/screening/screen.html (accessed 16 January 2011).

"multiple marker screening results."[19] Women older than forty years at the estimated date of delivery should be told of "the option of invasive testing on the basis of age alone."[20]

In a study conducted by Boyd et al. mapping the state of prenatal testing in eighteen countries in Europe, the authors note that in eleven of the countries (Belgium, Denmark, England and Wales, Finland, France, Germany, Italy, Poland, Portugal, and Switzerland) there was an official countrywide policy or recommendation for a Down syndrome screening test to be offered to all women.[21]

Thus, it seems clear that across the developed world, prenatal screening and testing of pregnant women operate on the premise that all pregnancies are presumed to be at risk and that all women should routinely be offered screening and diagnostic testing for at least the most common fetal aneuploidies/chromosomal abnormalities. The prevalence of risk discourse in the context of pregnancy is thus unsurprising and makes its deconstruction even more important. Elizabeth Ettorre argues, for instance, that "[t]hrough the workings of prenatal politics, biomedical discourses transform women's wombs into highly managed social spaces – sites of discourses about 'good' genes, women-as-foetal-incubators, 'good enough' foetal bodies and disability"[22] and that women take on a "genetic risk identity" as a consequence of their participation in "the production of a repertoire of risks."[23] She identifies this as a particularly

---

[19] Society of Obstetricians and Gynaecologists of Canada (SOGC), *Practice Guideline on Prenatal Screening for Fetal Aneuploidy* (February 2007), at http://www.sogc.org/guidelines/documents/187E-CPG-February2007.pdf.

[20] Society of Obstetricians and Gynaecologists of Canada (SOGC) Practice Guideline, *Prenatal Screening for Fetal Aneuploidy* (February 2007), at http://www.sogc.org/guidelines/documents/187E-CPG-February2007.pdf.

[21] P. A. Boyd et al., "Survey of Prenatal Screening Policies in Europe for Structural Malformations and Chromosome Anomalies, and Their Impact on Detection and Termination Rates for Neural Tube Defects and Down's Syndrome" (2008) *Fetal Medicine* 689, at 692.

[22] E. Ettorre, *Reproductive Genetics: Gender and the Body* (London: Routledge, 2002), at 21.

[23] E. Ettorre, *Reproductive Genetics: Gender and the Body* (London: Routledge, 2002), at 31.

gendered phenomenon involving as it does women's embodied identity. In the context of ART the attribution of risk extends to the period prior to gestation to include the bodies of both genetic progenitors (as potential carriers of recessive genes).

1.2 Preimplantation Testing

In the case of a woman or couple attending an ART clinic, there are three stages when testing may take place. The first stage is prior to attending the ART clinic. Sometimes a woman or couple planning to use the services of an ART clinic will first seek clarification of genetic status through genetic testing and counseling. This usually occurs when one of the potential parents is a known carrier for a genetic condition or has a close relative with a genetic condition. Indeed, in some Australian states access to IVF, in the absence of infertility, may be limited by law to those individuals who are at risk of transmitting a genetic abnormality or genetic disease to a child born as a result of a pregnancy conceived naturally.[24] In these cases the woman or couple may be attending the clinic with the specific purpose of accessing PGD.[25] Where this is the case, much of the information and advice given to the couple regarding their risk of passing on a genetic abnormality will have been conveyed in the context of genetic counseling more generally, or through a general practitioner (GP). The second point at which testing might take place is at the end of the process when the woman is pregnant. It is likely that even though her pregnancy has been conceived with the assistance of an ART clinic, she will nevertheless undergo the full battery of prenatal tests that

[24] Assisted Reproductive Treatment Act 2008 (Vic), s 10(2)(a)(iii); Assisted Reproductive Treatment Act 2008, (SA), s 9(1)(c)(iii); Human Reproductive Treatment Act 1991 (WA), s 23(1)(a)(ii).

[25] Alternatives such as the use of donor sperm or eggs are also reasons for using IVF in these circumstances; however, for our purposes we are interested in the circumstance in which embryo selection using PGD occurs.

are typically undertaken by women who do not use ART services to become pregnant. As this circumstance has been covered previously, we do not need to say much more about how this testing works. The third point at which testing might occur, however, is between the two previous times just described, namely, when in vitro fertilization has been used to create embryos for transfer to the woman's uterus. In this case, there will be an opportunity for investigation of those embryos prior to implantation. Depending on the legal regimes and best practice guidelines in place in the relevant jurisdiction, not all women who undergo IVF will have access to, or wish to undergo, preimplantation testing or screening of embryos.[26] Unlike screening in the prenatal context, preimplantation screening and diagnosis are not routine in all of the various jurisdictions considered in this book. In Australia, they are considered specialized procedures reserved for patients who have identified a history of a particular disorder in the family or who have a high rate of early miscarriage. In these circumstances, a woman may be advised of the availability of preimplantation genetic screening (PGS) or preimplantation genetic diagnosis (PGD).[27] As will be discussed in later chapters, rather

[26] PGD began as a technology aimed at diagnosis of gene disorders in embryos via cell biopsy but has increasingly been used to screen the embryos of infertile patients undergoing IVF treatment for chromosomal abnormalities. These abnormalities can lead to developmental arrest, implantation failure, and recurrent miscarriage: see Monash IVF, "Pre-implantation Genetic Diagnosis" http://www.monashivf.com/Services/Pre-implantation_Genetic_Diagnosis__PGD_.aspx. It should also be noted that, in the jurisdictions under consideration in this book, PGD is less likely to be covered by public health benefits: see, for example, Centre for Genetics Education, "Preimplantation Genetic Diagnosis" http://www.genetics.edu.au/pdf/factsheets/fs18.pdf (accessed 16 January 2012), and Genea, "PGD Fees" www.genea.com.au/How-we-can-help/Our-Fees/PGD-Fees (accessed 16 January 2012), but cf. Assisted Conception Unit, "FAQ" http://www.ivfdirect.com/information/faqpage.aspx (accessed 16 January 2012).
[27] Wesley Monash IVF, "Genetic Screening and Diagnosis: Preimplantation Genetic Screening and Preimplantation Genetic Diagnosis" (October 2009), http://wesley.monashivf.edu.au/WESLEY%20NEWSLETTER_Oct%2009.pdf; Monash IVF, "Pre-implantation Genetic Diagnosis," http://www.monashivf.com/Services/Pre-implantation_Genetic_Diagnosis__PGD_.aspx (accessed 16 January 2012).

than making PGD routine, it is more typical for PGD to be constrained by legal regulation and ethical guidelines. In Australia, for instance, the use of PGD is limited by the National Health and Medical Research Council's *Ethical Guidelines on the Use of Assisted Reproductive Technology in Clinical Practice and Research* (hereafter NHMRC ART guidelines) to instances of serious genetic conditions.[28] Furthermore, there is evidence that suggests that the pathway to PGD for some women is not as well established as it might be. Our empirical research[29] and an examination of Australian clinic policy materials indicate that most of the patients who undertake PGD self-identify as "at risk" by notifying the IVF clinic of a history of genetic illness in their family (or this is done for them during the referral process from their GP or genetic counselor).[30] These individuals may consider PGD as another reproductive option available to them apart from prenatal diagnosis and termination. As one genetic counselor in our study described it:

> Usually the early stage enquiries would be handled here ... or at one of our [genetic counseling] clinics. So usually by the time people get to the PGD clinic, they've already been given the basic infor-mation and they've been aware of their options. And a lot of that,

---

[28] National Health and Medical Research Committee, *Ethical Guidelines on the Use of Assisted Reproductive Technology in Clinical Practice and Research* (2007 (rev. edition)). See section 12.2 (at page 55), which states that PGD "must not be used for ... preven-tion of conditions that do not seriously harm the person to be born." See also Human Reproductive Technology Act 1991 (WA), s 14(2b)(a)(ii) and Assisted Reproductive Treatment Act 2008 (Vic), s 10(2)(a)(iii). For a more detailed analysis see Chapter 4.

[29] Four of the clinicians we interviewed for our study indicated this was the practice in their clinic.

[30] PGD is one of the reasons for referral included on the Genea (formerly Sydney IVF) GP referral form, available at http://www.genea.com.au/How-we-can-help/Your-first-appointment/Your-First-Appointment (last reviewed 19 November 2011). See also J.C. Karatas et al., "Women's Experience of Pre-implantation Genetic Diagnosis: A Qualitative Study" (2010) 30 *Prenatal Diagnosis* 771, at 771, 773, and 776. At 776, the authors state that among the Australian PGD users who had participated in their study: "[t]he motivation to use PGD was consistent, ... to avoid a severely debilitating and life-threatening illness in their children and avoid repetition of past pregnancy loss."

basically, what's happened with PGD, it's just an addendum to the list of reproductive options that couples have previously been offered as part of genetic counselling. So in the past they would have been offered take the chance, prenatal diagnosis and termination of pregnancy, not have children, adoption, donor gametes and so forth. And PGD is just another thing on that list. So that would routinely be discussed with couples who attend genetic counselling about reproductive risk.[31]

This is borne out by the various documents available from IVF clinics themselves. For instance, Australian clinics provide a great deal of information on their websites. Genea, formerly Sydney IVF, notes that "[m]ost commonly, PGD is used where a couple is aware of the possibility that their offspring will inherit a genetic disease,"[32] while Melbourne IVF suggests that "[c]ouples who have a serious inherited genetic condition, or a family history of such, or who are at a higher risk of having chromosomal abnormalities in their embryos may consider PGD."[33]

A similar situation exists in the United Kingdom and Canada, while in the United States, as noted later, there are a few instances of clinics that offer PGD to all patients who attend.

In the United Kingdom, for example, PGD may be used to test for disability with a view ultimately to selecting against it,[34] and the

---

[31] As noted in the introduction due to the small number of participants we offer these excerpts as anecdotal accounts only as they offer individual insights not otherwise accessible. Participants will be referred to by number and either the letter *C* for "Clinician" or *R* for "Regulator."

[32] Genea, website, "PGD Overview" http://www.genea.com.au/How-we-can-help/ Our-Services/Genetic-Disorders/PGD-Overview/PGD-overview (last reviewed 19 Novembr 2011).

[33] Melbourne IVF, "Genetic Testing (PGD)" http://www.mivf.com.au/ivf-fertility-treatments/genetic-testing-pgd.aspx (last reviewed 19 Novembr 2011).

[34] The effect of sections 13(9) and (10) of the Human Fertilisation and Embryology Act 1990 (UK) is that PGD may be used to select against disability where there is (a) "a particular risk that an embryo may have a gene, chromosome or mitochondrion abnormality" (Human Fertilisation and Embryology Act 1990 (UK),

Royal College of Obstetricians and Gynaecologists has indicated that they support this limited use for PGD. In their briefing on the Human Fertilisation and Embryology Bill, for instance they state: "The RCOG believes that in special cases, as set out in the Bill, PGD should be allowed in fertility treatment to establish whether the embryo has an abnormality that will result in the child developing a serious physical or mental illness."[35] It is currently used in eight centers in the United Kingdom for the purpose of preventing a serious genetic condition.[36]

PGD is regulated far less prescriptively in Canada and the United States than it is in the United Kingdom. While the Canadian Assisted Human Reproduction Act 2004 prohibits PGD's use for sex selection for social reasons (see article 5(e)), it places no further restrictions on PGD. Nevertheless, the Society of Obstetricians and Gynaecologists of Canada (SOGC) has published guidelines regarding the use of PGD that indicate that PGD is offered in much the same circumstances as it is generally offered in the United Kingdom: that is, as "an alternative to prenatal diagnosis for the detection of genetic disorders in couples at risk of transmitting a genetic condition to their offspring."[37]

Schedule 2 1ZA(1)(b)), and (b) "a significant risk that a person with the abnormality will have or develop a serious physical or mental disability, a serious illness or any other serious medical condition" (Human Fertilisation and Embryology Act 1990 (UK), Schedule 2 1ZA(2)(b)).

[35] Royal College of Obstetricians and Gynaecologists, "Briefing on HFEA Bill: RCOG Parliamentary Briefing on the Human Fertilisation and Embryology Bill (HL) 2007–8, http://www.rcog.org.uk/what-we-do/campaigning-and-opinions/briefings-and-qas-/human-fertilisation-and-embryology-bill/brief.

[36] K. Ehrich and C. Williams, "'A Healthy Baby': The Double Imperative of Preimplantation Genetic Diagnosis" (2010) *Health*, at 14:41. For a comprehensive account of women's access to PGD in the United Kingdom see S. Franklin and C. Roberts, *Born and Made: An Ethnography of Preimplantation Genetic Diagnosis* (Princeton: Princeton University Press, 2006), chapter 3.

[37] "SOGC Technical Update: "Preimplantation Genetic Diagnosis" (No. 232, August 2009), at http://www.sogc.org/guidelines/documents/gui232TU0908.pdf.

In the United States, professional organizations have created guidelines.[38] These guidelines clearly contemplate that PGD is to be offered to prevent the transmission of genetic disease by those who are at increased risk of doing so. For instance, in *Preimplantation Genetic Testing: A Practice Committee Opinion*,[39] the American Society for Reproductive Medicine (ASRM) provides that "PGD is indicated for couples at risk of transmitting a specific genetic disease or abnormality to their offspring." On the other hand, the Ethics Committee of the ASRM has stated that the use of PGD for non-medical sex selection "should not be encouraged."[40]

Nevertheless, these professional guidelines are not binding, and some U.S. practitioners offer PGD to people who wish to use the technique to select the sex of their baby for personal reasons.[41] Indeed, 42 percent of the PGD clinics that took part in a 2006 survey conducted by the Genetics and Public Policy Center of the Johns Hopkins University said that they provided PGD for "non-medical sex selection,"[42] and there is also evidence that PGD has been offered to select in favor of disabilities.[43]

[38] See Genetics and Public Policy Center John Hopkins University, "Reproductive Genetic Testing: A Regulatory Patchwork" http://www.dnapolicy.org/policy.international.php?action=detail&laws_id=63.

[39] See http://www.asrm.org/uploadedFiles/ASRM_Content/News_and_Publications/Practice_Guidelines/Committee_Opinions/Preimplantation_genetic_testing(1).pdf).

[40] The Ethics Committee of the American Society of Reproductive Medicine, "Sex Selection and Preimplantation Genetic Diagnosis" (1999) 72(4) *Fertility and Society* 595, at 598.

[41] S. Baruch, D. Kaufman, and K. L. Hudson, "Genetic Testing of Embryos: Practices and Perspectives of US IVF clinics" (2008) 89(5) *Fertility and Sterility* 1053; see also S. Baruch, "PGD: Genetic Testing of Embryos in the United States" (presentation, 15 February 2009), at http://ec.europa.eu/dgs/jrc/downloads/jrc_aaas_2009_03_baruch_pgd.pdf.

[42] S. Baruch, D. Kaufman, and K. Hudson, "Genetic Testing of Embryos: Practices and Perspectives of US IVF Clinics (2008) 89(5) *Fertility and Sterility* 1053, at 1056.

[43] See S. Baruch, D. Kaufman, and K. Hudson, "Genetic Testing of Embryos: Practices and Perspectives of US IVF Clinics" (2008) 89(5) *Fertility and Sterility* 1053, at 1056. See also our discussion of this practice in Chapter 4.

Because of the highly specified nature of many of the PGD tests, PGD cannot function in a generalist screening capacity. This means that in many cases patients will need to have knowledge of their risk factors in order to make use of the service.[44] However, if women/couples do not know their genetic "risk profile" or are not considering IVF and have a GP who is unfamiliar with PGD, they may never become aware that PGD is an option. This possibility is reflected in a study conducted by Karatas et al. of Australian women's experiences of PGD, in which three of the women interviewed expressed frustration that they had only learned about PGD through their own research or the media.[45]

Nevertheless, if one knows to look for it, information on PGD is widely available. As noted previously, most of the major Australian clinics have comprehensive materials online regarding the availability of testing, and this may have some passive influence over a patient's decision to undergo testing. Genea, for instance, lists on its website all the conditions for which PGD is available. They state: "Genea has developed tests for more than 130 inherited diseases. New tests can be developed as needed."[46] Similarly, Melbourne IVF notes on its website: "It is now possible to test for many hundreds of single gene disorders with Preimplantation Genetic Diagnosis (PGD). Hundreds of genetic disorders have been diagnosed by PGD around the world.... We have developed tests for over 60 genetic disorders, which are

---

[44] Monash IVF, for instance, requires one or both partners seeking PGD for single gene disorders to have had a previous genetic test to determine the specific gene causing the genetic condition. If a couple goes to Monash IVF without this testing they will be referred to Genetic Health Services Victoria for that testing before the PGD process can begin. See http://www.monashivf.com/site/DefaultSite/filesystem/documents/Preimplantation Genetic Diagnosis for single gene disorders.pdf (access 16 January 2012).

[45] J.C. Karatas et al., "Women's Experience of Pre-implantation Genetic Diagnosis: A Qualitative Study" (2010) 30(8) *Prenatal Diagnosis* 771, at 773.

[46] Genea, "PGD for Inherited Disease" http://www.genea.com.au/How-we-can-help/Our-Services/Genetic-Disorders/PGD-for-Inherited-Disease/PGD-for-Inherited-Disease (last reviewed 19 November 2011).

designed specifically for the needs of each couple."[47] Furthermore, general education materials may also filter through to women or couples. For instance, NSW Health's Centre for Genetics Education has provided a fact sheet for the public that states, "[PGD] can help couples who are at risk of having a child with a genetic condition avoid doing so without the need for decisions regarding termination of an affected pregnancy," and, further on, "Like any IVF procedure, stress and often disappointment can accompany PGD. Couples will need to balance the financial and emotional burden of the IVF procedure followed by PGD with that of termination of an affected child conceived naturally."[48]

In this document, we can identify a different kind of "risk calculus." The NSW Health fact sheet draws a distinction between the risk of PND (the emotional trauma of a potential termination) versus the risk of PGD (the stress of the IVF process and the potential for disappointment). As we shall discuss in the next section, these other contextual measures of risk complicate reliance on a simple epidemiological or clinical approach to risk measurement.[49]

Furthermore, despite the claim made in the NSW Health fact sheet that the use of PGD may eliminate the stress of termination after prenatal testing, it should be noted that in most instances, when a woman

---

[47] Melbourne IVF, "Chromosomal Abnormalities," http://www.mivf.com.au/about-fertility/how-to-get-pregnant/chromosomal-abnormalities (accessed on 16 January 2012).

[48] Centre for Genetics Education, "Preimplantation Genetic Diagnosis" (Fact Sheet 18, June 2007), http://www.genetics.com.au/pdf/factsheets/fs18.pdf.

[49] The fact sheet is adverting to two kinds of disappointment that are attendant upon IVF with PGD. The first is the one that is commonly discussed, namely, the low chance of a successful transfer that leads to a pregnancy. The second is that people who use IVF PGD and produce only affected embryos will not be allowed to use those embryos. As the fact sheet correctly notes, "Only those embryos that do not have the specific genetic condition that was tested for will be transplanted into the woman's uterus." This is quite different from the case in which a woman is pregnant and then discovers her fetus is affected with the anomaly. In such a case the woman will be allowed to make the choice whether to continue her pregnancy or not. We will return to this point in later chapters.

becomes pregnant she will be advised to undergo the usual prenatal screening and testing even if she has already used PGD to select an unaffected embryo for a specific condition. This is because PGD is typically used to identify the presence of a specific genetic disorder known to be carried by one or both of the parents. While PGD can also be used to diagnose chromosomal abnormalities and translocations, abnormalities involving other untested chromosomes cannot be excluded.[50] Monash IVF is careful in its fact sheets to recommend post pregnancy prenatal testing in all cases, not just when PGD is used for chromosomal screening. They state in their fact sheet "Confirmatory Prenatal Diagnosis Following Preimplantation Genetic Diagnosis (PGD)": "[y]ou should be aware that the results obtained from PGD are **NOT** 100% accurate. At best, the accuracy of the test is approximately 90% if you have had PGD or chromosomal screening or up to 98% if you have had PGD for a specific genetic condition. Consequently there may be up to a 10% error rate associated with any test performed."[51] The point to note here, as we move forward with our discussion of the construction of risk, is that even a 2 percent risk is construed as too high. Rather than reducing interventions, the development of more and more "technological fixes" seems to lead to even more risk evasion strategies. This point is further reinforced in our analysis of future technologies in Chapter 6. There is, thus, an alignment between the use of PGD and the routinization of confirmatory prenatal screening and testing.

[50] See Monash IVF, "fact Sheet: Preimplantation Genetic Diagnosis with Sex Selection for X-linked Genetic Disorders" (May 2009) http://www.monashivf.com/site/DefaultSite/filesystem/documents/PGD-with-sex-selection.pdf and Monash IVF, "fact sheet: Preimplantation Genetic Diagnosis with Chromosome Screening" (May 2009) http://www.monashivf.com/site/DefaultSite/filesystem/documents/PGD-for-chromosome-screening.pdf. Cf. Melbourne IVF, "New IVF Technique: Testing of Every Chromosome Embryos" (25 October 2010), http://www.mivf.com.au/ivf-latest-news/new-ivf-technique-testing-of-every-chromosome-embryos.aspx.

[51] Monash IVF, "fact Sheet: Confirmatory Prenatal Diagnosis Following Preimplantation Genetic Diagnosis (PGD)" (November 2006), http://www.monashivf.com/site/DefaultSite/filesystem/documents/confirmatory-Prenatal-Diagnosis-following-PGD.pdf.

1.3 How Is Risk Measured and Managed?

The way in which risk is measured is dependent upon the field of study in which it is used. Hunt et al. note that in epidemiology, risk refers to the statistical associations found within a population, while in the clinic risk is the probability of the occurrence of a particular disease or outcome for an individual.[52]

As we have seen in the previous section, there has been a trend toward making prenatal testing and screening for certain anomalies routine. Some would argue that the risk of these conditions in population terms is, however, very low. For instance, in Australia the overall rate of trisomy 21 for 2002–3 was 11.1 per 10,000 births, while 26.3 per 10,000 pregnancies were affected.[53] In the clinic where what is measured is individual risk, the conceptualization of statistical risk in general terms as either low, increased, or high is a typical means used to translate risk into accessible knowledge. The Royal College of Obstetricians and Gynaecologists has developed a table that is contained in their fact sheet "Understanding How Risk Is Discussed in Healthcare," in which they quantify the risk in community group terms (see Risk Table).

They also note in their opening two paragraphs that "[h]ow you view risk depends on one or more of the following:

- the chance of the event occurring (frequency)
- the chance of a condition being detected by a screening test (detection rate)
- the benefits of the treatment or screening
- how much harm may be caused
- if it is life-threatening

[52] L.M. Hunt et al., "Do Notions of Risk Inform Patient Choice? Lessons from a Study of Prenatal Genetic Counseling" (2006) 25 *Medical Anthropology* 193, at 195.

[53] Australian Institute of Health and Welfare, *Congenital Anomalies in Australia 2002–2003* (2008), http://www.preru.unsw.edu.au/PRERUWeb.nsf/resources/CA+2/$file/ca3a.pdf, at 140.

Risk

Table 2.1 *Risk table*

Verbal	Risk description[a]	Risk description[b]
Very common	1/1 to 1/10	A person in family
Common	1/10 to 1/100	A person in street
Uncommon	1/100 to 1/1000	A person in village
Rare	1/1,000 to 1/10,000	A person in small town
Very rare: less than	1/100,000	A person in large town

[a] EU-assigned frequency.
[b] Unit in which one adverse event would be expected.
Source: Royal College of Obstetricians and Gynaecologists, 'Understanding How Risk Is Discussed in Healthcare," available at http://www.rcog.org.uk/understanding-how-risk-is-discussed-healthcare (last reviewed 19 January 2011).

- if it is short-term (temporary) or long-term (permanent)
- how much you feel in control of the decision
- how much you trust the person discussing the risk with you
- whether you feel you understand the situation sufficiently."

As is clearly acknowledged, risk will have a varying meaning depending on the personal context and experience of the individual in question.

Take, for example, the words of Ms. Green, reflecting on the experience of having a fetal anomaly detected during prenatal testing, which resulted in the termination of her previous pregnancy.[54] Green's reflective letter to her genetic counselor was excerpted in a NSW government patient publication as illustrative of patient risk perception:

My perception of risks has changed. When one looks at a group of a hundred or a thousand women of a certain age, it makes sense to say "About 1% of these women will get a bad outcome on an amniocentesis." But, for me as an *individual* woman, facing another

[54] N.B.: *Green* is a pseudonym. Green's letter was originally published in the inaugural edition of the *Journal of Genetic Counseling*: R. Green, "Letter to a Genetic Counselor" (1992) 1(1) *Journal of Genetic Counseling* 55. It was republished in *NSW Health* (SAFDA), "Diagnosis of Abnormality in an Unborn Baby: The Impact, Options and Afterwards" (August 2006), at 20.

pregnancy, the risk, at the emotional level is simply 50%. That is, a bad outcome either *will* happen again or it *won't*.[55]

From this excerpt we can see that this woman has filtered her interpretation of risk statistics through her own personal experience, and Hunt et al. have found that this is not uncommon. They take the view that the perspective from which the risk is viewed inflects the nature and extent of risk. They state that "[f]or patients, the *value* of the pregnancy is in the foreground, while for clinicians the *disvalue* of the anomaly is in the foreground."[56] This has a direct impact, for instance, on how a clinician might evaluate the significance of a risk of a miscarriage versus an anomaly. Hunt et al. suggest that a clinician might view the calculation as simple – if the risk of the anomaly is greater than the risk of miscarriage, then it makes sense to consider prenatal diagnosis. However, they point out that, in fact, these two types of risk are not comparable.[57]

Jane Hansen, writing in 2008 for the Australian *Women's Weekly* about her own experience with amniocentesis, describes precisely this problem:

> I was 38 and my test showed I had a one in 186 chance of carrying a Down syndrome baby. This was considered quite high, although I didn't feel that way. At this point, I was faced with a thoroughly modern dilemma: carry on with the pregnancy after being flagged at high risk or opt for a diagnostic test that carried a small risk of miscarriage, but could give me a definitive answer.[58]

When interpreting her statistics, it is notable that the risk of Down syndrome (1 in 186) is characterized as high whereas the risk of

---

[55] R. Green, "Letter to a Genetic Counselor" (1992) 1 (1) *Journal of Genetic Counseling* 55, at 68.

[56] L.M. Hunt et al., "Do Notions of Risk Inform Patient Choice? Lessons from a Study of Prenatal Genetic Counseling" (2006) 25 *Medical Anthropology* 193, at 206.

[57] L.M. Hunt et al., "Do Notions of Risk Inform Patient Choice? Lessons from a Study of Prenatal Genetic Counseling" (2006) 25 *Medical Anthropology* 193, at 207.

[58] J. Hansen, "My Parental Nightmare" *Australian Women's Weekly*, August 2008.

miscarriage (1 in 200) is described as small. Despite herself using these descriptors, Hansen had thought that the risk of miscarriage from amniocentesis (1 in 200) cancelled out the risk of having a child with Down syndrome. However, she says, "Despite that [calculation], I was still deemed 'high risk.'"[59]

The continued classification of her pregnancy as "high risk" transformed the almost equally high risk of miscarriage into a "necessary risk," which Hansen ended up taking. To her relief she was found to be carrying an unaffected fetus, but then she tragically lost the pregnancy. It is difficult to imagine an alternative form of risk analysis that would allow Hansen to register the outcome of her calculation in her risk status. The use of the language of "increased risk" rather than high risk does not really seem to solve the problem. As noted earlier, the RANZCOG College Statement on *Prenatal Screening Tests for Trisomy 21 (Down Syndrome), Trisomy 18 (Edwards Syndrome) and Neural Tube Defects* (Statement no. C-Obs 4, 2007) describes risk in terms of "increased" rather than high risk. So, for instance, they state that in first trimester screening: "[a]n increased risk should be considered as a risk of 1 in 300." In second trimester maternal serum screening, they state that "[a]n increased risk should be considered as a risk of 1 in 250 or greater at term." For Hansen, though, it might have made more sense to characterize the 1 in 186 risk of Down syndrome as not worth the 1 in 200 risk of miscarriage. But "not worth the risk" is not one of the clinically available descriptions. In this case the statistics did not have any bearing on the reality of her individual situation. This kind of story, though only one example drawn from many thousands that no doubt have varied and differing responses from Hansen's, nevertheless usefully illustrates the way that measurements of risk status are fundamentally reductive and inadequate.

In fact, the designation of Hansen's status as "high risk" is intimately tied to the social and cultural construction of the harm to be avoided.

---

[59] J. Hansen, "My Parental Nightmare" *Australian Women's Weekly*, August 2008.

Risk, in this instance, is understood through a particular social/cultural and political lens. As Douglas puts it, "the institutional filter through which risks are perceived imposes a consistent distortion upon the probabilities."[60] Only certain kinds of disabilities or anomalies present in risk terms at all. Once they do, only a certain number of those will prompt the development of tests to avoid these "risks." A key question is who determines that the condition is one for which a test should be developed.

As we have seen, once a disability is identified as one for which a test is available, then the risk that your pregnancy might test positive for that trait will be described in population terms – 1 in 100 or 1 in 1,000 and so on. However, it is much more difficult to provide statistical information about the nature of the condition itself or its severity. This kind of information is usually conveyed in the context of counseling. Once designated a risk that prompts counseling, however, as Hunt et al. suggest, an "at risk" status is likely to be understood as an existing danger and may promote fear and anxiety rather than enhancing informed decision making, and there is evidence of this in the preceding anecdote. The statistics are irrelevant if the harm to be avoided is preemptively construed as unassailable.

The trend toward routine screening continues to intensify and to expand to include more and more potential diseases. It is clear that this trend registers a shift in thinking that has occurred over the last two decades.[61] We might argue that this trend suggests that the risk of an imperfect pregnancy is preemptively considered a worse risk than having no pregnancy at all and leads to a situation in which risk itself becomes the pathology.

---

[60] M. Douglas, *Risk Acceptability According to the Social Sciences* (New York: Russell Sage Foundation, 1985), 92.

[61] M. Gidiri et al., "Maternal Screening for Down Syndrome: Are Women's Perceptions Changing?" (2007) 114 *British Journal of Obstetrics and Gynaecology* 458, at 458–9.

2 RISK AS PATHOLOGY

2.1 What Is Normal?

With the increasing sophistication of prenatal tests and their proliferation, the ("normal") pregnant and pre-pregnant body is rendered a
pathological site.

As noted at the start of this chapter, as early as 1999 Abby Lippman
was arguing that increasing testing capacity leads to a decreased range of
normal pregnancies.[62] More than a decade later, testing has become widespread, and the number of different screening and diagnostic tests has
also increased. This has occurred alongside the development of simpler
and faster testing technologies. The effect of these kinds of "easy" technological fixes to a problem that in statistical terms is very unlikely to exist is
to pathologize normalcy itself. The normal pregnant woman is registered
in these moments as a site of inevitable vulnerability that is always potentially subject to illness, genetic mutation, injury, and surprise.

As Lupton notes, there is no such thing as a "no risk" pregnancy.
A woman might be considered a "low risk" but remains the subject of high levels of expert surveillance[63] and is expected to exert
continuing surveillance of her own body.[64] Samerski aptly describes

---

[62] A. Lippman, "Choice as a Risk to Women's Health" (1999) 1(3) *Health, Risk &
Society* 281, at 284.

[63] While not necessarily unwanted, it is worth noting the detailed and lengthy maternal
shared care guidelines produced by some health departments and public hospitals
that are specifically directed at women with "low risk" pregnancies. In Victoria, see
Shared Maternity Care Collective, "Guidelines for Shared Maternity Care Affiliates"
(2010), available at http://www.health.vic.gov.au/maternitycare/smcaguidelines-2010.
pdf, which totals 103 pages; in South Australia see ACT Health, "Maternity Shared
Care Guidelines" (May 2008), available at http://health.act.gov.au/c/health?a=dlpol&
policy=1150856562, 130 pages.

[64] D. Lupton, "Risk and the Ontology of Pregnant Embodiment" in D. Lupton
(ed.), *Risk and Sociocultural Theory: New Directions and Perspectives* (Cambridge:
Cambridge University Press, 1999), 64.

this phenomenon when she says, "Today ... sick people, pregnant women and perfectly healthy people all live in the shadow of their potential risk."[65] Furthermore, what constitutes a "risk" keeps changing, depending upon the developing technology. Best practice (as it develops) becomes a driver that doctors have little control over themselves. If offering a test is best practice, then any departure could be construed as negligence. Even before a test reaches the stage of being identified as best practice – (i.e., is merely available), doctors who are aware of it might feel exposed to potential liability if they fail to offer it.

When calculating risks in the prenatal context, there is a certain amount of settled reliance on the view that the thing about which the risk is calculated is a potentially intolerable deviation from the norm. However, when the range of possible tests keeps increasing the pool of potential harms, identification of a range of tolerable deviations from the "norm" poses greater and greater challenges. Ulrich Beck notes that "[a]s the possibility of genetic prediction grows, so too, paradoxically, does biographical uncertainty,"[66] and, in this way, we suggest that prenatal testing technology generates nonnormative identities.

As we shall see in Chapters 3 and 4, the concept of seriousness is used as a legal limit to restrain or at least inhibit reproductive decisions to terminate or select against particular kinds of nonnormative embodiment. In the context of risk analysis then, it is necessary to find a way to measure seriousness. A problem arises because of the inevitable feedback loop that operates. Once a risk is identified, its very articulation may constitute the harm to be avoided as serious. Indeed, our research has shown that seriousness may be cast very broadly and measured against the idea of the *trivial*. In our interviews with both clinicians and regulators detailed in Chapters 4 and 5, trivial concerns

[65] S. Samerski, "The Unleashing of Genetic Terminology: How Genetic Counselling Mobilizes for Risk Management" (August 2006) 25(2) *New Genetics and Society.*

[66] U. Beck and E. Beck-Gernsheim, *Individualization: Institutionalized Individualism and Its Social and Political Consequences* (London: Sage, 2002), 140.

are sometimes described as a preference for certain traits where there is no "clinically" measurable deficit that is being remedied.

Arguing that the "characteristic striving for health in the modern world" is part of the global project of modernity, Beck views this as a sign of the "new malleability of life with all its opportunities, checks and pressures."[67] However, Kerr and Cunningham-Burley argue that rather than finding a reflexive form of modernity characterized by reorganization and reform in the context of genetic testing, we find instead science and technology operating along old lines of modern and countermodern discourse. They say: "Reductionism and determinism continue to infuse contemporary methods and theories. Scientific and social progress are collapsed anew. Certitude and surveillance remain powerful guiding principles."[68] And as they also point out, "[d]espite the inevitable uncertainties in genetic knowledge and the testing process, the clinical setting often requires that genetic knowledge and test results are unreflexively applied and interpreted."[69] This certitude enables the development of what some legal scholars have described as "techniques of risk governance," which operate within the neoliberal project to "individualize risk" and generate legal claims[70] and liability. As we have noted, once a test is available, doctors may feel exposed to potential liability if they fail to offer it. And this may occur where the harm to be avoided is not serious or is even trivial. Mykitiuk and Scott put it like this: "Governing with risk is seen as a means of channelling

---

[67] U. Beck and E. Beck-Gernsheim, *Individualization: Institutionalized Individualism and Its Social and Political Consequences* (London: Sage, 2002), 141.

[68] A. Kerr and S. Cunningham-Burley, "On Ambivalence and Risk: Reflexive Modernity and the New Human Genetics" (2000) 34(2) *Sociology* 283, at 290.

[69] A. Kerr and S. Cunningham-Burley, "On Ambivalence and Risk: Reflexive Modernity and the New Human Genetics" (2000) 34(2) *Sociology* 283, at 289.

[70] See K. Hannah-Moffat and P. O'Malley, "Gendered Risks: An Introduction" in K. Hannah-Moffat and P. O'Malley, *Gendered Risks* (New York: Routledge-Cavendish, 2007) and R. Mykitiuk and D. N. Scott, "Risky Pregnancy: Liability, Blame and Insurance in the Governance of Prenatal Harm" (2010–2011) 43 *University of British Columbia Law Review* 311.

institutional practices and systems into a pattern that begins with *assessment* and moves through *prediction* to *management.* The technique of risk governance is often viewed as a mechanism for making people more individually accountable for risk .... "[71] What seems clear is that new testing technologies create uncertain biographies as they give rise to increasing risk pathologies. The category of risk, however, is derived from certainties about what constitutes a harm, and we argue this is misplaced.

Risk only makes sense in a world where it is clear what we are risking or, in other words, where we have a concept of what constitutes a "good" or a "bad" outcome and thus a good or a bad risk. It is impossible to interrogate the institutionalization (medical, social, or legal, for example) of risk management in pregnancy without at the same time unpacking the conceptual apparatus that has created the normative framework within which that analysis of risk takes place. Here, of course, we are drawn back into the discussion that we canvassed in Chapter 1, namely, the way in which disability and normality are framed and constructed. The achievement of a "normal"/ "healthy"/ "nondisabled" baby is dependent upon momentary alignments of medicolegal, social, historical, and biotechnological discourses that work in tandem to stabilize shifting normative ideals. In the context of reproduction we have groups (doctors, counselors, nurses, patients, partners, legislators) all transacting in particular ways to create a form of self and future subjectivity via minute calculations of risk and probability. This is similar to what Nikolas Rose describes, when writing about the use of psychiatric drugs and the medicalization of sadness, as "a political economy of subjectification."[72] He describes the way in which we are entangled within "a public habitat of images of the good life for identification, a plurality of pedagogies of everyday existence,

---

[71] R. Mykitiuk and D. N. Scott, "Risky Pregnancy: Liability, Blame and Insurance in the Governance of Prenatal Harm" (2010–2011) 43 *University of British Columbia Law Review* 313–314.

[72] N. Rose, "Beyond Medicalization" (2007) 369 *Lancet* 700, at 702.

which display, in meticulous if banal detail, the ways of conducting oneself that make possible a life that is personally pleasurable and socially acceptable."[73]

A similar architecture of "normal (good)" health is created in the context of pregnancy.

In the clinic, risk is pivotal in strategies of normalization to identify deviations from the norm. Lupton, for example, notes that one method of achieving normalization "involves the gathering of information about populations and subpopulations and subjecting it to statistical analysis."[74] She goes on:

> These approaches serve to render the risks attendant upon pregnancy as calculable and governable, thus bringing them into being as problems that require action. Clinical risk is based upon the characteristics of case studies of individuals observed by experts. Epidemiological risk is calculated through the observation of patterns in anonymous populations of disease and identification of risk factors .... Both types of risk knowledges are normalizing, locating the individual woman within a framework of comparisons to many other women.[75]

Outside the clinic, scientific literature is matched by a vast body of lay literature including parenting books, newspapers, TV stories, women's magazines, websites, and blogs. The proliferation of these texts both tells us what constitutes a particular kind of good life and good pregnancy and provides a critique of the way in which our existences fall short of that ideal. The complex calculations we are offered in the context of prenatal testing are also a critique of how

---

[73] N. Rose, "Beyond Medicalization" (2007) 369 *Lancet* 700, at 702.

[74] D. Lupton, "Risk and the Ontology of Pregnant Embodiment" in D. Lupton (ed.), *Risk and Sociocultural Theory: New Directions and Perspectives* (Cambridge: Cambridge University Press, 1999), 61.

[75] D. Lupton, "Risk and the Ontology of Pregnant Embodiment" in D. Lupton (ed.), *Risk and Sociocultural Theory: New Directions and Perspectives* (Cambridge: Cambridge University Press 1999), 63.

(the degree to which statistically) our reproductive selves fall short. These, together with one's own half-formed hopes and aspirations, form the context in which risk calculations are often undertaken. This is framed (in the clinic) in terms of science and not morality, but the effect is, arguably, to create a moral zone of action or inaction. Hunt et al. note, for instance, that in their study "many women interpreted the at-risk status of their pregnancy not as a probability but, rather, as indicating that their baby was in fact ill."[76] They state that "[t]his distinction is generally left out of discussions of risk assessment in clinical settings and has resulted in a widespread, but erroneous notions that risk is an intrinsic property of an individual."[77] Hunt et al.'s confidence that this is an erroneous notion, however, is, we think, hopeful. If we return to the quoted excerpt with which we began this chapter, it is worth recalling the advice offered by the Royal College of Obstetricians and Gynaecologists that there "is no such thing as a zero risk." Indeed, what is clear is that it is "normal" to be at risk in pregnancy. It is not surprising, then, that it becomes increasingly difficult for women to dissociate risk from a state of disease. Rose has described this as the "performative injunction" of risk – that it is "something to be guarded against, avoided, managed, reduced if not eliminated."[78] Risk, then, is, in Rose's words, a disease – "the disease of risk of disease."[79]

A number of feminist scholars have made similar arguments. Lippman, discussing the work of Lynn Morgan, argued as early as 1999 that "changing concepts of risk and risk management ... frame the

---

[76] L. Hunt et al., "Do Notions of Risk Inform Patient Choice? Lessons from a Study of Prenatal Genetic Counseling" (2006) 25 *Medical Anthropology* 193, at 210.

[77] L. Hunt et al., "Do Notions of Risk Inform Patient Choice? Lessons from a Study of Prenatal Genetic Counseling" (2006) 25 *Medical Anthropology* 193, at 212.

[78] N. Rose, "In Search of Certainty: Risk Management in a Biological Age" (2005) 4(3) *Journal of Public Mental Health* 14, at 14.

[79] N. Rose, "In Search of Certainty: Risk Management in a Biological Age" (2005) 4(3) *Journal of Public Mental Health* 14, at 15.

body as a site of 'virtual pathology.'"[80] In more recent work Lippman has returned to this theme and argued that "the emphasis on one's supposed risk of developing a problem,… in its most pernicious form … makes being 'at risk' itself a disease state."[81] She says that "given that there are more healthy than diseased people in the world, offering a product that is claimed to help manage their risks can capture increasing numbers of those in need of some treatment. Finding the 'not-yet-sick' and the 'worried well', who could be offered some drug or device, is the goal."[82]

Thus the construction of risk is complicated by the sense that being at risk is itself a problem. In addition to this, however, the way individuals perceive their own risk status varies.

2.2 Risk Perception and the Need to Test

It is difficult to distinguish the offer of testing from the claim to its necessity. In Chapter 1, we noted that the literature in which testing is presented to women asserts the desirability of their being "informed" about the risks that are involved in their pregnancy in order that they may make an informed choice – should "disability" be detected – about whether their pregnancy should continue. As we have seen in this chapter, in most developed countries, medical colleges, government health departments, and government funding bodies view all pregnant women as presumptively at risk of having a child with a disorder.

[80] A. Lippman, "Choice as a Risk to Women's Health" (1999) 1(3) *Health, Risk & Society* 281, at 283, quoting K.P. Morgan, "Contested Bodies, Contested Knowledge: Women, Health, and the Politics of Medicalization" in S. Sherwin (coord.), *The Politics of Women's Health: Exploring Agency and Autonomy* (Philadelphia: Temple University Press, 1998), 64–82.

[81] A. Lippman, *The Inclusion of Women in Clinical Trials: Are We Asking the Right Questions?* (Toronto: Women and Health Protection, 2006), 18.

[82] A. Lippman, *The Inclusion of Women in Clinical Trials: Are We Asking the Right Questions?* (Toronto: Women and Health Protection, 2006), 19.

These messages about the risks attending pregnancy must create (or perpetuate) in the minds of the women receiving them the idea that testing is, if not compulsory, only refused by the reckless. While these same organizations are at pains to make clear that the decision whether to undergo screening or diagnostic testing lies with the woman, it is hard to deny that the very offer of testing itself, though couched in terms of voluntarism, justifies its very existence.[83]

Abby Lippman carefully unpacked precisely how this process works when she showed how the availability of a particular test constructs the "need" for that test. She says:

> We must first identify the concept of need as itself a problem and acknowledge that needs do not have intrinsic reality. Rather, needs are socially constructed and culture bound, grounded in current history, dependent on context and therefore, not universal.
>
> With respect to prenatal diagnosis, "need" seems to have been conceptualized predominantly in terms of changes in capabilities for

---

[83] RANZCOG suggests, as best practice, that information provided to pregnant women should include "[t]he understanding that screening is entirely voluntary and that there will be no change to pregnancy management if a woman and her partner choose not to have any screening tests." RANZCOG, "Prenatal Screening Tests for Trisomy 21 (Down Syndrome), Trisomy 18 (Edwards Syndrome) and Neural Tube Defects" (Statement no. C-Obs 4 July 2007), 2. See also, for example, the NSW Health booklet "Prenatal Testing: Special Tests for Your Baby during Pregnancy" (March 2010), at http://www.genetics.com.au/pdf/pntbooklet2010. pdf, which notes at p. 2 that "the decision to undergo testing during a pregnancy is a very personal one and a decision best made based on all the available information. It is important to remember that you do not have to have prenatal testing if you do not wish to." Also see the Murdoch Children's Research Institutes Decision Aid "Your Choice Screening and Diagnostic Tests in Pregnancy," at http://www. mcri.edu.au/Downloads/PrenatalTestingDecisionAid.pdf, which says at p. 2 that "prenatal testing is made available because of the small risk that *all* women have of having a baby with a major problem" [our emphasis]. In bold letters at the end of the same page is the statement "Testing for fetal abnormality is not compulsory for anyone."

fetal diagnoses: women only come to "need" prenatal diagnosis after the test for some disorder has been developed.[84]

This is further reinforced by the doctor's approach to the pregnant woman, ensuring that she is informed about available tests and their advantages and disadvantages. The RANZCOG statement says, for example, that "[i]nformation on the relative advantages and disadvantages of the available screening tests should be provided to pregnant women (and their partners)."[85] Lippman ties the concept of need to women's role as primary caregivers and argues that "to the extent that she is expected generally to do everything possible for the fetus/child, a woman may come to 'need' prenatal diagnosis, and take testing for granted."[86] In this way the proposition that one can either choose to act (agree to be screened, undergo further diagnostic testing, terminate a pregnancy) or choose not to act (in the full knowledge that there "is no such thing as a zero risk")[87] is heavily value laden. Ulrich Beck, too, writing about genetic technology, has described its process as "spiral-like." He says technology "appears as both the product and the instrument of social needs, interests and conflicts. Technology is effect and cause at the same time."[88] Indeed, there is a central tension between the conceptualization of reproductive choice (informed or otherwise) and the push toward *informed* reproduction that we might characterize as responsible or civic reproduction. One might argue, for instance, that the very idea of informed

---

[84] A. Lippman, "Prenatal Genetic Testing and Screening: Constructing Needs and Reinforcing Inequities" (1991) 17 *American Journal of Law and Medicine* 15, at 27.

[85] RANZCOG, "Prenatal Screening Tests for Trisomy 21 (Down Syndrome), Trisomy 18 (Edwards Syndrome) and Neural Tube Defects" (Statement no. C-Obs 4 July 2007), 2.

[86] A. Lippman, "Prenatal Genetic Testing and Screening: Constructing Needs and Reinforcing Inequities" (1991) 17 *American Journal of Law and Medicine* 15, at 28.

[87] RCOG, "Understanding How Risk Is Discussed in Healthcare" February 2010, http://www.rcog.org.uk/understanding-how-risk-isdiscussed-healthcare.

[88] U. Beck and E. Beck-Gernsheim, *Individualization: Institutionalized Individualism and Its Social and Political Consequences* (London: Sage, 2002), 141.

choice is a means to make women (and their partners) culpable for the decisions they make. Mykitiuk and Scott argue that "risk conscious-ness is universally growing in response to scientific and technological advances,"[89] and we are replacing "social" or "collective" forms of risk governance with "individualising forms."[90] This has a twofold effect. Women find themselves not only expected, as Hannah-Moffatt and O'Malley put it, to "exhibit some sort of responsibility for, and even expertise in managing risk,"[91] but to go further and, where possible, perfect their pregnancies. Andre et al. state that "the increasing capac-ity to choose the genetic endowment of children brings with it a corre-sponding responsibility to do so. And when people – i.e., parents – do not do so, some accuse them of being irresponsible."[92] Julian Savulescu, director of the Oxford Uehiro Centre for Practical Ethics in England, has actively argued in favor of what he calls "procreative beneficence" in which parents are obliged to select a child, out of a range of possi-ble children, who will be most likely to live the "best life." He believes parents have a responsibility not just to screen out disease and dis-ability, but to choose personality traits like high IQ to advance society further.[93]

While there are an equal number of bioethicists and scholars arguing against a responsibility to pursue perfectionism,[94] popular

[89] R. Mykitiuk and D. N. Scott, "Risky Pregnancy: Liability, Blame and Insurance in the Governance of Prenatal Harm" (2010–2011) 43 *University of British Columbia Law Review* 315.

[90] R. Mykitiuk and D. N. Scott, "Risky Pregnancy: Liability, Blame and Insurance in the Governance of Prenatal Harm (2010–2011) 43 *University of British Columbia Law Review* 315.

[91] K. Hannah-Moffat and P. O'Malley, *Gendered Risks* (New York: Routledge-Cavendish, 2007), 2.

[92] J. Andre, L.M. Fleck, and T. Tomlinson, "On Being Genetically 'Irresponsible'" (2000) 10(2) *Kennedy Institute of Ethics Journal* 129, at 129.

[93] See J. Savulescu and G. Kahane, "The Moral Obligation to Create Children with the Best Chance of the Best Life" (2009) 23(5) *Bioethics* 274.

[94] M. Sandel, *The Case against Perfection: Ethics in the Age of Genetic Engineering* (Cambridge, Mass.: Harvard University Press, 2009) and R. Sparrow, "A Not-So-

discourse seems to echo the responsibility line. Kathy Evans, writing for the *Sunday Age*, says:

> With routine screening comes a feeling that choosing to have an affected baby is selfish, self-indulgent even, not fair on the child and definitely not on those whose taxes go to support it. My decision not to have testing in pregnancy implied my willingness to give birth to a faulty child and I have many times felt the reproachful eyes of the medical hierarchy upon me.[95]

Nevertheless, reproductive choice is said to be enhanced by the development of new and more sophisticated prenatal screening and testing technologies when matched with appropriate risk analysis information and genetic counseling. The view offered is that, used in the right way, these technologies allow women and couples to make "informed choices" about the management of risk in their pregnancies.

This is certainly true for some women, especially women who enter the process of prenatal testing and preimplantation testing after significant encounters with serious disability. Sarah Franklin and Celia Roberts conducted a number of interviews with women and couples who had undergone PGD to avoid a known disability. In this instance, the sense of responsibility felt by some of the participants to avoid having a child with a known disability is palpable. For example, they interviewed a couple known as Anne and Daniel who had lost their first child at the age of one to spinal muscular atrophy. They say, "but we would know that if we got pregnant naturally and you know, we had another child, we would know that we'd, we had the choice, and we've produced another child with SMA!"[96] Franklin and Roberts

New Eugenics: Harris and Savulescu on Human Enhancement" (February 2011) 41(1) *Hastings Center Report* 32–42. See also chapter 4 of B. Bennett, *Health Law's Kaleidoscope: Health Law Rights in a Global Age* (Aldershot: Ashgate, 2008).

[95] K. Evans, "The Gene Genie" *Sunday Age*, 14 March 2010, 11. This is one of many examples we found in a media search conducted over a five-year period. Database on file with the authors.

[96] S. Franklin and C. Roberts, *Born and Made: An Ethnography of Preimplantation Genetic Diagnosis* (Princeton, NJ: Princeton University Press, 2006), 117.

describe Anne's position as follows: "To look at such a child, Anne explains, would inevitably involve a deep sense of regret, of irresponsibility and of culpability."[97] Franklin and Roberts note, however, that they only interviewed people who had opted for PGD, not those who had rejected it, people they call "PGD refusers and it is clear that another couple might have had a very different response to the risk they were taking."[98] Putting aside questions of the voluntary nature of that decision, there is also a clear disconnection between the technology of risk analysis and the way in which real life decisions (choices) are made. In her 1985 book *Risk Acceptability According to the Social Sciences*, Mary Douglas describes the way in which risk calculation, as a scientific practice, depends on the idea of rational decision makers. She says, "the rational choice philosophers claim to use a neutral objective conceptual scheme to solve problems by sheer power of reason"[99] and, further on, "[t]he theory of choice applies a logic to the act of choosing. The rational argument is one that is not self-contradictory and likewise the rational choice."[100] However, reproductive decisions are made in the context of multiple and conflicting claims and expectations, in a world in which perception is mediated by and through social, cultural, and political discourses.

Douglas again is useful here, when she says: "On the one hand analysis of risk within the theory of choice … clears away all adhering real world considerations; understandably, a pure theory of risk separates its topics from prejudices entertained by the decision-maker and from institutional and historical contingencies. On the other hand, in the real

---

[97] S. Franklin and C. Roberts, *Born and Made: An Ethnography of Preimplantation Genetic Diagnosis* (Princeton, NJ: Princeton University Press, 2006), 117.

[98] S. Franklin and C. Roberts, *Born and Made: An Ethnography of Preimplantation Genetic Diagnosis* (Princeton, NJ: Princeton University Press, 2006), 117.

[99] M. Douglas, *Risk Acceptability According to the Social Sciences* (New York: Russell Sage Foundation, 1985), 13.

[100] M. Douglas, *Risk Acceptability According to the Social Sciences* (New York: Russell Sage Foundation, 1985), 41.

world the perception of probably natural losses is freighted with moral associations and institutional bias."[101]

One of the concerns that feminists have raised relates to the impact of this tension on pregnant women. Barbara Katz Rothman makes the point that the calculations required of pregnant women within the context of risk culture entail a "contradiction of demands."[102] Women are asked to "accept their pregnancies and their babies, to take care of the babies within them, and yet be willing to abort them."[103] This contradiction becomes especially acute when the decision whether to undergo amniocentesis is confronted. In this moment women may "want to have amniocentesis to identify and be able to abort a damaged *fetus*, but are afraid of the procedure's possible harm to their *baby*." Thus, women must balance two, perhaps equally terrifying risks, in order to reach a decision. One of the ways in which the contradiction is managed, suggests Katz Rothman, is via the device of personhood. She observes:

> If it is healthy, if it is genetically acceptable, then it is a person, her baby. If it is not, then it is just a fetus, a genetically damaged fetus.[104]

This raises the question of how the various pathways open to women in constructing risk and personhood affect the experience of pregnancy and parenthood. Katz Rothman notes that although the fear that a child may not meet parental expectations is not new, prenatal testing technologies have been transformative. She says: "Never before have we asked women to make rational, intellectual determinations based on that fear. What does it do to motherhood, to women, and to

---

[101] M. Douglas, *Risk Acceptability According to the Social Sciences* (New York: Russell Sage Foundation, 1985), 91.

[102] B. Katz Rothman, *The Tentative Pregnancy: Prenatal Diagnosis and the Future of Motherhood* (Viking, New York, 1986) at 6.

[103] B. Katz Rothman, *The Tentative Pregnancy: Prenatal Diagnosis and the Future of Motherhood* (New York: Viking, 1986) at 6.

[104] B. Katz Rothman, *The Tentative Pregnancy: Prenatal Diagnosis and the Future of Motherhood* (New York: Viking, 1986), at 6.

men as fathers too, when we make parental acceptance conditional, pending further testing?"[105] Samerski has argued more recently that prenatal counseling has a particularly significant role to play in directing women's understandings of risk in these situations of impossible contradiction.[106] Counselors are called upon, she suggests, to bridge the gap between their own expert statistical knowledge and understanding and the lay understanding of the expectant mother. However, Samerski claims this often leads patients into a "decision trap" that forces them to choose between precalculated risks. This imposition of a managerial rationality is arguably inappropriate for the kinds of decisions that are being made. Instead, she argues, the effect is often to turn an abstract probability into a personal threat. She notes that "genetic counselling can be understood as a ritual which introduces pregnant women to this managerial rationality. They are asked to anticipate their coming child in terms of a distribution of possible outcomes and follow the rationale of decision theory for reducing risks and making the optimal choice."[107] It is particularly interesting, therefore, to track the contemporary importance being placed on access for women to counseling when faced with these kinds of decisions. A quick survey of government, hospital and medical college guidelines in Australia suggests that counselling – and in some cases genetic counselling – has been thoroughly integrated into their prenatal testing methodologies. This counselling is to be offered at every step of the prenatal testing process – before and during PGD, before prenatal screening, after receipt of an "increased risk" screening result, before diagnostic testing, and when an anomaly is found and termination

---

[105] B. Katz Rothman, *The Tentative Pregnancy: Prenatal Diagnosis and the Future of Motherhood* (New York: Viking, 1986), at 7.

[106] S. Samerski, "The 'Decision Trap': How Genetic Counselling Transforms Pregnant Women into Managers of Foetal Risk Profiles" in K. Hannah-Moffat and P. O'Malley (eds.), *Gendered Risks* (New York: Routledge-Cavendish, 2007).

[107] S. Samerski, "The 'decision Trap': How Genetic Counselling Transforms Pregnant Women into Managers of Foetal Risk Profiles" in K. Hannah-Moffat and P. O'Malley (eds.), *Gendered Risks* (New York: Routledge-Cavendish, 2007), 70.

is considered.[108] In this last scenario, the offer of counseling is a legislative requirement in some Australian jurisdictions.[109]

Research focusing on risk perception in the context of disability, however, found that "[o]verall, individuals often have inaccurate perceptions about their risk which are more likely to be overestimations."[110]

---

[108] See, for example, the Victorian Shared Maternity Care Collective, "Guidelines for Shared Maternity Care Affiliates" (2010), available at http://www.health.vic.gov.au/maternitycare/smcaguidelines-2010.pdf, which notes at p. 60 that "[c]ommunity providers are encouraged to offer early advice and counselling around all tests but this is especially pertinent for screening and diagnostic tests for fetal abnormalities"; also see the NSW Health policy "Prenatal Testing/Screening for Down Syndrome and Other Chromosomal Abnormalities" (8 August 2007), available at http://www.health.nsw.gov.au/policies/pd/2007/pdf/PD2007_067.pdf, which requires that "offers of screening need to be accompanied by sufficient information and counselling" at 3. The RANZCOG policies "Prenatal Screening Tests for Trisomy 21 (Down Syndrome), Trisomy 18 (Edwards Syndrome) and Neural Tube Defects" (July 2009), "Prenatal Screening for Fetal Abnormalities" (March 2010), and "Prenatal Diagnosis Policy" (November 2006) also all recommend counselling as part of best practice.

[109] In Western Australia, the Health Act 1911 requires that women requesting an abortion (prior to 20 weeks gestation) give "informed consent," and section 334(5) notes that "informed consent means consent freely given by the woman where –

(a) a medical practitioner has properly, appropriately and adequately provided her with counselling about the medical risk of termination of pregnancy and of carrying a pregnancy to term;

(b) a medical practitioner has offered her the opportunity of referral to appropriate and adequate counselling about matters relating to termination of pregnancy and carrying a pregnancy to term; and

(c) a medical practitioner has informed her that appropriate and adequate counselling will be available to her should she wish it upon termination of pregnancy or after carrying the pregnancy to term."

Tasmania has a similar requirement: see the Criminal Code Act 1924 (Tas), s 164.

[110] S. Sivell et al., "How Risk Is Perceived, Constructed and Interpreted by Clients in Clinical Genetics, and the Effects on Decision Making: Systematic Review" (2008) 17 *Journal of Genetic Counseling* 30, at 56, referring to the work of P. Hopwood, "Breast Cancer Risk Perception: What Do We Know and Understand" (2000) 2(6) *Breast Cancer Research* 387, and R.T. Croyle and C. Lerman, "Risk Communication in Genetic Testing for Cancer Susceptibility" (1999) 25 *Journal of the National Cancer Institute, Monographs* 59.

In the context of prenatal testing, Sivell et al. found that there was a shift toward more accurate risk perceptions after genetic counseling but still not to the correct level. They conclude that "[t]he tendency of some individuals to continue to overestimate their risk indicates that being able to understand and reiterate an objective numerical risk estimate is not necessarily their primary goal; rather they are seeing ways in which they can manage and cope."[111]

It is possible, too, that overestimation of risk is tied to an overestimation of potential harm. If we return to the disability literature we discussed in Chapter 1, it is clear that perceptions of disability differ among those who experience disability themselves and those who do not. Earlier we referred to the Albrecht and Devlinger study that described a disability paradox whereby those with disabilities described their sense of life satisfaction in more positive terms than those without disabilities.[112] When an individual woman or a couple is faced with a statistical account of risk in relation to a disability, then, it may be that the conceptualization of the harm that could flow from that disability has an effect on the way in which the statistics are understood. Experience of disability or prior experience of an abnormality in pregnancy may also have an impact on the way those risks are weighted.

If Rose is right that "risk thinking" is "not about 'learning to live with uncertainty' – it is about refusing to live with uncertainty,"[113] then it is difficult to see how the provision of information about risk calculations and population statistics can ever enhance a person's capacity to make an informed decision. Rather (and this is one of the arguments we canvass in this book), risk information is intimately tied to reproducing responsibly.

---

[111] S. Sivell et al., "How Risk Is Perceived, Constructed and Interpreted by Clients in Clinical Genetics, and the Effects on Decision Making: Systematic Review" (2008) 17 *Journal of Genetic Counseling* 30, at 56.

[112] G.L. Albrecht and P.J. Devlieger, "The Disability Paradox: High Quality of Life against All Odds" (1999) 48 *Social Science & Medicine* 977. See also Chapter 1.

[113] N. Rose, "In Search of Certainty: Risk Management in a Biological Age" (2005) 4(3) *Journal of Public Mental Health* 14, at 18.

2.3 Reproducing Responsibly?

The concept of responsible reproduction operates in the frame of an expectation, namely, that women (and their partners) will "choose" both to utilize available testing technologies to enable rational risk based calculations and that they will act on those calculations to ensure the birth of a "healthy" baby.

This kind of discourse of responsible reproduction is similar to what Elisabeth Ettorre describes as a "type of reproductive asceticism and a discourse on shame."[114] She argues that "[w]hen pregnant bodies undergo ... invasive tests, this austere self-disciplining of reproductive asceticism can be viewed and experienced as necessary for the over-all, external regulation of 'fit' populations in consumer culture. In this regime, the female body emerges as a reproductive resource."[115]

By drawing attention to these practices we can see that there is a cultural push, as Ettorre puts it, to "separate ... ourselves as social and moral actors from our bodies."[116] Lippman too has made this point. She says that "[p]renatal testing separates a single entity, a pregnant woman, into two: herself and her fetus. And by shaping the fetus as separate and separable from the woman, an opportunity is provided to assign independent interests (and/or rights) to it – interests not just attached through the mother. Suddenly 'fetal abuse' becomes a thinkable concept, and a pregnant woman can be subjected to rules, regulations, and duties established by those seeking to protect fetal interests. With this division a responsible mother therefore becomes one that does everything – takes all tests – to ensure fetal health."[117]

[114] E. Ettorre, "Reproductive Genetics, Gender and the Body: 'Please Doctor, May I Have a Normal Baby?'" (2000) 34 *Sociology* 403, at 408.

[115] E. Ettorre, "Reproductive Genetics, Gender and the Body: 'Please Doctor, May I Have a Normal Baby?'" (2000) 34 *Sociology* 403, at 408.

[116] E. Ettorre, *Reproductive Genetics: Gender and the Body* (London: Routledge, 2002), 6.

[117] A. Lippman, "The Genetic Construction of Prenatal Testing: Choice, Consent or Conformity for Women?" in K.H. Rothenberg and E.J. Thomson (eds.), *Women and*

The addition of the option of PGD for those identified as at increased risk of passing on a genetic anomaly has added to the menu of potential risk avoidance strategies available to the pregnant, and the potentially pregnant, woman. However, in the case of PGD, it might be argued that the balance of pressures is slightly altered by the fact that in most jurisdictions it is hard to access compared with prenatal testing with laws limiting who may use it and why.[118] Further, it is often the woman or couple who seeks PGD on the basis of past experience with a disabling condition or because of being part of a disability support network that advocate its use. Franklin and Roberts note, for instance, that "patient groups for diseases such as thalassemia formally petitioned the government for research on PGD during public debate of the Human Fertilisation and Embryology Bill."[119] It is not surprising, then, that risk has taken on a new valency for women that precedes even the preimplantation stage. Perhaps more interestingly, we now see a situation in which women are increasingly called upon to interrogate their bodies before conception and, in some cases, as soon as it is possible for them to become pregnant.

3 PRECONCEPTION AND PRENATAL RISK AVOIDANCE STRATEGIES.

In April 2007, the United States Centers for Disease Control and Prevention (CDCP) released health guidelines for all women who could become pregnant, even those who had no plans to become a parent. Women from their midteens to their midforties were to be targeted in a campaign to provide risk assessment and counseling to all women of childbearing age to reduce risks related to the outcomes of

Prenatal Testing: Facing the Challenges of Genetic Technology (Columbus: Ohio State University Press, 1994), 22.

[118] this will be discussed in detail in Chapter 4.

[119] S. Franklin and C. Roberts, *Born and Made: An Ethnography of Preimplantation Genetic Diagnosis* (Princeton, NJ: Princeton University Press, 2006), 127.

pregnancy. The aim of the preconception health care interventions was to "allow women to maintain optimal health for themselves, choose the number and spacing of their pregnancies and, when desired, prepare for a *healthy baby* [our emphasis]."[120]

The lack of emphasis on male responsibility is notable. Perhaps more concerning is the focus of the interventions on the health of those persons not yet conceived and those whose conception has not even been contemplated. The inclusion of all women from "menarche to menopause" insists on creating a holding place for the preconceived embryo in an imaginary family yet to be constructed.[121]

Similar, although not identical, moves have been taken in other countries.

The Health Council of the Netherlands, for example, produced a report in 2007 called *Preconception Care: A Good Beginning.*[122] The aim of preconception care is described in this report as "promoting the health of the expectant mother and her child," and the period of preconception care is crafted more narrowly, as "some months before conception to the first few weeks thereafter."[123]

---

[120] U.S. Department of Health and Human Services, Centers for Disease Control and Prevention, "Recommendations to Improve Preconception Health and Health Care" (21 April 2006, Vol. 55, No. PR-6:7).

[121] I. Karpin, "The Uncanny Embryos: Legal Limits to the Human and Reproduction without Women" (2006) 28(4) *Sydney Law Review* 599, at 607. On this point see also the South Australian Department of Health's "Perinatal Practice Guidelines" available at http://www.health.sa.gov.au/PPG/Default.aspx?tabid=222 (see Section 1, chapter 1, "Preconception Advice"), which note in the introduction that "[l]ife and career plans are best made with knowledge of the impact of increasing maternal age on future reproduction" thereby recasting all major life decisions as part of preconception planning.

[122] Health Council of the Netherlands, *Preconception Care: A Good Beginning* (2007) 24 para 2.2, available for download at http://www.gezondheidsraad.nl/sites/default/files/200719E.pdf.

[123] Health Council of the Netherlands, *Preconception Care: A Good Beginning* (2007) 24 para 2.2, available for download at http://www.gezondheidsraad.nl/sites/default/files/200719E.pdf.

The Public Health Agency of Canada has in the *Family-Centred Maternity and Newborn Care: National Guidelines* described the preconception period as "incapable of neat definition" and states that "most women never really 'know' when, or if, they will become pregnant," and "clearly preconception care should be considered throughout one's life."[124] Similarly, a Queensland Health website on preconception care notes that

> conception occurs about 2 weeks before your period is due. That means you may not even know you're pregnant until you're more than 3 weeks pregnant. Yet your baby is most sensitive to harm 2 to 8 weeks after conception. This is when your baby's facial features and organs, such as the heart and kidneys, begin to form. Anything you eat, drink, smoke or are exposed to can affect your baby. That's why it's best to start acting as if you're pregnant before you are.[125]

In the United Kingdom, the National Service Framework for Children, Young People and Maternity Services, provides the following in its Maternity Services Standard 11: "All NHS maternity care providers, Primary Care Trusts and Local Authorities ensure that: Local multi-agency health promotion arrangements include health promotion for pregnancy" and "Campaigns and materials are targeted towards women in groups and communities who under-use maternity services or who are at greater risk of poor outcomes." The kinds of issues that are canvassed are the importance of:

[124] Government of Canada, Family-Centred Maternity and Newborn Care: National Guidelines (2000), at 3.5.

[125] Queensland Government, "Topic: Preconception" (last updated 28 April 2008) available at http://access.health.qld.gov.au/hid/WomensHealth/PregnancyandChildbirth/preconception_ap.asp. Other Australian government guidelines on preconception care include the South Australian Department of Health's "Perinatal Practice Guidelines" available at http://www.health.sa.gov.au/PPG/Default.aspx?tabid=222 (see Section 1, chapter 1, "Preconception Advice") and the Western Australia Department of Health's Webpage "Planning to Get Pregnant" available at http://www.health.wa.gov.au/havingababy/before/planning.cfm.

a) preconceptual folic acid
b) minimizing intake of alcohol
c) not using recreational drugs
d) not smoking during pregnancy and having a smoke-free environment
e) pre-pregnancy rubella immunization, and
f) seeing a healthcare professional as early in pregnancy as possible

In all these examples women's bodies are constructed within a culture of reproductive risk management.

Considering the growing interest and investment of time and money in embryo-testing technologies, it is not surprising that pre-pregnancy or preconception healthcare to ensure the conception of "healthy embryos" has become a focus. For example, *The Australian Doctor* magazine describes an emphasis on "preconception healthcare" as involving "assessing the level of risk of an adverse reproductive outcome in women or couples."[126]

However, what constitutes an adverse reproductive outcome needs to be more clearly articulated. Furthermore, the degree of risk that the outcome will occur also needs to be addressed. Instead, routinization and normalization of risk aversion rely on the assumption of a shared understanding of "health" and a community in consensus about which outcomes must be avoided at all costs. This scenario is, however, far from the case. Disability critiques such as those discussed in the previous chapter challenge assumptions made about desirable and undesirable health outcomes in the context of selecting and deselecting embryos and fetuses. Furthermore, risk avoidance is not universally viewed as a self-evident good. Many women choose to have children despite their own ill health or without regard to constraining lifestyle

---

[126] L. Cotterell, "Preconception Health Care" (18 June 2004) *Australian Doctor*, 35, at 35, available for download at www.australiandoctor.com.au/htt/pdf/AD_HTT_035_042__JUN18_04.pdf.

advice. Some women decide to conceive knowing that they may pass on a hereditary condition, and some will continue a pregnancy in which a disability has been detected. Other women, where it is permissible, decide, in the in vitro fertilization (IVF) context, to implant an embryo that has tested positive for an anomaly via preimplantation genetic diagnosis (PGD). Unless we embark on a more nuanced and complex account of both risk and disability, all of these women could be considered failed targets of preconception intervention and, as we shall see in the chapters that follow, failed targets of prenatal and preimplantation testing technologies.

Given the way in which this discourse of risk and shame and self-regulation is circulating – so that it is increasingly difficult to talk about pregnancy without being fluent in the language of "nuchals" and "amnios" and now, increasingly, PGD, and preconception health – it is worth asking whether or not there is a balance that can be struck between good surveillance and bad surveillance, and here we return to our central tension between reproductive choice (freedom) and reproductive responsibility (social expectation of conformity to normative conceptions of healthiness). To answer this question we find ourselves returning once again to the question of what is the norm (or normative) against which risk is being measured. In the next four chapters we explore the way in which risk is measured against the ideal of avoiding disability as refined through the (shifting) concept of seriousness. We ask whether seriousness as a conceptual tool can provide a useful limit to excessive regulatory surveillance and medical intervention.

As was stated in Chapter 1, the law's specification that a disability must be "serious" before abortion for that disability or selection against that disability is lawful is premised on the assumption that the phrase "serious disability" can be given meaning. However, as we shall see in the chapters that follow, the opposite may in fact be true, and our very inability to give a definitive account of "serious disability" may be precisely why it is a valuable regulatory tool. We consider this possibility while remaining alive to concerns that the imposition of a "seriousness" threshold before permitting abortion or embryo selection, rather than limiting surveillance of pregnant women, may in fact enable its proliferation.

3

Terminations

Abortion has been practiced in conjunction with prenatal screening and diagnosis for at least four decades and, when used in this way, can be described as technology deployed to prevent serious disability. In the previous chapters we critically examined the conceptualization of both risk and disability in contemporary discussions about prenatal testing technologies. In this chapter, we build on that analysis by closely examining how these concepts came to be, and are, configured in the legal and regulatory frameworks around abortion. We will do this across a range of jurisdictions, most notably Australia and the United Kingdom, but also comparator jurisdictions from around the world.

In many jurisdictions, abortion has been, or continues to be, prohibited unless legal exceptions apply. A notable exception to this approach can be found in the United States, where women have a constitutional right to privacy that encompasses the right to terminate a pregnancy (at least until viability, when the state's interest becomes compelling). However, in many jurisdictions where no such right is recognized, lawful abortion has historically been tethered to assessments of the danger posed by the pregnancy to the life or health of the woman. Although this "maternal health" exception has been interpreted as broad enough to encompass abortion for serious fetal abnormalities, some jurisdictions have created a distinct exception to permit abortion to avoid the risk of "serious handicap." The impetus for such an exception has resulted from the tremendous recent advances in prenatal diagnosis. Although such advances have enabled these abortions to take place earlier in pregnancy, they have also enabled doctors to detect serious conditions only diagnosable later in pregnancy. Because these abortions sometimes occur after viability, arguments about "serious handicap" as a regulatory concept tend to converge upon arguments about the status of the fetus as birth approaches.

In this chapter we examine three specific questions with which legislators have wrestled in their efforts to craft legal frameworks that are responsive to prenatal diagnosis. The first of these questions is whether the law should recognize fetal abnormality, as distinct from the woman's life, health, or preference, as a basis for abortion. The second is whether the law should provide some guidance concerning the scope and meaning of legal phrases like "serious/severe" "handicap/disability/impairment." The third is whether the law should permit abortion for fetal abnormality without time restriction (even where restrictions apply for other reasons). In examining these three areas of legislative contention, we particularly wish to interrogate the meaning of seriousness as a qualifier for disability and better understand the legislative intent behind the language of "serious handicap."

1 OVERVIEW OF THE LEGAL FRAMEWORKS GOVERNING ABORTION TO AVOID SERIOUS DISABILITY

The relevance of disability to the abortion decision is widely recognized by legislators around the world. Serious disability or some variant of this concept appears in the abortion laws of many nations, including the United Kingdom,[1] some Australian[2] and

---

[1] Abortion Act 1967 (as amended by the Human Fertilisation and Embryology Act 1990 (UK)) s1(1)(d).
[2] Criminal Law Consolidation Act 1935 (SA), s 82A; Medical Services Act (NT), s 11; Health Act 1911 (WA), s 334(7)(a).

U.S. jurisdictions,[3] New Zealand,[4] South Africa,[5] India,[6] Italy,[7] Poland,[8] Hungary,[9] Norway,[10] Greece,[11] Spain,[12] and the Czech Republic.[13]

1.1 United States

In *Roe v Wade*,[14] the U.S. Supreme Court held that women have a constitutionally protected right to an abortion until fetal viability. However, in *Planned Parenthood v Casey*[15] the Court limited this right, holding that the states may restrict women's access to abortion by imposing parental notification requirements on minors seeking the procedure, providing for compulsory waiting periods for those seeking abortion, and limiting public funding for abortion. Thus, while

---

[3] Maryland Code Ann., Health-General, § 20–209(b); Texas Health and Safety Code, §170.002(b)(3); Utah Code Ann., § 76–7-302(3)(b)(B)(ii).

[4] Crimes Act 1961 (NZ) s 187A (1)(aa).

[5] The Choice on Termination of Pregnancy Act 1996, s 2(1)(b)(ii).

[6] The Medical Termination of Pregnancy Act 1971, s 3(2)(b)(ii).

[7] Legalization of Abortion: Law 194 of the Italian Republic (1978), s 6.

[8] The Act of 7th January 1993 on Family-Planning, Human Embryo Protection and Conditions of Legal Pregnancy Termination, s 4a.1.2.

[9] Law No 79 of 17 December 1992 on the Protection of the Life of the Fetus, ss 6(1)(b), 6(3) and 6(4)(b).

[10] Law Number 50 of 13 June 1975 on the Termination of Pregnancy (as amended by Law Number 66 of 16 June 1978), s 2(c).

[11] Penal Code (as amended by Law No. 1609 of 28 June 1986 on Voluntary Termination of Pregnancy, Protection of Women's Health and Other Provisions), s 304(4)(2).

[12] The new law, which took force in July 2010, allows abortion until twenty-two weeks where the fetus has "serious abnormalities." There is no time limit if the fetus has abnormalities that are "incompatible with life" or has an "extremely serious incurable illness": see M de Lago, "Spain Allows Abortion on Demand up to 14 Weeks" (2010) 340 *British Medical Journal* 559.

[13] Law No. 66 of 20 October 1986 of the Czech People's Council Concerning the Artificial Termination of Pregnancy, s 5.

[14] 410 U.S 113 (1973).

[15] 505 U.S 833 (1992).

abortion may be available before viability, only nineteen states (and the District of Columbia) provide funding for abortions in cases that could include fetal abnormality.[16] Two states specifically provide funding for abortions that have been obtained on the grounds of fetal abnormality. Virginia provides funding for "certain abortions where the fetus is believed to have incapacitating physical deformity or mental deficiency,"[17] and Mississippi provides that abortion funding will be granted where "there is a fetal malformation that is incompatible with the baby being born alive."[18] The remaining seventeen states (and the District of Columbia) that provide funding do so for "all or most medically necessary" abortions[19]; we presume that this includes abortions for fetal abnormality where the abnormality poses a threat to the woman's health.

After viability, abortion is more restricted. Of the forty states that prohibit abortion after a certain point in a pregnancy (twenty states initiate prohibitions at "fetal viability"; five states do so in the third trimester; and fifteen states initiate prohibitions after a certain number of weeks – either twenty or twenty-four), many (twenty-nine) provide an exception where the procedure is necessary for the preservation of the mother's life or health. Only eleven states provide a

---

[16] See Guttmacher Institute, "State Policies in Brief: State Funding of Abortion under Medicaid as of November 1 2011," at http://www.guttmacher.org/statecenter/spibs/spib_SFAM.pdf (accessed on 21 November 2011).

[17] Virginia Code Ann., § 32.1–92.2 provides: "From the moneys appropriated to the Department from the general fund, the Board shall fund abortions for women who otherwise meet the financial eligibility criteria of the State Medical Assistance Plan in any case in which a physician who is trained and qualified to perform such tests certifies in writing, after appropriate tests have been performed, that he believes the fetus will be born with a gross and totally incapacitating physical deformity or with a gross and totally incapacitating mental deficiency."

[18] Mississippi Code of 1972, § 41–41–91.

[19] See Guttmacher Institute, "State Policies in Brief: State Funding of Abortion under Medicaid as of November 1, 2011," at http://www.guttmacher.org/statecenter/spibs/spib_SFAM.pdf (accessed on 21 November 2011).

narrower exception to the prohibition. New York, Rhode Island, and Michigan provide for an exception only where the procedure is necessary for the preservation of the mother's life.[20] Alabama, Indiana, Idaho, Kansas, Missouri, Ohio, Oklahoma and Nebraska provide for an exception only where the procedure is necessary for the preservation of the mother's life or *physical* health.[21] This means that in most U.S. states, postviability abortion is available where necessary to preserve the mother's mental health, and fetal abnormality may be relevant when determining whether the procedure is necessary for this purpose.

In addition to this, three states expressly allow abortion after viability where serious abnormality in the fetus is detected. Maryland provides that abortion is lawful at any time during the woman's pregnancy if the procedure is necessary to protect her "life or health" or "the fetus is affected by genetic defect or serious deformity or abnormality."[22] The Utah Criminal Code allows for postviability abortions where "two physicians who practice maternal fetal medicine concur, in writing, in the patient's medical record that the fetus has a defect that is uniformly diagnosable and uniformly lethal."[23] Finally, the Texas Health and Safety Code provides that postviability abortion in the third trimester of pregnancy is permitted "if at the time of the abortion the person is a physician and concludes in good faith according to the physician's best medical judgment that ... the fetus has a severe and irreversible abnormality, identified by reliable diagnostic procedures."[24]

---

[20] See Guttmacher Institute, "State Policies in Brief: State Policies on Later–Term Abortions as of June 1, 2011," at http://www.guttmacher.org/statecenter/spibs/spib_PLTA.pdf (accessed on 21 November 2011).

[21] See http://www.guttmacher.org/statecenter/spibs/spib_PLTA.pdf.

[22] Maryland Code Ann., Health-General, § 20–209(b).

[23] Utah Code Ann., § 76-7-302(3)(b)(B)(ii).

[24] Texas Health and Safety Code, §170.002(b)(3).

1.2 United Kingdom

In the United Kingdom, sections 58 and 59 of the English Offences against the Person Act 1861 create offenses relating to abortion. Section 58 provides that it is an offence for a person – that is, the pregnant woman or a third party – "unlawfully" to use an instrument with intent to cause a miscarriage. Section 59 prohibits the unlawful supply of abortifacient means in the knowledge that it is intended to be used or employed with intent to procure a woman's miscarriage. However, medical termination of pregnancy is permitted if the requirements of the Abortion Act 1967 are satisfied. Section 1(1)(a) of this Act allows abortion "if two registered medical practitioners are of the opinion, formed in good faith … that the pregnancy has not exceeded its twenty-fourth week and that the continuance of the pregnancy would involve risk, greater than if the pregnancy were terminated, of injury to the physical or mental health of the pregnant woman or any existing children of her family." Section 1(2) permits doctors, when assessing the risk to the woman, to take account of her "actual or reasonably foreseeable environment." After twenty-four weeks gestation, an abortion may still be performed on maternal health grounds, but the threshold of risk of harm is much higher. Thus, unless it is an emergency situation, two medical practitioners must form the good faith opinion that the termination is necessary to prevent grave permanent injury to the physical or mental health of the pregnant woman[25] or the continuance of the pregnancy would involve risk to her life greater than if the pregnancy were terminated.[26] Most relevantly, a pregnancy may also be terminated if two doctors are of the opinion, formed in good faith, that "there is a substantial risk that, if the child were born, it would suffer from such physical or mental abnormalities as to be seriously handicapped."[27]

---

[25] Abortion Act 1967 (UK), s 1(1)(b).
[26] Abortion Act 1967 (UK), s 1(1)(c).
[27] Abortion Act 1967 (UK), s 1(1)(d).

1.3 Australia

In all but two of the Australian jurisdictions (Australian Capital Territory [ACT] and Victoria), unlawful abortion remains a criminal offense. Nevertheless, all jurisdictions recognize that abortion is lawful in some circumstances. There is considerable variation in the detail of the law, but, in effect, there are three lawful bases for abortion recognized within and across the Australian jurisdictions, and any one of these could encompass an abortion to prevent the birth of a child with disabilities. Some jurisdictions specifically provide for medical termination of pregnancy to avoid "serious disability." Others provide for abortion where the woman's life or health is at risk or where appropriate in all the circumstances. Alongside these exceptions, a few jurisdictions permit abortion on informed request (WA up to twenty weeks, Victoria up to twenty-four weeks, or in the case of ACT without time limitation).

Three Australian jurisdictions specifically address the issue of abortion for fetal abnormality. In South Australia (SA) the legislation is based on the UK model. Thus, an abortion is permitted if, in the good faith opinion of two doctors, "there is a substantial risk that, if ... the child were born ... the child would suffer from such physical or mental abnormalities as to be seriously handicapped."[28] However, this ground is limited to abortion performed before the fetus is capable of being born alive (there is a presumption that this occurs at twenty-eight weeks gestation).[29]

The Northern Territory legislation makes special provision for abortion on the grounds of "serious handicap," although its scope is more limited than the South Australian provision. Abortions on this

---

[28] Criminal Law Consolidation Act 1935 (SA), s 82A(1)(a)(ii).

[29] Criminal Law Consolidation Act 1935 (SA) s 82A(8). Under the Abortion Act 1967 (UK), abortion on the grounds of "serious handicap" is permissible at any stage until birth.

ground are permissible until fourteen weeks into the pregnancy.[30] In Western Australia (WA), abortions are permissible up to twenty weeks gestation if the woman has given informed consent to the procedure.[31] However, an abortion may be performed after twenty weeks gestation if two or more members of a ministerially appointed panel agree that the mother or the unborn child "has a *severe medical condition* that ... justifies the procedure"[32] and the procedure is carried out in a facility approved by the minister for the purposes of the section. In this sense, the WA approach mirrors the UK model by providing for a lower time limit for abortions carried out on the grounds of maternal preference than for fetal abnormality. However, it specifies a higher threshold of risk, requiring the presence of a "severe medical condition" rather than a substantial risk of a serious handicap.

In the remaining Australian jurisdictions, there are no legislative provisions that specifically address abortion on the grounds of fetal abnormality. Among these jurisdictions, once again, approaches differ. The Australian Capital Territory (ACT) and Victoria have decriminalized abortion.[33] In the ACT abortion is permitted on the informed request of the woman provided it is performed by a doctor in an approved facility.[34] In Victoria, abortions are permitted up to twenty-four weeks gestation on the woman's informed request.[35] However, after twenty-four weeks, greater restrictions apply; termination is allowed after this time if the medical practitioner reasonably believes the termination is "appropriate in all the circumstances" and has obtained a concurring opinion from a second medical practitioner.[36] In considering "whether the abortion is appropriate in all the circumstances, a registered medical

---

[30] Medical Services Act (NT), s 11.
[31] Health Act 1911 (WA), s 334(3).
[32] Health Act 1911 (WA), s 334(7)(a) [emphasis added].
[33] Health Act 1993 (ACT), ss 80–83; Abortion Law Reform Act 2008 (Vic), ss 4–5.
[34] Health Act 1993 (ACT), ss 81–82.
[35] Abortion Law Reform Act 2008 (Vic), s 4.
[36] Abortion Law Reform Act 2008 (Vic), s 5(1).

practitioner must have regard to (a) all relevant medical circumstances; and (b) the woman's current and future physical, psychological and social circumstances."[37] This is broad enough to encompass abortion for fetal abnormality; indeed, as we will see, the Victorian Parliament clearly intended that such abortion would be authorized in appropriate circumstances. The Explanatory Memorandum states that "[t]he reference to all the relevant medical circumstances is intended to ensure that the medical condition of the foetus and the woman are to be taken into account."[38]

New South Wales (NSW), Queensland, and Tasmania all have offenses concerning unlawful abortion[39] and, with the exception of NSW, additional offenses relating to "killing an unborn child."[40] Nonetheless, medical termination of pregnancy is lawful in certain circumstances in each of these jurisdictions.[41] In Queensland, abortion is lawful if the doctor holds an honest belief, based on reasonable grounds, that the abortion is necessary to avert the risk of serious danger to the woman's life or physical or mental health, beyond the normal dangers of pregnancy and childbirth, and that abortion is a proportionate response to the danger to be averted.[42] This defense has been interpreted to cover dangers arising during the course of the pregnancy.[43] NSW also recognizes a defense of necessity to a

---

[37] Abortion Law Reform Act 2008 (Vic), s 4(2).

[38] Abortion Law Reform Bill 2008 (Vic), Explanatory Memorandum, Part 2, Clause 5.

[39] See Crimes Act 1900 (NSW), ss 82–84; Criminal Code 1899 (Qld), ss 224–226; Criminal Code Act 1924 (Tas), ss 134–135.

[40] Jurisdictions other than NSW and Victoria have separate offenses relating to "killing an unborn child," "causing the death of a child before birth," or "child destruction": see Crimes Act 1900 (ACT), s 42; Criminal Code Act 1983 (NT), s 170; Criminal Code 1899 (Qld), s 313; Criminal Code Act 1913 (WA), s 290; Criminal Code Act 1924 (Tas), s 165. It is not entirely clear whether these offenses set "upper limits" on the medical termination of pregnancy in the jurisdictions in which they apply.

[41] See *R v Wald* (1971) 3 DCR (NSW) 25; *R v Davidson* [1969] VR 667; *R v Bayliss and Cullen* (1986) 9 Qld Lawyer Reps 8; Criminal Code 1924 (Tas), s 164.

[42] *R v Bayliss and Cullen* (1986) 9 Qld Lawyer Reps 8.

[43] *R v Bayliss and Cullen* (1986) 9 Qld Lawyer Reps 8.

charge of unlawful abortion. This defense has been interpreted more broadly to allow the woman's social and economic circumstances, as well as purely medical matters, to be taken into consideration when determining whether the pregnancy might present a serious danger to a pregnant woman's physical or mental health.[44] The danger to her health may exist at the time of the abortion decision, at some other stage during the pregnancy,[45] or after the birth of the child.[46] In the 2006 trial of a doctor for unlawful abortion, a NSW court clarified that there are three bases upon which a doctor might be held to have performed an unlawful abortion: (i) if he or she did not form an honest belief that "termination of pregnancy was necessary in order to protect the mother from serious danger to her life or health, whether physical or mental;" (ii) that if "such a belief were held, it was not based upon reasonable grounds;" or (iii) "that a reasonable person in the position of the [doctor] would have considered that the risk of termination was out of proportion to the risk to the mother of the continuation of the pregnancy."[47] This makes it clear that, in NSW, the proportionality limb of the defense requires an objective weighing of the relative dangers of the termination procedure and the continuation of the pregnancy as far as the health of the woman is concerned.

2 FRAMING "SERIOUS DISABILITY" IN LAW

Although the idea of providing abortion for fetal abnormality now seems ubiquitous, the language, mechanisms, and legal limits drawn around this concept vary in a range of ways. As we have just seen, some

---

[44] *R v Wald* (1971) 3 DCR (NSW) 25.
[45] Ibid.
[46] *CES v Superclinics (Australia) Pty Ltd* (1995) 38 NSWLR 47 at 60.
[47] *R v Sood* [2006] NSWSC 1141 at [17].

jurisdictions no longer criminalize abortion so that abortion may be lawfully performed on the woman's request (which may of course be motivated by a wish to avoid a known abnormality). Of those that retain prohibitions or restrictions, some have specific provisions dealing with abortion for fetal abnormality, while others provide for a more open-ended exception encompassing risk to maternal life or health. In these latter situations, abortions will be lawful where the doctor is of the opinion that the pregnancy poses a risk to the mental or physical health of the woman. Although in this setting the law does not expressly acknowledge fetal abnormality as a reason for abortion, it is or may be a matter that doctors take into account in reaching a view about the necessity and, therefore, lawfulness of an abortion in the circumstances. In this sense, the meanings given to "disability" and its "seriousness" will be determined in accordance with the judgment of medical practitioners.

Among jurisdictions that do provide a specific exception in law, there seem to be three important framing concepts – risk, disability, and gestational stage – and there is some variability in how these concepts are deployed. Thus, provisions vary as to whether there need only be a quantifiable risk of disability in the child if born, or whether there must be a confirmed diagnosis of serious fetal abnormality. Regimes also vary in the nature and scope of validation of risk required. For instance, under Hungarian law, a risk of malformation or serious lesion could justify an abortion before the twelfth week; the "probability of a genetic or teratological lesion exceed[ing] 50%" is the basis for a lawful abortion up to the twentieth week; and where "the foetus presents a malformation that renders any form of postnatal life impossible" an abortion can occur up until birth.[48]

Further, the legislative language used to describe "disability" is highly variable. Most jurisdictions use the word "serious," "severe," or "grave" to qualify the term handicap, disease, or abnormality. For example,

---

[48] Law No 79 of 17 December 1992 on the Protection of the Life of the Foetus, ss 6(1) (b), (3) and (4).

the language used by UK law (also adopted by some Australian jurisdictions and India) is "such physical or mental abnormalities as to be
seriously handicapped."[49] Norwegian law uses the phrase "serious disease as a result of its genotype, a disease, or harmful influences during
pregnancy,"[50] and Greek law applies where "the conceptus is suffering
from a serious abnormality which would result in a serious congenital defect in the child and the pregnancy."[51] Some jurisdictions refer to
irreversibility or incurability, for instance, "severe and irreparable handicap of the foetus or an incurable illness threatening its life,"[52] "severe and
irreversible abnormality,"[53] and "a defect that is uniformly diagnosable
and uniformly lethal."[54] Thus, within this spectrum of seriously disabling
traits and conditions, distinctions may be drawn among disabilities that
are incompatible with life/lethal abnormalities, abnormalities that are
irreversible or irreparable, and serious diseases or genetic conditions. On
the other hand, some jurisdictions do not appear to require the disability
to be serious or grave at all. For example, Czech law will permit a termination where the "health or the healthy development of the foetus are
endangered, or if foetal development manifests genetic abnormalities."[55]

Finally, the time limits associated with abortion on this ground are
not uniform. In the examples just cited, the "upper" gestational limit for
abortion on disability grounds ranges from twenty weeks to birth. As
we have just seen in the case of Hungary, the time limit might increase

[49] Abortion Act 1967 (UK), s 1(1)(d); Criminal Law Consolidation Act 1935 (SA), s
82A(1)(a)(ii); Medical Services Act (NT), s 11(1)(b)(ii) (similar but not identical
language); Medical Termination of Pregnancy Act 1971 (India), s 3(2)(b)(ii).
[50] Law Number 50 of 13 June 1975 on the Termination of Pregnancy (as amended by
Law Number 66 of 16 June 1978), s 2(c).
[51] Penal Code (as amended by Law No. 1609 of 28 June 1986 on Voluntary Termination
of Pregnancy, Protection of Women's Health and Other Provisions), s 304(4)(2).
[52] The Act of 7th January 1993 on Family-Planning, Human Embryo Protection and
Conditions of Legal Pregnancy Termination, s 4a.1.2 (Poland).
[53] Texas Health and Safety Code, §170.002(b)(3).
[54] Utah Code Ann., § 76–7-302(3)(b)(B)(ii).
[55] Law No. 66 of 20 October 1986 of the Czech People's Council Concerning the
Artificial Termination of Pregnancy, s 5.

as the condition that has been diagnosed becomes more serious. Other examples of this approach include Spain, which permits abortions for "serious abnormalities" up until twenty-two weeks but imposes no limits on abortions for abnormalities that are "incompatible with life," and Utah, which makes an exception to its general prohibition on postviability abortions where "two physicians who practice maternal fetal medicine concur, in writing, in the patient's medical record that the fetus has a defect that is uniformly diagnosable and uniformly lethal."[56] Under South African law, after twenty weeks gestation, a pregnancy may be legally terminated if a "medical practitioner, after consultation with another medical practitioner or a registered midwife, is of the opinion that the continued pregnancy ... (ii) would result in a severe malformation of the fetus."[57]

Despite these variations, it is clear that there are also remarkable similarities in approach. These provisions all seek to set "thresholds" of one sort or another with respect to the degree of risk required, the magnitude of disability predicted, and the gestational stage before, at, or after which the provision will be triggered. All of these matters are, however, contentious and, in the case of risk and disability, particularly difficult to describe and translate into legislation. Thus, we now turn to interrogate in some detail this process of translation in the context of the UK and comparator Australian jurisdictions.

3 PARLIAMENTARY DEBATES ABOUT THE MEANING AND FUNCTION OF "SERIOUS HANDICAP"

Although "serious disability" seems to be a crucial regulatory concept for those jurisdictions that have incorporated it into abortion law, few

---

[56] Utah Code Ann., § 76–7-302(3)(b)(B)(ii).
[57] The Choice on Termination of Pregnancy Act 1996, s 2(1)(c)(ii).

if any parliaments have attempted to define what is meant by the term. This leaves the scope of these provisions somewhat uncertain, a matter that has drawn criticism from both liberal and conservative quarters.[58] In this section, we interrogate the question of why legislators have adopted "serious disability" as a regulatory concept and further why its scope has not been defined. We do this by analyzing parliamentary debates from two Australian state jurisdictions and the United Kingdom. We begin with the parliamentary debates that preceded the introduction of these provisions in the late 1960s, before turning our attention to more recent debates.

3.1 1960s Legislative Reform: United Kingdom and South Australia

In the late 1960s both the United Kingdom and South Australia undertook substantive reforms of the law relating to abortion. Both jurisdictions had criminal offenses relating to abortion, but, at least in the United Kingdom, these had been the subject of judicial interpretation that allowed a limited defense of necessity. At the time, the leading authority was *R v Bourne*, a case concerning an eminent doctor who was charged with offenses in connection with an abortion on a thirteen-year-old girl who had been raped.[59] Dr. Bourne did not deny that he had performed the procedure but asserted that it was necessary to preserve the young woman's life. The trial judge, Macnaghten J., directed the jury that abortion would not be "unlawful" within the meaning of s 58 of the Offences against the Person Act 1861 if the operation was performed for the purpose of protecting the pregnant

---

[58] For an overview of this criticism see: K. Savell, "Turning Mothers into Bioethicists – Late Abortion and Disability" in B. Bennett, T. Carney, and I. Karpin (eds.), *Brave New World of Health* (Annandale: Federation Press, 2008), 93–111.

[59] [1939] 1 KB 687 (this is a report of the trial judge's direction to the jury at the trial; the relevant direction on the meaning of "unlawful" appears at 694).

woman's life. He held that if the jury was satisfied that the doctor had formed an honest belief "on reasonable grounds, and with adequate knowledge, that the probable consequence of the ... pregnancy" would be to leave the woman a "physical or mental wreck," then it was entitled to accept that the doctor had acted for the purpose of preserving the mother's life.

The Medical Termination of Pregnancy Bill (which was subsequently enacted as the Abortion Act 1967) was introduced into the UK Parliament in a social climate that was receptive to legal reform. In the second reading speech in the House of Commons, Mr. Steel noted "a growing tide of public opinion in favour of such a change."[60] He also adverted to the delicate balancing act that framed the 1967 abortion law reform, stating, "we want to stamp out the back street abortions, but it is not the intention of the Promoters of the Bill to leave a wide open door for abortion on request."[61] The Bill proposed to declare the existing law as interpreted in *R v Bourne*. It would thus make provision for abortion where two doctors acting in good faith agreed that the abortion was needed to safeguard the life or health of the woman. But the Bill also sought to extend and clarify the law. This would be achieved by the introduction of three further measures: (i) to allow doctors to take account of the existing children of the woman's family in determining the balance of risks, (ii) to permit consideration of the actual or reasonably foreseeable environment of the woman in determining the risk to the woman or her children, and (iii) to allow for abortion where there was a substantial risk that if the child were born, it would suffer from such physical or mental abnormalities as to be seriously handicapped. This last ground was evidently the subject of strong public support, with one national opinion poll showing that the serious handicap clause was supported by a substantial majority

---

[60] *Hansard,* HC, vol. 732, col. 1071, 22 July 1966 (Mr. David Steel).
[61] *Hansard,* HC, vol. 732, col. 1075, 22 July 1966 (Mr. David Steel).

(80.5 percent) of the public.[62] The Bill passed, and when the Act first came into force, the serious handicap clause – then section 1(1)(b) – read as follows:

1. Subject to the provisions of this section, a person shall not be guilty of an offence under the law relating to abortion when a pregnancy is terminated by a registered medical practitioner if two registered medical practitioners are of the opinion, formed in good faith –
   a. that the continuance of the pregnancy would involve risk to the life of the pregnant woman, or of injury to the physical or mental health of the pregnant woman or any existing children of her family, greater than if the pregnancy were terminated; or
   b. that there is a substantial risk that if the child were born it would suffer from such physical or mental abnormalities as to be seriously handicapped.

Two years later, in 1969, the South Australian Parliament debated and passed an amendment to the Criminal Law Consolidation Act 1935, which substantially reformed the abortion law of that state. On the second reading of this Bill, the Attorney General, the Honorable Robin Millhouse, adverted – as Lord Silkin had done in the UK debates – to the strong public support for abortion law reform. He cited an Australian Gallup poll that found that

> About two out of three Australians would make abortion legal on four grounds. They are when: a woman's mental and physical health is threatened; the child is likely to have serious mental or physical deformities; pregnancy is the result of rape or incest; or the woman is intellectually defective or mentally ill.[63]

Relevantly for our purposes, the South Australian Parliament also debated and passed a provision, s 82A(1)(a)(ii), that made abortion

---

[62] As quoted by Lord Silkin in *Hansard*, HL, vol. 285, col. 264, 19 July 1967.
[63] *Hansard*, Legislative Assembly, 21 October 1969, 2319 (The Hon Robin Millhouse).

lawful where, in the opinion of two medical practitioners, formed in good faith, there is a substantial risk that the child if born would suffer from such physical or mental abnormalities as to be seriously handicapped.

3.2 The "Serious Handicap" Provisions

In the late 1960s, birth defects arising from maternal exposure to rubella and the teratogenic effects of thalidomide had emerged as issues of public concern in Australia and the United Kingdom. In the SA Parliament, Mr. Corcoran noted that "the most common case connected with this paragraph is rubella, although other conditions can lead to a handicapped child being born."[64] There had been a serious epidemic of rubella in the United States in 1964, affecting about 4 percent of pregnancies, and although the development of a vaccine was in progress, it was not commercially available at the time of the debates.[65] The effects of thalidomide had also recently become apparent. Accordingly, it was disabilities caused by rubella and thalidomide that were the paradigmatic examples of "serious" disability used by members during these debates.

Although the need for such a provision was challenged in both Parliaments, there was very considerable sympathy for the idea that it could achieve the "very real relief of human suffering."[66] Both in the United Kingdom and in South Australia, supporters of the respective serious handicap provisions made statements demonstrating strong convictions that any measure leading to the prevention of "serious handicap" or "deformity" was self-evidently compassionate. In the SA Parliament, one member exclaimed:

> Are we ... to deny these things?... Shall we say "the child shall be deformed and subhuman?"... To deny that is to deny the very

[64] *Hansard*, Legislative Assembly, 29 October 1969, 2599 (Mr. Corcoran).
[65] *Hansard*, Legislative Assembly, 21 October 1969, 2418 (Mr. Casey).
[66] *Hansard*, HC, vol. 749, col. 1058, 29 June 1967 (Dr. Winstanley).

import of life and to regard it as a fairytale. But it is no fairy tale – it is reality. These things must be dealt with.[67]

In the UK debate, Lord Molson posed the question "Is it not right that, subject to all necessary safeguards, a life should be prevented from coming into existence if it is going to be handicapped and unhappy?"[68] Baroness Elliot articulated the confluence of interests that she believed would be served by the provision:

> I think it will be disastrous if we were to allow paragraph (b) to be deleted from the Bill. It is an essential part of it, it is of vital importance to the family, to the mother and, what is more, to society – because no one can think it is good for the community that one mother should go on bearing mentally deficient children…. It is in the interests of the community and the mother, and clearly it must be in the interests of unborn children, since no one would wish a child to come into the world very severely handicapped, either mentally or physically in the way in which we know from long experience is often the case.[69]

Thus, in addition to emphasizing the burdens imposed on *the child born with serious disabilities*, supporters of the measure referred to the burden imposed by seriously disabled children *on their parents*, particularly their mothers. In the UK debate, Lord Somers pointed out the difficulty of disentangling the child's disabilities and the mother's mental health, observing that "if the children are severely affected then it is more than likely – in fact it is practically inevitable that the mother will be affected mentally."[70] Baroness Elliot thought it impossible to "exaggerate the terrible anxieties and difficulties that come as a result of having mentally defective children."[71] Concerns

---

[67] *Hansard*, Legislative Assembly, 21 October 1969, 2337 (Hon R. S. Hall).
[68] *Hansard*, HL, vol. 285, col. 347, 19 July 1967 (Lord Molson).
[69] *Hansard*, HL, vol. 285, col. 1038–1039, 26 July 1967 (Baroness Elliot).
[70] *Hansard*, HL, vol. 285, col. 1043, 26 July 1967 (Lord Somers).
[71] *Hansard*, HL, vol. 285, col. 1038, 26 July 1967 (Baroness Elliot).

were also raised about the burden on siblings. Lord Somers adverted to the possibility that "other children will be neglected ... because the mother has to look after and devote her whole time to the abnormal child."[72]

Similar themes emerge from the SA debate. For instance, Mr. Banfield encouraged members to "put themselves in the position of a mother having to feed her child for the rest of its life, having it slobber all over the place and having to carry it to and from the bathroom, morning and night, until it reaches the age of 50 or 60."[73] In the view of the provisions' supporters, this was too great a burden to impose on women; abortion was clearly presented as an appropriate response to the risk of such outcomes.

In the UK it was stated that the provision was "justified in the light of more recent medical developments."[74] Mr. Steel elaborated:

> For example, machines are now being developed in the United States which can determine if the chromosomes of a foetus are so severely disordered that no human being recognizable as such could be born as a result of the conclusion of the pregnancy.[75]

Thus, there is some suggestion that the UK Parliament was responding to technological developments that were already increasing – and might continue to increase – the power and sophistication of prenatal diagnosis of abnormality. Similarly, in SA it was mentioned that although with medical advances congenital rubella was likely to become less of a problem, the teratogenic effects of drugs and food and hereditary causes of abnormality might become a greater concern:

> It is probable that in a few years' time, after a greater study has been made of genetics, more statistics will come to light and we shall know that certain other defects and diseases are due to inherited

---

[72] *Hansard*, HL, vol. 285, col. 1044, 26 July 1967 (Lord Somers).

[73] *Hansard*, Legislative Assembly, 3 December 1969, 3511 (Hon V. G. Springett).

[74] *Hansard*, HC, vol. 732, col. 1073, 22 July 1966 (Mr.David Steel).

[75] *Hansard*, HC, vol. 732, col. 1073, 22 July 1966 (Mr.David Steel).

factors that the mother or the father cannot help transmitting to the child.[76]

It is reasonable to suggest that the medical and genetic advances that have occurred since these debates took place have far exceeded the expectations of these Bills' supporters, including the medical profession of the time. But it is noteworthy that the British Medical Association, the Royal College of Obstetricians and Gynaecologists, and the Australian Council of the Royal College of Obstetricians and Gynaecology all supported these provisions. Indeed, it was mentioned in the SA debates that the latter body's policy supported induced abortion where "there is documented medical evidence that the infant may be born with incapacitating physical deformity or mental deficiency."[77] This support for the Bill from the medical profession was due partly to a concern that medical professionals, acting in good faith, be protected from criminal sanction. As Dr. Winstanley pointed out in the UK debate, "they feel that doctors at the moment taking steps which they sometimes feel to be necessary are in jeopardy because of the lack of clarity in the law. They feel that the matter should be cleared up and the profession safeguarded."[78] Similarly, Mr. Lyons lamented a legal landscape that sought "to force the production of blind and twisted babies and drives members of a high and proud profession in fear to shifts and evasions."[79]

3.3 Opposition to the Provisions

As its supporters in both Parliaments emphasized, the provision would not "force" anyone to have or perform an abortion. In the UK, Mr. Lyons

---

[76] *Hansard*, Legislative Council, 3 December 1969, 3511 (Hon V. G. Springett).

[77] *Hansard*, Legislative Assembly, 5 November 1969, 2777 (Mr.Hudson).

[78] *Hansard*, HC, vol. 749, col. 1055, 29 June 1967 (Dr.Winstanley).

[79] *Hansard*, HC, vol. 732, col. 1090, 22 July 1966 (Mr.Edward Lyons).

observed that "the Bill is purely permissive. It requires no one to act in a way that his or her conscience forbids, yet for those embraced by its provisions this is a wholesome, glorious and compassionate Measure."[80] Similarly, in SA, Dr. Banfield noted that the provision would be "availed of only if, after a person's soul-searching and after the advice she had received, it was decided that it was in the best interests of everyone."[81] Supporters of the measures thus presented it as desirable that women be able to make a decision to avoid serious disability, however difficult that decision might be. Any suggestion that the provisions would or could lead to coercive practices was summarily dismissed:

> All it does it alleviate the fears of some people and prevent the disasters that we see as a result of some pregnancies that have to go to the end. I say again that the woman and her doctor should have the right to make the decision.[82]

However, this framing of the provisions as compassionate measures that were self-evidently necessary and desirable was challenged. In the United Kingdom, Mr. St. John-Stevas pointed out that the serious handicap provision "introduces a new principle into the law, namely, that one human being can make a judgment about another as to whether that human being's life is worth living."[83] A very similar challenge was made in SA:

> If we introduce legislation which says that the State may legislate against a person's life on the ground that he or she may be physically handicapped in some way, we have introduced a major change in the law and we have established a precedent that will lead to the application of the same argument against other groups in the community.[84]

---

[80] *Hansard*, HC, vol. 732, col. 1090, 22 July 1966 (Mr.Edward Lyons).

[81] *Hansard*, Legislative Council, 25 July 1969, 3214 (Hon D. H. L. Banfield).

[82] *Hansard*, Legislative Council, 25 July 1969, 3214 (Hon D. H. L. Banfield).

[83] *Hansard*, HC, vol. 732, col. 1156, 22 July 1966 (Mr.St John-Stevas).

[84] *Hansard*, Legislative Assembly, 29 October 1969, 2604 (Mr.Corcoran).

It should be recognized that many of the provisions' opponents were opposed to abortion more generally. Nevertheless, their particular objections to the serious handicap provisions bear striking similarities to the contemporary debates discussed in Chapter 1, which considered the appropriateness of quality of life judgments in the context of prenatal diagnosis and the negative assumptions made about the lives of people with disabilities. In both Parliaments, opponents drew attention to the fact that many "seriously handicapped" people enjoyed a quality of life thought impossible, or at least very unlikely, by citizens who were not disabled. According to Mr. Hughes in the SA debates, "[d]eformed people have testified before committees that they value their lives and strongly resent the suggestion that unborn babies with deformities should be aborted."[85] Other members in the SA Parliament referred to the evidence of a deaf couple (both affected by congenital rubella) who told the select committee that "had this provision been in force they would not have had the opportunity to enjoy the perfectly happy life they were enjoying."[86] Mr. Casey said, "I think we must be guided by these people who are gaining much from life."[87]

There were other similarities with contemporary disability rights debates; for instance, concerns were voiced about the limits of one's capacity to know whether another person's life will be full of suffering. In the House of Lords, the Earl of Dundee challenged the assumption that disability necessarily involved unhappiness, declaring that "there are thousands of children in this country and in other countries, deformed, without eyesight, maybe without arms or legs, and with all kinds of the gravest abnormalities, who have been born, cared for and loved and lived happier lives, and more socially useful lives, than millions of normal, healthy people."[88] This questioning of the elision of disability and unhappiness has now become familiar.

[85] *Hansard*, Legislative Assembly, October 22 1969, 2418 (Mr.Hughes).
[86] *Hansard*, Legislative Assembly, October 29 1969, 2599 (Mr.Corcoran).
[87] *Hansard*, Legislative Assembly, October 29 1969, 2602 (Mr.Casey).
[88] *Hansard*, HL, vol. 285, col. 276, 19 July 1967 (Earl of Dundee).

3.4 Legislative Conceptualization of Risk: "Substantial Risk"

A significant issue in the debates concerned the *limitations* of prenatal diagnosis, and especially its inability to diagnose positively the conditions that were then matters of social concern. Legislators noted that the effect of congenitally acquired rubella is contingent on a range of factors, most importantly the age of gestation at the time of maternal exposure. This raised the difficulty that even where maternal exposure was demonstrated, the effect of that exposure on the unborn child could not be predicted with any degree of certainty. As Viscount Waverley explained to the Lords:

> In the first six weeks rubella carries an over 50 per cent risk of abnormality, but this varies with the strength of the virus, though this is not known at the time. After the first three months, there is really hardly any risk at all. After the first six weeks, but within the first three months, the overall risk is 14%. It falls rapidly after the first six weeks.[89]

This and other forms of diagnostic uncertainty were to be addressed by the language of "substantial risk." Thus, the framers of the UK provision acknowledged openly the limitations of prenatal diagnosis. Indeed, the threshold of "substantial risk" was a *concession* to diagnostic imprecision. As Dr. Winstanley explained in the context of rubella:

> No precision can be applied to this at all. Early tests cannot reveal anything of that kind except on a statistical basis.... We are only able to say that certain kinds of abnormality result from certain diseases or circumstances.... I accept that and all the limitations which surround it. But I ask the House to understand that it is necessary to have this provision in the Bill both for the protection of members of the medical profession, who are at present doing this in good faith

[89] *Hansard*, HL, vol. 285, col. 1042, 26 July 1967 (Viscount Waverley).

because they believe it is necessary, and also for the very real relief of human suffering.[90]

Nevertheless, there was some dissatisfaction with the use of the words "substantial risk" in the provision. Members proposed amendments that included replacing "substantial risk" with either "certainty" or "probability."[91] There were two principal objections to the language of "substantial risk." The first was that this was insufficiently precise and would therefore create legal uncertainty. Mr. English stated:

> There is in the Bill a complete vagueness, and presumably in the end the courts will have to interpret what is a substantial risk. Meanwhile each individual doctor will have to determine it for himself, and he must run the risk of being wrong.... My suggestion ... is to import a 50 per cent probability, but the Minster for Health has said that a 50 per cent probability is beyond the reach of medical science at this time.[92]

This concern prompted extended discussion about the quantification of the risk. The sponsor of the Bill in the Lords, Lord Silkin, attempted to clarify the meaning of "substantial risk" by suggesting that a risk of one in three or four might be substantial but a risk of one in seven or

---

[90] *Hansard,* HC, vol. 749, col. 1058, 29 June 1967 (Dr.Winstanley).

[91] Mr. St. John-Stevas moved that "substantial risk" in s 1(1)(b) of the Bill be replaced with "certainty": *Hansard,* HC, vol. 749, col. 1047, 29 June 1967. This was debated at the same time as proposed amendment 21, which sought to replace "substantial risk" with "probability" in s 1(1)(b): *Hansard,* HC, vol. 749, col. 1061–1064, 29 June 1967. Had the latter amendment been passed, the following would also have been inserted into s 1: "(ii) in determining whether or not there is such a probability, a child shall be deemed to be seriously handicapped if it would be so ... physically sub-normal as to be incapable of existence otherwise than in a hospital or similar institution": *Hansard,* HC, vol. 749, col. 1062–1063, 29 June 1967. Members voted to put the question of whether "substantial risk" should remain in the bill to a vote and voted that "substantial risk" should remain: *Hansard,* HC, vol. 749, col. 1091, 29 June 1967. On 13 July 1967, the House voted that the Bill be read a third time and passed.

[92] *Hansard,* HC, vol. 749, col. 1075–1076, 29 June 1967 (Mr.English).

eight might not. In any event, "it would be for the doctor to decide. He would have all the facts before him. He would have discretion to agree in a particular case that there is a substantial risk."[93]

It was also objected, more fundamentally, that risk was an inadequate threshold and that a higher threshold of "certainty" should apply. This stemmed in part from the concern that without certainty in diagnosis, healthy fetuses would be aborted to prevent the births of abnormal children. The Earl of Dundee identified the problem in the following terms:

> What does a serious risk mean? Does it mean that the doctor can tell that there is a 50 per cent risk, or a 30 per cent risk or what does it mean? If it is 50 percent, it means that we should be destroying 50 unborn children in the hope that the other 50 might be saved from a life of abnormality. If it is 30 percent, it would mean destroying 70 potential lives in order that 30 not be abnormal.[94]

This seems somewhat remote from contemporary discussions about this (and similar) provisions. As we will see, these current discussions are more focused on the scope of serious handicap. Nonetheless, it is possible to detect some understandings about risk that continue to resonate. For example, Dr. Winstanley observed that "one does not make the decision purely on a statistical probability but on what is going to happen if the woman has an abnormal child. Once she has it, what the particular risk was before is of no great moment to her."[95]

The disagreement about whether abortion should be lawful provided that there was a risk (as opposed to the certainty) of handicap and, if so, how great that risk was required to be was ultimately resolved in favor of retaining the term "substantial risk." This implies that the significant concern about the termination of "normal" pregnancies for the sake of avoiding abnormal ones was overcome by

[93] *Hansard,* HL, vol. 285, col. 1055, 26 July 1967 (Lord Silkin).
[94] *Hansard,* HL, vol. 285, col. 275–276, 19 July 1967 (Earl of Dundee).
[95] *Hansard,* HC, vol. 749, col. 1058, 29 June 1967 (Dr. Winstanley).

stronger countervailing factors. These included an acknowledgment that diagnostic technology was rudimentary and so often could not predict serious handicap with any certainty; a desire to provide some level of protection for doctors who, together with pregnant women, formed the view that serious disability should be avoided; and, perhaps most significant, a desire to relieve the burden – both social and familial – that children with serious handicaps were thought to impose. The particular burdens that women endured led supporters of the Bill to give precedence to the mother's wishes by allowing her, in consultation with her doctor, to decide whether or not to terminate a pregnancy for this reason.

3.5 Legislative Conceptualization of Seriousness

The discussion about risk is of course tied to the substantive nature of the thing to be avoided, in this case "serious handicap." The language is again significant. It is noteworthy that both Bills' sponsors sought to refine and narrow the class of traits or conditions caught by the provision, and by the qualifying term "serious." But what was meant by "serious handicap"?

There can be no doubt the term "serious handicap" evoked a sense of the monstrous for some. In the Commons, Mr. McNamara referred to "certain forms of growth abnormality" in which the child was not viable and "a full monster."[96] In the Lords, Viscount Dilhorne used the terms "wholly abnormal" and "monstrosity" interchangeably.[97] Other terms no longer commonly heard in public discourse – such as "deformity,"[98] "malformed,"[99] "seriously mentally defective,"[100] and even the "village

---

[96] *Hansard*, HC, vol. 732, col. 1128, 22 July 1966 (Mr.McNamara).
[97] *Hansard*, HL, vol. 285, col. 1030, 26 July 1967 (Viscount Dilhorne).
[98] *Hansard*, HL, vol. 285, col. 1026, 26 July 1967 (Earl of Dundee).
[99] *Hansard*, HL, vol. 285, col. 1048, 26 July 1967 (Lord Leatherland).
[100] *Hansard*, HL, vol. 285, col. 289, 19 July 1967 (Viscount Dilhorne).

idiot" – appear in the UK debate.[101] As we have already mentioned, the impacts of rubella and thalidomide were of particular concern. Accordingly, there were numerous references to the complications of prenatal exposure, for example, deafness, blindness, limb malformation, and mental deficiency. Other conditions mentioned included muscular dystrophy, anencephaly and hydrocephaly, Huntingdon's chorea, and some sex-linked conditions such as hemophilia.[102] In both SA and the United Kingdom, sponsors were pressed for more specific definitions of the term "serious handicap." In SA, the Attorney General claimed that "[t]he phrase seriously handicapped cannot be further defined. One cannot define it exactly."[103] Nevertheless, he proceeded to elaborate:

> In my view "seriously" adds to "handicapped"; it means a serious handicap. This is a matter of judgment in every case and one cannot define it any more than we can define "substantial risk." It cannot be precisely defined *in vacuo*. It can be done much more easily in a specific case."[104]

---

[101] *Hansard,* HL, vol. 285, col. 1049, 26 July 1967 (Lord Leatherland).

[102] See, for example, deafness: *Hansard,* HL, vol. 285, col. 1045, 26 July 1967 (Viscount Barrington); *Hansard,* HC, vol. 732, col. 1089, 22 July 1966 (Mr.Lyons); *Hansard,* HC, vol. 749, col. 1056, 29 June 1967 (Dr.Winstanley); blindness: *Hansard,* HL, vol. 285, col. 1033, 26 July 1967 (Baroness Stocks); *Hansard,* HC, vol. 732, col. 1089, 22 July 1966 (Mr.Lyons); *Hansard,* HC, vol. 749, col. 1056, 29 June 1967 (Dr.Winstanley); limb malformation: *Hansard,* HC, vol. 749, col. 1055, 29 June 1967 (Dr.Winstanley); mental deficiency: *Hansard,* HL, vol. 285, col. 1042, 26 July 1967 (Viscount Waverley); *Hansard,* HC, vol. 749, col. 1056, 29 June 1967 (Dr. Winstanley); muscular dystrophy: *Hansard,* HL, vol. 285, col. 1042, 26 July 1967 (Viscount Waverley); *Hansard,* HC, vol. 749, col. 1052, 29 June 1967 (Mr.St John-Stevas); anencephaly and hydrocephaly: *Hansard,* HC, vol. 749, col. 1052, 29 June 1967 (Mr.St John-Stevas); Huntingdon's chorea: *Hansard,* HL, vol. 285, col. 1042, 26 July 1967 (Viscount Waverley); *Hansard,* HC, vol. 749, col. 1052, 29 June 1967 (Mr.St John-Stevas); hemophilia: *Hansard,* HL, vol. 285, col. 1042, 26 July 1967 (Viscount Waverley).

[103] *Hansard,* Legislative Assembly, 29 October 1969, 2603 (The Hon Robin Millhouse).

[104] *Hansard,* Legislative Assembly, 29 October 1969, 2603 (The Hon Robin Millhouse).

It was implied that "serious" could mean something that was not minor and that, taken together, the words meant "utterly and completely" handicapped:

> We are not concerned here with whether John Willie will have weak flat feet or weak arms; we are concerned with whether he will be born with some sort of disease or deformity that will handicap him completely and utterly. In other words, we are concerned here with the quality of life.[105]

When pressed, the Attorney General offered the example of Huntington's chorea as a condition that would clearly fall within the scope of the phrase "serious handicap." He read the following description of the condition to the Assembly:

> Huntington's chorea is a progressive degenerative disease of the central nervous system characterized by involuntary jerking movements of body and limbs. It causes the gradual impairment of affected persons, both physically and mentally and ultimately leads to death, often after an interval of 10 or more years.[106]

However, it was not noted that the disease was a late onset condition and so the intersection between time of onset and seriousness was not addressed directly. The Attorney General did go on to say that although he regarded Huntington's as a serious handicap, "some doctors or lay people may say that is not serious and that a thalidomide case is not serious."[107] He concluded by declaring that "it is a subjective test."[108]

---

[105] *Hansard*, Legislative Assembly, 3 December 1969, 3511 (The Hon V.G. Springett).

[106] *Hansard*, Legislative Assembly, 29 October 1969, 2603 (The Hon Robin Millhouse).

[107] *Hansard*, Legislative Assembly, 29 October 1969, 2603 (The Hon Robin Millhouse).

[108] *Hansard*, Legislative Assembly, 29 October 1969, 2603 (The Hon Robin Millhouse).

When one considers that s 82A(1)(a)(ii) forms part of a larger legislative scheme that attempts to specify authoritatively the circumstances in which abortion will and will not be lawful, it is curious that the Attorney General should have stated that the meaning of the term "serious handicap" is to be determined subjectively. It is also curious that supporters of the provision regarded "serious" as qualifying the word "handicap" even though it was acknowledged in the debates that "serious" defied precise definition. This formulation left little guidance for doctors seeking to conform with the law. It is as though the Parliament, having decided to regulate abortion in a way that was responsive to the increasingly sophisticated methods of prenatal diagnosis, then resiled from doing so directly, preferring instead to leave this gatekeeping function to the medical profession. Nevertheless, a similar approach is discernible in the UK debates. Lord Silkin observed that "one must allow a certain amount of elasticity in this.... I would say that a serious handicap is a handicap such as would make a person incapable of carrying out any normal activity."[109] Significantly, it was thought that a more precise definition of seriousness could thwart the legislative intent. Thus, Lord Stonham stated:

> I do not think a doctor can decide whether an eight weeks' foetus will have a reasonable enjoyment of life, but I do think that in these matters we ought not to define it too clearly. I think we ought to give the doctor a chance to exercise his professional skill in good faith.[110]

In other words, the clear legislative purpose was to allow the medical profession to make good faith determinations about which conditions constituted "serious handicaps."

Needless to say, opponents of the provision in the UK debate were not satisfied by assurances that seriousness did not require further

---

[109] *Hansard,* HL, vol. 285, col. 1057, 26 July 1967 (Lord Silkin).
[110] *Hansard,* HL, vol. 285, col. 1037, 26 July 1967 (Lord Stonham).

refinement or definition. Speaking of the phrase "serious handicap" Viscount Dilhorne asked:

> What does that amount to? Some people would say that to be born with a club foot was a serious handicap; to have one leg or one arm was a serious handicap. But is it really intended by the sponsors of this Bill that an abortion can take place lawfully if there be a substantial risk of a child's being born with one leg shorter than the other?... It seems to me if that is not the intention of the sponsors of the Bill ... the language ought not to enable abortions to take place for that kind of physical handicap.[111]

Opponents in the United Kingdom were not content to let the matter of definition rest there; they moved a number of amendments to the provision. These included attempts to substitute for "seriously handicapped" the words "completely handicapped"[112] or, alternatively, "deprived of reasonable enjoyment of life."[113] The gist of the opposition was that the term "serious handicap" was too vague to guide doctors and the law should expressly state some higher threshold. Significantly, neither of these proposed amendments succeeded,[114] but nor were these matters put to rest – as we will see in the following section.

4 CONTEMPORARY REFORMS – "LATE" ABORTION AND SERIOUS DISABILITY

When it entered into force the UK Abortion Act 1967 contained no specific time limits for abortion, but it was subject to the provisions of the Infant Life Preservation Act 1929 (ILP Act). The ILP Act made it a criminal offense to destroy a child capable of being born alive, except

[111] *Hansard,* HL, vol. 285, col. 1479, 23 October 1967 (Viscount Dilhorne).
[112] *Hansard,* HC, vol.749, col. 1052, 29 June 1967 (Mr.St John Stevas).
[113] *Hansard,* HL, vol. 285, col. 1479, 23 October 1967 (Viscount Dilhorne).
[114] *Hansard,* HC, vol. 749, col. 1091, 29 June 1967; *Hansard,* HL, vol. 285, col. 1485, 23 October 1967.

where necessary to preserve the mother's life. In addition, it contained a presumption that a child was capable of being born alive at twenty-eight weeks gestation. A similar system was in place in South Australia. In that jurisdiction, there was (and remains) a statutory presumption that a child is capable of being born alive at twenty-eight weeks.[115] Abortions are only lawful after a child is capable of being born alive where the procedure is necessary to preserve the woman's life *or* where the act bringing about the termination of pregnancy is done without intent to destroy the life of the child.[116]

By the 1990s, however, a consensus had developed within the medical profession that, because of improvements in neonatal intensive care, the time limit of twenty-eight weeks was no longer appropriate in the standard case of abortion.[117] But while it was widely accepted that the time limits in abortion law should be aligned with fetal viability, there was – and is still – disagreement about whether the limit should be set at twenty-four weeks or some earlier point. Furthermore, new questions arose for those who sought to achieve an alignment. Should exceptions apply to the twenty-four-week limit? How should those exceptions be phrased?

In the wave of regulation and reform that began in the 1990s in the United Kingdom and occurred in Western Australia in 1998, the Northern Territory in 2007, and Victoria in 2008, debate has ensued about whether gestational limits should apply to abortion for fetal abnormality. Provisions for these gestational limits, and for exceptions to them, have in effect created the new category of "late abortion." In the United Kingdom, the Abortion Act 1967 was amended by the Human Fertilisation and Embryology Act 1990 (HFE Act).[118] The House of Lords Select Committee on the ILP Act had, just two years

---

[115] Criminal Law Consolidation Act 1935 (SA), s 82A(8).

[116] Criminal Law Consolidation Act 1935 (SA), s 82A(7).

[117] *Hansard*, HC, vol. 171, col. 172, 24 April 1990 (Secretary for Health, Mrs. Virginia Bottomley).

[118] Human Fertilisation and Embryology Act 1990 (UK).

earlier, recommended that the ILP Act be removed from the ambit of abortion law. In moving that the HFE Bill be read for a third time, Lord Houghton observed that in 1967 little thought was given to the concurrent operation of the ILP Act and the Abortion Act. This, he said, "turned out to be a serious mistake because it meant that a doctor carrying out a perfectly lawful abortion under the Abortion Act could be exposed to prosecution under the *Infant Life (Preservation) Act 1929*. That fear has been something of a bugbear to the medical professional for years past."[119] During the passage of the HFE Bill, the principal issue debated regarding serious handicap was whether abortion for this reason should be exempted from the twenty-four-week limit, and, if so, whether there should be a limit set somewhere between twenty-four weeks and birth. This was ultimately resolved in favor of there being no limit for abortions on this ground.[120]

WA also underwent significant reform in 1998 with the introduction of provisions that would allow abortion on a woman's request up to twenty weeks gestation. The law of that jurisdiction now provides that a post–twenty-week abortion cannot be lawfully performed unless (1) two medical practitioners from a ministerially appointed panel of six have first agreed that the child has a severe medical condition that in their clinical judgment justifies the procedure and (2) the procedure is performed in an approved facility. In this section then we will compare and contrast the manner in which "late" abortion for fetal abnormality was discussed in the UK and WA parliamentary debates of the 1990s.

4.1 Differential Time Limits for Serious Handicap Abortions

In the United Kingdom, the concern that very serious abnormalities might not be detected before twenty-four weeks gestation was the

---

[119] *Hansard*, HL, vol. 516, col. 1245, 7 March 1990 (Lord Houghton of Sowerby).
[120] See Abortion Act 1967 (UK), s 1(1)(d).

main reason for the 1990 proposal to remove time limits for abortion on the grounds of serious handicap. It was thought that the twenty-four-week limit would leave some women in the distressing position of desperately needing an abortion but being unable to have one.[121] The House of Lords Select Committee Report on the ILP Act had concluded that

> if ... an unborn child were diagnosed as grossly abnormal and unable to lead any meaningful life, there is, in the opinion of the Committee, no logic in requiring the mother to carry her unborn child to full term merely because the diagnosis was too late to enable an operation for abortion to be carried out before the 28th completed week.[122]

Supporters of the provision referred to very grave abnormalities. Lord Walton observed that "they may include occasionally anencephaly and microcephaly. That is a foetus with a beating heart and a functioning circulation but either without a face and brain or with a tiny brain. It may also be true of severe degrees of spina bifida."[123] Lord Brightman, chair of the House of Lords Select Committee, added that where a child is "only going to live for a matter of minutes or hours ... it is lacking in humanity to require the mother, against her will, to suffer the agony of carrying the child to full term."[124]

Supporters also argued that women would be extremely reluctant to undergo late termination of pregnancy and would only do so where the disability was extremely grave. Mr. MacKay, for instance, stated that "no woman wants or welcomes the need to terminate a pregnancy, still less to have a late abortion. Very late abortions are the most traumatic and usually the most needed."[125] It was also suggested that

---

[121] *Hansard, HC,* vol. 171, col. 263, 24 April 1990 (Ms Harriet Harman).

[122] Cited by Sir David Steel in *Hansard,* HC, vol. 174, col. 1184, 21 June 1990.

[123] *Hansard,* HL, vol. 522, col. 1050–1051, 18 October 1990 (Lord Walton of Detchant).

[124] *Hansard,* HL, vol. 522, col. 1064, 18 October 1990 (Lord Brightman).

[125] *Hansard,* HC, vol. 171, col. 245, 24 April 1990 (Mr.MacKay).

the removal of a time limit in such cases would remove time pressure from the decision to terminate, so that an adequate period of reflection after diagnosis was possible.[126] Ms. Richardson spelled out the consequences of being too restrictive:

> We do not want women who are carrying babies who turn out to be damaged to have a pistol at their heads and to be told, "you are going to have a physically or mentally handicapped baby and you must have an abortion tomorrow or you will not be within the time limit". That could happen if our attitude is too tight and not relaxed enough. We must ensure that it will turn out the best for those women.[127]

It was also suggested that the absence of a time limit for fetal abnormality abortions would actually lower the number of terminations on this ground, as women would be able to wait for diagnostic confirmation rather than terminating the pregnancy for a risk of serious abnormality.[128] Lord Rea made the further observation that allowing late termination for serious handicap was not the same as forcing women to have such a termination. He noted that parents "are perfectly at liberty to continue with the pregnancy if their conscience dictates that the mother should give birth and they should look after a very severely handicapped child until it dies, possibly after few hours or maybe a few years depending on how serious is the handicap."[129] But he went on to say that "I believe that the majority of parents in that position will opt for a termination and will not want the child to survive. After a period they will try again with the strong expectation of conceiving another normal child in its place."[130]

Thus, the decision to avoid disability was presented as the normative choice by many of those who supported the proposal. For some of

---

[126] *Hansard*, HL, vol. 522, col. 1064, 18 October 1990 (Lord Brightman).
[127] *Hansard*, HC, vol. 171, col. 188, 24 April 1990 (Ms Richardson).
[128] *Hansard*, HC, vol. 171, col. 263, 24 April 1990 (Ms Harman).
[129] *Hansard*, HL, vol. 522, col. 1076, 18 October 1990 (Lord Rea).
[130] *Hansard*, HL, vol. 522, col. 1076, 18 October 1990 (Lord Rea).

the proposal's supporters, however, the proposal did more than simply acknowledge this reality – it was guaranteeing that women have a *right* to terminate in the case of serious fetal handicap. For instance, Mr. MacKay said, "I ... believe that it is the right of parents to decide whether to have an abortion if the child would be grossly disabled."[131] This construction of the choice to avoid disability as a "right" was more evident in these debates than it was in the parliamentary debates of the 1960s, which touched more lightly on the question of women's rights in the abortion decision. A concern for women's rights became even clearer in later parliamentary debates, such as the debate that took place in 2008 in Victoria. The language of choice in the context of changing social realities was highlighted:

> We have to recognize as legislators that many women are choosing to have children at a later stage in their lives, and that sometimes means there is an increased risk of abnormalities affecting that much wanted child. Medical advances mean that miscarriages can be stopped and so too nature's way of saying that the pregnancy was not right. This can mean that pregnancies will progress and a mother will find out that she is carrying a child with a profound disability. I would never judge a woman who made the decision to abort then.[132]

For supporters of the 1990 UK reform, it appears that the argument that the law should not intrude on a woman's right to control her bodily integrity and reproductive future has even stronger than usual force where a fetal abnormality is diagnosed. Compelling a woman to continue with a pregnancy and give birth to a disabled child risks harming her psychological health and imposes unreasonable social and economic burdens on her and her family. Some commentators agree; for instance, Lee has observed that "the law recognises that there is a difference between becoming a parent to a child with a disability and

---

[131] *Hansard,* HC, vol. 171, col. 245, 24 April 1990 (Mr.MacKay).
[132] *Hansard,* Legislative Assembly, 9 September 2008, 3347 (Ms Green).

becoming a parent to a child without a disability. And a good thing this is, too."[133] She defends a woman's right to end a pregnancy on the grounds of fetal abnormality "because it is the woman's pregnancy, her future and her family that will be affected by the choice she makes. She will live with the consequences of what she decides to do; and she must have the right to make a choice that others disagree with."[134]

Many of these themes also emerged in the WA parliamentary debate. Just as supporters of the 1990 UK reform had done, supporters of the Western Australian fetal abnormality provision emphasized that post-viability abortions would only occur for diagnoses of extremely severe cases of disability – that is, anencephaly or other "gross deformity." As the Honorable Cheryl Davenport explained, "the abnormalities are generally incompatible with life – for example, in the case of anen-cephalitis [sic] – so that the mother is not forced to carry the foetus to term, knowing that it will die at birth."[135] As well as desiring to spare the mother the trauma of continuing a pregnancy in such circumstances, some members were persuaded that it was morally superior to termi-nate a pregnancy rather than to allow the birth of a seriously disabled child. The Honorable Peter Foss observed that "there is as much, if not more, to criticize in creating and knowingly perpetuating a potentially miserable and terrible life as terminating a life."[136]

Against this, there remained concerns in both jurisdictions that the proposed law conveyed negative ideas about disability. In the Lords, the Earl of Perth noted that "we should never forget that often seriously handicapped children have compensating gifts which make life worth-while from their point of view."[137] In the UK debates, it was alleged that the legal exception to the twenty-four-week limit for disabled

---

[133] E. Lee, "Who's Afraid of Choice?" (2003), http://www.prochoiceforum.org.uk/ocrabortdis3.asp (accessed on 8 June 2011).

[134] Ibid.

[135] *Hansard*, Legislative Council, 1 April 1998, 1203 (Hon Cheryl Davenport).

[136] *Hansard*, Legislative Council, 1 April 1998, 1205 (Hon Peter Foss).

[137] *Hansard*, HL, vol. 522, col. 1079, 18 October 1990 (The Earl of Perth).

fetuses was unfair and discriminatory toward people with disabilities and/or those fetuses who, if normal, would have received the law's protection. Mr. Alton declared: "If a normal baby counts as human and is protected in the last two months of pregnancy, why should not a handicapped baby be protected as well?"[138] Others were concerned about the hurt or offense that the provision would, or could, cause to people with disabilities and their families. Miss Widdecombe put this argument forcefully:

> It is a gross insult that disabled people could switch on their televisions and radio at any hour of the day or night during the past few months and hear politicians arguing about whether they have the right to be born. We would not offer that insult to any racial or religious group, so we should not offer it to disabled people. It is wrong.[139]

This argument seems to be very similar to the "expressivist objection," which we discussed in Chapter 1. This is the claim that "many people with disabilities hold the view that selective abortion ... does convey a message, or otherwise imply that it would have been better had they not been born."[140] A closely related argument is that allowing the abortion of a disabled fetus in circumstances where it would not be permitted if the fetus were not disabled confers a greater level of legal protection on nondisabled fetuses and is, therefore, discriminatory. This too was raised as an issue in the UK debate. The UK Disability Rights Commission has since issued a statement indicating concern about the implications of s 1(1)(d) of the Abortion Act 1967:

> The section is offensive to many people; it reinforces negative stereotypes of disability and there is substantial support for the view

---

[138] *Hansard,* HC, vol. 174, col. 1208, 21 June 1990 (Mr. Alton).

[139] *Hansard,* HC, vol. 174, col. 1193, 21 June 1990 (Miss Widdecombe).

[140] S.D. Edwards, "Disability, Identity and the 'Expressivist Objection'" (2004), 30 *Journal of Medical Ethics* 418, at 418.

that to permit terminations at any point during a pregnancy on the ground of risk of disability, while time limits apply to other grounds set out in the *Abortion Act*, is incompatible with valuing disability and non-disability equally.[141]

The complaint that postviability abortion for serious abnormality is discriminatory has become a perennial theme in public discourse in the United Kingdom. Indeed, the matter was raised again in 2007 in the debates on the HFE Bill, where Baroness Masham declared, "I can think of no greater affront to equal opportunities for those who are disabled than the denial of the right to life itself."[142]

4.2 Incompatible with Life? Postviability Abortions and Further Refinement of Serious Handicap

Because those who participated in both the WA and UK debates considered whether abortion for serious handicap should be permitted after viability, questions about the seriousness of the disability became intertwined with concerns about the moral and legal status of late term fetuses. This was clearest in the Western Australian debates in the discussion about what would be serious enough to justify "killing a child."[143] Opponents in both Parliaments were concerned about the lack of specific guidance to medical practitioners about which conditions the law would accept fell within the exception. In the WA debate, one member observed:

As this legislation stands the Chamber is offering no guidance for what is a sufficiently severe medical condition to justify killing that or any other child. My great fear is that as the understanding of

---

[141] Disability Rights Commission, "Statement on s 1(1)(d) of the *Abortion Act*," 5 July 2003, http://www.drc-gb.org/library/policy/health_and_independent_living/drc_statement_on_section_11.aspx accessed on 5 May 2007.

[142] *Hansard*, HL, vol. 696, col. 726, 19 November 2007 (Baroness Masham).

[143] *Hansard*, Legislative Council, 1 April 1998, 1205 (Hon B. M. Scott).

genetics advances it will be possible to determine prior to birth a wider and wider range of conditions.[144]

There was what was by now a familiar dissatisfaction about the imprecision of the term "severe medical condition," and several attempts were made to improve, or tighten the scope of, the exception. One such attempt in WA involved the proposed promulgation of a list of conditions to which the exception would apply. This would have provided certainty about the meaning of "severe medical condition" and would, of course, have ensured that little discretion was left with doctors. However, the proposal did not command general support. As one member explained:

> It was the general view of members ... that that was not an appropriate way to proceed, partly because it would be difficult to define properly; it would also be a proposition that could cause a great deal of angst and harm to people in society who perhaps have those conditions now, and that is not something anyone wished to do.[145]

The idea of listing conditions was therefore specifically rejected on two grounds: first, that it was impossible to provide "a proper and exhaustive list"[146] and, second, that creating such a list of "severe medical conditions" might convey a negative message to members of the community with those conditions. Both arguments were thoughtful and had a sound basis. Nonetheless, the provision's opponents appear to have sensed a contradiction between this concern not to offend members of the community *living* with the specified conditions and earlier verbal assurances that the provision would chiefly apply where a "baby [is] ... suffering from gross deformity which *is not likely to enable the child to live*."[147] There was a clear concern

---

[144] *Hansard,* Legislative Council, 1 April 1998, 1204 (Hon E. R. J. Dermer).

[145] *Hansard,* Legislative Assembly, 1 April 1998, 1299 (Mr. Prince).

[146] *Hansard,* Legislative Assembly, 6 May 1998, 2481 (Mr. Prince).

[147] *Hansard,* Legislative Assembly, 1 April 1998, 1299 (Mr. Prince) [emphasis added].

that conditions that did not fit the description of "gross deformity" might be included:

> Is Down syndrome one of the severe medical conditions? What other severe medical conditions will justify the killing – the taking of human life? Many severe medical conditions, if we are to use the language in the normal sense, are capable of being corrected. Much of the work that is being done at King Edward Memorial Hospital will enable the correction of many defects and ailments. I am not concerned about the good work, but about the killing, the taking of human life for, frankly, no good reason whatsoever.[148]

A second strategy used by the measure's opponents, which was evident in both the UK and WA debates, was to state that only disabilities that were "incompatible with life" would justify postviability abortion. The rationale for this was seemingly that only a condition that would ultimately result in death is significant enough to justify killing a post-viability fetus. Opponents in both the WA and UK Parliaments moved amendments that would have seen the language of the relevant sections changed to provide a higher threshold of severity for postviability abortions. In WA, the amendment proposed would have allowed abortion for fetal abnormality after twenty weeks gestation where "the unborn child, has a severe medical condition that, in the clinical judgment of those two medical practitioners, justifies the procedure and ... is incompatible with life."[149] As Mr. Pendal explained:

> The amendment is not seeking to define those conditions. It is seeking to say that if the severe medical condition is incompatible with life an abortion under this proposed subsection would be lawful. The obverse is that if it is not a severe medical condition that is incompatible with life and it is a child with Down syndrome or other similar affliction an abortion would clearly be prevented because those conditions are compatible with life.[150]

[148] *Hansard*, Legislative Council, 20 May 1998, 2821 (Hon N. D. Griffiths).
[149] *Hansard*, Legislative Assembly, 6 May 1998, 2487 (Mr.Pendal).
[150] *Hansard*, Legislative Assembly, 6 May 1998, 2487 (Mr.Pendal).

In the United Kingdom opponents proposed an amendment whose effect would have been to compel doctors to take reasonable steps to secure a live birth whenever performing an abortion for a serious disability that was compatible with life.[151] Although the amendment was awkwardly drafted, the intent was to ensure that postviability abortions were only lawful under s 1(1)(d) where performed for fetal disabilities that were "incompatible with life," as distinct from disabilities that render the sufferer "unable to live a reasonable life" or handicaps "that make ... life difficult but not insupportable or unenjoyable."[152] At the very least, under this provision, a doctor would only be permitted to use feticide (lethal injection into the fetal heart prior to induced labor) if the serious handicap was "incompatible with life."[153] As Baroness Cox explained: "what kind of message are we sending to handicapped people if we choose to agree that late abortions, once a child is viable, may be granted on the ground of handicap, physical or mental, which is not incompatible with life?"[154]

Interestingly, the proposed amendment implied that "serious handicap could exist and yet be compatible with life."[155] As the Lord Chancellor pointed out, "[that] may not be entirely in accordance with the thrust and spirit of the amendment."[156] A more straightforward objection was that "incompatible with life" is subject to the same problems of definition as "serious handicap." This point was raised in both debates. In the United Kingdom, Lord Brightman stated:

> What is meant by "a handicap incompatible with life" as distinguished from a handicap compatible with life? Compatible with

---

[151] *Hansard*, HL, vol. 522, col. 1087, 18 October 1990 (Baroness Cox).

[152] *Hansard*, HL, vol. 522, col. 1092, 18 October 1990 (Lord Elton).

[153] *Hansard*, HL, vol. 522, col. 1096, 18 October 1990 (Archbishop of York).

[154] *Hansard*, HL, vol. 522, col. 1089, 18 October 1990 (Baroness Cox).

[155] *Hansard*, HL, vol. 522, col. 1099, 18 October 1990 (The Lord Chancellor, Lord Mackay of Clashfern).

[156] *Hansard*, HL, vol. 522, col. 1099, 18 October 1990 (The Lord Chancellor, Lord Mackay of Clashfern).

life for how long – life for a month or a year; until adolescence; until the age of 40; or until some other period, perhaps an hour or minute?[157]

When pressed for examples of conditions that would fall within the postviability exception, the amendments' opponents referred to conditions that would indeed result in death at or shortly after birth (for instance, anencephaly). Further, they emphasized that the conditions that the movers of the amendments sought to ensure would not be able to form the basis for a fetal abnormality abortion – such as Down syndrome, clubfoot, cleft lip and palate, and autism – would fall outside the scope of the provision. Nonetheless, neither Parliament was prepared to refine the meaning of "serious handicap" or "severe medical condition" further to put these matters beyond doubt. This was undoubtedly because the majority understood that contextual matters would be significant in determining the meaning of "severe medical condition" or "serious handicap." As one member of the WA Parliament said:

> It is not appropriate to define in legislation the abnormalities that we are talking about. This is such a sensitive subject that it should be up to the parents to talk with the expert clinicians who can give them advice in this field and to make this extraordinarily difficult decision.[158]

The implication is that the meaning of seriousness is not necessarily to be solely determined by the medical condition itself, but that other factors may be important, such as the "human feelings of the woman who is suffering anxiety over whether her child will have a problem."[159] The UK amendment was defeated in the Lords by a substantial majority (133–89).[160]

---

[157] *Hansard,* HL, vol. 522, col. 1090, 18 October 1990 (Lord Brightman).

[158] *Hansard,* Legislative Assembly, 6 May 1998, 2482 (Ms Warnock).

[159] *Hansard,* Legislative Assembly, 6 May 1998, 2487 (Mr. Marshall).

[160] *Hansard,* HL, vol. 522, col. 1086–1087, 18 October 1990.

4.3 Trusting Doctors to Interpret the Scope of "Seriousness"

Both Parliaments' clear position was that doctors would decide what the terms "serious handicap" and "severe medical condition" meant. This would of course be subject to a "good faith" requirement. Most parliamentarians were entirely satisfied with such an arrangement, the obvious advantage of which was its capacity to be sensitive to the nuances of particular situations. As a member of the WA Parliament observed:

> Politicians do not have the rights to take the moral high ground and determine what is incompatible with life, when we cannot understand the circumstances that exist. I cannot believe that some people think that they can put their opinions above those of the medical professionals who will make this assessment.[161]

The WA legislation is structured differently from the UK legislation in that the two doctors who must form the relevant opinion must be drawn from a ministerially appointed panel of six doctors. In this way, the WA Parliament could exercise greater control over subsequent interpretation of the phrase "severe medical condition." Although some members were still concerned about how doctors might interpret "severe medical condition," the Honorable Peter Foss pointed out:

> The system of setting up an approved institution and panel of doctors – using their medical ability and their standing in the profession – will make that a serious decision. That is a far better guarantee of propriety than any words in an Act defining it in greater detail. If the member does not trust those doctors and institutions then he is not trusting the very thing that should give him the greatest guarantee. We will not achieve more by including more words.[162]

---

[161] *Hansard*, Legislative Assembly, 6 May 1998, 2487 (Mr.Marshall).
[162] *Hansard*, Legislative Council, 1 April 1998, 1208 (Hon Peter Foss).

The same issue of trust in doctors' decisions arose in the UK parliamentary debates; again, this seemed to coalesce around the prospect that some doctors would interpret "serious handicap" too broadly. Once again, supporters resisted this suggestion and commented on the effectiveness of the regime. Mr. Doran quoted at length from a professor of obstetrics:

> The point here is that doctors have developed self-imposed guidelines that have emerged from their experience of current clinical practice. Thus, the perception has grown that it would be quite inappropriate for a variety of reasons to terminate pregnancies approaching the age of viability for reasons other than where ... there is a lethal ... foetal abnormality. This self-imposed, unwritten code of practice is evident on scrutiny of recent figures.[163]

Nonetheless, an amendment was proposed to require doctors to record and report the diagnosis made in cases of termination on the grounds of serious handicap.[164] The clear purpose was to keep a record of s 1(1)(d) abortions so as to ensure that abortions for "trivial reasons" were not occurring. Miss Widdecombe observed:

> If ... the medical profession has nothing to hide, and the Act is working well, there could be no possible objection to asking the profession to tell us how often it routinely aborts for a minor defect. If we have a requirement that the nature of the disability should be specified on the form, we shall be able to see whether doctors are aborting for spina bifida, hydrocephalus and cystic fibrosis or for hare lip and club foot.[165]

The amendment was narrowly defeated in the Commons on the casting vote of the acting speaker, Sir Paul Dean.[166] However, the spirit

---

[163] *Hansard*, HL, vol. 174, col. 1189, 21 June 1990 (Mr.Doran).
[164] *Hansard*, HC, vol. 174, col. 1178, 21 June 1990 (Deputy Speaker, Mr.Harold Walker); *Hansard*, HC, vol. 174, col. 1189, 21 June 1990 (Miss Widdecombe).
[165] *Hansard*, HC, vol. 174, col. 1190, 21 June 1990 (Miss Widdecombe).
[166] *Hansard*, HC, vol. 174, col. 1221, 21 June 1990.

behind the amendment garnered broad acceptance, and the regulations now make provision for the kind of reporting by doctors that supporters of the measure were seeking.[167]

The paradigmatic example dominating this discussion was cleft lip/palate. Miss Widdecombe claimed that abortions for this reason were not merely theoretical. She had been advised by a plastic surgeon who performed prenatal corrective surgery for cleft lip and palate at a London hospital that "mothers not only have abortions but that they are routinely offered" for such conditions.[168]

She went on to say "[t]hat should be a cause of worry because the legislation says that abortions should not be offered routinely in the case of minor defects but that there should be a substantial risk of serious disability."[169] Professor John Finnis and Dr. John Keown had also drawn attention to the assumed dangers associated with leaving doctors to decide what constituted a serious handicap. In a pamphlet circulated to parliamentarians, they argued that there was nothing to prevent doctors from concluding in good faith that "hare lip" was a serious handicap. This elicited a fierce reaction from supporters of the provision who regarded the suggestion as a "smear on the medical profession."[170]

Nevertheless, there has been continued concern about "late" abortion for "minor" defects. In 2003, for example, controversy followed media reports about a late abortion for cleft lip and palate.[171] This case resulted in both judicial and parliamentary consideration of the scope of serious disability. The English High Court found that the question of whether a condition's (ir)remediability determined whether or not

---

[167] See the Abortion Act 1967 (UK), s 2(1) and the Abortion Regulations 1991 (UK), regs 3(1)(a) and 4(1) and Schedules 1 and 2.

[168] *Hansard*, HC, vol. 174, col. 1190, 21 June 1990 (Miss Widdecombe).

[169] *Hansard*, HC, vol. 174, col. 1190, 21 June 1990 (Miss Widdecombe).

[170] *Hansard*, HC, vol. 174, col. 1187, 21 June 1990 (Mr.Doran).

[171] R. Savill, "Curate takes Police to Court over Abortion of Cleft-Palate Foetus" *Telegraph*, 19 November 2003, http://www.telegraph.co.uk/news/main.jhtml?xml=/ news/2003/11/19/npalat19.xml (accessed on 20 December 2005); J. Jepson,

it was a "serious disability" raised "serious issues of law and issues of public importance."[172] The House of Lords subsequently participated in a more nuanced and sophisticated debate about the meaning of serious disability for the purposes of the UK abortion legislation. Proponents of a narrow construction argued that a "serious disability" was one in which the affected person would be "unable to lead a meaningful life"; accordingly, bi-lateral cleft lip and palate was contended not to be a serious disability.[173] However, others argued that the nature of the condition was not a decisive consideration. Severity, diagnostic and prognostic uncertainty,[174] and the pain and difficulty of surgical repair[175] were all factors that might be relevant in determining whether in a particular case there was a substantial risk of "serious handicap."[176] For example, Lord Warner noted that the Royal College of Obstetricians and Gynaecologists' guidelines[177] regard the availability of treatment as merely one of a range of factors that doctors should take into account. Remedial treatment may be "prolonged, painful, subject to delays and doubts as to success, as well as dependent on the co-operation of the parents involved and the nature of the condition in question."[178]

"Murder, Even in Good Faith, Is Still Murder" *Telegraph*, 20 March 2005 http://www.telegraph.co.uk/opinion/main.jhtml?xml=/opinion/2005/03/20/do2001.xml (accessed on 5 May 2007). For an extended discussion of this case, see K. Savell, "Turning Mothers into Bioethicists: Late Abortion and Disability" in B. Bennett, T. Carney, and I. Karpin (eds.), *Brave New World of Health* (Annandale: Federation Press, 2008), 93–111.

[172] *Jepson v The Chief Constable of West Mercia Police Constabulary* [2003] EWHC 3318 (Admin).

[173] *Hansard*, HL, vol. 659, col. 215, 16 March 2004 (Lord Alton).

[174] *Hansard*, HL, vol. 659, col. 223, 16 March 2004 (Lord Craigavon).

[175] *Hansard*, HL, vol. 659, col. 229, 16 March 2004 (Lord Warner).

[176] *Hansard*, HL, vol. 659, col. 223, 16 March 2004 (Lord Craigavon).

[177] Royal College of Obstetricians and Gynaecologists, *Termination of Pregnancy for Fetal Abnormality in England, Wales and Scotland: Working Party Report* (London: RCOG, 1996). This report is discussed in more detail in the following two chapters.

[178] *Hansard*, HL, vol. 659, col. 229, 16 March 2004 (Lord Warner).

The issue of definition surfaced yet again in 2007 during the passage of the Human Fertilisation and Embryology Bill, which is discussed in more detail in the next chapter. Baroness Masham moved an amendment that would have removed s 1(1)(d) and section 5(2)(a) from the Abortion Act.[179] The effect would have been to disallow abortions after twenty-four weeks on the grounds of serious handicap. In her words, "the amendment would right a tragic discrimination concerning babies in the womb ... With equal opportunities legislation, anti-discrimination legislation and human rights legislation for disabled people, I cannot understand why this legislation does not also protect babies before they are born."[180] Opponents of the measure pointed to opinion polls demonstrating that only a minority of the British public (5–6 percent) felt that it was always wrong to terminate a pregnancy for serious mental or physical disability that would preclude independent living,[181] that the majority of women opt into the testing process, and that those who choose termination do so after careful consideration.[182] Nonetheless, familiar arguments ensued about the discriminatory impact of the law and its inability to guide and constrain doctors appropriately in these settings. Earl Howe made the point that "it ought to be possible to improve on existing BMA and Royal College guidelines by specifying exactly what clinical information should be available to all clinicians and mothers before final decisions are taken."[183] Further, it "ought to be possible for Parliament to set out more precisely what it means by the word 'seriously' ... do we mean 'serious' in terms of the foetus's viability; 'serious' in terms of the disability that the child, if born, will have to live with; or 'serious' in terms of the prospects of the disabled

---

[179] This section clarifies that the abortion of any fetus in a multiple pregnancy will be lawful if section 1(1)(d) "applies in relation to any foetus and the thing is done for the purpose of procuring the miscarriage of that foetus."

[180] *Hansard*, HL, vol. 697, col. 302, 12 December 2007 (Baroness Masham).

[181] *Hansard*, HL, vol. 697, col. 303, 12 December 2007 (Baroness Gould).

[182] *Hansard*, HL, vol. 697, col. 304, 12 December 2007 (Baroness Gould).

[183] *Hansard*, HL, vol. 697, col. 307, 12 December 2007 (Earl Howe).

child being accepted and properly cared for?"[184] These distinctions would seem again to be reiterating the worry not only that some handicaps might not be sufficiently serious to justify abortion after viability, but that there is nothing in the law to stem these perceptions of expansive interpretation of the provision by doctors and parents. Lord Alton, rehearsing statistics and cases concerning abortion for conditions such as Down syndrome, cardiovascular anomalies, spina bifida, and cleft palate, said:

> One of the most important points to note is that many of these conditions are not life-threatening.... Due to the vague and poorly defined wording of the 1990 Act, terminations for such minor, and easily treatable, conditions take place as a matter of course. Is it truly just or fair that we operate a kind of crude quality control over human beings, discarding them if they do not measure up to some arbitrary standard of physical perfection.[185]

5 SERIOUSNESS, NORMALCY, AND PERFECTION

An abortion for a "minor" defect, such as cleft lip/palate or clubfoot, emerged from these debates as the dystopic late abortion par excellence. Indeed, stories of such abortions have been persistently deployed by opponents of "serious handicap" abortion provisions to illustrate the inappropriate elasticity of the term "serious disability" in the hands of some doctors and the eugenic dangers lurking within the law. We suggest that the cleft lip/palate example is important precisely because this condition signifies the instability of disability, normalcy, and even perfection. Cleft palate might mean a physical imperfection, or it might mean a stressful and painful set of surgeries, recoveries, and breathing problems. It might mean a malformation as part of a larger syndrome. The anxiety embodied by the cleft palate example is the concern that

[184] *Hansard*, HL, vol. 697, col. 307–308, 12 December 2007 (Earl Howe).
[185] *Hansard*, HL, vol. 697, col. 310, 12 December 2007 (Lord Alton).

"serious handicap" might turn out to include anything that parents wish to avoid in their offspring and that the law might ultimately prove an unreliable bulwark against this drive for perfection. This connection is clearly made by Baroness Masham in the 2007 parliamentary debates on further amendments to the HFE Act. Addressing the issue of abortion for cleft palate, she said:

> Modern medicine can alleviate these conditions with relative ease. In my view, aborting foetuses with these minor, curable disabilities contravenes the Abortion Act in its own terms.... Many of these conditions are not serious. The law is being abused even in its own terms. Equal value is something we must seek to defend and promote.... But the law as it currently stands imposes a perfection test on life. None of us is perfect; we all have our constraints and our strengths.[186]

This takes us even closer to the difficulty posed by serious handicap as a regulatory concept. The relationships among disability, normalcy, and perfection are inherently unstable, and perhaps this is the unarticulated point that emerges from the cleft palate example. Is "disability" the presence of some undesired variation? Or is it in the absence of undesired variation that we find normalcy or even perfection? Uncertainty about the answers to these questions (or even the appropriate starting point) makes it difficult to judge when our choices are decisions to avoid disability and when they are decisions to pursue perfection (assuming that we care to make this distinction). Throughout the parliamentary debates, supporters and opponents of the provisions seem to be viewing disability from these vastly different vantage points. Opponents of the provisions worry that serious disability will be interpreted as any imperfection. They remind us that disability is part of the human condition and can never be cast out entirely. As Mr. Alton observed:

> Handicap and disability are also put in our midst as a way of challenging us. Each of us in our own way is handicapped and disabled. We

---

[186] *Hansard*, HL., vol. 696, col. 726, 19 November 2007 (Baroness Masham).

might conceal some of our disabilities better than others, but there is not a single hon Member who does not have a disability. If there were to be a perfection test on life, many of us would have to watch out.[187]

While this may be true, it does not engage with the extreme sacrifice borne by some families and people with disabilities whose life circumstances are extremely difficult and who struggle with the effects of serious disability. Supporters of the provisions take these situations as their frame and thus understand serious disability as a state so thoroughly abject that the only compassionate and human response to it is avoidance. They are thus speaking not to imperfection, but to human suffering.

As this chapter has shown, it is within and between these positions that legal frameworks to enable abortion for fetal abnormality have been forged. Kumari Campbell has argued that "legal responses to the challenges of disablement persistently demonstrate a *performative passion for sameness*" and that law attempts "to create order out of disorder (ie diversity and difference) through the process of purification – the establishment of distinct zones (disabled/abled, human/non-human)"[188] and in this sense we can read the parliamentary debates as instances of law seeking to establish just these kinds of limits. Although the legal frameworks considered possess some distinctive features, the overall thrust of law's engagement with this practice remains the same. In the jurisdictions considered, the law acknowledges that serious disability can be a sound reason for abortion, even after viability. Furthermore, it has been accepted that "serious handicap" or "severe medical condition" should not be further refined. A prescriptive approach to this question – either by listing "serious" conditions or by using different language such as "lethal," "life threatening," or "incompatible with life" – has been considered, debated, and rejected.

[187] *Hansard*, HC, vol. 171, col. 226, 24 April 1990 (Mr. Alton).
[188] F Kumari Campbell, *Contours of Ableism – The Production of Disability and Abledness* (New York: Palgrave Macmillan, 2009), 32.

Nevertheless, it is important to recognize that these debates were also characterized by ambivalence about the certitude of these limits and their larger social meanings and effects. Thus, the opponents of the fetal abnormality provisions were not only concerned to criticize what they perceived to be the deficiencies in legislative language but also to challenge the very legitimacy of a legal project that seeks to distinguish between "normal" and "disabled" in this way. Strikingly, these parliamentary debates traversed much of the ground covered in the contemporary philosophical, feminist and disability rights literature canvassed in Chapters 1 and 2, signaling at the very least that competing claims about disability, health, and rights have a history and place within the law itself. Indeed, the legal limits eventually enacted tend to signal this underlying ambiguity by characterizing the determination of seriousness as sufficiently contingent to make inadvisable attempts at precise definition. In this matter, parliaments have left the definition of "seriousness" to the judgment of clinicians in the context of the woman requesting abortion. As a result, the legislative parameters drawn around serious disability are highly dependent on the ethical sensibilities of women and medical practitioners (both as individuals and as a group). Just how clinicians are arriving at these determinations is taken up in Chapter 5.

4

Deselections

1 PREIMPLANTATION GENETIC DIAGNOSIS

In this chapter we continue our examination of what might controversially[1] be called "disability avoidance technologies" with an in-depth analysis of the history of preimplantation genetic diagnosis (PGD) and the laws that regulate it. We examine trends in a number of key comparator jurisdictions including the United Kingdom, Australia (our primary investigation site), Canada, New Zealand, and the United States, as well as providing a brief consideration of European approaches.

The basic technology of preimplantation genetic testing is about twenty years old. It has undergone rapid development in that time so that it is now able to detect more than 150 chromosomal and genetic abnormalities.[2] The technique involves taking a biopsy sample (removing one or two cells) from an embryo that has developed to a minimum of five cells. The biopsied cells then undergo a genetic analysis. There are essentially two kinds of preimplantation testing: that used

---

[1] Some would argue that as a technology of selection, PGD is not just used to avoid disability but might also be used to select for non-medical traits, to achieve a desired sex for a child, and in rare instances to select in favor of a disability.

[2] The UK Human Fertilisation and Embryology Authority (HFEA) maintains a list of conditions for which PGD is authorized (and additional conditions currently under consideration). The list is available online at http://www.hfea.gov.uk/cps/hfea/gen/pgd-screening.htm (accessed 19 June 2011).

for chromosomal analysis to detect aneuploidy or other chromosomal abnormalities (sometimes called preimplantation genetic screening or PGS)[3] and that used to detect genetic abnormalities (preimplantation genetic diagnosis or PGD). Both are expensive technologies that tend not to be covered by national health programs and so are still only used by small numbers of people worldwide. However, those numbers are growing, particularly as some clinicians are now suggesting that patients who have experienced recurrent miscarriages undergo pre-implantation testing[4] to assist in the identification of embryos with the

[3] There is no consensus about the language; however, the United Kingdom HFEA Code of Practice (8th edition) distinguishes PGS from PGD and defines the process as "checking the chromosomes of embryos conceived by in vitro fertilisation (IVF) or intra-cytoplasmic sperm injection (ICSI) for common abnormalities"; see http://www.hfea.gov.uk/70.html. Furthermore, in the Code of Practice (8th edition) PGS is specifically permitted but limited to testing for a chromosomal abnormality only if (a) that abnormality may affect its capacity to result in a live birth, or (b) there is a par-ticular risk that it has that abnormality, and where the Authority is satisfied that there is a significant risk that a person with that abnormality will have or develop a serious medical condition." See the HFEA Guidance, "The Use of PGS" 9A at http://www.hfea.gov.uk/495.html (last accessed 20 November 2011). The American Society for Reproductive Medicine also describes as PGS the examination of embryos to identify and transfer only euploid embryos and thereby to improve the likelihood for a successful pregnancy. See the Practice Committee of the Society for Assisted Reproductive Technology and the Practice Committee of the American Society for Reproductive Medicine, "Preimplantation Genetic Testing: A Practice Committee Opinion" (November 2008) 90, Suppl 3 *Fertility and Sterility* 136; available online, at http://www.asrm.org/uploadedFiles/ASRM_Content/News_and_Publications/Practice_Guidelines/Committee_Opinions/Preimplantation_genetic_testing(1).pdf (accessed on 10 June 2011). However, Melbourne IVF has just announced a new technology they call "Advanced Embryo Selection,™" which continues their work using "PGD" to "screen … all the chromosomes in a developing embryo, … to pre-cisely select the embryo with the greatest likelihood of pregnancy success": see http://www.mivf.com.au/ivf-fertility-treatments/genetic-testing-pgd/advanced-embryo-selection.aspx (accessed on 19 June 2011).

[4] Because there are differing views about the nomenclature, we will use the term "PGD" unless the particular regulatory body we are referring to uses distinguishing language. In that case we will identify the distinction made.

greatest chance of successful implantation.[5] Our focus in this chapter and throughout the book is on PGD to avoid serious disability in the future child rather than its use to prevent recurrent miscarriage.

PGD is used in a number of circumstances:

- to test for chromosomal abnormalities;
- to test for a known genetic condition (sometimes referred to as the "condition of interest");
- to test for sex where the specific gene cannot be identified but the disorder is established to be sex-linked; and
- to test for a tissue match with an existing seriously ill child with the intention of harvesting stem cells from cord blood upon birth to treat the existing child.[6]

Apart from those circumstances where there is a problem of recurrent miscarriage, the decision to use PGD is usually prompted by a patient query regarding concern over the presence of a hereditary genetic condition in his or her family. Because PGD is expensive and invasive and often subject to restrictive regulatory regimes, it has not been taken up as an alternative to routine prenatal screening and testing for the more common genetic disorders where there is no family history and thus no known risk.

In the jurisdictions analyzed in this chapter several regulatory responses to PGD can be identified. Most jurisdictions use some combination of responses 2 to 5:

1. laws that prohibit the use of PGD as a diagnostic tool. Countries prohibiting PGD fall into two categories – those with a history of eugenics, such as Germany, and those like Ireland, with a Catholic framework that give strong recognition to the status of the embryo as a human life. Notably, however, Germany has

---

[5] See http://www.mivf.com.au/ivf-fertility-treatments/genetic-testing-pgd/advanced-embryo-selection.aspx (accessed on 19 June 2011).

[6] This is referred to in the popular media as the creation of a "savior sibling."

recently (2011) revised its legislation and now allows PGD in limited circumstances;

2. laws that place limits on the circumstances when PGD might be used to avoid disability in the child to be born; for example, by making access to PGD conditional on the genetic "disease" or "defect" being "serious," "severe," or "grave";

3. laws that place limits on the circumstances when PGD might be used to select a matched embryo to treat an illness in a related child;

4. laws that prohibit the use of PGD for non-medical reasons; for example, for non-medical sex selection or non-medical trait selection (also referred to in popular discourse as creating "designer babies");

5. laws that prohibit the use of PGD to select in favor of a disability. This is what Karpin has described elsewhere as "negative enhancement" – a form of enhancement in favor of traits that are otherwise generally considered socially undesirable.[7] The most well-known example of this, in the non-PGD context, is the deaf lesbian couple who sought to reproduce a deaf child and recruited a sperm donor with several generations of deafness in the family;[8] and

6. jurisdictions that do not place *any* limits on the use of PGD.

In this chapter, our primary focus will be on the kinds of laws that fall into the second category, namely, those that make access to PGD to avoid a disability in a future child conditional on there being a "serious," "severe," or "grave" condition. Of the twenty-one jurisdictions we have examined, thirteen directly or indirectly limit the use of PGD in this way.[9] We will focus primarily on five jurisdictions: the United Kingdom and Australia and the Australian states of Victoria, South

---

[7] I. Karpin, "Choosing Disability: Preimplantation Genetic Diagnosis and Negative Enhancement" (2007) 15 *Journal of Law and Medicine* 89.

[8] J. Savulescu, "Deaf Lesbians, 'Designer Disability' and the Future of Medicine" (2002) 325 *British Medical Journal* 771. Note this category might be considered to be a subset of the previous category.

[9] The 21 jurisdictions are the *United Kingdom, Australia,* Victoria, *South Australia, Western Australia,* the United States, Canada, *New Zealand, Greece, Spain, France,*

Australia, and Western Australia. Of the nine jurisdictions that do not impose a seriousness limit, Victoria is constrained indirectly by federal guidelines, the United States appears to have no specific legislative limits on PGD at the federal level and varying indirect laws at the state level.[10] Canada and the Netherlands limit PGD only with respect to non-medical sex selection,[11] Switzerland prohibits PGD except for sex linked disorders,[12] and Ireland prohibits PGD outright. Italy has legislation that, on its face, prohibits most kinds of PGD (although recent case law has suggested some flexibility of interpretation), and Belgian law appears to authorize PGD for therapeutic purposes with no seriousness threshold in place.[13] *None* of the thirteen jurisdictions that use

Denmark, Sweden, Norway, the Netherlands, *the Czech Republic*, Switzerland, Belgium, Ireland, *Germany*, and Italy. The 13 that directly or indirectly limit access to PGD on the grounds of seriousness or its cognates are listed in italics.

[10] However, the American Society for Reproductive Medicine (ASRM) has published Practice Guidelines regarding the use of PGD: see the Practice Committee of the Society for Assisted Reproductive Technology and the Practice Committee of the American Society for Reproductive Medicine, "Preimplantation Genetic Testing: A Practice Committee Opinion" (November 2008) vol. 90, Supp. 3 *Fertility and Sterility* 136: http://www.asrm.org/uploadedFiles/ASRM_Content/News_and_Publications/Practice_Guidelines/Committee_Opinions/Preimplantation_genetic_testing(1).pdf (accessed on 10 June 2011). See also the American College of Obstetricians and Gynaecologists' Committee on Ethics, in ACOG Committee on Ethics Opinion, "Sex Selection," (February 2007) vol. 360: http://www.acog.org/from_home/publications/ethics/co360.pdf (accessed on 10 June 2011)

[11] Assisted Human Reproduction Act 2004, Art. 5(e) (Canada).

[12] Swiss Law on Reproductive Medicine of 18 December 1998, Article 5(2). The Swiss Federal Council plan to change Article 119 of the Constitution in order to allow PGD. The discussion stage of this proposal began on 29 June 2011 and finished on 30 September 2011. A report is not expected before mid-2012 see http://www.bag.admin.ch/themen/medizin/03878/index.html?lang=de (accessed 20 November 2011).

[13] In Ireland, see Article 40(3)(3) of the Irish Constitution. In Germany, the prohibition was found in section 2 of the Act for Protection of Embryos of 13 December 1990. However, on 7 July 2011, the German Parliament voted in favor of limited use of PGD (see Federal Ministry of Education and Research, "German Bundestag Permits Preimplantation Genetic Diagnosis" at http://www.biotechnologie.de/BIO/Navigation/EN/news,did=128614.html?listBlId=77908&

the "seriousness"/"gravity" limit offer a definition of this term in their legislation.[14] The closest we come to finding regulatory definitions is in documents that are supplementary to formal legislative instruments. For example, in the United Kingdom, the HFEA Licence Committee has developed an explanatory memorandum to aid in determinations of seriousness, and this will be discussed in detail in Part 2.

We think that the imposition of a seriousness threshold can be traced to two pressure points: historical concerns over the appropriate limits on the use of abortion for disability, on the one hand, and future-oriented anxieties over the potential to create designer babies, on the other. We are interested in the way seriousness seems to operate both as a bulwark against accusations of perfectionist eugenics and as a reassurance for those who view embryos as a form of life requiring some measure of respect.

In Part 2 of this chapter, we examine PGD regulation in the United Kingdom, where the first use of PGD resulting in a pregnancy occurred. It was also in the United Kingdom where the first detailed regulatory scheme that both facilitated and restricted the development and use of PGD (the Human Fertilisation and Embryology Act 1990 (HFE Act)) was introduced. In the years that followed, the HFE Act was supplemented by the Human Fertilisation and Embryology Authority Code of Practice (HFEA Code); this code is now in its eighth edition.

(accessed on 16 November 2011). The new law is called "Gesetz zur Regelung der Präimplantationsdiagnostik (Präimplantationsdiagnostikgesetz – PräimpG)," translated as Law for the Regulation of PGD." See http://www.bundesrat.de/ cln_117/nn_2034972/SharedDocs/Drucksachen/2011/0401–500/480–11,template Id=raw,property=publicationFile.pdf/480–11.pdf. In Italy, see article 13 of Law No. 40 of 19 February 2004, Regulating Medically Assisted Reproduction. In Belgium see the Law on IVF Embryo Research of 11 March 2003.

[14] We have focused our examination of the law in Anglophone jurisdictions and in those instances have been able to examine regulations, codes of practice, and guidelines that operate in tandem with legislation. We have been unable to do this for the non-Anglophone jurisdictions.

In 2008 comprehensive amendments were made to the HFE Act that further refined and codified the law concerning the use of PGD.

In part 3 we examine the Australian regulatory framework, which draws heavily on the UK precedent. As early as 1982, the National Health and Medical Research Council (NHMRC) had provided guidelines on "human experimentation" in the context of IVF and embryo transfer.[15] This was followed in 1984 by the Victorian state government introducing legislation regulating IVF and assisted reproduction, including the use of technology to avoid an "undesirable hereditary disorder."[16] In 1988, South Australia introduced legislation requiring the licensing of persons undertaking artificial fertilization procedures including to avoid "a risk that a genetic defect would be transmitted."[17] None of these early guidelines and pieces of legislation contemplated the capacity to test embryos and transfer them to the woman post testing. In other words, until 1991 there were no federal or state laws in Australia that directly addressed the use of PGD. This changed in 1991 when Western Australia passed

[15] NHMRC, "Statement on Human Experimentation and Supplementary Notes 1982: Supplementary Note 4 – In Vitro Fertilisation and Embryo Transfer" (February 1984) 28(1), *Australasian Radiology* 65. At that early stage, those performing experimental procedures using PGD would have been guided by the fifth "particular matter" that the note stated must be taken "into account when ethical matters are being considered." This "matter" was stated as follows: "(5) Research with sperm, ova or fertilized ova has been and remains inseparable from the development of safe and effective IVF and ET; as part of this research other important scientific information concerning human reproductive biology may emerge. However, continuation of embryonic development in vitro beyond the stage at which implantation would normally occur is not acceptable."

[16] Infertility (Medical Procedures) Act 1984 (Vic). The Artificial Conception Act 1984 (NSW) focused on the use of donor gametes and regulated parental status.

[17] Reproductive Technology (Clinical Practices) Act 1988 (SA). The South Australian legislation was broader than had been previous Australian legislation in this area. While the Act did not directly mention PGD, nothing in it prohibited such procedures; indeed, the licensing system set up under the Act may have facilitated such research. See our discussion of the Reproductive Technology (Clinical Practices) Act of 1988 in Part 3.

its legislation prohibiting diagnostic testing of the embryo.[18] Over the years that followed, Victoria and South Australia began to regulate assisted reproductive technology (including authorizing PGD) comprehensively and to implement regulatory oversight provisions. More recently, though, both have loosened regulatory controls and devolved much of the decision making to the practitioners of IVF. Western Australia, on the other hand, finally permitted PGD testing in 2004, imposing detailed regulatory oversight that continues today.[19] Part 3 will trace the development of these laws and the decision (or not) to use a threshold of seriousness. We also examine the implementation of the NHMRC guidelines on Assisted Reproductive Technology and the role of federal legislation governing cloning and embryo research in regulating ART.[20]

In Part 4 we examine the scope of regulation in Canada, New Zealand, the United States, and several European jurisdictions. While these jurisdictions vary greatly, we note two important common themes. First, more often than not a seriousness threshold is included, and, second, the determination of what "serious" means falls to clinicians and clinical geneticists rather than the legislature.

[18] The Human Reproductive Technology Act 1991 (WA) was the first piece of Australian legislation to be introduced directly after the first successful use of PGD had been announced in the United Kingdom. See additional discussion in part 3.

[19] Victoria introduced the Infertility Treatment Act in 1995, which overhauled the earlier Act, and later made substantial changes via the Assisted Reproductive Treatment Act in 2008. Western Australia amended its legislation in 2004, and the South Australian legislation was amended in 2008. For more information, see our detailed discussion in Part 3.

[20] The Prohibition of Human Cloning Act 2002 (Cth) (later the Prohibition of Human Cloning for Reproduction Act 2002, and as amended in 2007) and the Research Involving Human Embryos Act 2002 (Cth). As we shall discuss in Part 3, the NHMRC Guidelines were amended in 1996, 2004, and 2007 (when they were renamed the Ethical Guidelines on the use of Assisted Reproductive Technology in Clinical Practice and Research). The latter two iterations of these guidelines, which were developed after the introduction of the federal legislation regulating cloning and embryo research, specifically refer to PGD.

2 UNITED KINGDOM

2.1 The Beginnings of PGD

The first successful use of PGD occurred in the United Kingdom in April 1990 when two couples at risk of transmitting what was referred to in the journal *Nature* as "adrenoleukodystrophy and X linked mental retardation"[21] were able to have their embryos sexed to prevent the transfer of an affected male embryo. Alan Handyside and Robert Winston from London's Hammersmith Hospital announced the successful transfer[22] at the same time that debate over the Human Fertilisation and Embryology Bill (HFE Bill) was in full swing in the House of Commons. The HFE Bill was the product of years of discussion. It followed the 103-page Warnock Report in 1984,[23] the first Department of Health and Social Security consultation paper in 1986,[24] and the resulting White Paper in 1987.[25] One of the primary motivating forces for the HFE Bill was a desire to remedy a lack of regulatory oversight of ongoing experimental technologies, including those used in the treatment of infertility. It was argued that these laws would enable the continuation of embryo "research," but under strictly controlled conditions. By the time the HFE Bill reached Parliament, the research of the Hammersmith team was already well known. For

---

[21] A.H. Handyside et al., "Pregnancies from Biopsied Human Preimplantation Embryos Sexed by Y-specific DNA Amplification" (1990) 344 *Nature* 768.

[22] A.H. Handyside et al., "Pregnancies from Biopsied Human Preimplantation Embryos Sexed by Y-specific DNA Amplification" (1990) 344 *Nature* 768.

[23] Department of Health and Social Security, *Report of the Committee of Inquiry into Human Fertilisation and Embryology*, Cmnd 9314 (1984) (the report is known colloquially as "The Warnock Report" after the chair of the committee, Dame Mary Warnock).

[24] Department of Health and Social Security, Legislation on Human Infertility Services and Embryo Research: A Consultation Paper, Cmnd 46 (1986).

[25] Department of Health and Social Security, Human Fertilisation and Embryology: A Framework for Legislation, Cmnd 259 (1987).

instance, in the House of Lords in December 1989, PGD was referred to as a technology with the potential to allow the early detection of "serious genetic diseases" including Duchenne muscular dystrophy and cystic fibrosis,[26] Tay-Sachs disease, Lesch-Nyhan disease, Down syndrome, Hunter's syndrome, Hurler's syndrome, and Huntington's chorea.[27] Therefore, it was not surprising that when the successful implantation was announced four months later, the debate turned to a discussion of the arguments for and against PGD.

During the debate there were numerous references to the Hammersmith announcement; most of those who spoke of this success did so in acclamatory and admiring terms. In the House of Commons the development was described as a "breakthrough" and a "world first,"[28] and Dafydd Wigley, the member for Caernarfon, himself the father of two sons who had died of "severe genetic disability,"[29] asked "[c]an the House in all conscience, even contemplate a legal ban on such marvellous pioneering work?"[30] When the Parliament ultimately voted on the HFE Bill, about a month after the Hammersmith announcement, an overwhelming majority supported its passage; some commentators have argued that the timing of the announcement was carefully planned to give the HFE Bill a final push over the line. Two members of the House of Commons, McNair Wilson and Alan Amos, described with some measure of apparent sarcasm the announcement of the breakthrough as "extraordinarily convenient" and a "lucky coincidence."[31]

---

[26] *Hansard*, HL, vol. 513, col. 1006, 7 December 1989 (Lord Mackay of Clashfern).

[27] *Hansard*, HL, vol. 513, col. 1014, 7 December 1989 (Lord Ennals).

[28] *Hansard*, HC, vol. 171, col. 46, 23 April 1990 (Ms Richardson).

[29] *Hansard*, HC, vol. 170, col. 946, 2 April 1990 (Mr. Dafydd Wigley).

[30] *Hansard*, HC, vol. 170, col. 948, 2 April 1990 (Mr. Dafydd Wigley).

[31] Sir Michael McNair Wilson stated, "It would be churlish of me to wonder why that knowledge came to light just before today's debate. One might describe it as a lucky coincidence. However, is that the whole story?" *Hansard*, HC, vol. 171, col. 91, 23 April 1990. Shortly afterward Mr. Alan Amos commented, "We were told last week, with extraordinarily convenient and suspicious timing, that sex can be identified

Sarah Franklin and Celia Roberts argue in their ethnography of PGD that the *Nature* report and the media coverage that followed, together with the proliferation of lobbying from representatives of communities affected by genetic disease, resulted in the solidification of a connection between "a moral obligation to explore new avenues of preventing early childhood death and suffering from a range of conditions" and "the prospects of human embryo research."[32] It is also important to consider the broader context in which these events were occurring. The 1990s were a period in which there was a massive global cultural, political, and scientific embrace of the power of the "gene." The "new genetics" was heralded as an infinitely powerful discourse holding the key to the secrets of life. The year 1990 also marked the start of the Human Genome Project (HGP).[33] This was a major U.S. government sponsored initiative to study the entire human genetic inheritance and was part of "a wide range of scientific activities related to genomics" budgeted to cost upward of U.S.\$3 billion.[34] The aim of the HGP was to analyze the structure of human chromosomes, to sequence the genes in that structure, to locate and map the structure, and to find the location of defective genes that cause or contribute to human genetic disease. At the time, it was claimed that the HGP would provide us with the definitive story of human identity and would allow us to locate the gene for all sorts of hitherto elusive problems. There were visions of genes for alcoholism, unemployment, domestic and social violence, as well as drug addiction and

---

three days after fertilisation, and that male embryos were already being destroyed." *Hansard*, HC, vol. 171, col. 104, 23 April 1990.

[32] S. Franklin and C. Roberts, *Born and Made: An Ethnography of Preimplantation Genetic Diagnosis* (Princeton, NJ: Princeton University Press, 2006), 59–60.

[33] The project was undertaken cooperatively by the National Institute of Health and the U.S. Department of Energy; for more information see http://www.ornl.gov/sci/techresources/Human_Genome/home.shtml.

[34] The U.S. government reports the total cost of the HGP (excluding construction costs) at U.S.\$437 million: see http://www.ornl.gov/sci/techresources/Human_Genome/project/budget.shtml.

homelessness.[35] It was in this context that the UK Parliament was considering this expansive new legislation that would revolutionize the framework for genetic research and provide a structure governing research involving genetic diagnosis of human embryos.

While PGD was seemingly instrumental in ensuring the successful passage of the HFE Bill in 1990, it was not mentioned directly in the original text of the Act.[36] Instead, under ss 3(1)(b) and 11(1) of the HFE Act, the capacity to authorize the use of PGD was devolved to the licensing authority, the Human Fertilisation and Embryology Authority (HFEA). Schedule 2 of the Act set out the activities for which a license may be granted; this included under s 1(1)(d) "practices designed to secure that embryos are in a suitable condition to be placed in a woman or to determine whether embryos are suitable for that purpose." Subsections 3(2)(b) and (e) allowed a license to be authorized for the purpose of, respectively, "increasing knowledge about the causes of congenital disease" and "developing methods for detecting the presence of gene or chromosome abnormalities in embryos before implantation."

Despite the absence of any direct reference to PGD in the HFE Bill, it is clear from the debates that – within a rhetorical economy of worthiness – PGD's capacity to prevent disablement was used as a trump card to persuade parliamentarians to support the Bill's authorization of embryo research. It is argued by some that by using the language of "risk" and exploiting fear of disability, the Bill's supporters secured

---

[35] D. Koshland, "Sequences and Consequences of the Human Genome" (1989) 246 *Science* 189. The project was finally completed in 2003 – it took 13 years. Since the development of Next Generation Sequencing, the amount of time required to sequence a whole human genome has been considerably reduced. The first genome sequenced using this technology, that of James Watson, who codiscovered the double helix structure of DNA, took approximately two months and was published in 2008: David A. Wheeler et al., "The Complete Genome of an Individual by Massively Parallel DNA Sequencing" (2008) 452 *Nature* 872.

[36] Its first mention in the HFE Act itself is in the 2008 amendments; these amendments are discussed in more detail later.

the legalization of controversial or innovative biotechnologies.[37] We noted similar rhetorical maneuvers in the abortion debates canvassed in Chapter 3. As we observed, in those debates concerns about the harms associated with disability were persuasive enough to override anxieties about "late" termination of pregnancy. Both cases are prime examples of one of the issues that we are exploring in this book – namely, the way in which the concept of disability (more commonly referred to in the early debates as "handicap") operates as an *enabling* idea to confer legitimacy on technologies that would otherwise be seen as transgressive and highly problematic. These are very often experimental technologies, such as PGD, that push the boundaries of what is normal and natural. If we analyze this language (as we did the language used in the abortion debates – see Chapter 3), we can better understand how the concept of disability is used to justify technological developments that might otherwise be met with greater resistance.

2.2 Disability in the UK Debates

In arguing in favor of the HFE Bill's passage, Parliamentarians used disability and the risk that it might develop as a flashpoint requiring urgent legislative action.[38] To achieve this, many examples used to support the Bill conjured up images or stories about the most extreme forms of disability. For example, Lord Glenarthur describes the "awful risk to children and their parents of distressing and life-threatening congenital handicaps"[39] and Viscount Caldecote talks of the need to prevent "the creation of grossly deformed and mentally handicapped

---

[37] The latest examples of such experimental biotechnologies – including IGM and cytoplasmic oocyte donation – are discussed in more detail in Chapter 6.

[38] In Part 3 of this chapter we will examine similar approaches used in the Australian parliamentary debates.

[39] *Hansard*, HL, vol. 513, col. 1042, 7 December 1989 (Lord Glenarthur).

babies."[40] These characterizations persist throughout the debates, even though the range of diseases and conditions described, in fact, vary quite markedly in their severity.[41] One particularly illuminating example is that provided by Sir Charles Morrison in the House of Commons. He tells a personal story of coming face to face with people with disabilities and presents this story as a kind of terrifying fable:

> Just over 20 years ago I visited a hospital in my constituency for the mentally subnormal. I was taken round by the doctor in charge and I remember passing a door to a ward through which the doctor did not lead me. I asked what was in there, but the doctor told me that we were not going into that particular ward.
>
> I persisted with my questioning and I was told that it was a children's ward. I said that I should like to visit that ward, but the doctor told me that I would not. I persisted in my desire to see it and the doctor told me that, if I insisted, I should take a grip of myself. He was right to give me that advice, because when I went into that ward I saw human beings, none of them over the age of 10, who were virtually unrecognizable as such. Nowadays, that ward does not exist because of research undertaken in the past.[42]

By telling this tale, Sir Charles fills the imaginary space of the unknowability of disability with the spectacle of dehumanized monsters who have been kept hidden from our view. The excerpt also suggests the role that doctors have in being privy to the secrets of the claimed "true" horror of disablement and sets the framework for the

---

[40] *Hansard*, HL, vol. 513, col. 1056, 7 December 1989 (Viscount Caldecote).

[41] At various points members refer to the potential to eliminate spina bifida (which involves varying degrees of disability from very mild to severe), hemophilia (a manageable disorder), epidermolysis bullosa (a skin disorder that leads to internal blistering and ultimately results in death), and retinitis pigmentosa (which can lead to blindness), and, perhaps more surprisingly, asthma (a respiratory disorder that is generally manageable with drugs). See, among others, *Hansard*, HC, vol. 171, col. 79, 23 April 1990 (Mrs. Currie); *Hansard*, HC, vol. 170, col. 980, 2 April 1990 (Ms Harman); *Hansard*, HC, vol. 170, col. 963, 2 April 1990 (Mr. Kevin Barron); and *Hansard*, HC, vol. 171, col. 120, 23 April 1990 (Ms Harmon).

[42] *Hansard*, HC, vol. 170, col. 938, 2 April 1990 (Sir Charles Morrison).

Bill (and the regulations that will follow) as facilitating medical judgment about disability. Furthermore, by using extreme examples such
as this, supporters of the Bill engaged in a descriptive mustering of
evidence where extremity became the norm of disability. Congenital
disease or genetic or chromosomal abnormalities operate here as open
signifiers. Though they need not always refer to the most severe and
distressing kinds of disablement, in the context of the debate, the magnitude of potential disability is signaled, and ideas of suffering, the
immense burden of care, and grief over loved ones are foregrounded.
Lord Carter is one of the members of Parliament who provided a
mediating counterdiscourse. Referring to Schedule 2 of the Bill, which
provided for the grant of licenses for "increasing knowledge about the
causes of congenital diseases," he asks what is included within the definition of congenital diseases: "Is that meant to cover all congenital
diseases, including those which are not life-threatening but which are
disabling to a greater or lesser extent?"[43] To overcome this uncertainty,
Lord Carter[44] moved an amendment whose effect would have been to
qualify the phrase "congenital disease" with the words "which are life-
threatening or severely disabling."[45] Once again, we see a mirroring

---

[43] *Hansard*, HL, vol. 513, col. 1083, 7 December 1990 (Lord Carter).

[44] Lord Carter, it is interesting to note, is himself the parent of a child with a genetic
disease.

[45] *Hansard*, HL, vol. 515, col. 1006, 8 February 1990 (Lord Carter). Similarly, the Duke
of Norfolk moved that the word "suitable" in Schedule 2 be more clearly defined
(Schedule 2 provided, relevantly, that a license may authorize "practices designed to
secure that embryos are in a suitable condition to be placed in a woman"). He was
concerned that, to some, "only a child with the qualities that the parents wanted was
suitable" and that this might lead to preferences for "a boy or a girl or a blond child or
a blue-eyed child": *Hansard*, HL, vol. 515, col. 996, 8 February 1990. Ultimately, the
amendment was withdrawn on the basis of advice received from the Parliamentary
Under-Secretary of State, Department of Health, Baroness Hooper, that the word
"suitable" did not mean "that they conform to the desire of the woman for a baby with
blue eyes or other such characteristics, but are suitable for the purpose of implantation and creating a viable embryo": *Hansard*, HL, vol. 515, col. 997, 8 February 1990.
Here again we see how the deference to medical judgment is paramount.

of the concerns articulated and strategies deployed in the abortion debates. In those debates, we saw similar efforts to impose a higher disability threshold; attempts were made to provide that abortions of a "child capable of being born alive" were lawful only where that child was suffering from a handicap "incompatible with life."[46] Moreover, as was the case in the abortion debates, the possibility of compiling a list of conditions was discussed as one way of resolving the uncertainty that Lord Carter had identified. When arguing for the amendment, Lord Carter quotes Baroness Mary Warnock, the chair of the body that wrote the report[47] that underpinned much of the content of the Bill, as saying, "I think we need to have an agreed list, by society as a whole, of which of the conditions that are so disabling lead to such a short life on the part of a child who suffers from them that medicine and common humanity must work together to eliminate these if possible."[48] Further, he notes that while color blindness is an inherited disorder that might be researched under the legislation, it would not, in his view, qualify as serious enough to warrant the devotion of "scarce research resources."[49]

Lord Carter's amendment was rejected on the basis that it was a practical impossibility to "decide which diseases came into any particular category, whether it was phrased in the actual wording proposed in this amendment or indeed any other similar wording."[50] Interestingly, however, once the Bill passed through the two Houses of Parliament, the HFEA immediately drew on the qualifying language of seriousness used in the abortion context when authorizing PGD licenses. Notably when the HFE Act was amended in 2008, similar language did finally appear in the amended terms. This suggests, perhaps, that while the

---

[46] See our discussion in Chapter 3.
[47] Department of Health and Social Security, Report of the Committee of Inquiry into Human Fertilisation and Embryology, Cmnd 9314 (1984).
[48] *Hansard*, HL, vol. 515, col. 1007, 8 February 1990 (Lord Carter).
[49] *Hansard*, HL, vol. 515, col. 1007, 8 February 1990 (Lord Carter).
[50] *Hansard*, HL, vol. 515, col. 1007–1008, 8 February 1990 (Baroness Hooper).

specter of extreme disability proved a useful rhetorical maneuver for the purposes of ensuring the HFE Bill's initial passage, Lord Carter's more nuanced approach was ultimately more useful to those charged with the responsibility of applying the HFE Act in practice (this will be discussed in more detail in Section 2.3).

So far we have examined the views of those who supported the HFE Bill and those who wished to define its outer limits. But there were also some parliamentarians who opposed the Bill either because of a fundamental position that viewed embryos as life or because of concerns that the authorization of PGD would amount to state-based eugenics. These members repeatedly noted that the research being facilitated by the legislation was not going to offer a cure for disease and disability but would only offer the opportunity to prevent it.[51] Lord Ashbourne states, for example: "What is meant by prevention? It is another word for destruction. In short, embryo research is merely a screening process to detect abnormalities."[52] Viscount Sidmouth too was concerned with the morality of the decision to destroy so-called defective embryos:

> The ability to identify these disorders in embryos within 14 days would no doubt make it possible to destroy them at an early stage. Such a policy of extermination might eventually reduce the number of born sufferers, but who could claim this as treatment let alone as a cure? If such a claim is seriously made, I believe we are in sight of the slippery slope. Other supposedly undesirable genetic characteristics might be put forward and the same logic would apply.[53]

This vocabulary of "extermination" and eugenics harks back to the earlier discussion in debates around abortion,[54] so it is not surprising that one of the rhetorical strategies employed by proponents of the Bill

---

[51] In Chapter 6 we explore the claimed benefits of inheritable genetic modification, which would enable treatment of the biological individual rather than selection against that entity or termination.

[52] *Hansard*, HL, vol. 513, col. 1049, 7 December 1990 (Lord Ashbourne).

[53] *Hansard*, HL, vol. 513, col. 1079, 7 December 1990 (Lord Ashbourne).

[54] See chapter 3.

was to emphasize the role that PGD would play in eliminating abortion. First, it was noted that to prevent research into genetic disorders would "prevent the reduction of late abortion."[55] Second, it was noted that to ban PGD to prevent the birth of children with the conditions identified would be hypocritical if abortion continued to be authorized for those purposes.[56] In this way, the Bill's supporters sought to minimize the emotional power of these references to eugenics by constructing PGD as being less morally offensive than the abortion practices that the Parliament had already legitimized.

Here we might fast-forward twenty years to consider whether, in fact, the kinds of conditions that currently justify abortion are the same as those that justify PGD. The answer is not straightforward. In most of the jurisdictions we analyze, access to an early termination of pregnancy (i.e., prior to twenty weeks) is less difficult than access to PGD. For example, while it would be possible to use early abortion to terminate an unwanted pregnancy on the grounds of gender alone, it would not be possible to use PGD to deselect an embryo on the same grounds.

2.3 The Law up to 2008

When the HFE Bill eventually went to a vote it was passed by a large majority. This was considered an extraordinary victory given that only five years earlier the efforts of those opposed to embryo research had "very nearly...[outlawed] embryo research and almost all IVF treatment."[57] Once the Bill was passed and the HFEA was established,

---

[55] *Hansard*, HL, vol. 513, col. 1103, 7 December 1989 (Lord Meston quoting Viscount, Lord Caldecote); *Hansard*, HL, vol. 171, col. 107–108, 23 April 1990 (Mr. David Martin).

[56] *Hansard*, HC, vol. 171, col. 38, 23 April 1990 (Sir David Steel); *Hansard*, HC, vol. 171, col. 44, 23 April 1990 (Ms Richardson).

[57] See E. Jackson, *Regulating Reproduction: Law, Technology and Autonomy* (Oxford and Portland, OR: Hart Publishing, 2001), at 183, where she notes that Enoch Powell's

the HFEA moved quickly to undertake a number of consultations that would create a more detailed framework for the provision of PGD. It also specifically aligned PGD's availability with the availability of abortion for disability. That is, PGD was authorized to test for conditions that involved a "substantial risk of a serious handicap."[58] Of course, as we have outlined in Chapter 3,[59] this language is by no means transparent in the abortion context.[60]

In 1993 when the HFEA conducted its consultation on sex selection it was clearly stated that "pre-implantation diagnosis is ethically acceptable where there is a *risk* of a *life threatening* disease."[61] In 1999, when it conducted its broader Consultation on PGD (with the Advisory Committee on Genetic Testing), it stated that it was "implicit in the legislation" that Parliament made the decision to

1985 Bill outlawing the creation of embryos unless they were to be implanted into an identifiable woman passed its first reading 238 to 66 and only failed because it was talked out of time.

[58] E. Jackson, *Regulating Reproduction: Law, Technology and Autonomy* (Oxford and Portland, OR: Hart Publishing, 2001), at 243. See also Human Fertilisation and Embryology Authority and Advisory Committee on Genetic Testing, *Consultation Document on Preimplantation Genetic Diagnosis* (1999), which states at para. 34: "at present (1999) where the suitability of PGD is being considered, centres are understood to be applying the criteria for termination of pregnancy for fetal abnormality published by the Royal College of Obstetricians and Gynaecologists": http://www.hfea.gov.uk/cps/rde/xbcr/hfea/PGD_document.pdf (accessed on 10 June 2011).

[59] See our discussion in Chapter 3.

[60] Furthermore, as we shall discuss later, in adopting this alignment strategy the HFEA's subsequent change from the language of "substantial risk" to that of "significant risk" is not noted; this, despite the lengthy discussion of the difference between "substantial risk" and other nomenclature – such as "certain risk" – in the abortion debates. Other phrases that are used, such as "life-threatening" and "severe" do little to assist in identifying the relevant criteria. See edition 6 of the HFEA Code, released in 2003, where "substantial" is changed to "significant" risk; paragraph 14.22 states, "It is expected that PGD will be available only where there is a significant risk of a serious genetic condition being present in the embryo."

[61] Human Fertilisation and Embryology Authority, *Sex Selection Public Consultation Document* (1993), para. 28 [our emphasis].

allow PGD for "certain severe or life-threatening disorders."[62] The meanings of disability and seriousness were considered in this 1999 consultation report, and it was queried whether PGD should be used to select against late onset disorders, carrier embryos, and genetically complex disorders. The lengthy discussion of seriousness in the RCOG statement on Termination of Pregnancy for Fetal Anomaly, which used the World Health Organization (WHO) scale for severity of the disability, was also mentioned.[63] Furthermore, this was all considered against the backdrop of section 13(5) of the HFE Act, which required that treatment only be offered after taking into account the welfare of any child who might be born as a result of the treatment and the larger question of whether this "principle of the welfare of the child [can] ever be compatible with a decision to begin a pregnancy knowing that a child will be born with a genetic disorder?"[64]

Beyond this, however, the 1999 Consultation Report offers limited guidance concerning the specific boundaries of PGD use. The report does note that the most common reasons worldwide for using PGD are to sex an embryo to avoid X-linked disorders and to test for age related

---

[62] Human Fertilisation and Embryology Authority and Advisory Committee on Genetic Testing, *Consultation Document on Preimplantation Genetic Diagnosis* (1999), para 10.

[63] They note that only individuals with a disability at the third or higher points on the WHO scale of the severity of a disability would be considered by most people to be seriously handicapped. Points 3 and 4 are defined as follows: 3 "Assisted performance. Includes the need for a helping hand (i.e., the individual can perform the activity or sustain the behavior, whether augmented by aids or not, only with some assistance from another person), and 4 Dependent performance. Includes complete dependence on the presence of another person (i.e., the individual can perform the activity or sustain the behavior, but only when someone is with him most of the time)." Human Fertilisation and Embryology Authority and Advisory Committee on Genetic Testing, *Consultation Document on Preimplantation Genetic Diagnosis* (1999), Annex C, at 23.

[64] Human Fertilisation and Embryology Authority and Advisory Committee on Genetic Testing, Consultation Document on Preimplantation Genetic Diagnosis (1999), para. 38.

aneuploidy.[65] In addition, it does at various points identify disorders considered "serious," including single gene disorders such as cystic fibrosis, Duchenne muscular dystrophy, hemophilia, Huntington's chorea, the thalassemias, sickle cell disease, and a number of uncommon hereditary cancers.[66] However, it is unclear whether these conditions fall within the definition of "severe" or "life-threatening" so as to authorize PGD. This vagueness is perhaps made explicable by the fact that this was a consultation document, which aimed (among other things) to discover people's views about whether PGD *should* be offered for these, or any, conditions.

At the same time, though, the Consultation Report does suggest some limits. First, it raises the concern that PGD may devalue the lives of those with the condition for which PGD is sought and suggests that any conclusion about what is and is not a serious disability must be contextually based. For instance, at paragraph 21 it is noted that

> the impact on the quality of life of a child born with a disability, as well as their families will depend on a number of factors. These will include the seriousness of the disability, the circumstances of the family, as well as the emotional and material support available.

The report goes on to state that "[e]ach family should be free to make their own choices in this respect and their view will be *one* of the most important determining factors in assessing the justification for PGD."[67] Second, it is made clear at paragraph 22 that "the HFEA and

---

[65] Human Fertilisation and Embryology Authority and Advisory Committee on Genetic Testing, Consultation Document on Preimplantation Genetic Diagnosis (1999), para. 11. The term *aneuploidy* refers to the existence of more or less than the usual number of chromosomes.

[66] Human Fertilisation and Embryology Authority and Advisory Committee on Genetic Testing, Consultation Document on Preimplantation Genetic Diagnosis (1999), para. 5.

[67] Human Fertilisation and Embryology Authority and Advisory Committee on Genetic Testing, Consultation Document on Preimplantation Genetic Diagnosis (1999), para. 21.

the ACGT do not think it would be acceptable to test for any social or psychological characteristics, normal physical variations, or any other conditions which are not associated with disability or a serious medical condition." This is a direct response to concerns that clinicians and patients might try to use the technology to create so-called designer babies selected on the basis of socially desirable traits, rather than simply to deselect on the basis of ones that are socially undesirable.[68]

So while the Consultation Report was vague concerning the conditions for which PGD would be authorized, it also acknowledged that it was not socially acceptable to provide the medical profession with an unfettered discretion to use PGD. Interestingly, this approach differs from that adopted in the abortion context, where the Parliament seemed happy from quite early on to give the medical profession a wide discretion in determining what amounted to a "serious" handicap. Other acts by the HFEA suggest a similar degree of initial caution about the medical profession's role. In a 1999 Clinical Guidance Letter,[69] the HFEA had required clinics, when applying to test for a new disorder, to provide the On Line Mendelian Inheritance in Man System (OMIM) number so that the HFEA could make certain determinations about the nature of the disorder – its prevalence, its severity, and so on. Where there was no OMIM number the HFEA required clinics to submit information about "the known risk," the "severity of the particular case," "the way it affects the family," and "the mode of inheritance."[70] This was to enable the HFEA to determine whether it was appropriate to allow testing for the condition requested.

However, the difference between the approach in the abortion context and that in the PGD context may only have been superficial, as

[68] This concern recalls the Duke of Norfolk's unease about what he terms "a Brave New World scenario" – see footnote 45.

[69] Human Fertilisation and Embryology Authority, "Clinical Guidance Letter," 13 August 1999: see http://www.hfea.gov.uk/3219.html (accessed on 24 June 2011).

[70] Human Fertilisation and Embryology Authority and Advisory Committee on Genetic Testing, *Consultation Document on Preimplantation Genetic Diagnosis* (1999), para. 28.

clinical practice at the time that the Consultation Report was written was to apply the RCOG criteria for termination of pregnancy for fetal abnormality when determining whether to use PGD. This is described in the Consultation Report as limiting PGD's use "to cases where there is a precise diagnosis and a substantial risk of serious handicap."[71] The Consultation Report goes on to query whether it is proper to limit PGD to a prescribed number of specific serious inherited conditions and, specifically, whether "the seriousness of a genetic condition be a matter of clinical judgment based on general guidance? If so, what aspects might such general guidance cover?"[72]

The problems identified by the Consultation Report with having "serious" defined – either by doctors or regulators – ultimately led to the HFEA opting for a third approach, which could be described as a patient autonomy focus. In 2001 the HFEA and the Human Genetics Commission (successor to the ACGT) reported on the outcomes of their public consultation on PGD.[73] Consistently with the abortion regulations regarding late termination for disability, seriousness was considered to be an important factor when authorizing PGD. Recommendation 10 indicated that the guide to clinics should state "that indications for the use of PGD should be consistent with current practice in the use of PND."[74] Despite this, the language of Recommendation 11 provided that "[t]he guidance should indicate that PGD should only be available where there is a *significant* risk of

---

[71] Human Fertilisation and Embryology Authority and Advisory Committee on Genetic Testing, Consultation Document on Preimplantation Genetic Diagnosis (1999), para. 34.

[72] Human Fertilisation and Embryology Authority and Advisory Committee on Genetic Testing, Consultation Document on Preimplantation Genetic Diagnosis (1999), paras. 28, 35.

[73] Human Fertilisation and Embryology Authority and Human Genetics Committee, *Outcome of the Public Consultation on Preimplantation Genetic Diagnosis* (2001).

[74] Human Fertilisation and Embryology Authority and Human Genetics Committee, Outcome of the Public Consultation on Preimplantation Genetic Diagnosis (2001), para. 26.

a serious *genetic condition being present in the embryo*."[75] In contrast, termination for fetal abnormality required a "substantial" risk; moreover, that risk related to the likelihood that a child who was born would "suffer from such physical or mental abnormalities as to be seriously handicapped" rather than simply a genetic condition present in the fetus.[76] It is debatable whether the effect of these changes in the language is to allow PGD for more or fewer potential conditions than termination for fetal abnormality. In any case, the 2001 Outcome Report partly resolved its own problem of meaning by insisting that "a central role in the judgement about the significance of the risk and the seriousness of the condition should be given to the people seeking the treatment" and recommended accordingly (see Recommendation 13).[77]

By 2003 this shift in emphasis to the patient decision-making context had been firmly established. Although a 2003 Clinical Guidance Letter and the sixth edition of the HFEA Code of Practice both indicated that the use of PGD "is expected to be consistent with current practice in the use of (post-implantation) prenatal diagnosis (PND)"[78] – thus retaining the alignment with abortion practices – it is also clear in both documents that the concept of seriousness was now tied to the patient's perception of seriousness and the likely impact of the condition on the family. The 2003 Clinical Guidance Letter states, for instance, that "the decision to use PGD is expected to be made in consideration of the unique circumstances of those seeking treatment, rather than the fact that they carry a particular genetic condition," and there is an extensive list of information that must be provided

---

[75] Human Fertilisation and Embryology Authority and Human Genetics Committee, Outcome of the Public Consultation on Preimplantation Genetic Diagnosis (2001), para. 28.

[76] Abortion Act 1967 (UK), s 1(1)(d).

[77] Human Fertilisation and Embryology Authority and Human Genetics Committee, *Outcome of the Public Consultation on Preimplantation Genetic Diagnosis* (2001), para. 33.

[78] Human Fertilisation and Embryology Authority, "Guidance on Preimplantation Testing" (CH(03) 04), 15 May 2003, at3, and Human Fertilisation and Embryology Authority, *Code of Practice* (6th edition, 2003), 124.

to patients in order to ensure they are fully informed.[79] Most notable perhaps is the requirement that "where the family has no direct experience of the condition, the testimony of families and individuals about the full range of their experiences of living with the condition" should be provided to those seeking the treatment. Further, consistently with the recommendations in the 2001 Outcomes Report, the 2003 Clinical Guidance Letter and the sixth edition of the HFEA Code of Practice Guidance both indicate that the following should be considered when deciding the appropriateness of PGD:

(i) The view of the people seeking treatment of the condition to be avoided
(ii) Their previous reproductive experience
(iii) The likely degree of suffering associated with the condition
(iv) The availability of effective therapy, now and in the future
(v) The speed of degeneration in progressive disorders
(vi) The extent of any intellectual impairment
(vii) The extent of social support available and
(viii) The family circumstances of the people seeking treatment.[80]

These criteria have persisted through all subsequent iterations of the HFEA Code Guidance notes.[81] But, perhaps more important, the requirement of seriousness has now been thoroughly codified and included in the body of the amended HFE Act itself, not just in the HFEA Code

---

[79] Human Fertilisation and Embryology Authority, "Guidance on Preimplantation Testing" (CH(03) 04), 15 May 2003, at 3.

[80] It should be noted that over the years several other policy advice documents and guidance notes have been issued by the HFEA regarding preimplantation testing, for example, with respect to tissue typing (2004 http://www.hfea.gov.uk/2677.html) and with respect to processing applications to undertake PGD for a condition already previously authorized (2005http://www.hfea.gov.uk/1193.html). While we have tried to be comprehensive, we have primarily focused our analysis on those policy and regulatory documents that specifically relate to the question of a seriousness threshold.

[81] Human Fertilisation and Embryology Authority "Guidance on Preimplantation Testing"[CH (03) 04], 15 May 2003 at 4 and Human Fertilisation and Embryology Authority *Code of Practice* (6th edition, 2003), 124.

as was previously the case. Furthermore, the HFEA's PGD licensing committee has developed an explanatory memorandum for the committee to use when making determinations as to the seriousness of the relevant condition. This is discussed in detail in the following section.

2.4 The 2008 Amendments to the HFE Act

A crucially important amendment in 2008 was the addition of a specific provision concerning authorization for genetic testing using PGD. The rules are set out in Schedule 2 of the amended HFE Act. Testing is allowed where there is a "particular risk that the embryo may have any gene, chromosome or mitochondrial abnormality, [for the purpose of] establishing whether it has that abnormality or any other gene, chromosome or mitochondrion abnormality" (Schedule 2, para. 1ZA(1)(b)) *and* "there is a *significant* risk that a person with the abnormality will *have or develop a serious* physical or mental disability, a *serious* illness or any other *serious* medical condition" (Schedule 2, para. 1ZA(2)(b)). This language, not surprisingly, generated a great deal of debate.

By 2008, the discussion had become significantly more sophisticated. For instance, as we discussed in Chapter 3, some members argued, with respect to abortion, that to allow abortion for fetal abnormality after twenty-four weeks was discriminatory, since abortion of a non-disabled fetus is not available at this stage of gestation.[82] Though it was conservatives who argued this position, these members nevertheless referred to policy documents from the Disability Rights Commission and quoted the Universal Declaration of Human Rights. This argument was also used in the context of PGD in the House of Commons, with Geraldine Smith stating that "embryo selection could be classed as the ultimate form of disability discrimination."[83]

---

[82] *Hansard*, HL, vol. 696, col. 726, 19 November 2007 (Baroness Masham); *Hansard*, HL, vol. 697, col. 305, 12 December 2007 (Baroness Wilkins).

[83] *Hansard*, HC, vol. 475, col. 1099, 12 May 2008 (Geraldine Smith).

While these groups had modernized or refined their tactics by aligning themselves with disability rights activists, those who favored PGD in its broadest sense continued to use the rhetorical power of extreme disability to argue their case. In language echoing that used by Sir Charles Morrison some eighteen years earlier, Baroness Tonge claimed that it was possible to distinguish between "disabled human beings" and "grossly abnormal human beings; many of ... whom bear little resemblance to human beings."[84]

When the debate turned later to a discussion of the meaning of "serious," it was in the context of the new provisions explicitly authorizing the use of PGD to create so-called savior siblings. Savior siblings are children conceived specifically because a couple has an existing child with a serious medical condition that could be treated by umbilical cord blood stem cells, bone marrow, or other tissue from a matching donor. In some very limited cases parents have sought permission to use PGD to create embryos that are a tissue match for their existing ill child. The HFEA had already approved human leukocyte antigen (HLA) tissue typing in the limited circumstances where the embryo was already being selected to avoid the relevant condition.[85] It had, however, refused to approve the use of the technique when the embryo to be selected was not itself being chosen to avoid the condition.[86] In response to significant pressure from the public, professionals, and academics, the HFEA reviewed its 2001 interim policy in 2004 to allow HLA tissue typing in

---

[84] *Hansard*, HL, vol. 698, col. 528, 28 January 2008 (Baroness Tonge); Norman Lamb did attempt to respond directly to the disability rights claims by making a distinction between embryo selection, on the one hand, and discrimination against living individuals, on the other, but he made this point only very briefly. He said, "It must surely be preferable to avoid babies being born with very serious disabling conditions. That seems quite different from doing everything possible to avoid any discrimination against an individual who has a disability": *Hansard*, HC, vol. 475, col. 1087, 12 May 2008.

[85] Human Fertilisation and Embryology Authority, "Interim Policy on Preimplantation Tissue Typing" (November, 2001).

[86] S. Sheldon and S. Wilkinson, "Should Selecting Saviour Siblings Be Banned?" (2004) 30 *Journal of Medical Ethics* 533.

both circumstances.[87] The 2008 changes to the HFE Act formalized this by authorizing the use of PGD in such cases, provided that the existing child suffered from a "serious" medical condition. In both the House of Lords and the House of Commons, attempts had been made to introduce amendments that would qualify or define what "serious" meant in this context. In the House of Lords, one amendment sought to insert the words "and potentially life-threatening"[88] after "serious," while a second amendment would have introduced a subsection that defined "serious" as "life-threatening or impairing severely the quality of life of a person with the disability, illness or condition."[89]

Both amendments were discussed at length, and, although both were defeated, some interesting themes emerged in the discussion. For instance, even some of those who supported one or both of limiting amendments[90] indicated their support was contingent upon the wording being flexible enough to allow clinical judgment to prevail. For instance, Lord Winston stated, "this is a matter for decision at the time of the clinical involvement,"[91] and Lord Walton said, "The saving word in this amendment is 'potentially'. It does not indicate that the condition must be life-threatening, but it may be potentially life-threatening. That is sufficient qualification …"[92] Even Earl Howe, who proposed the second amendment, stated, in relation to the first amendment, "the reason I am not drawn to the noble and learned Lord's amendment is that there has to be some flexibility for the HFEA to decide upon each case on its individual merits."[93]

---

[87] Human Fertilisation and Embryology Authority, "Report: Preimplantation Tissue Typing" (2004): see http://www.hfea.gov.uk/docs/PolicyReview_Preimplantation TissueReport.pdf (accessed on 24 June 2011).

[88] *Hansard*, HL, vol. 698, col. 11, 21 January 2008 (Lord Lloyd).

[89] *Hansard*, HL, vol. 698, col. 23, 21 January 2008 (Earl Howe).

[90] Supporters included Lord Winston (one of the doctors who had been responsible for the Hammersmith PGD success in 1990) and Lord Walton of Detchant (the doctor who had given muscular dystrophy its name).

[91] *Hansard*, HL, vol. 698, col. 15, 21 January 2008 (Lord Winston).

[92] *Hansard*, HL, vol. 698, col. 15, 21 January 2008 (Lord Walton).

[93] *Hansard*, HL, vol. 698, col. 14, 21 January 2008 (Earl Howe).

So while it was agreed that creating a child to treat another child's relatively minor illness was not acceptable, there was considerable concern raised about how what was minor and what was serious was to be determined. For instance, Baroness O'Cathain drew the line at autism: "While I would never wish to minimize the significant difficulties that autism presents, it is not a condition for which the production of a tissue-typed child should be the solution,"[94] while Lord Alton reminded the House of the case of late abortion involving cleft palate to support his argument that the word "serious" was too broad and not adequately defined.[95]

Earl Howe continued to argue in favor of his definition (see previous discussion). He argued that such a definition would make it clear that "serious" meant serious for the child, not serious for the National Health Service (NHS) or for the parents. Baroness Finlay also argued in support of the amendment on the grounds that "what is serious to one person is not serious to another," and she used the example of the condition psoriasis to make her point. She stated that "[o]verwhelming psoriasis that affects the whole of a person's skin can be a devastating skin disease, but can amount to a few plaques on a person's elbows and knees." She proceeded to discuss recent advances that suggest the possibility of treatment using stem cells, noting that "you have to define how bad it is to warrant a saviour sibling" and arguing that that is why a qualifier such as "life-threatening" is necessary.[96]

In the end, as noted previously, the amendment to the "saviour sibling" provision failed, allowing it to pass through the Parliament unchanged. One reason for this seems to have been the force of arguments used by members such as Baroness Butler-Sloss, who provided a lawyer's perspective on the language. Her comments are particularly interesting because they suggest lawyers are more reluctant to

---

[94] *Hansard,* HL, vol. 698, col. 14, 21 January 2008 (Baroness O'Cathain).
[95] *Hansard,* HL, vol. 698, col. 15–16, 21 January 2008 (Lord Alton).
[96] *Hansard,* HL, vol. 698, col. 25–26, 21 January 2008 (Baroness Finlay).

state a definitive meaning for something such as "quality of life" than their medical colleagues. Speaking after Lord Winston had described with unqualified certainty the devastating nature of Lesch-Nyhan syndrome,[97] Butler-Sloss said:

> [i]t may be that doctors can come to understand what is meant by "quality of life" rather better than lawyers and judges. When I was a judge and I had to decide whether a very young baby or, at the other end of the spectrum, a severely ill elderly person, should be given treatment to keep them alive, I and the judges of the Court of Appeal … were … extremely careful not to use the phrase "quality of life"….What for some people would be a way of life that they absolutely could not endure would, for other people who had to endure it, be something worth living.[98]

Another area where the Parliament codified what had been the practice of the HFEA was in prohibiting patients from choosing to transfer an affected embryo – that is, selecting in favor of disability – where there were non-affected embryos that could be transferred. This was partly in response to U.S. reports that a desire to select in favor of deafness and dwarfism was one of the reasons why some individuals had undertaken PGD. But it was also in response to a clinical dilemma that had arisen: Some clinicians had been confronted with a woman who had produced otherwise viable embryos that were *all* affected by a particular condition such as the *BRCA* gene. Given that this is a late onset disease that may not even manifest and that both prophylactic and treatment options exist, questions were raised about whether patients should be denied the right to have such an embryo transferred. The response in the United Kingdom was quite complicated. Rather than prohibiting the choice in favor of an affected embryo altogether, the legislation stated:

[97] "They mutilate themselves; they bite their tongues off; they often have to have their teeth extracted to prevent that happening in case they die of the infection. It is the most brutally revolting disease, which I will not describe in detail because it really is that unpleasant": *Hansard*, HL, vol. 698, col. 27, 21 January 2008 (Lord Winston).

[98] *Hansard*, HL, vol. 698, col. 27, 21 January 2008 (Baroness Butler-Sloss).

13(9) Persons or embryos that are known to have a gene, chromosome or mitochondrion abnormality involving a significant risk that a person with the abnormality will have or develop –

    (a) a serious physical or mental disability,
    (b) a serious illness, or
    (c) any other serious medical condition,

must not be preferred to those that are not known to have such an abnormality.

Further, section 13(10) provided:

13(10) Embryos that are known to be of a particular sex and to carry a particular risk, compared with embryos of that sex in general, that any resulting child will have or develop –

    (a) a gender-related serious physical or mental disability,
    (b) a gender-related serious illness, or
    (c) any other gender-related serious medical condition,

must not be preferred to those that are not known to carry such a risk.

The HFEA Code (eighth edition)[99] makes it clear that if an unaffected embryo exists, it must be implanted first. But where there is no such embryo, paragraphs 10.17 and 10.18 of the code explain the process to be undertaken as follows:

10.17:The use of an embryo known to have an abnormality ... should be subject to consideration of the welfare of any resulting child and should normally have approval from a clinical ethics committee.

10.18: If a centre decides that it is appropriate to provide treatment services to a woman using an embryo known to have an abnormality as described above, it should document the reason for the use of that embryo.

NOTE: An example of an embryo not suitable for transfer in this context is one that has no realistic prospect of resulting in a live birth.

---

[99] See under "Embryo Testing and Sex Selection": http://www.hfea.gov.uk/496.html (accessed on 16 June 2011).

These provisions were clearly the result of some rather careful thinking. First, unlike in a number of other jurisdictions with similar provisions,[100] a seriousness threshold has been included. This makes possible the selection of an embryo affected by a genetic abnormality that would lead to a non-serious disability or illness. The feminist legal scholar Marie Fox has argued that the passing of the savior siblings provision alongside the express prevention of preferential parental selection of embryos known to have an abnormality suggests that much turned on "a narrow medical determination of the welfare of existing or potential children, which is arguably eugenicist."[101] She goes on to state, "Other choices are deemed frivolous by comparison, with the legislators keen to distance themselves from any notion of reproductive freedom to 'design babies' through screening and embryo selection."[102] And of course we are still left with the same question – what is a serious or severe disability? Nevertheless, the insertion of the new provisions provides a legislative basis for the HFEA to invite debate on these points.

It is possible, therefore, to discern the impact of eighteen years of negotiated understandings of disability. In these latest debates the question was not whether to regulate this technology but, rather, whether a law could be drafted that distinguished clearly between uses of the technology that were acceptable and those that were not. While the intervention of Baroness Butler-Sloss seems to have prevailed, it remained unclear after the debates what limits the word "serious" might impose. The HFEA Code and Guidance suggests that the patient autonomy focus has continued to prevail. More importantly, unlike in the abortion context, clinical judgment about what conditions are "serious" continues to be mediated through the

---

[100] See our later discussion in this chapter.
[101] M. Fox, "The Human Fertilisation and Embryology Act 2008: Tinkering at the Margins" (2009) 17 *Feminist Legal Studies* 333–44 at 339.
[102] M. Fox, "The Human Fertilisation and Embryology Act 2008: Tinkering at the Margins" (2009) 17 *Feminist Legal Studies* 333–44 at 339.

HFEA. Indeed, the codification of the "seriousness" requirement had the effect of making more official the HFEA's mediating role. Interestingly, however, in 2010 the Licence Committee of the Human Fertilisation and Embryology Authority produced an explanatory memorandum on PGD that was intended to "set out its approach to the statutory criteria of 'risk' and 'seriousness' which it is required to assess when considering applications to undertake PGD."[103] This note provides some guidance for committee members who might otherwise struggle with the language of seriousness and risk as it appears in the HFE Act. Most notably it distinguishes between a "particular risk," which is described as "an objectively measurable criterion," and a "significant risk," which refers to the penetrance of a condition and may be full or incomplete. Perhaps most important for our purposes, however, is the detailed account of factors that must be considered when assessing the seriousness of the disability, illness, or condition. Considerations taken into account include age of onset, symptoms of the disease, whether the condition is treatable, what type of treatment is available, the effect of the condition on quality of life, and the variability of the symptoms. The documents describe these in the following terms:

5.3 When assessing the seriousness of the disability, illness or condition, the Licence Committee will take into account the following factors:

    a) Age of onset: Is the condition congenital or does it manifest later in life? If it does manifest later, at what stage (childhood, early adulthood, later)?

    b) Symptoms of the disease.

What are the symptoms of the condition? Is the condition potentially fatal, life threatening or life limiting?

---

[103] Human Fertilisation and Embryology Authority, "PGD Explanatory Note for Licence Committee" (28 October 2010), available at http://www.hfea.gov.uk/docs/2010–10–28_Licence_Committee_PGD_Explanatory_note.PDF (accessed 16 November 2011).

c) Whether the condition is treatable

d) What type of treatment is available for those conditions that can be treated

What is the extent of the treatment available? How invasive is the treatment or likely treatment?

e) Effect of the condition on quality of life

This will include any evidence about the speed of degeneration in progressive disorders and the extent of any physical and /or intellectual impairment.

f) Variability of symptoms

Symptoms associated with the same condition can vary from family to family (and from individual to individual), and can range from the mild to the severe. Where the condition has variable symptoms, the Licence Committee will take account of:

what the range of variability is; and
whether the range suggests that some forms of the condition are so mild that they might not meet the 'serious' test.[104]

In addition, importantly, Section 5.4 of the document states that "where a condition has a range of penetrance … the Licence Committee will base its decision on the highest penetrance figure," and 5.5 states that "where a condition has variable symptoms, the Licence Committee will base its determination of how serious the disability, illness or condition is, on the worst possible symptoms." The effect of this is to take a "worst case scenario" approach to risk rather than weighing up statistical likelihood.

Unlike the 8th Code of Practice Guidance on factors to be taken into account when determining seriousness, which was discussed earlier, the Explanatory Memorandum does not mention familial context and patient perspectives as relevant factors. Nevertheless, we

[104] Human Fertilisation and Embryology Authority, "PGD Explanatory Note for Licence Committee" (28 October 2010), available at http://www.hfea. gov.uk/docs/2010–10–28_Licence_Committee_PGD_Explanatory_note.PDF, 2–3 (accessed 16 November 2011).

would still argue that the use of these criteria by the license committee recognizes that serious disability is a shifting normative ideal that must be measured contextually and temporally. For example, taking just one of the criteria that the committee considers – the treatability of the condition – we can see that as treatment technologies develop, some conditions that were once considered serious may no longer fit that typology. Thus it is difficult to see, as we have argued before, how determinations of seriousness in the context of disability could be other than plural and shifting. Treatment is just one factor that can change. Even seemingly objective criteria like age of onset will have to change as life expectancy increases. The sociocultural climate of normative ideals can also shift radically over time, changing the way we perceive and tolerate different bodily possibilities. The fact that legislatures and regulatory bodies continue to use the language of seriousness while resisting calls to provide clear definitive statements about its meaning suggests, as we will go on to show, that parliaments can and do sometimes view ambiguity constructively. Indeed, it is arguable that by not legislatively defining seriousness, they deliberately leave a space for what we might describe as a productive ambivalence.

In a number of the Australian state legislatures, for instance, there have been similar debates about the meaning of "seriousness." We now turn our attention to those debates. As will be seen, it is interesting that, unlike in the United Kingdom, intense regulatory oversight in these Australian jurisdictions has been replaced more recently by more facilitative rather than prescriptive regulation under which clinics have gained greater discretion.

3 AUSTRALIA

As noted at the outset, Australia was not far behind the United Kingdom either in undertaking PGD or in developing regulations to facilitate its use. While there is some disagreement about the precise order of events, it seems clear that one of the first successful births after PGD biopsy occurred in Australia a few years after the Hammersmith success. Researchers at the University of Adelaide Department of Obstetrics and Gynaecology, acting in conjunction with the Reproductive Medicine Unit at the Queen Elizabeth Hospital in South Australia, claim to have been the first to offer PGD in Australia in 1993 and to have been responsible for the first birth from PGD in Australia (about the sixth in the world) in 1995.[105] However, Monash IVF in Victoria claims the first Australian birth of an embryo that had undergone PGD using the fluorescence in situ hybridization (FISH) method.[106] While this competition might seem unimportant some fifteen years and one thousand plus PGD babies later,[107] we can track a clear legislative correlation between jurisdictions that were the front-runners in using the technology and those that were the first to regulate the practice supportively. This correlation supports our earlier claim that disability avoidance technologies tend to drive legislative reform and facilitate the introduction of highly experimental and innovative biotechnologies. In Australia, the acceptance of these technologies has reached a new peak as jurisdictions that previously maintained a high level of scrutiny over the practice of PGD no longer do so.

3.1 Western Australia (1991)

As noted earlier, the Australian National Health and Medical Research Council (NHMRC) had provided federal guidelines on "Human Experimentation" in the context of IVF and embryo transfer as early as

---

[105] Queen Elizabeth Hospital press release, "IVF Researchers Win Awards at International IVF Congress" May 1999, at www.tqeh.sa.gov.au/repositories/files/IVF%20Researchers%20win.doc (accessed on 16 June 2011).

[106] See http://www.monashivf.edu.au/site/DefaultSite/filesystem/documents/Preimplantation%20Genetic%20Diagnosis.pdf (accessed on 16 June 2011).

[107] See http://www.pgdis.org/history.html (accessed on 16 June 2011).

1982,[108] and the Victorian state government had introduced legislation regulating IVF and assisted reproduction in 1984.[109] However, the first Australian jurisdiction to refer explicitly to diagnostic testing of embryos was Western Australia (WA), which introduced its legislation at almost the same time as the UK legislation was enacted. As far as we can ascertain, no PGD had been trialed in Western Australia at that time, and this may explain why, by virtue of section 14(2) of the Western Australian Human Reproductive Technology Act (1991) (HRT Act), PGD was effectively prohibited.[110] The section provided that there could be no approval of

[108] NHMRC, "Statement on Human Experimentation and Supplementary Notes 1982: Supplementary Note 4 – In Vitro Fertilisation and Embryo Transfer" (February 1984) 28(1) *Australasian Radiology* 65. As noted earlier (footnote 15), those performing experimental procedures using PGD would have been guided by the fifth "particular matter."

[109] Infertility (Medical Procedures) Act 1984 (Vic). Notably, this Act did allow access to IVF or the use of donor gametes where an independent medical practitioner was "satisfied that it is reasonably established that if the woman were to become pregnant" from either her or her husband's gametes "an undesirable hereditary disorder may be transmitted to a child born as the result of the pregnancy."

[110] Records of the number of births from IVF using PGD in Australia seem to start from about 2002. See http://www.preru.unsw.edu.au/PRERUWeb.nsf/page/Assi sted+Reproduction+Technology+ and, specifically, J. Bryant, E. Sullivan, and J. Dean, "Assisted Reproductive Technology in Australia and New Zealand 2002: Supplement," (2004) AIHW, Sydney, 15; A. Wates, J. Dean, and E. Sullivan, "Supplement to Assisted Reproductive Technology in Australia and New Zealand 2003," (2006) AIHW National Perinatal Statistics Unit, Sydney, 18; Y. Wang, J. Dean, N. Grayson, and E. Sullivan, "Assisted Reproductive Technology in Australia and New Zealand, 2004" (2006) AIHW National Perinatal Statistics Unit, Sydney 10; Y. Wang, J. Dean, and E. Sullivan, "Assisted Reproductive Technology in Australia and New Zealand 2005," (2007) AIHW National Perinatal Statistics Unit, Sydney 8–9; Y. Wang, J. Dean, T. Badgery-Parker, E. Sullivan, "Assisted Reproductive Technology in Australia and New Zealand 2006" (2008) AIHW National Perinatal Statistics Unit, 27; Y. Wang, G. Chambers, E. Sullivan, and M. Dieng, "Assisted Reproductive Technology in Australia and New Zealand 2007 Supplement Tables" (2009) AIHW National Perinatal Statistics Unit, 8; Y. Wang, G. Chambers, E. Sullivan, and M. Dieng, "Assisted Reproductive Technology in Australia and New Zealand 2008" (2010) AIHW National Perinatal Statistics Unit, 4.

any research being conducted, or any diagnostic procedure to be carried out upon or with an egg in the process of fertilisation, or any embryo, unless the Council is satisfied – (a) that the proposed research or procedure is intended to be therapeutic for that egg or embryo and (b) that existing scientific and medical knowledge indicates that no detrimental effect on the well-being of any egg in the process of fertilisation or any embryo is likely to therefore occur.

Since PGD would not be therapeutic for the embryo carrying the genetic defect (but could in fact lead to its destruction), this was interpreted as prohibiting PGD.

There was some controversy surrounding the interpretation of this section, which arose because it provided that a "therapeutic" procedure was permissible. This was highlighted in 1999 when the WA government's Select Committee on Human Reproduction filed its final report.[111] That report refers to a submission made by Professor Cummins, who argued that the intended effect of the amendment that ultimately became the final section 14 (2) was not to prohibit PGD but, rather, to allow for genetic diagnosis so long as it was "non-harmful."[112] At the time the legislation was passed, there was still some concern about the safety of the embryos being tested; accordingly, it was argued that by moving this amendment, the minister (Mr. Wilson) had only intended to prohibit PGD until it was proved safe. There is some textual support in the parliamentary debates for Professor Cummins's view. The minister said, for instance, that "[t]he Act recognizes a role for IVF in the fight against genetic disease; it will allow the use of IVF for the benefit of couples whose children are likely to be affected by genetic disease. Those couples would benefit from ... in future, when preimplantation diagnosis of embryos is safe and acceptable under the law ... th[is] procedure also."[113] However, a careful reading of the

---

[111] Legislative Assembly of Western Australia, "Select Committee on the Human Reproductive Technology Act 1991 Report" (1999).

[112] Legislative Assembly of Western Australia "Select Committee on the Human Reproductive Technology Act 1991 Report" (1999), 92.

[113] *Hansard*, Legislative Assembly, 5 June 1991, 2741 (Mr. Wilson).

debates reveals that the minister was drawing a distinction between what he called "therapeutic specific" and "therapeutic general." The former, he defined as treatments directed at the "particular egg or embryo,"[114] while the latter referred to treatments directed at embryos in general. If "therapeutic" meant "therapeutic general," then procedures that involved "the loss of present embryos in order to benefit future embryos"[115] would have been lawful. However, the minister made it clear that "therapeutic" meant "therapeutic specific"; for instance, he stated that "[a]ll the other words included in my amendment make it quite clear that it is directed to the wellbeing and enhancing the life prospects of a particular egg or embryo."[116]

Many members of the WA Parliament were aware of both PGD and its potential benefits. However, contrary to what had happened in the UK Parliament, the majority of the WA Parliament was unconvinced that PGD was safe or that it would be beneficial. On the whole, those who argued in favor of PGD were not as emotive or detailed in their description of disability as their British counterparts had been. It may have been partly for this reason that their arguments had little impact on their colleagues. For instance, Mr. Wiese, perhaps the strongest advocate of more flexible laws enabling a broader range of embryo research, made his case in the following terms:

> As a result of using techniques associated with IVF and diagnostic techniques on embryos the medical profession is now able to identify embryos carrying diseases and *major* abnormalities. Therefore,

---

[114] *Hansard,* Legislative Assembly, 11 June 1991, 2992 (Mr. Wilson).

[115] *Hansard,* Legislative Assembly, 11 June 1991, 2993 (Mr. Wilson).

[116] *Hansard,* Legislative Assembly, 11 June 1991, 2992 (Mr. Wilson). The Select Committee had also received a Crown Solicitor's Office opinion, which confirmed that "the effect of section 14(2)(a) is to rule out the application of any diagnostic procedures including one that would not directly harm the embryo, if it was not 'intended to be therapeutic for that egg or embryo'": Legislative Assembly of Western Australia, "Select Committee on the Human Reproductive Technology Act 1991 Report" (1999), 93.

they are able to use the techniques related to IVF to prevent the implantation of embryos already carrying *dreadful* diseases which would if allowed to be implanted and reach maturity eventually result in the woman carrying that embryo giving birth to a child carrying some sort of *dreadful* genetic disease associated with those genes that carry diseases. [our emphasis][117]

On the other hand, arguments against embryo research highlighted the potential for discrimination against people with disabilities and portrayed as exaggerated their opponents' accounts of the impact of disability. For example, Mr. Wilson said that "genetic disease does not mean death.... Accepting that parents will have disabled children, we must allow for that position to be adopted by parents – unless we adopt an attitude which is totally discriminatory towards disabilities."[118]

In the Legislative Council, the Honorable P. G. Pendal compared his previous discomfort with disability with his current, more circumspect views:

One of my notes shows that [Father Walter Black, an ethicist from the L. J. Goody Bioethics Centre] said no human embryo should be denied the opportunity to develop merely because of a disability. I know that many Members had a few problems with that approach because it raised the question of what to do if one discovered an embryo had a terrible disability. I raise this matter not only because the principle is worth thinking about but also because it reminds me that in a world full of perfect people one would probably have no need for virtues such as compassion.[119]

In response, the Honorable Cheryl Davenport used rather more moderate language than that used in the UK debates, stating, "I believe that the pressure on parents and family members who must cope with children who have genetic diseases such as Down's syndrome, cystic

[117] *Hansard*, Legislative Assembly, 14 May 1991 (Mr. Wiese), 1827.
[118] *Hansard*, Legislative Assembly, 5 June 1991 (Mr. Wilson) 2741.
[119] *Hansard*, Legislative Council, 21 August 1991 (Hon P.G. Pendal), 3620.

fibrosis, muscular dystrophy and the like could be eliminated at an early stage by such a procedure."[120]

We focus on the language in these debates so as to illustrate that the way disability is discussed can shape the content of laws in this area. Emotive and personal narratives of horrendous hardship and struggle, such as those that we have noted in the UK debates, may capture the imagination of parliamentarians and influence them to permit technologies such as PGD. Although it is difficult to determine the extent to which the absence of this language in the WA debates influenced parliamentarians' votes, what is clear is that Parliament was not persuaded to allow PGD. It was not until 2004, as we will see later, that the legislation was amended to legalize PGD.

3.2 Victorian Developments (1995–2003)

Unlike WA, Victoria was a leader in the use of PGD technology. In 1995 new legislation introduced a system of regulatory oversight of PGD technologies.[121] However, as we will see, the system was designed so that significant regulatory responsibility was left with the medical profession.

Section 8(3)(b) of the Infertility Treatment Act(1995) (the IT Act) authorized a "treatment procedure" if "a doctor who has specialist qualifications in human genetics" was satisfied "that if the woman became pregnant from an oocyte produced by her and sperm

---

[120] *Hansard*, Legislative Council, 21 August 1991 (Hon Cheryl Davenport), 3622.

[121] Prior to the 1995 legislation, ART in Victoria had been governed by the Infertility (Medical Procedures) Act 1984. This legislation did not address diagnostic procedures such as PGD but did provide that donor sperm and/or eggs could only be used during IVF if a medical practitioner was satisfied that it was "reasonably established" that if these were not used, the IVF patient might transmit to her child "an undesirable hereditary disorder": see Infertility (Medical Procedures) Act 1984 (repealed), ss 11–13.

produced by her husband, a *genetic abnormality or a disease* might be transmitted to a person born as a result of the pregnancy" [our emphasis]. While the interpretation of "genetic abnormality" fell to a doctor with specialist qualifications in human genetics and there was no seriousness threshold, s 106(1) of the IT Act potentially placed limits on the exercise of that judgment. This section gave the newly established Infertility Treatment Authority (ITA) the capacity to impose conditions or restrictions on any license that it granted or renewed; these conditions could relate to "the manner in which diagnostic services related to infertility or treatments regulated by this Act for genetic abnormality or disease may be performed." Accordingly, the ITA developed a policy concerning PGD, which was adopted in 2003 and subsequently set up a system of lists.[122] Conditions requiring prior approval on a case-by-case basis for PGD were placed in List C. List C included:

- Autosomal recessive conditions where it was proposed to identify and select against carrier embryos, in addition to testing for the condition;
- Exclusion testing where a person is at risk of an autosomal dominant condition but does not wish to undertake direct testing; and
- Conditions where there is a higher instance in one sex, but there is inconclusive genetic evidence about the transmission of that condition (in 2008/2009 individual cases were presented to the authority, "complete with clinical evidence, family history, assessment by a medical geneticist, and peer-reviewed evidence to support the applications." Approvals were given for sex selection in these circumstances for autism – five cases, *BRCA*, hemophilia

---

[122] Infertility Treatment Authority, "Genetic Testing and the Requirements of the Infertility Treatment Act 1995: Policy in Relation to the use of Preimplantation Genetic Diagnosis" (2003) reviewed 2009 [no longer available electronically, on file with the authors].

A, paracentric inversion on X-chromosome, X-linked agamma-globulinemia (XLA), X-linked ichthyosis (steroid sulfatase deficiency), X-linked severe combined immunodeficiency disease (*IL2RG* gene)).[123]

Conditions that required no prior approval were set out in Lists A and B. List A included conditions that lead to pregnancy failure and chromosomal abnormalities. List B included sex-related disorders and single gene disorders.

In the debates that led to the passage of the IT Act, there was some objection to the non-inclusion of a specific seriousness threshold. For instance, Mr. Thwaites quoted a prominent Catholic bioethicist, Nicholas Tonti-Filippini, who had described the formulation in the IT Act in the following terms: "Every pregnancy might result in a child with a genetic abnormality or disease ... there is no such thing as 'genetic normality.' Each person is genetically unique and hence in some way 'abnormal.'"[124]

On the face of it, it is hard to deny Tonti-Filippini's point about the normality of abnormality. Genetic difference is of course entirely normal. However, the authors of the legislation considered "abnormality" to be synonymous with a "defect," "malformation," or "malfunction" rather than merely an anomaly or deviation. This linguistic interrogation is important. If we consider that difference is not only acceptable but also at some level normal, then it becomes even more important to find a way to ensure that one person's, or one expert group's, idea of what is normal and good and healthy is not imposed on those who do not share that view. These are complex negotiations, and the many legislative and quasi-legislative responses we are highlighting in this chapter demonstrate the varied ways in which law might respond to this task. In Victoria, while the ITA obviously felt it was necessary to

---

[123] Infertility Treatment Authority, "Annual Report 2009" s 08 at 14: see http://varta.org.au/annual reports/w1/i1003573/ (accessed on 24 June 2011).

[124] *Hansard*, Legislative Assembly, 1 June 1995, 2106–2107.

offer guidance about the provision of PGD, in practice the list and the approvals were heavily contingent upon clinical and scientific advice.

There is an interesting difference, too, between the way PGD was authorized for the purpose of selecting against embryos with abnormalities, the rules regarding PGD for HLA tissue typing to select a savior sibling and rules regarding choosing in favor of a disability. The ITA described its approach to the rules regarding PGD to select against a disability in its "Policy in Relation to the Use of Preimplantation Genetic Diagnosis" as follows:

> The authority's policy on PGD is designed to
>
> • Facilitate the use of PGD for direct testing to prevent the transmission of severe single gene disorders or sex-linked genetic diseases.[125]

Despite this they proceed to note that

> The provisions of sections 8 (3) (b) and 50 (2) do not specify what is considered to be "a genetic abnormality or a disease." Legal advice indicates that Parliament intended the words to receive a broad, purposive interpretation. Confirmation by a doctor with specialist qualifications in human genetics satisfies the condition for admission. Such a person will make each decision in the context of the medical expertise available to them. The responsibility is entrusted to the specialist with qualifications in human genetics, and such a specialist would be required to document the clinical grounds upon which admission to treatment is based. The Act therefore imposes the responsibility for gate-keeping on the doctor with specialist qualifications in human genetics.[126]

---

[125] Infertility Treatment Authority, "Genetic Testing and the Requirements of the Infertility Treatment Act 1995: Policy in Relation to the Use of Pre-implantation Genetic Diagnosis (PGD)" (2009) (2).

[126] Infertility Treatment Authority, "Genetic Testing and the Requirements of the Infertility Treatment Act 1995: Policy in Relation to the Use of Pre-implantation Genetic Diagnosis" (PGD) (2009) (4).

We interviewed Victorian regulators who were asked about the process undertaken by the ITA for approving a particular condition for PGD testing.[127] R5 stated:

> Really there were two elements to it. One perspective is that it was really the treating clinician and the advice from the clinical geneticist that performed a gate-keeping role in relation to the use of PGD... The other aspects of it were the health and welfare of the child.

R5 gave an example of requests to sex select girls in families that had a history of autism in the boy children, stating:

> For a while the Authority required an individual application in relation to genetic testing using sex selection to implant embryos that were female rather than male to reduce the risk of autism.... As time went on, the Authority decided to monitor the use of autism, rather than require an application, as more information came to light, and the use of PGD to eliminate, or to minimise the risk of autism became more common.... And so it was really in situations where genetic inheritance wasn't as clear or it was a novel use that an application was required.

When questioned further about whether the ITA considered the question of whether "those particular disorders" ought "to be tested for in the first place," R5 replied:

> We didn't get into degree of penetrance, as the regulator in New Zealand did in relation to the use of PGD but certainly considered the seriousness of the disease, whether it could be treated, whether the onset was in childhood or adulthood, what the prognosis was for the health and welfare of the child and the child as it became an adult.

---

[127] As noted in the introduction due to the small number of participants we offer these excerpts as anecdotal accounts only as they offer individual insights not otherwise accessible. Clinicians are represented by a *C* and regulators by an *R*.

R5 also indicated that, on some occasions, expert scientific and clinical advice would be sought; if there was still uncertainty, the matter would sometimes be put before a "properly constituted Ethics Committee." As there must be two laypeople (a woman and a man), a lawyer, and a minister of religion or appropriate equivalent on all Australian Ethics Committees,[128] this approach seems to have created an opportunity for broader input from those without clinical or scientific backgrounds. The ITA also had a medical and scientific representative on the panel of the licensing committee to provide technical assistance with questions around inheritance and the nature of the condition in question. R5 did state that "for the most part the Authority endorsed the decisions of the clinical geneticist and the clinician." Thus, under this scheme there was a sense in which the regulation of PGD operated in a "consultative manner, but in the best interests of the child to be born."

However, in the case of PGD for HLA tissue typing to select an embryo to save a sibling, the ITA's approach was more restrictive. The condition to be treated was required to be "severe or life threatening," and approval for the procedure had to be obtained from an Ethics Committee at the institution where the procedure was to be undertaken."[129] Of course, this contrasts with the UK Parliament's decision to avoid such qualifying language as "life-threatening"[130] because of the impossibility of defining that term. The reason for imposing a seriousness threshold in this instance, but not in the instance of "ordinary" PGD, was that here the interests of the child to be born were treated as being paramount. This procedure does not involve deselection of an affected embryo but rather selection of a tissue matched embryo *that will come to exist as a child.* Although the aim will usually be to harvest cord blood stem cells, some have suggested

---

[128] National Health and Medical Research Centre, "National Statement on Ethical Conduct in Human Research" (2007), 5.1.30.

[129] Infertility Treatment Authority, "Tissue Typing in Conjunction with Preimplantation Genetic Diagnosis" (January 2007, rev. ed.), 2.2.

[130] see earlier discussion in this section.

that, if not enough stem cells are harvested from the cord blood, the child might also be used later as a bone marrow donor. And while most clinicians would not allow such a child to become a solid organ donor for the sick sibling, there have been suggestions that this might eventually occur and that, in such a case, undue pressure might be placed on a child who had been created precisely for that purpose.[131] R5 indicated that the ITA did find the question of HLA matching more complex and therefore felt that the involvement of an Ethics Committee was appropriate.

The ITA PGD policy also addressed the question of whether it was permissible to transfer into the uterus an embryo that had been identified as carrying an abnormality. Again, the ITA took a strict approach, stating:

> Some prohibitions (like that on social sex selection) are contained in the statute. Others, like the prohibition on using PGD to select *for* disability, were not envisaged by the Victorian Parliament as legitimate uses of PGD, and are incompatible with the first Guiding Principle of the Act: that the welfare and interests of the child to be born are paramount.[132]

Further, section 4.3 of the policy provided that "[t]he use of PGD to select in favour of genetic disease or abnormality is prohibited by the Authority as inconsistent with the first guiding principle of the Act (section 5)."[133]

Thus, in Victoria there has never been a seriousness threshold in the case of selecting in favor of a disability. This contrasts with the most

---

[131] For a discussion of these and opposing views see S. Sheldon and S. Wilkinson, "Should Selecting Saviour Siblings Be Banned?" (2004) 30 *Journal of Medical Ethics* 533.

[132] Infertility Treatment Authority, "Genetic Testing and the Requirements of the *Infertility Treatment Act 1995*: Policy in Relation to the Use of Preimplantation Genetic Diagnosis (PGD)" (2002)(reviewed 2009), s 3 (2).

[133] Infertility Treatment Authority, "Genetic Testing and the Requirements of the *Infertility Treatment Act 1995*: Policy in Relation to the Use of Preimplantation Genetic Diagnosis (PGD)" (2002)(reviewed 2009), s 4.3(c) (4).

recent amendments to the UK provisions, which we discussed earlier. As we saw, in the United Kingdom choosing to transfer an affected embryo is only prohibited where a seriousness threshold has been met and, even then, only if there are other non-affected embryos available for transfer. In Victoria, however, it has to be presumed that an embryo identified as having *any identified* genetic disease or abnormality would be precluded from transfer.

R5 did suggest that a seriousness threshold, whether for selecting against or selecting in favor, was probably not necessary at the present time though it was possible as the technology developed that this would need to be revisited. Their reasoning was that "PGD is such an intrusive element of IVF treatment. It's so expensive that it's not going to be used frivolously."

There does seem to be an inconsistent approach to the role of the doctor as gatekeeper in both the IT Act and the ITA PGD policy. As we have seen, in some cases regulatory limits were imposed. For instance, s 50 of the IT Act prohibited non-medical sex selection,[134] and the ITA PGD policy imposed more stringent limits on some practices than others. This suggests that there was a felt need to limit clinical discretion. Yet, at the same time, regulators not only delegated decision-making power to the clinicians but often called on them as expert advisers in order to inform their own decision making. This means that clinicians have extraordinary influence over the definitions of what is and is not an abnormality/condition that is serious enough to warrant intervention. In Chapter 5 we examine just how clinicians interpret this role. But the following questions remain: (a) Should more detailed guidelines be provided to clinicians? and (b) if so, who should make those guidelines? We continue our exploration of the variety of initial legislative responses to PGD by viewing how these decisions were first managed in the state of South Australia.

[134] Infertility Treatment Act 1995 (Vic), s 50(2).

3.3 South Australia (1988–2004)

Between 1988 and September 2010, the Reproductive Technology (Clinical Practices) Act 1988 (RTCPA Act) regulated the provision of ART in South Australia. Enacted at a time when IVF was in its infancy, the RTCPA Act provided for the licensing of persons before they could carry out an artificial fertilization procedure (s 13(1)) and stated that any such license would be subject to a condition preventing the application of artificial fertilization procedures "except for the benefit of married couples in the following circumstances – … (ii) there appears to be a risk that a genetic defect would be transmitted to a child conceived naturally" (s 13(3)(b)(ii)).

The RTCPA Act also created the SA Council on Reproductive Technology (SACRT) (s 5). Among its other functions, SACRT was to formulate, and keep under review, a code of ethical practice to govern the use of artificial fertilization procedures (s 10(1)(a)(i)). In fulfillment of this requirement, in the early 1990s, SARCT developed the Code of Ethical Clinical Practice. The code was established as a regulation under the Act in 1995 (the Reproductive Technology (Code of Ethical Clinical Practice) Regulations 1995). It provided, in clause 11(1)(b)(i)(B), that where infertility treatment was sought to avoid a genetic disease the licensee must be furnished with a letter of referral signed by a medical practitioner, stating that "in his or her opinion, there is a risk that a genetic defect would be transmitted to any child conceived naturally by the wife and specifying the nature of that defect."

Section 13(3)(b)(ii) and cl 11(1)(b)(i)(B) had the effect of permitting PGD in South Australia. However, as stated by SACRT in its Memorandum 12, it was not clear what a "genetic defect" meant: "[w]hile the term may have some colloquial currency, it has no biological or medical meaning. The term is not defined in the Act, nor has the Council defined the term for inclusion in the Code of Ethical

Practice."[135] SACRT advised that, in interpreting s 13(3)(b)(ii), the term "genetic defect"

> is to be taken to refer to a single gene or chromosome disorder the likely effect of which is to seriously impair a person who inherits the disorder from one or both parents.[136]

It stated that it was "convinced" that to define "genetic condition" in this way was "consistent with the intention of the Act."[137] Significantly for our purposes, by providing for a seriousness threshold in Memorandum 12, SACRT imposed tighter regulation of PGD than had existed before.[138] Once again, however, there was little guidance concerning what "seriously" meant.

In interviews that we conducted with members and former members of SACRT and some members of the SA Department of Health, we explored what "seriously" did mean. One member, R1, considered that it was for those using the memorandum to determine what was meant by the word "seriously":

> And in fact, the role of the Council in South Australia is really not even to judge that. So it's kind of like if the Health Commission uses

[135] SARCT, "Memorandum 12 to Reproductive Medicine Units Re. Preimplantation Genetic Diagnosis (PGD) – Definition of "A Genetic Defect" for the Purpose of Determining Eligibility for Treatment" (reproduced in the SACRT Annual Report 2004, 39).

[136] SARCT, "Memorandum 12 to Reproductive Medicine Units Re. Preimplantation Genetic Diagnosis (PGD) – Definition of "A Genetic Defect" for the Purpose of Determining Eligibility for Treatment" (reproduced in the SACRT Annual Report 2004, 39).

[137] SARCT, "Memorandum 12 to Reproductive Medicine Units Re. Preimplantation Genetic Diagnosis (PGD) – Definition of "A Genetic Defect" for the Purpose of Determining Eligibility for Treatment" (reproduced in the SACRT Annual Report 2004, 39).

[138] It is worth noting that this tightening of regulation by SACRT did not extend to addressing the questions of HLA tissue typing and selecting for a disability, as the ITA did in Victoria.

that Memorandum or the clinics use the Memorandum and they interpret what that seriousness might mean.

R2, remarked that "seriously" was "meant to exclude something like sex, unless sex was relevant to an illness." When asked whether there was any further discussion about using the term "seriously" to ensure that PGD could not be used to prevent the transmission of minor disabilities, and, if so, what "minor" disabilities were understood to be, the regulator replied that it was assumed "that clinicians would have a fairly clear idea of the kind of thing. It was meant to, I suppose, exclude sort of trivial and arbitrary stuff. But again those words are value-laden words and they are open to interpretation."

However, in discussion with R4 it emerged that after the RTCPA Act had been passed there were concerns that there was no definition of what was a genetic defect. R4 noted that an expert clinician was consulted, who advised SACRT concerning both PGD and the kinds of conditions that might be detected. It was after those discussions that Memorandum 12 was drafted. But when attempting to explain what the word "seriously" was intended to mean, this regulator's comments were consistent with those made by the other interviewees. R4 stated: "And then the Council decided it had to be a serious defect, not just blue eyes" and later "the people who are dealing with those patients with their genetic history know what serious means ... so far as they were concerned, they didn't need to define serious, because the discussion about what was a serious genetic defect is a long-standing one that had been held in the genetics environment. And [the Clinician] managed to convince them – as he would – that this was a well-understood term and it was dependent upon a family, their situation and all those other factors. It was a social construct for each individual family, and not one that you should have a bunch of strangers laying down the law on."

When R4 was asked whether "the threshold of seriousness was put in place to ward off trivial things like eye colour, but not really considering different levels of disability" the response was: "No, because they were really saying the level of disability was what that family defined as serious. And because that was the philosophy of the genetics unit who was doing the testing, it became the accepted philosophy of the Council."

Two themes arise for us from these regulator comments. The first is a familiar theme, the negotiation between a legal limit and medical knowledge. In this instance, we assume on the basis of this small sample that SACRT felt that the clinical geneticists were best placed to determine the meaning of seriousness. Thus despite being sufficiently proactive to feel the need to introduce the threshold, they nevertheless felt that the clinicians did not need further guidance in understanding that threshold. It is clear that the clinicians are operating within a framework of trust based partly on their expertise. At the same time there is some concern registered in the regulators' comments that PGD might be used for selection of non-medical traits. Given that the same clinicians would be making the determinations in relation to these requests as well, SACRT's response seems slightly contradictory. However, it does add support to our conclusion that one impetus for the intense regulatory activity around PGD in its early stages was a concern with designer babies and enhancement.

Overall, the early patterns of PGD regulation in Australia suggest that the deciding factor in attempts to strike a balance between these two themes was the extent to which PGD was already in use in the jurisdiction. As noted, there is a tendency for those jurisdictions that had strong patterns of early PGD use to be most willing to legislate in favor of PGD, and to do so in a way that gave significant flexibility to the medical community to decide the meaning of qualifying terms like "seriousness." By contrast, in WA, where PGD was not in use, disability was not constructed as such a significant threat, and legalization was not seen as necessary.

However, the speed of technological progress in this area meant this distinction would not be decisive for long. As noted previously, the 1990s was an era of rapid expansion in scientific research on genes with the start of the Human Genome Project. Perhaps the most significant event of the 1990s, however, was the 1996 announcement that the first mammal – Dolly the Sheep – had been cloned. This prompted legislatures around the world to contemplate and, subsequently, restrictively regulate (prohibit) human cloning. As a result, not long after WA, Victoria, and SA were developing their initial regulatory frameworks around ART, there were moves afoot at the federal level to institute some degree of oversight over embryo research. Given that human cloning was seen as a potential reproductive technology, it is not surprising that ART was drawn into the net of this regulatory fervor.

3.4 Federal Law (2002–2008)

In Australia, there is arguably no direct constitutional head of power that would authorize federal legislation concerning assisted reproductive technology. Nevertheless, in 2002 the federal government introduced two pieces of legislation: the Prohibition of Human Cloning Act 2002 (PHC Act) (later known as the Prohibition of Human Cloning for Reproduction Act (PHCR Act)) and the Research Involving Human Embryos Act 2002 (RIHE Act). In order to avoid constitutional problems regarding the federal government's power to enact these laws, each of the states and territories agreed to enact mirror legislation.[139] The

---

[139] Because the federal government is limited in the areas over which it can legislate to those constitutionally allowed under s51 of the Constitution, it is not clear that the federal government has the power to regulate in this area. Therefore, it has requested that the states and territories pass uniform legislation replicating the federal legislation. Except for the Northern Territory, all state and territory jurisdictions have passed corresponding legislation: Research Involving Human Embryos and Prohibition of Human Cloning Act 2003 (QLD), Human Cloning and Other Prohibited Practices Act 2003 (NSW), Research Involving Human Embryos (New South Wales) Act 2003(NSW), Assisted Reproductive Treatment Act 2008 (VIC), Research Involving Human Embryos Act 2003 (SA), Human Cloning and Other Prohibited Practices Act 2003 (TAS), Human Embryonic Research Regulation Act 2003 (TAS), Human Cloning and Embryo Research Act 2004 (ACT), Human Reproductive Technology Act 1991 (WA).

PHC Act prohibited the creation of a human embryo for any purpose other than to enable pregnancy. In addition, it set out a list of potential embryonic creations that were not allowed, including clones, hybrids, chimeras, and embryos with different genetic manipulations.[140] The RIHE Act operated in tandem with the PHC Act to set up a regulatory regime to manage those embryos created in the context of assisted reproduction. Under certain circumstances and by license only, excess ART embryos (as defined in both acts) could be used for research.

Prior to its amendment, Part Two of the PHC Act contained far-reaching prohibitions. Most of those prohibitions remain, although significant amendments in 2006 allowed the creation of cloned embryos for research purposes. This will be discussed in Chapter 6.[141] For our purposes, the key regulatory impact of these acts for ART service providers was found in s 8 together with s 11 of the RIHE Act, which required accreditation of all ART clinics in Australia with the Reproductive Technology Accreditation Committee (RTAC). The RTAC Code of Practice stipulated that ART centers "must be directed by" the National Health and Medical Research Council Ethical Guidelines on the Use of Assisted Reproductive Technology in Clinical Practice and Research (NHMRC ART Guidelines), with departure from these guidelines permitted only in limited circumstances.[142]

[140] See generally Part Two of the original PHC Act.

[141] In November and December 2006, the landscape changed. New legislation was debated and passed, and therapeutic cloning or somatic cell nuclear transfer was given the green light. The amending legislation was a response to recommendations made by the Lockhart Committee Review, which had been set up to review the Prohibition of Human Cloning Act 2002 (PHC) and the Research Involving Human Embryos Act 2002 (RIHE). Further, s 15 of the Act continues to preclude inheritable genetic modification; however, somatic cell modification of an embryo of the kind that might be called gene therapy is not precluded.

[142] The RTAC requires all ART clinics to adhere to its Code of Practice. The Code of Practice, in turn, mandates compliance with relevant legislation: at [1.17] and that all ART clinics follow the NHMRC ART Guidelines: at [1.18]. Practices that depart from these ethical guidelines are only permitted in limited circumstances: see at [1.18]. Furthermore, ART-specific state regimes also mandate, directly or

The NHMRC ART Guidelines were developed in 2003 and made available in 2004[143] – about the same time that Western Australia was passing its legislation to lift the ban on PGD and SACRT was developing Memorandum 12.[144] As a consequence of the introduction of the NHMRC ART Guidelines, it now seems clear that clinics in all states and territories in Australia are limited to using PGD to select against a *serious* disease or illness.[145] The guidelines state specifically

indirectly, compliance with the NHMRC ART Guidelines. In Victoria, section 5.1 of VARTA's Information for Registered ART Providers (December 2009) notes that compliance with the NHMRC Guidelines is a condition of registration for ART providers. Similarly in South Australia s8(2)(a) of the Assisted Reproductive Treatment Regulations 2010 (SA) provides that the minister must impose upon the registration of ART providers a condition requiring that they comply with the NHMRC Guidelines. A condition of every Western Australian license is accreditation with the RTAC, which in turn requires compliance with the NHMRC ART Guidelines: see Human Reproductive Technology Act 1991 (WA), ss 33(2)(ea) and 29(5)(aa). The recent legislative amendments – Prohibition of Human Cloning for Reproduction and the Regulation of Human Embryo Research Amendment Act 2006 (Cth) – appear to have no impact on this position.

[143] The most recent version of the guidelines was published in 2007 after the changes to the federal legislation allowing cloning for research were introduced. The section dealing with PGD was not altered in the later version.

[144] The NHMRC ART Guidelines note that researchers also need to refer to the NHMRC National Statement: see National Health and Medical Research Council, Ethical Guidelines on the Use of Assisted Reproductive Technology in Clinical Practice and Research (2007) at [1.14]. The NHMRC National Statement is only relevant to ART clinics insofar as these clinics undertake research, as opposed to the clinical provision of PGD, and even then, the statement itself emphasizes that research involving the use of gametes or embryos is governed by the aforementioned NHMRC ART Guidelines: see NHMRC, National Statement on Ethical Conduct in Human Research (2007) 39 (Ch 3.4, Introduction).

[145] National Health and Medical Research Council, Ethical Guidelines on the Use of Assisted Reproductive Technology in Clinical Practice and Research (2007) at [12.2]: Pending further community discussion, PGD must not be used for (inter alia) the "prevention of conditions that do not seriously harm the person to be born." In relation to the timing of this prohibition, it is worth noting that because the RTAC Code of Practice was only revised in 2005, there was a gap in implementation of all the elements of the NHMRC ART Guidelines.

that "[p]ending further community discussion, PGD must not be used for (inter alia) the "prevention of conditions that do not *seriously harm* the person to be born."[146]

Despite the significant regulatory importance of these guidelines they are surprisingly nondirective, leaving open the question of what constitutes a disability and what constitutes seriousness. For instance, they state that

- what counts as a serious genetic condition is controversial;
- there are different perceptions of disability; and
- the practice of selecting against some forms of abnormality may threaten the status and equality of opportunity of people who have that form of abnormality.[147]

This is an interesting and vital piece of recuperative work aimed at contextualizing disability and acknowledging theoretical critiques expressing disability rights. R6, who was involved in drafting the guidelines, described the decision to include this as a matter of responsibility, saying: "It would be irresponsible of us to write a guideline not acknowledging that and not drawing people's attention to the fact that that's controversial."

R6 also commented on the use of the language of seriousness as a necessary qualifying tool. "But I don't think there would have been anyone in 2004 who would have just said genetic condition. Because I think by then we well knew that – well I might be going too far to say – we've all got a genetic condition. But by then we knew that there are early onset, middle onset, late onset, relatively trivial." R6 subsequently

This meant that some clinics continued to undertake non-medical sex selection up until 2004. See, for example, Genea at http://www.genea.com.au/How-we-can-help/Our-Services/Preimplantation-Genetic-Diagnosis--PGD-/Sex-selection-with-PGD/Sex-selection-with-PGD.

[146] At [12.2]. The "Explanation of Key Terms" in the NHMRC ART Guidelines does not attempt to define "serious."

[147] National Health and Medical Research Council, Ethical Guidelines on the Use of Assisted Reproductive Technology in Clinical Practice and Research (2007) at [12.1].

elaborated on this point: "But I don't think anyone would have been reluctant to put it in. I think what people might have wondered about was whether it did much good putting it in at all. I mean it was meant to flag something of ethical importance."

It is hard to identify the impact of these regulatory limits on the clinicians, the scientists, and the public. We address this question directly in Chapter 5, where we draw on existing empirical research and some interviews that we conducted with Australian clinicians.

However, the NHMRC ART Guidelines do operate on the basis that there is some level of shared understanding. For example, it is worth noting that when it came to using PGD to facilitate tissue typing to choose an embryo that would be a match for a sick sibling, the NHMRC ART guidelines were much more directive. Like the ITA policy in Victoria, the guidelines required that the condition of the sick child be "life-threatening." The process set down for approval for the use of PGD in these circumstances involves first requiring a clinic to seek approval from a clinical ethics committee or relevant regulatory authority. By virtue of section 12.3.1, before agreeing to the use of PGD, the ethics committee or relevant agency "should ascertain that:

- the use of PGD will not adversely affect the welfare and interests of the child who may be born;
- the medical condition of the sibling to be treated is life-threatening;
- other means to manage the medical condition are not available; and
- the wish of the parents to have another child as an addition to their family and not merely as a source of tissue."

As we have seen there is ongoing debate and discussion about whether the idea of "serious" or "severe" includes within it life-threatening or indeed life-shortening disorders. In the UK debates there was some discussion that suggested that a relatively minor disorder, such as asthma, might be life-threatening if not treated appropriately and that these words did not add much to our understanding of the kind of conditions in question.

Finally, the guidelines also specifically preclude (at [12.2]) the use of PGD to select "in favour of a genetic defect or disability in the person to be born."[148] Interestingly, while the drafters of the guidelines noted that PGD to select against an embryo should only be used for serious disability and that seriousness was a controversial question, in the case of those who might select in favor of an affected embryo, there is no qualifying language of seriousness. Selecting in favor of any genetic defect or disability is prohibited. Furthermore, unlike the recent amendment to the UK legislation discussed earlier, it is not clear whether a woman would be allowed to transfer an affected embryo if she had no others from which to choose. In our empirical research we were advised that the intention was only to limit a *preference* for an affected embryo and not to prohibit the transfer of an affected embryo where there were no unaffected embryos available. R6, referring to the potential scenario where a woman was faced with a situation where all her embryos were affected, stated:

> I'm very confident we didn't have that scenario in mind. Because you see, that wouldn't count as selection. The scenario we had in mind is you've got this array of embryos, this is the one with deafness and you choose that one because it's deaf. Or because it's going to be deaf. Or because its growth is going to be retarded. So I don't think what you're describing is prohibited.

However, there is some ambiguity in the NHMRC ART Guidelines, which are not written in statutory language. Furthermore, our empirical research suggests that clinicians are uncertain about how they ought to respond to this kind of scenario.

---

[148] National Health and Medical Research Council, Ethical Guidelines on the Use of Assisted Reproductive Technology in Clinical Practice and Research (2007) at [12.2].

C3 said:

> there's an IVF principle that the best interests of the child should be paramount or come above the parents. Rank more highly than the parents' wishes. And I think the reluctance to transfer known affected embryos, I think, is not based on the severity of the disorder. It's based on the best interests of the child, which once again are hard to define.

C1 referred to the well-known example of the deaf couple who deliberately chose a sperm donor to ensure the birth of a deaf child and stated:

> I have found this issue personally very difficult and I haven't resolved it in my mind.... I think if you look at it purely from the child's point of view and external society's point of you would argue is it right to actively create a child with a major sensory disability?... On the other hand my experience of the deaf is that it is to some extent a different culture, that communication is different, behaviour is different, sense of humour is different.... I just haven't resolved it.

The uncertainty expressed by the clinicians and the ambiguity recognized by the regulator in these quotes might be an argument in favor of more explicit regulatory controls. However, most regulators, as we have seen, and most clinicians, as we see in Chapter 5, do not favor more constraint but prefer to be able to make a decision based on the circumstances of the individual case. Indeed, in Australia it seems that the period of intense regulatory oversight is now waning.

As we have seen, there was a tremendous amount of regulatory activity in Australia in 2003/2004. Apart from the introduction of the NHRMC ART Guidelines, South Australia amended its regulations in line with Memorandum 12 to deal specifically with the circumstances under which PGD would be made available, and Western Australia introduced legislation that lifted the ban on PGD.

3.5 Western Australia (1998–2004)

The WA government began to review its decision to prohibit PGD shortly after the HRT Act was passed, although it was not until 2004 that the government actually changed this legislation. In 1998, it set up a Select Committee on the HRT Act, setting in train a series of events that led to the 2004 amendments to the Act. The Select Committee's Report recommended that "PGD with restrictions should be allowed."[149] Further, the report noted that in light of the recent changes to WA's abortion laws,[150] "it was preferable to be able to implant embryos that had been tested and found to be free of a genetic disease rather than a woman becoming pregnant, undergoing prenatal testing and subsequently choosing to have an abortion."[151] Here again we see PGD both aligned with, and distinguished from, PND and abortion. In this instance, however, an assumption is made that PGD is a better option than PND and abortion even though it is unclear why that would be so. Is PGD better for the woman, for the embryo/fetus, or for the future child? We will return to this important question in the next chapter when we look at the way that clinicians and patients view their options.[152]

Another issue that is raised in the WA Select Committee's Report is whether there should be a list of diseases that PGD can be used to detect. In answering this question the Select Committee considered the views of a forum conducted by the UK Progress Educational Trust. The forum concluded that decisions about testing should be left to the families "since they are the ones who often have experience of

---

[149] Legislative Assembly of Western Australia "Select Committee on the Human Reproductive Technology Act 1991 Report" (1999), 95.

[150] See Health Act 1911 (WA), s 334(7)(a). This made abortion lawful after 20 weeks gestation where two medical practitioners from a panel of at least six agreed that the "unborn child" had a "severe medical condition" that justified the procedure. These changes are discussed in more detail in Chapter 3.

[151] Legislative Assembly of Western Australia, "Select Committee on the Human Reproductive Technology Act 1991 Report" (1999), 95.

[152] See Chapter 5.

the disease in question and who will ultimately be left to deal with the consequences."[153] This is an interesting emphasis – rather than leaving it to the medical profession to determine, the WA Select Committee saw families' and patients' views as determinative. This emphasis was reflected in the way the WA Reproductive Technology Council (RTC) chose to implement the legislative amendments that were introduced in 2004. It is also consistent with the approach taken in the abortion context, where similar arguments for and against a list of diseases and disabilities were canvassed.[154]

The amendments to the HRT Act, which were eventually pro-claimed on 1 December 2004, permit the diagnostic testing of embryos (including PGD) in Western Australia. However, this permission is limited by section 14(2b), which requires that the RTC not grant approval for a diagnostic procedure unless "there is a significant risk of a serious genetic abnormality or disease being present in the embryo." This mirrored the UK HFEA guidelines at the time. Section 14(2b) was the subject of much parliamentary debate. One matter that was debated at length was whether or not the word "significant" should be altered to "substantial." Supporters of the amendment made the claim that inclusion of the word "substantial" would impose a more onerous test and would make it clear that PGD could not be used for non-serious conditions.[155] Parliamentarians referred to concerns raised by groups such as People with Disabilities (WA) that "people with Down's Syndrome will be weeded out" and the Deaf Society of WA that PGD would be used to select against deafness.[156] In response it was argued that "'[s]ignificant' in terms of risk is used by epidemi-

---

[153] Legislative Assembly of Western Australia, "Select Committee on the Human Reproductive Technology Act 1991 Report" (1999), 97 citing Progress Educational Trust Annual Review (1997) 3 "Issues in Public Policy and Ethics."

[154] See Chapter 3.

[155] *Hansard*, Legislative Assembly, 29 October 2003, 12749 (Mrs. C. L. Edwardes).

[156] *Hansard*, Legislative Assembly, 29 October 2003, 12751 (Mrs. C. L. Edwardes).

ologists, and is estimable in scientific terms … and I am told … that … 'substantial' … does not have a scientific meaning."[157]

In fact, the argument made by the amendment's supporters was misconceived; the word "significant" in s 14(2b) goes only to how likely the condition is to be transmitted and to manifest. It is the second part of the clause, which requires there to be a "serious genetic abnormality," that was the real object of the concern. Here we return to the same question – what is meant by "serious" and for whom must the abnormality or disease be "serious"?

The WA changes led to PGD being regulated in a way that bore more similarity to UK than Victorian PGD regulation. However, the WA amendments ultimately went considerably further than the UK legislation, allowing consideration of environment, family support structures, and attitudes to disability when determining whether a condition was "serious." As we shall see, when developing its policy determining what considerations must be taken into account when authorizing PGD, the RTC referred to the International Classification of Functioning Disability (ICF), which provides for these broader considerations.[158] So while the gatekeeper role of the clinician was emphasized in determining whether a condition was "serious," so too was the view of the patient or family of the potential child. The legislative debates give some indication of the reasons for this different approach because they demonstrate a legislature keenly attuned to the idea that different people have different perceptions of disability, quality of life, and seriousness.

One particularly interesting example involves a condition that was portrayed in a rather different way in the UK debates. When arguing the benefits of the 1991 HFE Act in the UK House of Commons,

---

[157] *Hansard,* Legislative Assembly, 29 October 2003, 12756 (Mr. J. A. McGinty).

[158] World Health Organisation, "International Classification of Functioning, Disability and Health" at http://www.who.int/classifications/icf/en/ (accessed on 17 June 2011).

Kevin Barron referred to the condition retinitis pigmentosa. He quoted from a letter in support of the Bill that had been written by constituents of his who had children suffering from the condition: "We are the parents of two sufferers of Retinitis Pigmentosa.... It can in the worst cases lead to total loss of sight in youth and is the second greatest cause of blindness in the country." Referring to the chance that the Bill might not pass, the letter goes on, "It would be a terrible blow to those of us who have come to hope that it might be feasible to end the transmission of the condition that so malignly affects us."[159]

This is to be contrasted with the way the same condition is used in the Western Australian debates. There Mr. J. B. D'Orazio says: "My family suffers from retinitis pigmentosa. My grandfather went blind, my dad is blind already and I will probably be blind. It is genetically transferred. I hate to think that on the basis that a disease may be hereditary or a gene may not exist, there will be a possibility that people like me will not be alive today. That is what it comes down to.... I do not think a disease, such as retinitis pigmentosa which causes blindness, does affect people's standard of living."[160]

Throughout the WA debates, members raised example after example of conditions that would need to be determined to be serious or not. These included diabetes (viewed as not serious),[161] attention deficit hyperactivity disorder (ADHD) (viewed as absurdly hypothetical for genetic testing),[162] hemochromatosis (viewed as serious but completely treatable),[163] hereditary cancer (viewed as serious but a matter for the family to decide),[164] Tay-Sachs disease, Huntington's chorea, achondroplasia, Duchenne's muscular dystrophy, and fragile X[165] (all viewed

---

[159] *Hansard*, HC, vol. 170, col. 963, 2 April 1990 (Mr. Kevin Barron).

[160] *Hansard*, Legislative Assembly, 23 October 2003, 12752 (Mr. J.B. D'Orazio).

[161] *Hansard*, Legislative Assembly, 23 October 2003, 12753 (Mr. P.G. Pendal).

[162] *Hansard*, Legislative Assembly, 23 October 2003, 12754 (Mr. P.W. Andrews).

[163] *Hansard*, Legislative Assembly, 29 October 2003, 12769 (Mr. M.P. Whitely).

[164] *Hansard*, Legislative Assembly, 29 October 2003, 12770 (Mr. J.A. McGinty).

[165] *Hansard*, Legislative Council, 8 April 2004, 1947 (Hon Robyn McSweeney).

as serious). There was even mention of the potential for a test for schizophrenia,[166] which was considered to be very concerning. The Honorable Kate Doust stated:

> In some information that came from the UK, a question was asked of someone who was involved with the equivalent council in the UK about whether it used prediagnostic testing for mental health problems such as schizophrenia, or any other mental health issues. Are they the sort of health issues that could potentially be given permission by the council to be tested for? I understand that a lot of mental health problems can be inherited. As there are no guidelines or parameters, does the potential exist for permission to be given to someone undergoing one of these procedures to have an embryo tested for a type of mental health problem?[167]

There was also some debate about the possibility of creating – either in the HRT Act itself or in regulations – a list of conditions that would be authorized for testing. This was unsuccessful, largely because concerns were raised that it was a cumbersome process incapable of adapting quickly enough to a technology that would continually develop new tests for new conditions. Nevertheless, the RTC Policy on Approval of Diagnostic Procedures Involving Embryos (March 2008) does elaborate upon when there will be a "significant risk of a serious genetic abnormality or disease." In relation to the circumstances in which there will be a "significant risk" of such a disease, the policy states:

5. It is not appropriate to specify a statistical probability as the sole criterion for the risk of a genetic abnormality or disease being present in the embryo to be "significant."

6. The level of risk should be measured against the risk of the disease or disability occurring in the general population. The Council should be satisfied that there is a higher risk of the embryo in question being affected by the abnormality or disease being tested for than embryos in the general population.

---

[166] *Hansard,* Legislative Council, 22 June 2004, 3970 (Hon Kate Doust).
[167] *Hansard,* Legislative Council, 22 June 2004, 3970 (Hon Kate Doust).

7. The significance of the risk for the persons seeking the testing may also be relevant, in that the persons seeking treatment may have varying perceptions of the significance of risk that need to be taken into account.

In relation to the circumstances in which a disease will be classified properly as a "serious genetic abnormality or disease," the policy provides:

8. In assessing whether a genetic abnormality or disease is serious it is appropriate to look at environmental and personal factors as well as the impairment to body functions and structures that may arise from the condition. The assessment should consider the limits that these factors impose on the extent to which a person can engage in activities or participate in life situations.

9. The *International Classification of Functioning Disability and Health* (ICF) developed by the World Health Organisation provides a broad overview for assessment of seriousness, which covers many different aspects of the disease, however, does not consider an individual's perspective of seriousness. The infrastructure of the ICF may be adapted to the assessment of the seriousness of a genetic abnormality or disease.

Further, on the question of providing a list, the guidelines state:

15. It is not appropriate to specify a list of conditions that could be tested for by PGD. Each application needs to be considered on its own merits, as the Council needs to be satisfied that the condition will be serious in the embryo (potential offspring).

16. The Council should evaluate PGD for individual cases based on support of a clinical geneticist (accredited by the Human Genetics Society of Australasia (HGSA)) who has assessed the risk and seriousness of the condition to be tested for and discussed relevant issues with the participants requesting the testing.

17. In making this determination the Council should also take into account that the genetic abnormality or disease in the embryo is not simply a defect in the genetic material, but is one associated with a known clinical defect.

18. Where approval for embryo diagnostic testing is being sought for a condition where there may be carrier embryos but no affected embryos (e.g. a male participant with an X linked recessive condition), Council must consider whether the condition will have a serious effect on the carrier embryo.

Clause 18 is particularly interesting because it returns to the question of serious for whom and answers it as serious for the embryo. That has not been the case elsewhere, where carrier testing has been more widely approved. Our interviews with WA regulators included one regulator who, when asked about this clause, gave voice to the idea of future psychological pain as something that might be considered as a serious disability for the future child for the purposes of PGD and clause 18 in particular. They stated:

> [The decision] is influenced by this issue of the welfare of the subsequent child so where the – if the subsequent child is going to be a carrier for a very serious condition then one of the concerns is that that effectively – it significantly impacts on the reproductive ability of that future child. We've certainly had instances where the parents are saying look, we've had significant problems with our ability to make reproductive choices and if we can prevent that pain being experienced by our children then we would very much like to do that.

While there are extensive and detailed policy guidelines on the use of PGD to select against a disability, there is very little information regarding the policy of the RTC in relation to HLA tissue typing. In relation to selection in favor of a disability, the policy does state: "Diagnostic testing carried out prior to implantation is generally intended to allow selection of embryos that do not have an abnormality or disease for implantation."[168] Thus it seems clear that selection in favor of an affected embryo would not be countenanced.

---

[168] Reproductive Technology Council, "Policy on Approval of Diagnostic Procedures Involving Embryos" March 2008, 2.

In both WA and the United Kingdom, then, more restrictive legislation has gradually been introduced. In Victoria, South Australia, Western Australia, and at the federal level (the NHMRC Ethics Committee) all the bodies involved in policy development have been appointed by the government to undertake the task. Some have argued that the legislature(s), as the elected representatives of the community, ought to have a greater role in determining the limits of the use of these technologies rather than leaving these decisions to expert committees or indeed clinicians and patients. However, interestingly, WA is the only state jurisdiction to maintain the oversight role of the statutorily constituted body. In Victoria and South Australia, recent legislative amendments have removed the regulatory oversight roles of the ITA (now Victorian Assisted Reproductive Treatment Authority [VARTA]) and the SACRT (now abolished). The effect of this is significant. It means that the NHMRC ART guidelines are now, via the accreditation process, the default regulation for all states and territories in Australia apart from Western Australia.[169]

3.6 Victoria (2008–2010)

As noted, regulatory oversight has been reduced under the new Assisted Reproductive Technology Act (2008) (ART Act). Under section 10(3) of the ART Act, the interpretation of the meaning of "genetic abnormality or genetic disease" falls to a geneticist or a doctor with specialist qualifications in human genetics, and there is no longer a provision for licensing oversight by a regulatory authority. Section 99 of the ART Act establishes (VARTA) to succeed the ITA. Section 74 provides essentially that VARTA must grant registration as an ART provider to a person who holds accreditation registration with the Reproductive Technology Accreditation Committee

---

[169] See our discussion of the Federal framework in section 3.4 of this chapter. The NHMRC Guidelines still apply in WA via accreditation requirements, however, clinics must also comply with state laws.

(RTAC). VARTA may impose conditions on a registered ART provider but only if this is in the public interest (s 75(1)). Moreover, any condition that VARTA imposes must not be inconsistent with the person's RTAC accreditation and is invalid to the extent of its inconsistency with such a condition (s 75(2)).

Our interviews with regulators suggested that the new role of VARTA is still being developed, and it is primarily engaged in public education. At the moment, VARTA is not applying the former three-tier list policy. However, as noted, Victorian ART providers must have RTAC registration. As RTAC registration is conditional upon compliance with the NHMRC ART Guidelines (see 3.4), it follows that Victorian PGD providers must comply with those guidelines.

The new legislation still directly outlaws sex selection for non-medical reasons (s 28(1)) but is silent on the use of PGD for HLA tissue typing for savior siblings and selection in favor of a disability. In these cases, the NHMRC ART Guidelines are applicable.

3.7 South Australia (2010)

As in Victoria, the most recent amendments to the South Australian legislation have removed regulatory oversight of PGD. Clause 8(2) (a) of the Assisted Reproductive Treatment Regulations 2010 (which took effect on the same day, 1 September 2010, as did the new Act), provides that the minister must impose a condition requiring all persons registered to provide ART to comply with the NHMRC ART Guidelines. Moreover, section 9(1)(c) of the Act (now renamed the Assisted Reproduction Treatment Act 1988) provides that the minister must impose on a person registered to provide ART a condition preventing the provision of ART except in specific circumstances, one of which is "(iii) if there appears to be a risk that a serious genetic defect, serious disease or serious illness would be transmitted to a child conceived naturally." Seriousness is not defined.

The new Act also abolished the SACRT. Despite this, however, it did impose a higher standard on access to IVF more generally where the aim was to avoid a disability. Previously the RCTA Act had conditioned the provision of PGD on there being a risk of the transmission of a "genetic defect"; in the new Act, the word "serious" has now been included before the words "genetic defect." There does not appear to have been any discussion of this insertion in the amendment debates, and most of the people we interviewed, who had previously been involved with the regulation of PGD via the SACRT and the Department of Health, confirmed that this had been changed without significant discussion.

One regulator did speculate that it was inserted to deal with concerns over non-medical trait selection. They stated: "And I think off the top of my head, I think it was more to remove the possibility that people would, if they thought that black hair was a genetic defect, that that couldn't be a reason to access treatment for example." The same regulator also speculated that the language was chosen to put the new Act in line with the NHMRC guidelines.

The new legislation is silent on PGD for HLA tissue typing for savior siblings and selection in favor of a disability. In these cases, the NHMRC ART Guidelines are applicable.

4 OTHER COUNTRIES

4.1 Europe

As noted previously, there are eight European countries that allow PGD but also impose a seriousness limit where it is used for selection against a disability.[170] Of these, four are especially worth mentioning.

---

[170] These are Greece, Spain, France, Denmark, Sweden, Norway, Germany and the Czech Republic.

Spain requires that testing for serious hereditary disease must involve an early onset condition.[171] This is a fairly unusual provision and would exclude the use of PGD to test for the breast cancer *BRCA 1* gene, possibly Alzheimer's disease, and also Huntington's disease (depending on the definition of early onset.) France allows PGD where there is a "high probability of giving birth to a child with a severe genetic disease, without any chance of successful treatment at the time of the diagnosis" and requires a "specialist physician qualified in medical genetics or having training or experience in this field" to certify that this is the case.[172] Here, as elsewhere, reliance is on the expertise of the clinician in determining the nature of the condition. Denmark too requires that the condition be a "serious hereditary condition"[173] but also allows HLA tissue typing for the treatment of a child with a "life-threatening disease."[174] The provisions list several conditions relating to the lack of available other treatments and the allowable interventions on the donor child to be born, but again a key element is "expert medical appraisal of the circumstances of the child and family."[175] Sweden specifically prohibits the use of PGD "to choose characteristics" and requires approval from the National Board of Health and Welfare before PGD can be used for tissue typing to select an embryo that will be a donor for a sick sibling.[176]

---

[171] Law No. 14 of 26 May 2006 on human reproduction procedures, article 12(1)1(a).

[172] Law No. 94–654 of 29 July 1994 governing the donation and use of elements and products of the human body, medically assisted reproduction, and prenatal diagnosis, article R. 2131–7.

[173] Law No. 460 of 10 June 1997 on artificial fertilization in connection with medical treatment, diagnosis, and research (research on embryonic stem cells), s 25(1)2.

[174] Law No. 460 of 10 June 1997 on artificial fertilization in connection with medical treatment, diagnosis, and research (research on embryonic stem cells), Chapter 2, s 7.

[175] Order No. 286 of 23 April 2004 on the use of preimplantation diagnosis in specific cases, s 1.

[176] The Genetic Integrity Act (2006:351), Chapter 4, s 2.

Apart from national laws, members of the European Union (EU) must comply with European Union law and the various European Conventions. Perhaps the most important European Convention in this area is the European Convention for the Protection of Human Rights and Dignity of the Human Being with regard to the Application of Biology and Medicine 1997 (the "Oviedo Convention"). However, many major European countries have decided not to ratify this convention, including five of the European jurisdictions we have selected for specific coverage in this book: the United Kingdom, France, Belgium, Sweden, and Germany.[177] Nevertheless, it is worth noting the convention's provisions because a number of the countries that have not ratified it have, nevertheless, incorporated similar provisions in their national laws that generally accord with the spirit of the treaty. Furthermore, the Closing Declaration of the Eighth Meeting of the 2005 Conference of National Ethics Committees (COMETH),[178] which is made up of representatives of national ethics committees (or equivalent bodies) from the Council of Europe, stated that it recognizes the Oviedo Convention as the "cornerstone" of European biomedical law and makes specific reference to the benefits of a pan-European debate relating to PGD.[179]

Of particular importance for our purposes are Articles 12, 14, and 18, which provide limits on predictive genetic tests, sex selection, and research on embryos, respectively. For instance, Article 12 provides that

> tests which are predictive of genetic diseases or which serve either to identify the subject as a carrier of a gene responsible for a disease or to detect a genetic predisposition or susceptibility to a

[177] Joint Research Centre of the European Commission, "JRC Scientific and Technical Reports: Preimplantation Genetic Diagnosis in Europe" (2007), 61: see ftp://ftp.jrc.es/pub/EURdoc/eur22764en.pdf (accessed on 19 June 2011).

[178] Held in Dubrovnik, Croatia, 25–26 April 2005.

[179] See Joint Research Centre of the European Commission, "JRC Scientific and Technical Reports: Preimplantation Genetic Diagnosis in Europe" (2007), 61: ftp://ftp.jrc.es/pub/EURdoc/eur22764en.pdf (accessed on 19 June 2011).

disease may be performed only for health purposes or for scientific research linked to health purposes, and subject to appropriate genetic counselling.[180]

Although "health purposes" is not defined, Article 12 clearly prohibits the use of predictive tests for non-medical trait selection. The Explanatory Report on the Convention states that "Article 12 as such does not imply any limitation of the right to carry out diagnostic interventions at the embryonic stage to find out whether an embryo carries hereditary traits that will lead to *serious* diseases in the future child."[181] Thus, while there is no threshold of seriousness in Article 12 itself, the explanatory material suggests in the case of serious disease there should be no question about the validity of undertaking predictive genetic testing. Article 14, which prohibits non-medical sex selection, does contain a seriousness threshold. Article 14 reads:

> The use of techniques of medically assisted procreation shall not be allowed for the purpose of choosing a future child's sex, except where *serious* hereditary sex-related disease is to be avoided.[182]

[180] The European Convention for the Protection of Human Rights and Dignity of the Human Being with Regard to the Application of Biology and Medicine 1997 (the "Ovideo Convention"), article 12, cited in Joint Research Centre of the European Commission, "JRC Scientific and Technical Reports: Preimplantation Genetic Diagnosis in Europe" (2007), 60: see ftp://ftp.jrc.es/pub/EURdoc/eur22764en.pdf (accessed on 19 June 2011).

[181] Council of Europe, "Explanatory Report to the European Convention for the Protection of Human Rights and Dignity of the Human Being with Regard to the Application of Biology and Medicine 1997"20 (paragraph 83) cited in Joint Research Centre of the European Commission, "JRC Scientific and Technical Reports: Preimplantation Genetic Diagnosis in Europe" (2007), 60: see ftp://ftp.jrc.es/pub/EURdoc/eur22764en.pdf (accessed on 19 June 2011).

[182] The European Convention for the Protection of Human Rights and Dignity of the Human Being with Regard to the Application of Biology and Medicine 1997 (the "Oviedo Convention"), article 14, cited in Joint Research Centre of the European Commission, "JRC Scientific and Technical Reports: Preimplantation Genetic Diagnosis in Europe" (2007), 60: see ftp://ftp.jrc.es/pub/EURdoc/eur22764en.pdf (accessed on 19 June 2011).

Interestingly, this goes further than prohibiting non-medical sex selection *using PGD*. It would also presumably prohibit the use of *prenatal testing* to determine sex for other than medical reasons. Therefore, it might be argued that to advise a couple of their future child's sex could lead to a contravention of this provision. The Explanatory Report does not explain the meaning of "seriousness" in this provision but does state at paragraph 94 that it is "for internal law to determine, according to the procedures applied in each state, the *seriousness* of a hereditary sex-related disease."[183]

4.2 New Zealand

Under s 38 of the Assisted Reproductive Technology Act 2004, the Advisory Committee on Assisted Reproductive Procedures and Human Reproductive Research is obliged to, "within time frames agreed with the Minister, provide the Minister with information, advice, and, if it thinks fit, recommendations on the following matters in relation to human assisted reproductive technology: ... (e) selection of embryos using pre-implantation genetic diagnosis." The National Ethics Committee on Assisted Reproduction (NECAR) duly developed guidelines in 2005. Those guidelines define PGD as a procedure used to test early human embryos for *serious* inherited genetic conditions and chromosomal abnormalities.[184] However, when it comes to the question of what "serious" means, the guidelines provide that "it

---

[183] Council of Europe, "Explanatory Report to the European Convention for the Protection of Human Rights and Dignity of the Human Being with Regard to the Application of Biology and Medicine 1997"22 (paragraph 94) cited in Joint Research Centre of the European Commission, "JRC Scientific and Technical Reports: Preimplantation Genetic Diagnosis in Europe" (2007), 60: see ftp://ftp.jrc. es/pub/EURdoc/eur22764en.pdf (accessed on 19 June 2011).

[184] National Ethics Committee on Assisted Human Reproduction, "Guidelines on Preimplantation Genetic Diagnosis" (March 2005), 2.

is the responsibility of PGD providers, in collaboration with a clinical geneticist, to determine whether a disorder is likely to be serious in the offspring."[185]

In this way, the New Zealand law and guidelines are similar to the laws that we have described elsewhere; they provide that PGD may only be used to prevent the transmission of "serious" conditions but stop short of defining that limit legislatively, instead devolving that responsibility to the clinicians providing PGD.

However, as do the Australian NHMRC ART Guidelines, the New Zealand guidelines refer to the impact of a determination that a condition is "serious" on members of the community with disabilities. They state: "Concern has been raised that PGD discriminates against people with disabilities, and promotes the view that the birth of people with disabilities should be prevented. However, it is important to distinguish between 'disability' and 'people with disabilities,' and that selecting against embryos with disabilities does not necessarily imply that those with disabilities are living lives that are either less valuable or less meaningful. NECAHR supports the *New Zealand Disability Strategy*."[186]

4.3 Canada

In Canada, apart from a prohibition of non-medical sex selection in the Assisted Human Reproduction Act 2004,[187] PGD is largely

---

[185] National Ethics Committee on Assisted Human Reproduction, "Guidelines on Preimplantation Genetic Diagnosis" (March 2005), Section 1, point 6, 6.

[186] National Ethics Committee on Assisted Human Reproduction, "Guidelines on Preimplantation Genetic Diagnosis" (March 2005), 3.

[187] Assisted Human Reproduction Act, SC 2004, c 2, s 5(1)(e): "No person shall knowingly ... for the purpose of creating a human being, perform any procedure or provide, prescribe or administer any thing that would ensure or increase the probability that an embryo will be of a particular sex, or that would identify the sex of an in vitro embryo, except to prevent, diagnose or treat a sex-linked disorder or disease." This Act received royal assent on 29 March 2004 but has yet to take full force.

unregulated. Regulations regarding the use of PGD are yet to be pro-mulgated despite having been the subject of a consultation undertaken by Health Canada in 2007.[188] This is because in the intervening period the province of Quebec successfully challenged the constitutionality of various provisions in the Act.[189]

Further, in a 2005 report, the Government of Canada dis-cussed "whether prospective parents, at risk of passing on a serious genetic disease to their offspring have a right to access PGD."[190] The report stated:

> One could argue that information about the genetic status of one's *in vitro* embryos is essential for reproductive autonomy. Such infor-mation may be necessary for some persons to assist in their deci-sion-making regarding reproduction. For example, if PGD revealed that one's *in vitro* embryos carried a genetic anomaly that would likely result in the child being born with a severely debilitating dis-ease, one might choose not to reproduce.[191]

---

[188] The Assisted Human Reproduction Agency of Canada (previously the Assisted Human Reproduction Implementation Office) has been created to conduct research and consultation so as to formulate regulations required under the Assisted Human Reproduction Act: see http://www.ahrc-pac.gc.ca/v2/aaa-app/index-eng. php (accessed 12 June 2011). Health Canada has previously called for comments – ending 30 January 2006 – in response to its PGD Issues Paper entitled "Issues Related to the Regulation of Pre-Implantation Genetic Diagnosis under the Assisted Human Reproduction Act" (2005).

[189] While the prohibitions set out in section 5 to 9 (including against social sex selection) are not in question, Health Canada is still deciding how to respond to the decision of the Supreme Court of Canada, http://www.hc-sc.gc.ca/hl-vs/reprod/hc-sc/legislation/ delay-interruption-eng.php. The Supreme Court of Canada opinion in Reference re the Assisted Human Reproduction Act [2010] 3 S.C.R. 457, published on December 22, 2010, see http://scc.lexum.org/en/2010/2010scc61/2010scc61.html.

[190] Government of Canada, "A Brave New World: Where Biotechnology and Human Rights Intersect" (July 2005).

[191] Government of Canada, "A Brave New World: Where Biotechnology and Human Rights Intersect" (July 2005), 3–5: see http://biostrategy.gc.ca/humanrights/ humanrightse/Biotech_CH1_E.pdf (accessed on 19 June 2011).

The report also discussed sex selection, selection in favor of deafness, and selection for "genetic compatibility to donate to a sibling who has a life-threatening disease."[192] It concluded that an "argument could be made that the state prohibition on PGD [for selection in favor of deafness] impacts negatively on the deaf woman's human dignity."[193] On the other hand, it observed that the courts might find that a state prohibition of sex selection for non-medical reasons "is in accordance with the principles of fundamental justice or is justifiable by the state under section 1 of the *Charter*."[194] As for tissue typing, the report, after acknowledging that "it is possible to select for and transfer only those *in vitro* embryos that have certain traits needed to provide a cell or tissue transplant for a seriously ill sibling, without harming the donor child" (note that the terms "life-threatening" and "serious" are used seemingly interchangeably), concluded that

> an argument could be made that a prohibition on the use of PGD to obtain information to select an *in vitro* embryo to become a donor child is more than just a decision respecting a lifestyle choice, it deprives the woman of critical information to make a decision relating to reproduction.... [In addition, t]he state prohibition would prevent the existing sibling from accessing a beneficial medical treatment, e.g. a transplant of histocompatible stem cells from a saviour child, for a condition that may pose a threat to his or her life.[195]

[192] Government of Canada, "A Brave New World: Where Biotechnology and Human Rights Intersect" (July 2005), 3–23: see http://biostrategy.gc.ca/humanrights/humanrightse/Biotech_CH1_E.pdf (accessed on 19 June 2011).

[193] Government of Canada, "A Brave New World: Where Biotechnology and Human Rights Intersect" (July 2005), 3–24: see http://biostrategy.gc.ca/humanrights/humanrightse/Biotech_CH1_E.pdf (accessed on 19 June 2011).

[194] Government of Canada, "A Brave New World: Where Biotechnology and Human Rights Intersect" (July 2005), 3–26: see http://biostrategy.gc.ca/humanrights/humanrightse/Biotech_CH1_E.pdf (accessed on 19 June 2011).

[195] Government of Canada, "A Brave New World: Where Biotechnology and Human Rights Intersect" (July 2005), 3–26: see http://biostrategy.gc.ca/humanrights/humanrightse/Biotech_CH1_E.pdf (accessed on 19 June 2011).

For as long as the process of developing regulations continues, clinicians will be guided by the Society of Gynaecologists and Obstetricians of Canada Guidelines regarding the use of PGD.[196] These provide that PGD is offered as "an alternative to prenatal diagnosis for the detection of genetic disorders in couples at risk of transmitting a genetic condition to their offspring" and recommend that couples should be informed that PGD "can reduce the risk of conceiving a child with a genetic abnormality carried by one or both parents if that abnormality can be identified with tests performed on a single cell." The guidelines do not specifically provide that the "genetic abnormality" must be "serious" before PGD should be offered.

4.4 United States

In the United States there is no federal regulation, and the only state that has indicated an intention to regulate PGD specifically is New York. Ten states have prohibited embryo research, but six of them exempt PGD from this prohibition.[197] A further four states restrict the use of PGD to where it is beneficial to the embryo.[198] Another state, South Dakota, prohibits "non-therapeutic research that destroys a human embryo"[199] or "subjects a human embryo to substantial risk of injury or death."[200]

---

[196] SOGC, "SOGC Technical Update: Preimplantation Genetic Diagnosis" (August 2009) 232 *Journal of Obstetrics and Gynaecology Canada* 761, at http://www.sogc. org/guidelines/documents/gui232TU0908.pdf (accessed on 10 June 2011).

[197] Mass Gen Laws Ch 112, § 12J(a)(I) (1996); Mich Comp Laws Ann § 333.2686 (1996); NH Rev Stat Ann § 168-B:15 (1994); NM Stat Ann §§ 24–9A-1, 24–9A-3, 24–9A-5 (1994); ND Cent Code § 14–02.2–01(3) (1991); RI Gen Laws § 11–54–1(b) (1994).

[198] LA Rev Stat Ann §§ 9:122, 9:129 (1991); ME Rev Stat Ann tit 22, § 1593 (1992); Minn Stat Ann § 145.422 subd 1, 2 (1989); 18 PA Cons Stat Ann §§ 3216(a), 3203 (1995).

[199] SD Cod. Laws 34–14–16.

[200] SD Cod. Laws 34–14–17.

In a major report by the President's Council on Bioethics, called "Reproduction and Responsibility,"[201] it was remarked that PGD had entered the American ART scene relatively unnoticed from a governance perspective. The authors of the report said:

> PGD represents the first fusion of genomics and assisted reproduction and the first reproductive technology that allows would-be parents to screen and select the genetic characteristics of their potential offspring, to a limited but growing degree. It is striking that this new capacity arrived with little fanfare – entering into routine practice essentially unmonitored, unstudied, and unregulated.[202]

It was also noted that "during his presentation to the Council in December 2002, [one doctor] speculated that one such application of PGD would be to screen for genetic markers correlated with higher IQ levels. While he expressed skepticism that such tests would be effective or reliable, he did think the demand for such tests would be high."[203]

Despite the concerns raised in the President's Council Report, there have been no legislative responses either at the federal or at the state level. There have, however, been moves to institute oversight in the form of data collection. The Genetics and Public Policy Center has been working with the American Society for Reproductive Medicine (ASRM) and the Preimplantation Genetics Diagnosis International Society (PGDIS) to establish a U.S. PGD database. They indicated in a news release in July 2007 that the database was "nearing fruition"

---

[201] The President's Council on Bioethics, "Reproduction and Responsibility: The Regulation of New Biotechnologies" (March 2004).

[202] The President's Council on Bioethics, "Reproduction and Responsibility: The Regulation of New Biotechnologies" (March 2004), 102.

[203] The President's Council on Bioethics, "Reproduction and Responsibility: The Regulation of New Biotechnologies" (March 2004), 91.

and would "permit robust research and enable studies that can track outcomes over time."[204]

In the absence of regulation, organizations such as the American College of Obstetricians and Gynaecologists (ACOG)[205] and the American Society for Reproductive Medicine (ASRM)[206] have published best practice guidelines regarding the use of PGD. The guidelines clearly consider that PGD is offered to prevent the transmission of genetic disease by those who are at a high risk of doing so. The ASRM guidelines provide that "PGD is indicated for couples at risk of transmitting a specific genetic disease or abnormality to their offspring"[207] and recommend that "PGD can reduce the risk for conceiving a child with a genetic abnormality carried by one or both parents if that abnormality can be identified with tests performed on a single cell."[208] While there is no specific requirement in the ASRM's guidelines that the "genetic abnormality" be "serious," the American College of Obstetricians and Gynaecologists' Committee on Ethics, in its ACOG Committee on Ethics Opinion, "Sex Selection," has stated (at p 3) that

[204] Genetics and Public Policy Center, "Oversight of PGD" (July 2007): see http://www.dnapolicy.org/images/issuebriefpdfs/Oversight_of_PGD_Issue_Brief.pdf (accessed on 18 June 2011).

[205] ASRM, "Preimplantation Genetic Testing: A Practice Committee Opinion," at http://www.asrm.org/uploadedFiles/ASRM_Content/News_and_Publications/Practice_Guidelines/Committee_Opinions/Preimplantation_genetic_testing(1).pdf (accessed on 18 June 2011).

[206] ACOG Committee on Ethics, "Committee Opinion on Sex Selection" (February 2007), at http://www.acog.org/from_home/publications/ethics/co360.pdf (accessed on 18 June 2011).

[207] ASRM, "Preimplantation Genetic Testing: A Practice Committee Opinion," at http://www.asrm.org/uploadedFiles/ASRM_Content/News_and_Publications/Practice_Guidelines/Committee_Opinions/Preimplantation_genetic_testing(1).pdf (accessed on 18 June 2011), 136.

[208] ASRM, "Preimplantation Genetic Testing: A Practice Committee Opinion," at http://www.asrm.org/uploadedFiles/ASRM_Content/News_and_Publications/Practice_Guidelines/Committee_Opinions/Preimplantation_genetic_testing(1).pdf (accessed on 18 June 2011), 142.

they "support, as ethically permissible, the practice of sex-selection for *serious* sex-linked genetic disorders" [emphasis added].[209]

Despite this clear guideline, a survey by the Genetics and Public Policy Centre found that 3 percent of IVF-PGD clinics in the United States report providing PGD to couples who seek to select an embryo *for* the presence of a particular disease or disability, such as deafness, in order that the child would share the characteristic with the parents.[210] In that same study 42 percent were recorded as using PGD to select a particular gender for social reasons.[211]

For our purposes, it is interesting to compare the situation in the United States – a mostly unregulated zone where clinicians are given free reign to undertake PGD – with the practice of PGD in those jurisdictions where it is regulated. It seems clear that where PGD is not regulated, a small number of clinicians are willing to offer the kinds of services that many jurisdictions have been unwilling to permit – such as selection in favor of a disability – and quite a large number (though not quite half) are willing to offer non-medical sex selection. This suggests that a number of the concerns raised by the members of the various parliaments we have been discussing have some foundation. Nevertheless, it seems clear that even in the regulated jurisdictions clinicians play a role as "gatekeepers" of access to PGD. Even where a legislature attempts to create limits, it is accepted that concepts such as "disability" and "normality" are fluid. They are ideas that are given meaning socially, politically, and contextually and their meanings are not fixed but change over time.

[209] ACOG Committee on Ethics, "Sex Selection" (February 2007) vol. 360: http://www.acog.org/from_home/publications/ethics/co360.pdf (accessed on 10 June 2011), 3.

[210] S. Baruch, D. Kaufman, and K. Hudson, "Genetic Testing of Embryos: Practices and Perspectives of US in Vitro Fertilization Clinics" (2008) 89(5) *Fertility and Sterility* 1053, at 1055: see http://www.dnapolicy.org/resources/GeneticTestingof Embryos.pdf.

[211] S. Baruch, D. Kaufman and K. Hudson, "Genetic Testing of Embryos: Practices and Perspectives of US In Vitro Fertilization Clinics" (2008) 89(5) *Fertility and Sterility* 1053, at 1056: see http://www.dnapolicy.org/resources/GeneticTestingofEmbryos.pdf.

5 CONCLUSION

In this chapter we have examined various pieces of legislation and guidelines as a stepping off point for our examination of the meaning of "serious" disability in the context of preimplantation genetic diagnosis. Our aim has been to indicate why different jurisdictions have decided to regulate PGD, thus limiting its use, and in particular, what is at stake in the use of the concept of seriousness as a threshold in the context of disability avoidance diagnostic technologies.

However, across all the jurisdictions we have examined, definitions or criteria that assist in understanding the concept of seriousness are rare, leaving us with the question; If these disability avoidance technologies are to be used in a way that involves some constraints, who is to establish the relevant criteria – patients, clinicians, legislators, judges, ethicists, disability communities, or no one? Placing legal limits on the use of prenatal testing technologies in response to these competing concerns raises a further set of issues. Kumari Campbell, for instance, argues that law "reflects a broader desire to *drive down disability* – thus ensuring that this class of enumerated persons remains problematically in a *state of exceptionality*, defined by law, rather than being a significant part of the country's population."[212]

What we have shown in Chapters 3 and 4, however, is that legal responses often contain a significant degree of "ambiguity" and "ambivalence" and that these uncertainties open up productive spaces for renegotiating ideas of normality and ablebodiedness. In many cases this has been achieved by incorporating the voices of patients, clinicians, and disability communities in the legal regimes for authorizing these technologies.

Disability studies critiques have raised serious concerns about the unlimited use of prenatal testing technologies, including PGD, because they claim that this has the potential to have a discriminatory impact

---

[212] Fiona Kumari Campbell, *Contours of Ableism: The Production of Disability and Abledness* (London: Palgrave, 2009), 30.

on people currently living with disabilities. Furthermore, social disability theorists argue that it is fundamentally misconceived to remove potential children from the human gene pool on the basis that, because of their particular embodiment, they are ill-equipped for the existing environment. They contend that, in fact, it is often the existing environment that is ill-adapted to people with disabilities and that technological effort should be applied to improving the environment with similar vigor to that currently applied to the development of technologies such as PGD. In other words, it is argued that it is fundamentally flawed to adjust future children to the existing world, particularly given our rapidly changing global landscape.

On the other hand, it is also clear that many women and men do wish to use these technologies to avoid having affected children. It is clear that many people would seek to avoid certain kinds of "serious" disabilities and that smaller numbers would seek to avoid all forms of abnormality or select in favor of some forms of abnormality. Sarah Franklin and Celia Roberts argue that the "lived complexity of PGD contrasts with the polarized characterizations the media often promote in 'for and against' stagings of the debate."[213] In support of this view they cite their own ethnographic study, which revealed PGD to be a "site of extreme ambivalences" for the people who undergo it.[214] If, as we are suggesting, legal responses are similarly ambivalent and devolve much of the final decision making about the use of PGD and other prenatal testing technologies to the clinicians, then it is useful to turn to an exploration of the way that determinations about disability and seriousness are being made in the clinical setting. In Chapter 5 we undertake that task.

---

[213] S. Franklin and C. Roberts, *Born and Made: An Ethnography of Preimplantation Genetic Diagnosis* (Princeton, NJ: Princeton University Press, 2006), 21.

[214] S. Franklin and C. Roberts, *Born and Made: An Ethnography of Preimplantation Genetic Diagnosis* (Princeton, NJ: Princeton University Press, 2006), 22, 107–24, 151–2.

5

Interpretations

As we saw in Chapter 3, the law has provided no specific guidance concerning what is a "serious handicap" or a "severe medical condition" in the fetus, or about which fetal abnormalities pose a danger to the physical or mental health of the woman, so as to justify termination. We have seen that in many of the jurisdictions under consideration access to PGD, too, is conditioned upon there being a risk that a "serious disability" will be transmitted. The inherent difficulty of setting such a threshold is that it immediately raises the question of where to draw the line between pregnancies, or prospective pregnancies, that might result in offspring with a serious disability and those that might not. How "serious" must a condition be to meet this threshold?

In this chapter, then, we turn our attention to the question of how decisions about serious disability are being made in the context of abortion and PGD. In the first part of this chapter we observe that there is divergent opinion among clinicians as to which conditions are serious and, furthermore, that often decisions and processes around the determination of seriousness are complex and contextual. Accordingly, the prospective child's prognosis may not alone determine whether a disability is serious. Although this is a crucial consideration, a host of other factors and pressures may bear upon decision making across these two fields. These include the attitudes, experiences, and resources of the family into which the child would be born;

the capacity of technology to detect abnormalities in utero or in vitro; the professional regulation of clinician discretion within clinics and hospitals; and the moral and social status of embryos compared with later term fetuses.

In the second part of this chapter, we consider some of the ways in which seriousness might be given further substance, and we identify three policy approaches to this question: creating a list of serious conditions, adopting a set of criteria to assist in determining whether a condition is serious, and/or requiring that a multidisciplinary assessment or review process be followed to arrive at decisions about seriousness. We compare and contrast these policy approaches to termination for fetal abnormality with the regulation of PGD, discussed in the previous chapter. Notably, we focus on terminations later in pregnancy, as it is in these contexts that the question of seriousness as a legal limit has tended to arise. However, it is worth noting that our focus on legal gestational thresholds is somewhat diverting. This narrower focus means that we do not address the equally important question of what (if any) regulation exists to ensure that access to prenatal diagnosis – performed and acted upon in the earlier stages of pregnancy – is subject to a seriousness threshold, as is the case for PGD.

We close this chapter with an examination of the seriousness threshold in the context of conditions that are not life threatening at birth. We do this by drawing upon a range of available material including published empirical research, reports by consultative bodies, media reports, and excerpts from interviews that we conducted with clinical geneticists and genetic counselors involved in the provision of prenatal testing and preimplantation genetic diagnosis in Victoria, South Australia, Western Australia, and New South Wales.[1] Here we are keen to

---

[1] As noted in the introduction, due to the small number of participants we offer these excerpts as anecdotal accounts only as they offer individual insights not otherwise accessible. The letter C denotes clinician.

develop a richer understanding of attitudes toward the use of selection practices to avoid conditions that are not life threatening at birth and to identify more clearly the areas of contention and agreement both within and between the medical profession and the community.

1 DIVERGENT OPINION AMONG CLINICIANS ABOUT WHAT CONSTITUTES A SERIOUSLY DISABLING CONDITION: A PROBLEM IN NEED OF A SOLUTION?

It will be recalled that during the UK parliamentary debates concerning the Abortion Act 1967, certain conditions were named as being serious handicaps. These included anencephaly, congenital rubella, and prenatal thalidomide exposure. By 2006, the issue of whether it was desirable to create a "list of conditions" that were "serious handicaps" for the purposes of s 1(1)(d) of the Abortion Act (either because the law was too vague to guide clinicians, or because in practice the provision was being interpreted too broadly), had gained further momentum. The challenge by Joanna Jepson to an abortion at twenty-eight weeks for cleft lip and palate generated intense public interest about how serious handicap was interpreted by doctors.[2]

Interestingly, there is some evidence that doctors do have significantly varying views concerning which abnormalities are serious enough to justify termination of pregnancy at or after viability. The Medical Practitioners Board of Victoria's 1998 "Report on Late Terminations of Pregnancy," noted that as early as 1993 Geller et al.

reported a study of the attitudes of French physicians and obstetricians towards late TOP for fetal abnormalities. 47 percent of

[2] See K. Savell, "Turning Mothers into Bioethicists: Late Abortion and Disability" in B. Bennett, T. Carney, and I. Karpin (eds.), *Brave New World of Health* (Sydney: Federation Press, 2008), 93.

participating physicians were Catholic. The majority supported third trimester TOP for severe abnormality, though support decreased with increasing gestational age. The majority supported TOP for spina bifida, trisomy 21 and microcephaly. There was considerable variation in attitudes toward less severe and treatable conditions such as Turner's syndrome and Klinefelter's syndrome. Those who supported TOP for these disorders supported the right of parents to choose.[3]

In a later Australian study of clinical geneticists and practitioners of obstetric ultrasound, it was found that although there was a high level of consensus about facilitating termination at twenty-four weeks for a lethal condition such as anencephaly (88 percent of obstetric ultrasound practitioners and 82 percent of clinical geneticists would facilitate termination), there was greater disagreement concerning other conditions. For instance, 76 percent of obstetric ultrasound practitioners would facilitate termination at twenty-four weeks for spina bifida, and this figure fell to 63 percent for Down syndrome, 60 percent for dwarfism, and 20 percent for cleft palate.[4] These results led the authors to conclude that "[t]here was a lack of consensus around which abnormalities were severe enough to warrant termination, and up to what gestation TOP is acceptable. This implies that the options open to a particular patient are likely to be determined by the subjective values of the practitioner she happens to see."[5]

---

[3] Medical Practitioners Board of Victoria, "Report on Late Terminations of Pregnancy" April 1998, 7, citing G. Geller et al., "Attitudes toward Abortion for Fetal Anomaly in the Second vs the Third Trimester: A Survey of Parisian Obstetricians" (1993) 13 *Prenatal Diagnosis* 707.

[4] J. Savulescu, "Is Current Practice around Late Termination of Pregnancy Eugenic and Discriminatory? Maternal Interests and Abortion" (2001) 27 *Journal of Medical Ethics* 165, 166–7.

[5] J. Savulescu, "Is Current Practice around Late Termination of Pregnancy Eugenic and Discriminatory? Maternal Interests and Abortion" (2001) 27 *Journal of Medical Ethics* 165, 167.

Savulescu found that his results were broadly consistent with the findings of a UK study conducted by Green, which was published in 1995.[6] The UK study also found a correlation between the perceived seriousness of the condition and the gestational stage at which abortion was considered appropriate by obstetricians. When asked about the latest stage at which they would offer termination for cystic fibrosis, 50 percent of the sample said that they would offer termination at twenty-four weeks, but this fell sharply to 8 percent after twenty-four weeks. By contrast, in the case of anencephaly, the proportion of respondents who would recommend termination after twenty-four weeks was 64 percent. This figure dropped to 21 percent for terminations after 24 weeks for spina bifida and further still to 13 percent after twenty-four weeks for Down syndrome.[7] As Green noted, these results imply that 92 percent of obstetricians surveyed "d[id] not think that cystic fibrosis qualifie[d] as a serious handicapping condition."[8] On this reasoning, only 21 percent and 13 percent, respectively, thought that spina bifida and Down syndrome were seriously handicapping conditions.[9]

Significantly, both Green and Savulescu found decreasing support for abortion for the same abnormalities as gestation progressed,

[6] J. Savulescu, "Is Current Practice around Late Termination of Pregnancy Eugenic and Discriminatory? Maternal Interests and Abortion" (2001) 27 *Journal of Medical Ethics* 165, 166–7; see J. Green, "Obstetricians' Views on Prenatal Diagnosis and Termination of Pregnancy: 1980 Compared with 1993" (1995) 102 *British Journal of Obstetrics and Gynaecology* 228.

[7] J. Green, "Obstetricians' Views on Prenatal Diagnosis and Termination of Pregnancy: 1980 Compared with 1993" (1995) 102 *British Journal of Obstetrics and Gynaecology* 228.

[8] J. Green, "Obstetricians' Views on Prenatal Diagnosis and Termination of Pregnancy: 1980 Compared with 1993" (1995) 102 *British Journal of Obstetrics and Gynaecology* 228, 232.

[9] J. Green, "Obstetricians' Views on Prenatal Diagnosis and Termination of Pregnancy: 1980 Compared with 1993" (1995) 102 *British Journal of Obstetrics and Gynaecology* 228, 230.

suggesting that obstetricians would offer termination for conditions that they did not think were seriously disabling, provided that the termination occurred earlier in pregnancy.[10] This serves to highlight the complexity of thinking about the seriousness threshold in relationship to gestational stage.[11] It suggests that maternal preference/health is a more influential factor than seriousness of abnormality for earlier terminations, and, indeed, this is reflected in the laws of many jurisdictions. These findings also suggest that obstetricians' perceptions of the fetus's status as pregnancy progresses and/or perhaps the increased risks associated with interruption of pregnancy at a later stage bear on their assessments as to whether a disability is sufficiently serious to justify abortion. Furthermore, the "seriousness" threshold may function as a means of enabling doctors to explain their lack of willingness to perform a termination where they feel a reluctance to assist. Thus, Wertz and Knoppers have commented that "the terms 'serious' and 'not serious' sometimes serve professionals' ethical needs to justify providing or withholding services."[12] The relationship between seriousness and gestational stage is also something to be borne in mind when considering the way in which determinations about "serious disability" are made in the context of PGD. As we will see later in section 3.3, some of the clinicians and counselors with whom we spoke noted

---

[10] J. Savulescu, "Is Current Practice around Late Termination of Pregnancy Eugenic and Discriminatory? Maternal Interests and Abortion" (2001) 27 *Journal of Medical Ethics* 165, 166–7; J. Green, "Obstetricians' Views on Prenatal Diagnosis and Termination of Pregnancy: 1980 Compared with 1993" (1995) 102 *British Journal of Obstetrics and Gynaecology* 228, 230.

[11] A different illustration of the same issue can be found in the 2010 RCOG report, "Termination of Pregnancy for Fetal Abnormality in England, Scotland and Wales," which states that "the decision to terminate a fetus with a severe isolated limb abnormality after 24 weeks clearly raises greater dilemmas than termination at an earlier stage of pregnancy." Royal College of Obstetricians and Gynaecologists, "Termination of Pregnancy for Fetal Abnormality in England, Scotland and Wales: Report of a Working Party' Party" (May 2010), 15.

[12] D. Wertz and B. Knoppers, "Serious Genetic Disorders: Can or Should They Be Defined?" (2002) 108 *American Journal of Medical Genetics* 29, 35.

that "seriousness" might be judged less strictly by prospective parents in the setting of deselecting an embryo compared with terminating an established pregnancy.

More recently, Habiba et al. conducted a European study of obstetricians' experiences with late termination of pregnancy.[13] This study asked participants which abnormalities were indications for abortion after twenty-three weeks. There was a high, though variable, proportion of respondents across the countries surveyed who agreed that "fetal congenital malformations" were an indication for late abortion: The percentage figures in the jurisdictions were 89 percent (Italy), 79 percent (Spain), 96 percent (France), 77 percent (Germany), 94 percent (Netherlands), 92 percent (Luxembourg), 99 percent (United Kingdom), and 86 percent (Sweden).[14] There was less consensus that Down syndrome was an indication for late abortion, where responses ranged from 17 percent among Dutch obstetricians to 89 percent among French obstetricians.[15]

Interestingly, only 50 percent of UK obstetricians in Habiba et al.'s study thought that Down syndrome was an indication for abortion after twenty-three weeks,[16] a figure significantly lower than that reported by Green fourteen years earlier. This gives some indication of the variability of perceptions about the disabling nature of conditions over time, an issue that squarely emerged in Statham et al.'s study of

---

[13] M. Habiba et al., "Late Termination of Pregnancy: A Comparison of Obstetricians' Experience in Eight European Countries" (2009) 116 *British Journal of Obstetrics and Gynaecology* 1340.

[14] M. Habiba et al., "Late Termination of Pregnancy: A Comparison of Obstetricians' Experience in Eight European Countries" (2009) 116 *British Journal of Obstetrics and Gynaecology* 1340, 1343.

[15] M. Habiba et al., "Late Termination of Pregnancy: A Comparison of Obstetricians' Experience in Eight European Countries" (2009) 116 *British Journal of Obstetrics and Gynaecology* 1340, 1343.

[16] M. Habiba et al., "Late Termination of Pregnancy: A Comparison of Obstetricians' Experience in Eight European Countries" (2009) 116 *British Journal of Obstetrics and Gynaecology* 1340, 1343.

UK obstetricians' experiences with late abortion in four maternal fetal units.[17] In this study, the authors found that

> [i]n each of the four units, at least one doctor observed ... that attitudes to terminating pregnancies for Down syndrome and for other conditions such as achondroplasia were changing ... [f]or achondroplasia, the changes appear to have been absolute, i.e., the condition is not deemed to meet the criteria for termination after 24 weeks whereas previously it would have and even though similarly affected pregnancies will be terminated ... earlier in pregnancy.[18]

These findings signal that the scope of seriousness is capable of contraction as well as expansion. In their international study of genetics professionals' understandings of the meaning of "serious genetic disorders," Wertz and Knoppers found a "wide overlap between the categories serious and nonserious," which they suggest could be attributed to "the effects of economic, cultural and social environment."[19] To illustrate the point, they go on to argue that

> [a] treatable condition, such as cleft palate, thalassemia or PKU, may be not serious if treatments are indeed available and affordable, but could be serious if the treatment or the special diet is unaffordable. Although many people think that disorders associated with mental retardation or neurological impairment are more serious than other conditions, there may be wide variations in economic support and social perceptions that transform serious into not serious.[20]

[17] H. Statham et al., "Late Termination of Pregnancy: Law, Policy and Decision-making in Four English Fetal Medicine Units" (2006) 113 *British Journal of Obstetrics and Gynaecology* 1402.

[18] H. Statham et al., "Late Termination of Pregnancy: Law, Policy and Decision-making in Four English Fetal Medicine Units" (2006) 113 *British Journal of Obstetrics and Gynaecology* 1402, 1407.

[19] D. Wertz and B. Knoppers, "Serious Genetic Disorders: Can or Should They Be Defined?" (2002) 108 *American Journal of Medical Genetics* 29, at 34.

[20] D. Wertz and B. Knoppers, "Serious Genetic Disorders: Can or Should They Be Defined?" (2002) 108 *American Journal of Medical Genetics* 29, 34.

Other factors, such as concerns about community disapproval or legal liability, might also impact on obstetricians' behavior, if not their attitudes. A majority of obstetricians in a study conducted by Savulescu and de Crespigny thought that patient management was affected by the lack of legal clarity about abortion in Victoria[21] (medical abortion has since been decriminalized in that jurisdiction, but it remains an offense in some circumstances in six other Australian jurisdictions). Further, a majority of respondents reported that they had "recently limited their offering of abortion for fetal abnormality" in response to factors such as "press coverage," the Victorian "late abortion case," and "increased concern about legal uncertainty."[22]

Levels of community support or tolerance for abortion compared with PGD may be a crucial point of distinction. Over time, the number of conditions that may be tested for by PGD have expanded fairly rapidly. At Genea (formerly Sydney IVF), for instance, the list of conditions tested for increased from 76 conditions in 2006 to 145 conditions in 2009. Although we can only speculate about the reasons for this, it would seem to reflect both the clinic's improving technological capability to detect genetic conditions and prospective parents' growing awareness of, and increased desire to use, this new technology. Against this, there may be limits on the use of PGD that are not specifically tied to perceptions of serious disability. PGD is expensive and dependent on the woman's willingness to engage in IVF, with all of its associated risks, stresses, and discomforts.[23] But the expansion might also point to

[21] J. Savulescu and L. J. de Crespigny, "Pregnant Women with Fetal Abnormalities: The Forgotten People in the Abortion Debate" (2008) 188 *Medical Journal of Australia* 100, 101.

[22] J. Savulescu and L. J. de Crespigny, "Pregnant Women with Fetal Abnormalities: The Forgotten People in the Abortion Debate" (2008) 188 *Medical Journal of Australia* 100, 101.

[23] Karatas, for example, has found that although PGD alleviated some stresses by giving women a sense of control about their reproductive options, the stress experienced by women undergoing PGD was nonetheless significant: Karatas et al., "Women's Experience of Pre-implantation Genetic Diagnosis: A Qualitative Study"

an absence of serious and/or widespread public concern about the use of PGD to select against a broader range of conditions. This may be because the practice of PGD is relatively unknown among members of the public or because the genetic deselection of embryos for "serious disability" is not seen as involving the same moral/social concerns as does terminating a pregnancy. It is interesting to note, however, that a recent U.S. study on public attitudes toward PGD found no necessary correlation between respondents' perceptions about the status of the embryo and their beliefs about the acceptability of PGD.[24] Thus, about half of the respondents who assigned maximum moral worth to an embryo in vitro nonetheless regarded PGD as acceptable to avoid a fatal childhood disease. By contrast, of the respondents who did not approve of PGD, only 38 percent rated the human embryo in vitro as having maximum moral worth.[25]

2 POTENTIAL SOLUTIONS: POLICY RESPONSES TO DETERMINING SERIOUS DISABILITY

In light of the lack of professional consensus about where to draw the line between serious and not serious conditions we might ask: Should

---

(2010) 30 *Prenatal Diagnosis* 771–7. See also Sarah Franklin and Celia Roberts, who comment that for women undertaking PGD "[t]he ... contrast, between chance and control, adds what is often referred to as a paradoxical dimension to PGD in that intensification of the power to diagnose is also, at another level, amplification of pathology ... since arrival at PGD confirms the presence of more serious disease, the prospect of 'greater control' is double-edged (possibly more control but only in relation to a worse set of prospects)": S. Franklin and C. Roberts, *Born and Made: An Ethnography of Preimplantation Genetic Diagnosis* (Princeton, NJ: Princeton University Press, 2006), 124–5.

[24] K. L. Hudson, "Preimplantation Genetic Diagnosis: Public Policy and Public Attitudes" (2006) 85(6) *Fertility and Sterility* 1638.

[25] K. L. Hudson, "Preimplantation Genetic Diagnosis: Public Policy and Public Attitudes" (2006) 85(6) *Fertility and Sterility* 1638, 1641.

seriousness be defined? Is there a place for further refining the correct approach to determining what is a serious condition?

In the field of PGD, various regulatory strategies have been used to assist with the determination of which conditions are serious. The strategy of producing a legislative list to define or prescribe which conditions are serious conditions was not favored in any of the Australian jurisdictions or in the United Kingdom. However, lists of conditions have been generated as a consequence of the licensing approval processes and annual reporting requirements undertaken by statutorily constituted regulatory bodies (such as the HFEA, the RTC in Western Australia and formerly the ITA in Victoria, and the SACRT in South Australia). In addition to this, lists of conditions have been made available by private clinics seeking to inform prospective clients about the services that they provide. While these lists do not fix the meaning of the phrase "serious disability" (or its variants) – and are open to revision and expansion (and, theoretically, contraction) – they do provide an indication of how this term has been, and is being, interpreted. The regulatory processes that have led to the development of these lists have themselves involved multidisciplinary discussions, first, at the level of the clinic, and, second, by the regulatory committee charged with the responsibility of issuing or refusing licenses for appropriate use.

Another approach (which may or may not operate in tandem with a list of serious conditions) is what might be termed a criteria-based approach. This approach seeks to articulate the factors that are to be considered by the regulators or clinicians, as appropriate, in reaching a decision about whether a condition is serious. As we examined in Chapter 4, this approach has been adopted by the HFEA and is also currently being used in some Australian jurisdictions, in compliance with the NHMRC ART guidelines and some state legislative requirements, and in New Zealand.

Do these approaches to refining the meaning of "serious" translate to the context of abortion? There are of course both similarities and differences between the regulatory frameworks and social consequences of these selection practices that need to be borne in mind. An obvious difference between the regulation of PGD, on one hand, and abortion for fetal abnormality, on the other, is that, in the case of the former, some jurisdictions have opted to create specially constituted regulatory bodies to take a more formal role in overseeing its use. Although such bodies have not been a feature in every jurisdiction, they are being used, or have been used, in the United Kingdom, Victoria, South Australia, Western Australia, and New Zealand. By contrast, abortion for fetal abnormality has never been regulated in this way. There are also, of course, some crucial practical differences between abortion and PGD that could account for these differences: The first leads to the end of a pregnancy that is no longer desired, and the second concerns the implantation of embryos unaffected by the serious condition about which the woman is concerned. We need to remember that the consequences of legal or regulatory limitations on access are different for these two groups of women. Although denial of access to PGD and termination both frustrate reproductive desires, the denial of access to PGD does not preclude the woman from becoming pregnant, whereas refusing access to termination requires the woman to proceed with the unwanted pregnancy.

Despite these differences, it is possible to draw some key comparisons between the policy approaches that have been taken to defining or assessing "serious disability" in the context of abortion and those just mentioned for PGD (and discussed in some detail in the previous chapter).

2.1 A List-based Approach to Determining Seriousness

The differing views among clinicians about the meaning of "serious disability" in the abortion context have led to suggestions that it is necessary that this phrase should be defined more tightly or a list of conditions be developed. In 2007, the House of Commons Science and Technology Committee on the Scientific Developments relating to the Abortion Act[26] considered some of these arguments.[27] The Committee's report noted the argument advanced by the Christian Medical Fellowship that a legal definition should be introduced "so that abnormalities are treated in the same way across the medical profession."[28] Further, it noted the view that "the wording [of the Act] could be made more precise to give [the profession a clearer understanding of] what Parliament's intention is as to what these words should mean."[29]

Drafting a list of seriously disabling conditions would remove some of the doubt surrounding the meaning of the phrase "serious disability." But while this would provide more certainty to clinicians, it would do this by removing or limiting their discretion to provide terminations for abnormalities that were not on the list. Although the Science and Technology Committee acknowledged that there was some evidence of public disquiet about the application of s 1(1)(d) of the Abortion Act and cited three "controversial" examples of the use of abortion for fetal abnormality (the abortion at twenty-eight weeks of a fetus with bilateral cleft lip and palate, the abortion of twenty fetuses between 1996 and 2006 for clubbed feet, and the rate of abortion following

[26] House of Commons Science and Technology Committee, "Scientific Developments Relating to the Abortion Act 1967: Twelfth Report of Session 2006–07 (Volume 1)": see http://www.publications.parliament.uk/pa/cm200607/cmselect/cmsctech/1045/1045i.pdf (accessed on 21 June 2011).

[27] House of Commons Science and Technology Committee, "Scientific Developments Relating to the Abortion Act 1967: Twelfth Report of Session 2006–07 (Volume 1)" para. 79.

[28] House of Commons Science and Technology Committee, "Scientific Developments Relating to the Abortion Act 1967: Twelfth Report of Session 2006–07 (Volume 1)" para. 74.

[29] House of Commons Science and Technology Committee, "Scientific Developments Relating to the Abortion Act 1967: Twelfth Report of Session 2006–07 (Volume 1)" para. 75.

diagnosis of Down syndrome [around 50 percent]), it was nevertheless not persuaded that a list would be helpful.[30]

In the United Kingdom and Australia, a list-based approach has not been adopted in the case of abortion. Indeed, the idea of adopting a list has been met with considerable resistance from professional bodies and commissions.[31] In its 2006 report *Making Babies: Reproductive Decisions and Genetic Technologies,* the Human Genetics Commission, when discussing the meaning of "seriously handicapped" in the UK Abortion Act, stated:

> [I]t has proved difficult to define what is meant by "serious." One way of doing this would be to draw up a list of conditions that are considered to lead to a very poor quality of life, and to restrict consideration to these conditions. However, this approach fails to recognise that *quality of life judgements are subjective,* and that genetic disorders are variable in terms of severity and health outcomes. There is evidence to suggest that people with genetic disorders, their families and professionals *all have different views about which conditions give rise to a poor quality of life...*For this reason, the decision about what counts as serious is in practice left to the judgement of prospective parents in consultation with medical staff. [emphasis added][32]

In 2010, the RCOG report entitled *Termination of Pregnancy for Fetal Abnormality in England, Scotland and Wales* (2010 RCOG report) also

---

[30] House of Commons Science and Technology Committee, "Scientific Developments Relating to the Abortion Act 1967: Twelfth Report of Session 2006–07 (Volume 1)" para. 73 and 79.

[31] It may be, however, that the practice of testing embryos for serious genetic conditions is more amenable than termination of pregnancy to a list-based approach. Factors that might impel regulators to use this approach include the scale and clinical organization of testing services and the relative certainty of prognosis for serious genetic conditions provided by PGD compared with that provided by ultrasound.

[32] Human Genetics Commission, "Making Babies: Reproductive Decisions and Genetic Technologies" (January 2006), 36–37.

rejected the efficacy and desirability of a list of "serious" conditions. The following reasons were offered:

> Precise definition is impractical for two reasons. Firstly, sufficiently advanced diagnostic techniques capable of accurately defining abnormalities or of predicting the seriousness of outcomes are not currently available. Secondly, the consequences of an abnormality are difficult to predict, not only for the fetus in terms of viability or residual disability but also in relation to the impact in childhood as well as on the family into which the child would be born.[33]

Of course, the law could conceivably provide answers to these questions: For example, the act could be drafted in such a way as to make it clear that "serious" was to be judged from a particular perspective, or from multiple perspectives. However, the crucial matter that this submission highlights is that the detection of fetal anomaly is just the starting point for deliberations about seriousness. Within such a framework, knowledge of what the abnormality is will not always be sufficient on its own to enable a judgment to be made about whether that condition is "serious." For example, in some cases the fetal abnormality itself might be determinative, but this cannot be assumed. Whereas most people would judge anencephaly to be serious enough to justify a termination late in pregnancy, for instance, not all prospective mothers do – and some will continue with the pregnancy in the belief that the condition does not justify abortion. Conversely, fewer people might regard a *correctable* cardiac malformation as serious enough to justify an abortion late in pregnancy. But, some women – perhaps because of existing responsibilities to other children, or to a lack of private health insurance, or to living a vast distance from the children's hospital where multiple surgeries would have to be performed, or to having been recently widowed – might regard the condition as a serious handicap.

---

[33] Royal College of Obstetricians and Gynaecologists, "Termination of Pregnancy for Fetal Abnormality in England, Scotland and Wales: Report of a Working Party" (May 2010), 9–10.

Consequently, "ordering" conditions from least to most severe in a linear fashion is not the favored policy approach to assessing which conditions are serious handicaps. This takes us back to our discussion in Chapter 1 about the highly varied and variable contributions of social arrangements and histories, perceptions, resources, and support, as well as impairments, to what constitutes a disability. Because disability is both more and less than an impairment of normal functioning in a person, its determination is not an abstract exercise. Thus, a contextually driven understanding of "serious" tends to militate against the use of lists to denote which conditions are serious.

There is evidence that this is acknowledged by the clinicians involved. In their study of health professionals in maternal-fetal units, Williams et al. found that most health professionals were not comfortable with the idea of drawing up a list of "serious" conditions.[34] Although a minority of participants thought that practitioners had a duty to "make sure lines were drawn, particularly around what they perceived as more minor conditions," a majority believed that "individuals should have the right to make the choice."[35] These beliefs seem to have arisen from a realization that there is much disagreement – even among clinicians – about which conditions are serious.[36] Similarly, Statham et al. found that there was little support among health professionals in four English fetal medicine units for creation of a list of conditions for termination after viability.[37] In this study, the authors found that "a list was seen to have an overwhelming

---

[34] C. Williams et al., "'Drawing the Line' in Prenatal Screening and Testing: Health Practitioners' Discussions" (2002) 4(1) *Health, Risk and Society* 61, 64.

[35] C. Williams et al., "'Drawing the Line' in Prenatal Screening and Testing: Health Practitioners' Discussions" (2002) 4(1) *Health, Risk and Society* 61, 67, and 68.

[36] See C. Williams et al., "'Drawing the Line' in Prenatal Screening and Testing: Health Practitioners' Discussions" (2002) 4(1) *Health, Risk and Society* 61, 69.

[37] H. Statham et al., "Late Termination of Pregnancy: Law, Policy and Decision-making in Four English Fetal Medicine Units" (2006) 113 *British Journal of Obstetrics and Gynaecology* 1402.

disadvantage."[38] The concerns raised by participants included that a list would constrain their ability to facilitate individualized decisions, could not take account of the range of severity of conditions, and might reduce the level of care available to infants born with a listed condition.[39] Statham at al. conclude:

> Overall, formal lists were not seen as a satisfactory solution, whereas "guidance" might be welcomed. A list could provide an indication of acceptability, which would give the practitioner the security of knowing they were acting within a framework accepted by peers. It could, however, act as a pressure for doctors to adhere to that list.[40]

One of the further themes that emerged from Statham's study is that a list of sorts is "evolving by consensus" despite the absence of a prescribed one. Making this point, one respondent remarked, "I'm completely opposed to lists for late terminations ... but a kind of unspoken list is beginning to develop, even if it's not a list, it's just areas of anxiety and areas of uncertainty and areas of no-go."[41]

The opposition from some maternal-fetal specialists to the idea of drafting a list of conditions to guide judgments about serious disabilities might stem from concerns about limiting patient autonomy and/ or professional discretion. Of course, the commitment to these values above others (for example, social or distributive justice) is also to

---

[38] H. Statham et al., "Late Termination of Pregnancy: Law, Policy and Decision-making in Four English Fetal Medicine Units" (2006) 113 *British Journal of Obstetrics and Gynaecology* 1402, 1407.

[39] H. Statham et al., "Late Termination of Pregnancy: Law, Policy and Decision-making in Four English Fetal Medicine Units" (2006) 113 *British Journal of Obstetrics and Gynaecology* 1402, 1407–8.

[40] H. Statham et al., "Late Termination of Pregnancy: Law, Policy and Decision-making in Four English Fetal Medicine Units" (2006) 113 *British Journal of Obstetrics and Gynaecology* 1402, 1408.

[41] H. Statham et al., "Late Termination of Pregnancy: Law, Policy and Decision-making in Four English Fetal Medicine Units" (2006) 113 *British Journal of Obstetrics and Gynaecology* 1402, 1408.

some extent socially and culturally bound. Wertz and Knoppers, for instance, found significant regional differences in the ways in which the geneticists in their study framed their support for or opposition to defining "serious." Thus, "American geneticists generally opposed list making, rejected the idea of limiting services, and thought that decisions should be made by individual patients. Their views were based in part on support for individual and family autonomy in a free market where everything should be available to those who can pay."[42] In contrast to this, the authors commented that in jurisdictions that possessed national health insurance schemes, such as Canada and parts of Europe, there was "an impetus to try to define serious, in genetics and other areas of medicine, in order to apportion services equally to all who need them."[43]

2.2 Abortion Statistics and Seriousness

Despite the rejection of a list in all Australian jurisdictions and the United Kingdom, it is still possible to gain an indication from the published data on terminations for fetal abnormality after or close to viability of the sorts of conditions that are regarded as serious by women with an affected pregnancy and their clinicians. However, we should also bear in mind that these serious conditions are to some extent an artifact of the technological means to detect them. Overwhelmingly, the conditions that are considered indications for late termination are those that the available technology is able to detect, that is, structural abnormalities detectable on ultrasound scan and certain chromosomal abnormalities detectable by CVS or amniocentesis.

---

[42] D. Wertz and B. Knoppers, "Serious Genetic Disorders: Can or Should They Be Defined?" (2002) 108 *American Journal of Medical Genetics* 29, 34.

[43] D. Wertz and B. Knoppers, "Serious Genetic Disorders: Can or Should They Be Defined?" (2002) 108 *American Journal of Medical Genetics* 29, 34.

The most recently published data in the United Kingdom for abortions under s 1(1)(d) group the conditions according to the World Health Organisation's International Classification of Diseases (10th revision).[44] These include abnormalities of the central nervous system (such as anencephaly, hydrocephalus, spina bifida, and other malformations of the brain). The 2010 RCOG report indicates that in 2008, "one third of terminations undertaken beyond 24 weeks [gestation] were for abnormalities of the central nervous system."[45] The report states further that "[t]his is likely to reflect the greater certainty that the abnormality would result in serious handicap."[46] Other categories include severe cardiac, renal, musculoskeletal, "other" structural (including facial clefting), and chromosomal abnormalities. Of the musculoskeletal abnormalities category, the report states that "[a]lthough many skeletal abnormalities are lethal, isolated absent or abnormal limbs and other skeletal dysplasias, such as achondroplasia, are often shocking to parents but not always associated with 'severe' handicap."[47] The fact that there were fewer than ten late term abortions in this category in 2008 may lend some support to the view expressed in the Statham study that achondroplasia is no longer regarded by many obstetricians in England as a "seriously handicapping condition."[48]

---

[44] World Health Organization, "International Statistical Classification of Diseases and Related Health Problems 10th Revision Version for 2007": see http://apps.who.int/classifications/apps/icd/icd10online/ (accessed on 21 June 2011).

[45] Royal College of Obstetricians and Gynaecologists, "Termination of Pregnancy for Fetal Abnormality in England, Scotland and Wales: Report of a Working Party" (May 2010), 13–14.

[46] Royal College of Obstetricians and Gynaecologists, "Termination of Pregnancy for Fetal Abnormality in England, Scotland and Wales: Report of a Working Party" (May 2010), 14.

[47] Royal College of Obstetricians and Gynaecologists, "Termination of Pregnancy for Fetal Abnormality in England, Scotland and Wales: Report of a Working Party" (May 2010), 14.

[48] Royal College of Obstetricians and Gynaecologists, "Termination of Pregnancy for Fetal Abnormality in England, Scotland and Wales: Report of a Working Party" (May 2010), 14.

Chromosomal abnormalities (including Down syndrome, Edwards' syndrome, and Patau's syndrome) only accounted for 22 percent of abortions after 24 weeks in 2008, after central nervous system abnormalities (34 percent) and "other" congenital malformations (35 percent). Equivalent national statistics for Australia are more difficult to obtain given the various and varied reporting regimes and data collection in operation.[49] However, the available statistics for most jurisdictions include neural tube defects and chromosomal abnormalities.[50] The Victorian perinatal data collection unit, for example, reported that in the period 2003–4, 86 percent of pregnancies affected by Edwards' syndrome (trisomy 18) were terminated. Further, 81 percent of pregnancies affected by neural tube defects (including 93 percent affected by anencephaly and 73 percent affected by spina bifida); 72 percent of

---

[49] On the patchiness of reporting and data analysis of the induced abortion and congenital abnormality rates across Australia, see the Australian Institute of Health and Welfare (AIHW) National Perinatal Statistics Unit Website available at http://www.preru.unsw.edu.au/PRERUWeb.nsf/page/ba3, as well as the AIHW reports *Use of Routinely Collected National Data Sets for Reporting on Induced Abortion in Australia* (2005) and *Recommendations for Development of a New Australian Birth Anomalies System* (2004) (both available at http://www.aihw.gov.au/publications-catalogue/?taxonomy_id=6442451339,6442451130). The national data set proposed in the latter report is now in the process of being set up: see http://www.npsu.unsw.edu.au/PRERUWeb.nsf/page/CADC. However, it seems this data consolidation effort is still a work in progress, as the most recent AIHW national report on congenital abnormalities, while published in 2008, only includes data collected from 2002–3 (see AIHW, *Congenital Abnormalities in Australia 2002–2003* (2008), available at http://www.aihw.gov.au/publications-catalogue/?taxonomy_id=6442451339,6442451130). The AIHW did, however, recently release a report looking specifically at the prevalence of neural tube defects (see *Neural Tube Defects in Australia: An Epidemiological Report* (2008), also available at http://www.aihw.gov.au/publications-catalogue/?taxonomy_id=6442451339,6442451130).

[50] Chapter 4 of the AIWH report *Recommendations for Development of a New Australian Birth Anomalies System* (2004) provides an overview of the reporting obligations and data collection practices in the various Australian jurisdictions, including which types of anomalies (structural, chromosomal, etc.) are included for the purposes of the relevant reporting requirements.

pregnancies affected by Down syndrome, and an unspecified number of pregnancies affected by cleft lip and palate were terminated.[51] The report does not specify at what gestational stage these terminations were carried out, and it is not possible to tell whether the relative rates of termination reflect clinician or parental ambivalence about these conditions or the stage at which they were detected.

The 2010 RCOG report concludes that the UK national statistics suggest some changing trends in abortion for fetal abnormality. These trends seem to have been influenced by technological improvements and by a changing cultural climate. The report speculates that the decrease in late terminations for hydrocephalus

> may be due to earlier diagnosis, the availability of better diagnostic and prognostic information ... and/or a more conservative approach to pregnancy termination after 24 weeks of gestation. Conversely, there seems to be an increase in terminations for cardiac abnormalities, probably reflecting the increasing emphasis on ultrasound screening for cardiac abnormalities and improving expertise in diagnostic fetal echocardiography.[52]

This reinforces the idea that the technology that is available, and health service providers' willingness to use it to detect particular abnormalities, both play a role in determining which conditions are "serious."

2.3 United Kingdom: Criterion-based Approach

In the absence of a list or a definition of "serious handicap," the consultative approach favored by the Human Genetics Commission provides little guidance to doctors as to what the legal limits are for

[51] Victorian Perinatal Data Collection Unit, "Summary of Ten Most Frequently Reported Birth Defects in Victoria 2003–2004."
[52] Royal College of Obstetricians and Gynaecologists, "Termination of Pregnancy for Fetal Abnormality in England, Scotland and Wales: Report of a Working Party" (May 2010), 15.

serious disability terminations. With this in mind, the Science and Technology Committee Report suggested that the Department of Health "commission work to produce guidance that would be clinically useful to doctors and patients."[53] Further, it noted that the production of such guidance would be "enhanced by better collection of data relating to the reasons for abortion beyond 24 weeks for foetal abnormality."[54]

An alternative approach to producing a list of conditions has been to identify the criteria relevant to the determination of whether a disability is "serious." Indeed, this was the approach taken by the Royal College of Obstetricians and Gynaecologists in 1996 when it first published its guidance on how members should interpret section 1(1)(d) of the Act (1996 RCOG guidelines).[55] Drawing upon the World Health Organization's definition of disability, the 1996 RCOG guidelines identified two categories of impairment that would capture what was meant by the term "seriously handicapped" as understood "by most people."[56] These reflect WHO points 3 and 4, namely:

3. Assisted performance: the need for a helping hand (i.e. the individual can perform the activity or sustain the behaviour, whether augmented by aids or not, only with some assistance from another person).

4. Dependent performance: includes complete dependence on the presence of another person (i.e., the individual can perform the

[53] House of Commons Science and Technology Committee, "Scientific Developments Relating to the Abortion Act 1967: Twelfth Report of Session 2006–07 (Volume 1)" para. 81: see http://www.publications.parliament.uk/pa/cm200607/cmselect/cmsctech/1045/1045i.pdf (accessed on 21 June 2011)

[54] House of Commons Science and Technology Committee, "Scientific Developments Relating to the Abortion Act 1967: Twelfth Report of Session 2006–07 (Volume 1)" para. 82: see http://www.publications.parliament.uk/pa/cm200607/cmselect/cmsctech/1045/1045i.pdf (accessed on 21 June 2011).

[55] RCOG, Termination of Pregnancy for Foetal Abnormality in England, Wales and Scotland (January 1996).

[56] RCOG, Termination of Pregnancy for Foetal Abnormality in England, Wales and Scotland (January 1996), para. 3.3.2.

activity or sustain the behaviour but only when someone is with him most of the time).[57]

The 1996 RCOG guidelines further state that "a person is only likely to be regarded as seriously handicapped if they need the support described in the WHO points 3 or 4."[58] However, in the case of forming an opinion about the likely "serious handicap" to be associated with a particular fetal abnormality, the guidance states that the following factors should be given careful consideration:

1. The probability of effective treatment, either *in utero* or after birth;
2. The probable degree of self awareness and of ability to communicate with others;
3. The suffering that would be experienced;
4. The extent to which actions essential for health that normal individuals perform unaided would have to be provided by others.[59]

These factors are consistent with those that have been identified elsewhere in the literature. Thus, to provide that there should be consideration of the potential for effective treatment is broadly consistent with attitudes that it is questionable whether cleft lip, clubfoot, or even hereditary cancer is a serious enough condition to justify abortion/selection against it.[60] The second and third factors seem to be crucial

---

[57] RCOG, Termination of Pregnancy for Foetal Abnormality in England, Wales and Scotland (January 1996), para 3.3.2.
[58] RCOG, Termination of Pregnancy for Foetal Abnormality in England, Wales and Scotland (January 1996), para. 3.3.3.
[59] RCOG, Termination of Pregnancy for Foetal Abnormality in England, Wales and Scotland (January 1996), para. 3.3.3.
[60] J. Fisher, "Termination of Pregnancy for Fetal Abnormality: The Perspective of a Parent Support Organisation" (2008) 16 (31 Supplement) *Reproductive Health Matters* 57, 59–60; G. Quinn, "Conflict between Values and Technology: Perception of PGD among Women at Increased Risk for Hereditary Breast and Ovarian Cancer" (2009) 8 *Familial Cancer* 441, 444, and 447; A. L. Bredenoord et al., "Dealing with Uncertainties: Ethics of Prenatal Diagnosis and PGD to Prevent Mitochondrial

to the characterization of diseases such as Tay-Sachs disease and anencephaly as "serious."[61] Finally, there is evidence that the fourth factor mentioned is also considered to be highly relevant in decisionmaking. Breslau, for example, measures the severity of particular handicaps by assessing how dependent on other people, in daily activities, a child suffering from such a handicap would be.[62]

The 1996 RCOG guidelines did not elaborate on whether these criteria were to be measured from the perspective of the prospective parents or the future child, although it did urge that, seeing as "seriously handicapped" had not been the subject of judicial interpretation, certifying doctors should take a "cautious" approach.[63] This was somewhat clarified in the 2010 revision of the RCOG guidelines,[64] *Termination of Pregnancy for Fetal Abnormality in England, Scotland and Wales: Report of a Working Party*, where the issue of interests involved – child (if born), family, and society – is addressed more directly. The 2010 RCOG report states that both "the size of the risk" and the "gravity of the abnormality" are important considerations and that doctors should consider the following factors:

1. the potential for effective treatment, either *in utero* or after birth
2. *on the part of the child*, the probable degree of self-awareness and of ability to communicate with others [our emphasis]
3. the suffering that would be experienced

Disorders" (2008) 14(1) *Human Reproduction Update* 83, 90; T. Krahn, "Where Are We Going with Preimplantation Genetic Diagnosis?" (2007) 176 (10) *Canadian Medical Association Journal* 1445.

[61] K. Evans, "The Gene Genie" *Sunday Age* (14 March 2010), 11.

[62] N. Breslau et al., "Abortion of Defective Foetuses: Attitudes of Mothers of Congenitally Impaired Children" 49(4) (1987) *Journal of Marriage and the Family* 839 at 843.

[63] RCOG, Termination of Pregnancy for Foetal Abnormality in England, Wales and Scotland (January 1996) para. 3.3.3.

[64] Royal College of Obstetricians and Gynaecologists, "Termination of Pregnancy for Fetal Abnormality in England, Scotland and Wales: Report of a Working Party" (May 2010).

4. the probability of being able to live alone and to be self-supportive as an adult
5. *on the part of society*, the extent to which actions performed by individuals without disability that are essential for health would have to be provided by others [our emphasis][65]

In comparing the two guidances, we can see that the first and third factors remain largely unchanged since the 1996 guidelines. The language "on the part of the child" has been added to the second factor, and "on the part of society" has been added to the fifth factor (with a slight alteration to the language). A new factor ("the probability of being able to live alone and to be self-supportive as an adult") has been added.

This raises two novel points of construction. First, the absence of language in factors 1, 3, and 4 indicating that those matters should be considered from a particular perspective suggests that these factors need not be assessed only from either the child's or the society's perspective. They are capable of encompassing the impact on the family as well as the child. Second, inclusion of societal interests in factor 5 suggests that matters such as the cost to the community of providing care related services to disabled citizens may be taken into consideration. The recognition of this interest in the multifactorial analysis clarifies and possibly extends the earlier guidance and conveys the sentiment that society has an interest in avoiding serious disability.

The 2010 report affirmed that "there is no legal definition of serious handicap," but this is not viewed as a problem.[66] Indeed the report concluded that there was "little reason to change the current law regarding the definition of serious abnormality" on the grounds that "it would

[65] Royal College of Obstetricians and Gynaecologists, "Termination of Pregnancy for Fetal Abnormality in England, Scotland and Wales: Report of a Working Party" (May 2010), 9.
[66] Royal College of Obstetricians and Gynaecologists, "Termination of Pregnancy for Fetal Abnormality in England, Scotland and Wales: Report of a Working Party" (May 2010), 10.

be unrealistic to produce a definitive list of conditions that constitute serious handicap."[67] The preferred approach was that clinicians would provide "[a]n assessment of the seriousness of a fetal abnormality ... on a case by case appraisal, taking into account all available clinical information"[68]

Unarguably, the criteria-based approach offers a flexibility that the list-based approach does not: It is adaptive to the individual circumstances of the woman seeking termination. This policy approach accords with that favored in the context of PGD in the United Kingdom and in some Australian jurisdictions. However, a notable difference between PGD and abortion guidelines is that the PGD criteria *expressly* note the consultative nature of the exercise. Thus, to take one example canvassed in Chapter 4, an early version of the HFEA Clinical Guidance Letter expressly stated that "[t]he decision to use PGD is expected to be made in consideration of the unique circumstances of those seeking treatment, rather than the fact that they carry a particular genetic condition."[69] More recently, in the eighth edition of the HFEA Code of Practice Guidance 10 it is stated that in determining whether PGD should be used, the center should take into account factors such as "the views of the people seeking treatment in relation to the condition" and "their previous reproductive experience."[70] It also makes explicit reference to some of the matters that are merely implicit in the RCOG guidances. In other words, it provides that the following matters should also be considered: "the extent of any intellectual

---

[67] Royal College of Obstetricians and Gynaecologists, "Termination of Pregnancy for Fetal Abnormality in England, Scotland and Wales: Report of a Working Party" (May 2010), 10.

[68] Royal College of Obstetricians and Gynaecologists, "Termination of Pregnancy for Fetal Abnormality in England, Scotland and Wales: Report of a Working Party" (May 2010), 10.

[69] HFEA, "Guidance on Preimplantation Testing" 15 May 2003: see http://www.hfea.gov.uk/2686.html (accessed on 21 July 2011).

[70] HFEA, "Code of Practice" (8th edition: 2009), 10.7(a).

impairment," "the social support available," "the speed of degeneration in progressive disorders," and "the family circumstances of the people seeking treatment."[71] Although on the face of this, it would appear that the clinical diagnosis receives more emphasis in the termination criteria than the PGD criteria, the HFEA guidance to clinics must still be read in the context of the overall HFEA licensing process. The PGD licensing committee, established by the HFEA to assess applications to undertake PGD, adopts an approach that seems less explicitly geared toward context based decisions. As discussed in Chapter 4, the approach to the statutory criteria of "risk" and "seriousness" set out in the explanatory note for the licensing committee adheres much more closely to statistical criteria and factors that might be objectively measurable.[72]

As we saw previously, despite the availability of the RCOG criteria for termination, doctors in the United Kingdom continue to have quite varied opinions about the extent to which conditions that are not life threatening are "seriously handicapping." These variations exist

---

[71] HFEA, "Code of Practice" (8th edition: 2009), 10.6(d),(e), (f), and (g).

[72] For instance, "particular" and "significant" risk are distinguished according to heritability and penetrance, respectively. Seriousness is determined on the basis of a number of factors including age of onset, symptoms, treatability, and quality of life. So, while the HFEA Code of Practice Guidance counsels clinics to have regard to the perspectives of those seeking treatment and the likely impact on the family of the condition in question, the PGD licensing committee appears to take a more scientific approach to questions of seriousness. "Quality of life," for instance, is described in the memo as including such matters as the speed of degeneration in progressive disorders and the extent of any physical and /or intellectual impairment. In some circumstances, it could be difficult to assess quality of life outside the family context into which the individual in question would be born. Therefore, it is highly likely that such issues are taken into the mix when the committee is weighing up its decision whether to authorize PGD for a particular condition or not. Human Fertilisation and Embryology Authority Preimplantation Diagnostic Testing ("PGD") Explanatory Note for Licence Committee 28 October 2010 at http://www.hfea.gov.uk/docs/2010-10-28_Licence_Committee_PGD_Explanatory_note.PDF (accessed 20 November 2011)).

between cultures as well as within them.[73] To take yet another example, the American Medical Association's (AMA's) policy (H-5.982 Late-term Pregnancy Termination Techniques)[74] recommends against third-trimester terminations for any conditions that are not life-threatening:

> In recognition of the constitutional principles regarding the right to an abortion articulated by the Supreme Court in *Roe v.Wade*, and in keeping with the science and values of medicine, the AMA recommends that abortions not be performed in the third trimester *except in cases of serious fetal anomalies incompatible with life*. Although third-trimester abortions can be performed to preserve the life or health of the mother, they are, in fact, generally not necessary for those purposes. Except in extraordinary circumstances, maternal health factors which demand termination of the pregnancy can be accommodated without sacrifice of the fetus, and the near certainty of the independent viability of the fetus argues for ending the pregnancy by appropriate delivery.[75] [emphasis added]

Thus, within the United States, an abortion after viability is not recommended by the AMA where the fetal abnormality is compatible with the child's survival, unless "extraordinary circumstances" exist.

2.4 Australia: Multidisciplinary Team Approach

The policy framework for termination of pregnancy in Australia does not, so far as we can tell, adopt the approach of listing conditions

---

[73] M. Habiba et al., "Late Termination of Pregnancy: A Comparison of Obstetricians' Experience in Eight European Countries" (2009) 116 *British Journal of Obstetrics and Gynaecology* 1340.

[74] American Medical Association, "Health and Ethics Policy of the AMA House of Delegates: H-5.982 Late Pregnancy Termination Techniques," available at http://www.ama-assn.org/ad-com/polfind/Hlth-Ethics.pdf.

[75] American Medical Association, "Health and Ethics Policy of the AMA House of Delegates: H-5.982 Late Pregnancy Termination Techniques" http://www.ama-assn.org/ad-com/polfind/Hlth-Ethics.pdf at 1.

nor does it provide criteria to be used in determining whether a condition is serious. This may be a consequence of the varied legal frameworks across the country, not all of which possess the seriousness threshold. The peak professional body, the Australian and New Zealand College of Obstetricians and Gynaecologists (RANZCOG), favors a multidisciplinary team approach. Rather than providing guidance on the meaning of serious abnormality, it recommends a process by which such determinations should be reached:

> Termination of pregnancy becomes more complex in the presence of late recognition of pregnancy, advancing gestational age, fetal abnormality and pre-existing maternal disease. The College supports a multidisciplinary approach in assisting women in such circumstances.[76]

Further guidance on the role and constitution of the multidisciplinary team can be found in the joint RANZCOG/HGSA statement on prenatal diagnosis.[77] This notes that "[e]ach specialised prenatal diagnostic service requires the services of a multi-disciplinary team of health professionals, whose specialities may be dependent on the setting."[78] However, a typical team "would comprise a clinical geneticist, genetic counsellor, midwife and/or nurse specialising in prenatal diagnosis, medical specialist in obstetric ultrasound, obstetrician specialising in prenatal diagnosis and management of fetal abnormality, paediatrician, social worker, a clinic coordinator, laboratory staff, and

---

[76] Royal Australian and New Zealand College of Obstetricians and Gynaecologists, "College Statement C-Gyn 17: Termination of Pregnancy" (2009), 1.

[77] Joint HGSA/RANZCOG Prenatal Diagnosis Screening Committee, "Joint HGSA/RANZCOG Prenatal Diagnosis Policy: College Statement C-Obs 5" (November 2006).

[78] Joint HGSA/RANZCOG Prenatal Diagnosis Screening Committee, "Joint HGSA/RANZCOG Prenatal Diagnosis Policy: College Statement C-Obs 5" (November 2006), 1.

secretarial assistance."[79] When prenatal diagnosis detects an anomalous condition, the guidance states that

> [i]nterpretation of results should be a team responsibility. The results should be communicated to the referring doctor and patient as soon as possible and in a manner that ensures clear understanding. The action to be taken on the basis of abnormal results is a decision for the couple concerned based on the information given with full counselling support. Where termination of pregnancy is undertaken because of an abnormal test the managing doctor must first sight a written report.[80]

The joint statement expressly aligns the approach to prenatal testing and diagnosis with preimplantation genetic diagnosis; thus, "[a]n appropriate level of assessment, counselling support and collaborating health professionals are required for preimplantation genetic diagnosis as listed here for prenatal diagnosis."[81]

This approach of multidisciplinary/shared decisionmaking is the dominant regulatory approach to late termination of pregnancy in the major institutions in which these terminations take place in the ACT, Victoria, and NSW.[82] The NSW Health Department policy provides that an "assessment of need" must be undertaken before termination. This entails a "consideration and documentation" of the following:[83]

- the patient's physical and psychological condition

[79] Joint HGSA/RANZCOG Prenatal Diagnosis Screening Committee, "Joint HGSA/RANZCOG Prenatal Diagnosis Policy: College Statement C-Obs 5" (November 2006), 1.

[80] Joint HGSA/RANZCOG Prenatal Diagnosis Screening Committee, "Joint HGSA/RANZCOG Prenatal Diagnosis Policy: College Statement C-Obs 5" (November 2006), 3.

[81] Joint HGSA/RANZCOG Prenatal Diagnosis Screening Committee, "Joint HGSA/RANZCOG Prenatal Diagnosis Policy: College Statement C-Obs 5" (November 2006), 3.

[82] D. Ellwood, "Late Termination of Pregnancy – an Obstetrician's Perspective" (2005) 29(2) *Australian Health Review* 139, 140.

[83] NSW Health, "Policy Directive: Pregnancy – Framework for Terminations in New South Wales Public Health Organisations" (2010), 3.2.

- assessment of gestational age
- in cases of birth defect diagnostic probability
- in cases of birth defect prognosis for the fetus

While the treating clinician may undertake the assessment of need in the first trimester and in consultation with counselors and other colleagues as necessary in the second trimester up to twenty weeks, the policy provides that a "multidisciplinary assessment" must be undertaken for all terminations after twenty weeks gestation:[84]

> In the case of post 20 weeks gestation a multidisciplinary assessment will be necessary. The AHS [Area Health Service] has an obligation to provide a multidisciplinary team, with a mix of skills and experience to provide advice to the treating medical practitioner so that he/she is able to undertake an informed assessment for need of termination of pregnancy. The multidisciplinary team may include experts in the areas of psychiatry or specialist mental health, fetal medicine, neonatology and the other specialty or specialties relevant to the woman's and fetus's medical condition.

The policy is silent on the question of whether all of the members involved in the multidisciplinary assessment must give approval for the termination to proceed, although Ellwood suggests that, in practice, these committees do operate as a formal review.[85] Ellwood also observes that a local ethics committee process is followed (mirroring the NSW policy) in the ACT.[86] Similar processes have been adopted at the two major hospitals in Victoria where late terminations of pregnancy occur. In these institutions, the treating clinician refers the abortion request to a "termination review panel," which decides

---

[84] NSW Health, "Policy Directive: Pregnancy – Framework for Terminations in New South Wales Public Health Organisations" (2010), 3.2.

[85] D. Ellwood, "Late Termination of Pregnancy – an Obstetrician's Perspective" (2005) 29(2) *Australian Health Review* 139, 140.

[86] D. Ellwood, "Late Termination of Pregnancy – an Obstetrician's Perspective" (2005) 29(2) *Australian Health Review* 139, 140.

whether to approve the request.[87] The Victorian Law Reform Commission noted that requests heard by these panels represent a small proportion of abortions performed in Victoria (most occur before thirteen weeks) and are "provided almost exclusively in cases of fetal abnormality."[88]

There is little publicly available information about how hospital ethics committees work. However, some insight can be gleaned from the Victorian Board of Medical Practitioners Report.[89] In its findings, with respect to late termination services in Victoria, the board states:[90]

> the majority of late term terminations that are performed are for severe fetal abnormalities. These include:
>
> • Conditions that are incompatible with life, such as anencephaly or renal agenesis;
>
> • Gross fetal abnormalities including some chromosomal abnormalities, severe congenital abnormalities that would require extensive surgery (eg cardiac) or gross physical deformities.

The findings go on to state that "[t]here are also circumstances where a termination may be requested on the grounds of fetal abnormality of a lesser degree but which may cause psychological harm to the mother. These situations are more difficult to deal with as the fetal condition may be treatable, at least in part, by surgery. Facial

---

[87] Woodrow, N.L. "Termination Review Committees: Are They Necessary?" (2003) 179 *Medical Journal of Australia* 92, 93; Victorian Law Reform Commission, "Law of Abortion: Final Report" (March 2008), 36–7.

[88] Victorian Law Reform Commission, "Law of Abortion: Final Report" (March 2008), 36.

[89] Medical Practitioners Board of Victoria, "Report on Late Terminations of Pregnancy in Victoria" (April 1998).

[90] Medical Practitioners Board of Victoria, "Report on Late Terminations of Pregnancy in Victoria" (April 1998), 37–8.

deformities such as cleft palate and limb deformities may fall into this category."[91]

Despite the lack of information about termination review panels or hospital ethics committees, it seems clear that, in some Australian jurisdictions, they have an important role to play in determining whether an abortion for fetal abnormality will be performed. These committees in effect are called upon to make or endorse judgments about what is a "serious disability" through a shared decision-making mechanism – whether or not the law of the jurisdiction in which the committee operates expressly recognizes fetal abnormality as a ground for termination. Interestingly, the obstetricians in Statham et al.'s UK study mentioned the value of collegial discussions in clarifying their views on whether to offer termination of pregnancy in difficult cases, and it may be that ethics committees could assist clinicians by providing a forum for this sort of discussion. Statham et al. write: "Where there was uncertainty about whether or not an abnormality meets the criteria, there appeared to be levels of debate and consideration: one is for the doctor to define his or her personal position within professional guidelines and responsibilities. Another may be discussion with other colleagues within the unit or other fetal medicine units."[92]

While the oversight of abortion decisions by a review panel may assist and support treating doctors by sharing responsibility with them,[93] it should also be noted that this oversight may nonetheless have unfavorable consequences. Woodrow, for instance, has commented that "[i]f a committee is set up to serve the interests of the hospital,

---

[91] Medical Practitioners Board of Victoria, "Report on Late Terminations of Pregnancy in Victoria" (April 1998), 38.

[92] H. Statham et al., "Late Termination of Pregnancy: Law, Policy and Decision-making in Four English Fetal Medicine Units" (2006) 113 *British Journal of Obstetrics and Gynaecology* 1402, 1406.

[93] N. L. Woodrow, "Termination Review Committees: Are They Necessary?" (2003) 179 *Medical Journal of Australia* 92, 93.

then it tends to err on the side of 'conservative' decision-making."[94] This could lead to concerns about whether women's interests are appropriately safeguarded, especially in the context of decisionmaking that is otherwise professionally regulated. Where access to termination for fetal abnormality is decided largely by doctors in consultation with ethics committees, a doctor's or committee's refusal to facilitate a termination leaves the woman who has sought the termination in a difficult position. Some women might indeed be in a better position if there were a list of conditions. Thus, although a list might constrain the discretionary decisionmaking of health professionals, as Emily Jackson points out, limiting clinician discretion does not necessarily operate to the disadvantage of women seeking termination:

> While women who can pay for specialist abortion services will not encounter hostile medical practitioners, women who depend upon NHS funding may discover that their GP and/or their health authority is uncooperative, in which case the need to satisfy two doctors may be both onerous and time consuming. Additionally, there are women from ethnic minority groups or women who are poorly educated who may not have the knowledge or the confidence to seek a second opinion if their GP is obstructive.[95]

Similar observations have been made in the Australian context. As mentioned previously, Savulescu and de Crespigny have argued that current abortion practice is inconsistent and "likely to be determined by the subjective values of the practitioner."[96]

---

[94] N. L. Woodrow, "Termination Review Committees: Are They Necessary?" (2003) 179 *Medical Journal of Australia* 92, 93.

[95] E. Jackson, "Abortion, Autonomy and Prenatal Diagnosis" (2000) 9(4) *Social and Legal Studies* 467, 471; see also L. de Crespigny and J. Savelescu, "Pregnant Women with Fetal Abnormalities: The Forgotten People in the Abortion Debate" (2008) 188 *Medical Journal of Australia* 100.

[96] See J. Savulescu, "Is Current Practice around Late Termination of Pregnancy Eugenic and Discriminatory? Maternal Interests and Abortion" (2001) 27 *Journal of Medical Ethics* 165, 166–7; see also; L. de Crespigny and J. Savelescu, "Pregnant

3 SERIOUSNESS AS A SPECTRUM: AREAS OF CONTENTION

As we have just seen, determinations about seriousness are contingent on a multidirectional flow of information between health professionals and prospective parents and, in turn, may occupy a range of different (nonlegal) spaces – doctors consulting their colleagues; consultations between doctors and their patients; prospective parents' talking to one another, to genetic counselors, and to disability support networks; deliberations of local hospital ethics committees, professional bodies, and regulators; and even hospital administration and regulatory bodies consulting the broader community. In this section, we will probe a little further the construction of serious disability in some of these spaces drawing upon published research and excerpts from interviews that we conducted with clinical geneticists and counselors.

3.1 Parental Perceptions of Seriousness

As mentioned previously, Wertz and Knoppers found little consensus among genetics professionals as to where to draw the line between serious and non-serious disorders. They concluded that

> [t]here appears to be a general spectrum of opinions, not a clear division, with greater agreement at the extremes (with anencephaly at the lethal end and clubfoot at the nonserious end).[97]

Scott too has observed that some conditions appear to be universally recognized as being serious, for example, include Lesch-Nyhan

Women with Fetal Abnormalities: The Forgotten People in the Abortion Debate" (2008) 188 *Medical Journal of Australia* 100 at 103.

[97] D. Wertz and B. Knoppers, "Serious Genetic Disorders: Can or Should They Be Defined?" (2002) 108 *American Journal of Medical Genetics* 29, 34.

syndrome and Tay-Sachs disease.[98] These conditions are characterized as "serious," she argues, because of the "significance of the potential losses – of experiences, activities or opportunities."[99] Even among disability rights scholars there is support for the view that these conditions are "serious." For instance, Shakespeare argues that "[i]n those rare cases where impairment causes inevitable neo-natal death or permanent lack of awareness, it might be more appropriate to screen out such conditions prenatally."[100] However, many conditions and disorders are not so easily classified. Scott describes these as "mid-spectrum" conditions.[101] Whether or not these disorders are serious is the "subject of reasonable disagreement,"[102] which as we have seen can be considerable. Scott notes that "the degree of disagreement, including among genetics professionals, about what counts as 'serious' is one of the most difficult issues in this context."[103] Moreover she says, a "complicating factor is the question of the *legitimacy of differing perspectives* on these issues – medical, parental and those of people with disabilities (who may in part 'speak' for or about the fetus). Importantly, we now see that the question of the meaning of seriousness is in part a question of 'serious for whom?'" [original emphasis].[104]

---

[98] R. Scott, "Prenatal Screening, Autonomy and Reasons: The Relationship between the Law of Abortion and Wrongful Birth" (2003) 11 *Medical Law Review* 265, 309.

[99] R. Scott et al., "The Appropriate Extent of Pre-implantation Genetic Diagnosis: Health Professionals' and Scientists' Views on the Requirement for a 'Significant Risk of a Serious Genetic Condition'" (2007) 15 *Medical Law Review* 320, 337.

[100] T. Shakespeare, "Choices and Rights: Eugenics, Genetics and Disability Equality" (1998) 13(5) *Disability and Society* 665, 670.

[101] R. Scott, "Prenatal Screening, Autonomy and Reasons: The Relationship between the Law of Abortion and Wrongful Birth" (2003) 11 *Medical Law Review* 265, 311.

[102] R. Scott, "Prenatal Screening, Autonomy and Reasons: The Relationship between the Law of Abortion and Wrongful Birth" (2003) 11 *Medical Law Review* 265, 312.

[103] R. Scott, "Prenatal Testing, Reproductive Autonomy and Disability Interests" (2005) 14 *Cambridge Quarterly of Healthcare Ethics* 65, 73.

[104] R. Scott, "Prenatal Screening, Autonomy and Reasons: The Relationship between the Law of Abortion and Wrongful Birth" (2003) 11 *Medical Law Review* 265, 311.

Scott concludes that while in some cases of "mid-spectrum disorders," the child

> may well have a good or reasonable quality of life his condition
> may still impact significantly on his parents, perhaps because he
> has learning difficulties or often requires hospitalisation. Arguably,
> parents do have an interest in choosing whether to continue a preg-
> nancy with these kinds of implications.... In these kinds of cases,
> then, the point of recognising that parents will be the most impor-
> tant judges of the impact on them of a given fetal condition is to
> suggest that, given that there is *room for doubt* about seriousness in
> the mid-spectrum area, parents' perceptions may legitimately *tip the
> balance.*[105] [original emphasis]

This serves further to reinforce the point that the question of what is serious may not be a purely clinical determination, as parents will have views about whether or not the disability being described to them is one with which they feel they can cope. However, even this analysis may not do justice to the complexities that inform the interpretive matrix. The multiple factors that bear upon parental perceptions of seriousness was a theme in our discussions with clinicians. For instance, C2 thought that the way in which parents process the clinical information presented to them is highly contingent:

> So what I believe is that we can say, "okay, well this is this condi-
> tion, and this is how severe it is. And this is what is most likely the
> existence of a person with this." But I believe that the people sit-
> ting there will interpret it within the framework of their own lives.
> So if they've watched a family member raise a child with Down
> syndrome and have had a pretty good life, and their perception
> is that they've coped really well and that is hasn't had a massive
> impact on their family, then they'll interpret what I'm saying within
> the framework of that perception of a child with Down syndrome.
> And if another person has seen someone raise a child and that child

---

[105] R. Scott, "Prenatal Screening, Autonomy and Reasons: The Relationship between the Law of Abortion and Wrongful Birth" (2003) 11 *Medical Law Review* 265, 312.

required multiple surgeries and the relationship fell apart, then of course that's going to impact on ... they'll be interpreting what I'm saying ... and we do talk about that. That's where that conversation about their perception of severity comes up very much.... But they don't happen in isolation. They don't just listen to me talking about a particular condition and go "oh yeah that's right. And I'm not going to worry about the fact that my cousin had to raise this child and it died at three because it got pneumonia or whatever." All of that stuff obviously does impact and play a role.

This understanding of the contextual/reflexive nature of prospective parents' approach to serious disability accords closely with the views expressed by C1, a health professional involved in prenatal diagnosis and PGD. This respondent stated:

There is a component of perception of medical severity. But many of these decisions are made in that social context of "Am I single? Am I poor? Do I feel I can cope? What will the effect be on my existing children? Will my family support me if I do this or don't do that?" Those sort of social contexts or issues are clearly terribly important. Would I use PGD if my parents and siblings were strongly opposed on an ethical, moral or religious ground? And so on. All of those things definitely come into it, as well as one's personal morality and so on. And I think that the concept of severity is one component of that, is one thing in addition to that. And then within severity there are all the usual things of length of life, pain and suffering, the actual quality of the symptoms – a whole range of factors – treatability, disfigurement. There are a whole lot of things that come into that severity. That's why it's so hard to define.

C1 suggests that severity is difficult to define, precisely because of the contextual factors that influence parents' perceptions about disability and the decisions that follow. This is consistent with the dominant policy approaches to prenatal and preimplantation genetic diagnosis, as discussed in the previous section and Chapter 4. C4 had a similar experience:

I've seen families where there's been an early death from diabetes in [a] young adult, where that family, if you asked them to say that's not a serious condition, they would look at you with surprise that you would even bother to bring up the notion that it's not a serious condition.

3.2 Seriousness as a Limit in Practice

Notwithstanding this recognition of the impossibility of precisely defining seriousness, there remains a question as to whether a limit of some sort is important. Should the use of PGD be subject to a threshold of "seriousness"? C1 commented that

> the law uses a word which creates an image that one shouldn't be doing these things for trivial reasons. I quite like that concept. On the other hand, I believe that you can't define what is severe, slightly severe, moderately severe, mildly severe, severely severe. To me, it's just something that you can't do, partly because I don't think it's appropriate to do it ... I think it's something individual families should decide ... they should decide where in the spectrum of undefined severity their family problem resides.

This brings forth an interesting tension and suggests, once again, that a limit may be important even if no one is able to say exactly where it lies. As we saw in Chapter 3 and 4, a number of jurisdictions have imposed a seriousness threshold for terminations later in pregnancy and PGD even though it has been clearly recognized by the framers of such laws that the limit could not be specified with any precision. In other words, it is the idea of a limit, rather than its reality, that is being relied upon to provide coherence to these regulatory frameworks.

However, as we noted in our discussions of the parliamentary debates, the imprecision of the limit also creates anxiety. Conditions such as Down syndrome and cleft palate seem to cause particular anxiety – are these conditions serious? The existing literature suggests that there is some social disapproval of abortion for aesthetic defects such as cleft lip/palate. For instance, Dery compared attitudes about the social acceptability of abortion for various conditions and found that respondents were least likely to approve of abortion for a "severe aesthetic defect."[106] Similarly, Drake et al. found that, while the majority of respondents accepted abortion for anencephaly, Down syndrome, and spina bifida, there was considerably less support for abortion for cleft lip (and for Alzheimer's disease and Turner's and Klinefelter's syndromes).[107] In the context of parental choices about whether to undertake prenatal diagnosis for clefting, Sagi et al. found that "[w]hile most parents (78%) indicated that they would probably or definitely choose the option of prenatal diagnosis of clefts, 57% of them reported that they would probably or definitely not choose to terminate" for the condition.[108] Similarly, there is some evidence that the parents of children with cleft lip/palate are averse to abortion for the condition. In Nusbaum et al.'s study, most respondents reported that they did not think about aborting the pregnancy as a cleft was "not significant enough to warrant consideration of abortion."[109]

One of the difficulties thrown up by conditions such as cleft lip/palate and, as we will see, Down syndrome is that it is less clear that these conditions will preclude a satisfying and worthwhile life, and so, in a sense, these conditions threaten to destabilize a threshold that is ostensibly reliant on this understanding of the negative impact of

[106] A. M. Dery et al., "Attitudes towards the Acceptability of Reasons for Pregnancy Termination Due to Fetal Abnormalities among Prenatal Care Providers and Consumers in Israel" (2008) 28 *Prenatal Diagnosis* 518, 522.

[107] H. M. Drake et al., "Attitudes towards Termination for Fetal Abnormality: Comparisons in Three European Countries" (1996) 49 *Clinical Genetics* 134, 138.

[108] M. Sagi et al., "Application of the Health Belief Model in a Study on Parents' Intentions to Utilize Prenatal Diagnosis of Cleft Lip and/or Palate" (1992) 44 *American Journal of Medical Genetics* 326, 330.

[109] R. Nusbaum et al., "A Qualitative Description of Receiving a Diagnosis of Clefting in the Prenatal or Postnatal Period" (2008) 17 *Journal of Genetic Counselling* 336, 344.

serious disability. We explored the case of Down syndrome with C1, who said:

> Is Down syndrome a serious disorder? Now, what is the quality of life for a child with Down syndrome in our modern society? I think the answer is that it's very good, provided your health is good. If your congenital heart abnormalities aren't too severe, you live a very good social life, provided your family supports you and loves you and brings you up and all of that. You interact with other people, you can participate very fully in life. And so that if you write legislation in terms of – is Down syndrome a disorder that harms a child with Down syndrome? I think one could quite legitimately say no. And yet, prospectively, families asked whether they would accept a child with Down syndrome, would like to have a child with Down syndrome etc, would in general say no. Not everybody of course.

There is evidence to suggest that Down syndrome's seriousness is somewhat contentious. It will be recalled that the House of Commons Science and Technology Committee specifically mentioned the high rate of termination following detection of this condition as a matter of concern to some members of the community. Ward observes that Down syndrome is one of the conditions that are most often tested for prenatally "despite the fact that [it] … is not a life-threatening condition and many people with Down's Syndrome live full and happy lives."[110] The Down syndrome NSW Information and Services director, Jill O'Connor, whose son has Down syndrome, is quoted as saying that she was "not convinced that people are getting all the information that they might like to have when they are making these decisions…We want them to know what Down syndrome is and we'd also like to see people not being made to make quick decisions."[111] A similar view is expressed by Dixon, who argues that doctors may not be giving patients an "accurate

---

[110] L.M. Ward, "Whose Right to Choose? The 'new' Genetics, Prenatal Testing and People with Learning Difficulties" (2002) 12(2) *Critical Public Health* 187 at 194.

[111] J. Maher, "From Disbelief at Down Diagnosis to Joy and Delight" *Sun Herald*, 11 November 2009, 25.

picture" of Down syndrome.[112] Roberts notes that while "most prospective parents seem to consider Down syndrome as involving severe mental retardation. In actuality, 90% of all individuals with Down syndrome fall within the mild to moderate range of functioning."[113] Thus, there remains some uncertainty about how informed parents are when making these decisions.

The framing of Down syndrome as a troubling condition in terms of prenatal diagnosis finds expression in the media, too, where the severity of the syndrome has been questioned. As Evans notes:[114]

> Prenatal testing for Down syndrome is now routine and 95 per cent of affected pregnancies are terminated. There are many arguments attempting to justify the eradication of the condition – such as the prevention of unnecessary suffering – but I wonder if some are intellectual smokescreens for a rather more unpalatable truth: the fear of being unable to love something that is not perfect.

In C1's experience, women tend not to openly express such fears, though they may have them:

> We talk to lots of people about testing in pregnancy and so on, but I don't know that I have ever heard anybody say "I don't want this pregnancy to continue because I am enjoying my life and I don't want to have a disabled child." I don't know that I've actually heard that. People don't say it. They couch their decisions in a different way. And they couch it in terms of the effect on the child, family and so on.

Despite concerns about whether Down syndrome is seriously disabling among some members of the community, there is evidence of

---

[112] D. Dixon, "Informed Consent or Institutionalized Eugenics? How the Medical Profession Encourages Abortion of Fetuses with Down Syndrome" (2008) 24(1) *Issues in Law and Medicine* 3, 55.

[113] C. Roberts et al., "The Role of Genetic Counselling in the Elective Termination of Pregnancies Involving Fetuses with Disabilities" (2002) 36(1) *Journal of Special Education* 48], 50.

[114] K. Evans, "The Gene Genie" *Sunday Age*, 14 March 2010, 11.

widespread social acceptance of termination for Down syndrome (at least in the early stages of pregnancy). Bell et al.'s respondents thought that abortion was more acceptable for Down syndrome than it was for either spina bifida or hemophilia,[115] and Dery found that most respondents considered mental retardation to be "acceptable for TOP."[116] Further, C1 highlighted the difficulties associated with a restrictive approach to termination, while appreciating some of the tensions this produces:

> It's good that the lawmakers, in terms of a statement about the community position, don't want these things to be used or terminations to occur for truly trivial reasons. The family should decide. You see, we have these really interesting conflicts, that we have social termination "on demand" and yet we agonise when couples make decisions about children with disabilities. And it's really interesting. Why should we subject the parents who are wishing to terminate a pregnancy with Down syndrome or cleft palate or one missing kidney, why should we be more restrictive and more trying to determine what they do than termination of pregnancy when there's no reason to believe there's any abnormality in the baby? ... And presumably, it's founded in I guess, the difference between a wanted and an unwanted pregnancy ... But for a wanted pregnancy, now something's been found, and somehow that particular foetus has more rights than the one who was unwanted. I think it's really interesting, because I think it is a real contrast.

This response raises a fascinating point, which, in a sense, inverts the claim advanced by Asch and Parens that, when a disabling trait is

---

[115] M. Bell et al., "Reactions to Prenatal Testing: Reflections of Religiosity and Attitudes toward Abortion and People with Disabilities" (2000) 105(1) *American Journal on Mental Retardation* 1.

[116] A. M. Dery et al., "Attitudes towards the Acceptability of Reasons for Pregnancy Termination Due to Fetal Abnormalities among Prenatal Care Providers and Consumers in Israel" (2008) 28 *Prenatal Diagnosis* 518, 522.

detected, the risk is that "a single trait stands in for the whole"[117] and in effect engulfs the full potentiality and makeup of the future child. As the foregoing passage suggests, the detection of a trait can also bring a "future child" into focus in a manner that does not occur with an unwanted pregnancy. In the case of an unwanted pregnancy, the future child as an abstraction is rejected. In the case of termination of a pregnancy after the detection of fetal anomaly, a particular "future child" is rejected. Thus, somewhat ironically, it seems that a limited personification is achieved through the testing process.

3.3 Seriousness and Gestational Stage

Perhaps this is another aspect that is crucial in distinguishing prenatal testing and PGD for some people. In respondent C3's experience, prospective parents commonly express their motivation for seeking PGD along the following lines: "I wouldn't feel comfortable terminating a pregnancy. But at the same time, I would really rather not pass this on to my child." Such responses imply that PGD, unlike termination, is seen by prospective parents as avoiding a particular condition rather than deselecting a "future child." Respondent C2, who was generally cautious about the benefits of PGD, seemed to affirm this point:

> I think for some people, yes, it [PGD] is a better option. And I don't think that those couples are basing that on the severity of what they're testing for. I don't think they're making a judgment to go down that road because what they're testing for is considered to be more severe. I think it's just because the process of pregnancy and testing and termination, they just can't do it anymore.

---

[117] E. Parens and A. Asch, "Disability Rights Critique of Prenatal Genetic Testing: Reflections and Recommendations" (2003) 9 *Mental Retardations and Developmental Disabilities Research Reviews* 40, 42.

Thus, another of the crucial "contextual matters" when determining where the seriousness threshold lies is what woman are prepared to do to prevent the birth of a child who has an abnormality or genetic condition or disease. As we have seen in section 1 above, there is evidence that the stage of gestation correlates with clinicians' willingness to facilitate termination for certain disabilities. We postulated that this interaction between severity and gestational age might also work in reverse, that is, that the threshold for seriousness might be lower early in pregnancy or before pregnancy. When asked about whether the value of seriousness as a limit decreases as the technology allows abnormality to be detected earlier, C1 said:

> As the pregnancy proceeds, the willingness to terminate that pregnancy decreases … but I personally would have no doubt that there will be the overlapping bell curves where it's sort of very serious for prenatal diagnosis with – let's say, if amniocentesis was the only test, so you'd be terminating at 20 weeks – people will build in a greater severity of disorder or impact or whatever it is before they'd consider that. CVS – termination of pregnancy around 12 weeks – a bit more acceptable. Getting DNA from maternal blood – I don't know whether that would be 5 weeks or 6 weeks … even more likely. And then you get to PGD where disorders at the lesser severe end of the scale would be acceptable for couples.

The suggestion here is that women might be willing to use PGD to select against conditions that they would not judge to be serious enough to warrant having an abortion. C3 lent some support to this theory:

> I'm relaying what my experience is with patients. So within the PGD population, there is a proportion of couples where the risk is for adult onset disorders, and they are coming and saying, "I wouldn't feel comfortable terminating a pregnancy. But at the same time, I would really rather not pass this on to my child." So there's no question. I mean it's a generalisation but couples are more accepting of termination of pregnancy for a lethal early childhood disorder, for example, or even something like cystic

fibrosis – manageable to some extent, but causes someone to die when they're 40 or so these days. They're more accepting of termination in that context than for an adult-onset disorder. So there's a threshold effect somewhere.

But, as C2 remarked, PGD can also be a complex and difficult decision for couples:

I think that the problem is that there's a perception of PGD as being the solution to the dreadful problem that we have of terminating foetuses and, in actual fact, it's very complicated. It's complicated, it's complex, it's expensive.... It's quite hard and it's prohibitive for some people. The cost is prohibitive.

So, while some have presented PGD as a better option for avoiding serious disability than prenatal diagnosis and termination, it may be that this idea needs to be appropriately contextualized. Although PGD technology has the capacity to avoid disability and abortion, the woman still must make a significant physical, psychological, and financial investment. These barriers may have a self-limiting effect, which makes fears or concerns about "inappropriate uses" of the technology somewhat fanciful. On the current state of technology, this effect provides an important counterweight to concerns about the burgeoning use of PGD for designing children and the interpretive openness of "serious genetic condition." Respondent C3 felt that there was no legitimate cause for concern about PGD practices being used too liberally or for perfecting progeny:

... certainly [here] the system works, and I can't see any major risk of harm. And I guess part of that is just because it's a big undertaking to do PGD, and people don't enter into it lightly. There is not a whole queue of people saying, "I want a baby with blue eyes and blonde hair." It's just a fantasy.

Nevertheless, other respondents mentioned the increasing range of the conditions that PGD may be used to test for, and this is a discussion to which we now turn.

4 EXPANDING HORIZONS? PGD FOR LATE ONSET, LOW PENETRANCE CONDITIONS

As we saw in Chapter 4, in the initial stages of PGD regulation, an attempt was made to align the sorts of "serious" conditions for which PGD would be performed with those for which abortion was available under s 1(1)(d) of the Abortion Act. However, Aarden et al. argue that "both kinds of indications have started to diverge."[118] This, they suggest, has been driven by "couples increasingly seeing PGD as a better option than prenatal diagnosis and abortion for preventing diseases with a later onset or less immediate and serious consequences."[119]

4.1 PGD – A Better Option for Parents?

The framing of PGD as "a better option" for some couples was a feature of some of our discussions. As mentioned previously, PGD was seen as preferable for couples who could not, often for very complex reasons, face termination but who nonetheless wanted to have an unaffected child. One example given was the one of parents who already have an affected child. C4 said:

> In thinking about … seriousness, I think there is a really important distinction between prenatal and preimplantation genetic diagnosis … and … so I think the notion of terminating a pregnancy that's – take your example of Fragile X syndrome – where the child may be like that sibling, who those parents love and adore … to terminate the pregnancy is a very different – and you used the word

---

[118] E. Aarden et al., "Providing Preimplantation Genetic Diagnosis in the United Kingdom, the Netherlands and Germany: A Comparative In-depth Analysis of Health-care Access" (2009) 1(1) *Human Reproduction* 1, 2.

[119] E. Aarden et al. "Providing Preimplantation Genetic Diagnosis in the United Kingdom, The Netherlands and Germany: A Comparative In-depth Analysis of Health-care Access" (2009) 1(1) *Human Reproduction* 1, 2.

"threshold" – very different decision from starting a pregnancy knowing that that's not there.

Thus, PGD might enhance the reproductive options of parents who already have an affected child by enabling them to avoid the disability without having to face the difficult decision of terminating the pregnancy for a condition affecting their existing child.

PGD was also described as a superior option on the basis that it might allow more conditions to be avoided than might prenatal testing. For C2, this was directly relevant to the question of seriousness:

> So you have disability then you have serious disability, and within serious disability you have serious disability that it not life-shortening, and then you have serious disability that is life-shortening or lethal, and so, stepping away from being a genetic counsellor, the group that causes me most concern is the concept of a serious disability that is not life-shortening. And it seems to me that if you were going to test for anything or offer PGD for anything, that this is the group that needs it most of all, because you're talking about a serious disability for 30, 40, 50, 60 years of life as opposed to serious disability with maybe just a short number of years.

C1 also discussed the idea that a lower threshold of seriousness or severity might operate in the context of PGD compared with prenatal diagnosis, partly because many women see embryonic deselection as less morally problematic than abortion:

> I think that's generally true, that in terms of people's selection of those reproductive options, the disorder would have to be more severe, in general, for couples to choose prenatal diagnosis – like CVS and amniocentesis – than disorders where they would choose PGD, where the severity would be less.... If you draw your bell shape curve, I think it would be just that little bit down to the milder end, or towards the milder end for PGD compared to prenatal. Because I think people do have very significant concerns about termination of pregnancy and for some disorders, they simply wouldn't contemplate it, but would contemplate PGD because they don't see disposing of

unwanted embryos in the same light as terminating the pregnancy of a baby at 12 weeks or 18 weeks or whatever.[120]

4.2 Expanding Notions of Seriousness

The suggestion that the threshold of severity or seriousness is lower in the case of PGD again raises the issue of limits. As we saw earlier, a number of the clinicians we spoke to thought that seriousness could not be defined. However, C5 thought there was a role for a definition of the word "serious":

> I think having a definition is valuable. It would be valuable for some-one like myself who is not a doctor. I think it provides a framework for discussion that would be useful, for example, in counselling.

When pushed a little further on the reasons why a definition of the word "serious" or the phrase "significant disability" would be useful, C5 raised concerns about eugenics and the pursuit of perfection, and, in particular, the challenges presented by using technology to avoid a late onset, low penetrance condition such as bowel cancer:

> So more and more as we've moved into this field we talk about mak-ing sure the patients really understand ... that it's not a guarantee. It provides information on the status of the embryo with what we now know about these chromosomes. The other thing too which I raise more and more in my sessions ... are they after the perfect child? We all want perfect children but how far will they go with this? Does

---

[120] This accords with the findings of Klitzman, who surveyed individuals at risk for Huntington's disease about their reproductive options/behavior: "Some have had, or would have amniocentesis, followed by abortion if the fetus were found to have the mutation [for Huntington's disease]. Yet moral concerns often arose ... concern-ing these procedures ... terminating a pregnancy was felt to be morally problem-atic and left many uncomfortable." See R. Klitzman R et al., "Decision-Making about Reproductive Choices among Individuals At-Risk for Huntington's Disease" (2007) 16 *Journal of Genetic Counselling* 347, 355.

their mind allow them to understand that life isn't perfect at times and that even with what appears to be a clear embryo, other things may happen along the way?

There is, of course, some disagreement about whether lower penetrance, later onset genetic conditions such as inherited breast, bowel, and ovarian cancer are serious genetic conditions. The main argument in favor of characterizing later onset genetic conditions as serious is that they are or may be fatal. However, some argue that they are not serious genetic conditions on the grounds that they (a) are treatable; (b) will be contracted, if at all, during adulthood; and (c) have incomplete penetrance.[121] Thus, Quinn interviewed 975 members of a Website that aims to provide support to women who, because of their genes, are at high risk of developing breast or ovarian cancer. She found that of the 446 respondents who wrote detailed comments, many expressed anger about using PGD for hereditary breast and ovarian cancer (HBOC) as the condition is "treatable, unlike other diseases with no options for prevention or treatment."[122] Similarly, Callaghan writes that "the idea that the mere risk – heightened as it may be – of breast cancer is enough for scientists to write off embryos that could one day lead otherwise brilliant and productive lives, seems terribly wrong."[123]

Nevertheless, in a recently published study on the attitudes of clinicians, Brandt et al. found that doctors generally approved of PGD for hereditary cancer syndromes, although they noted that the American Medical Association states that "selection to avoid a genetic disease may

[121] See A. L. Bredenoord et al., "Dealing with Uncertainties: Ethics of Prenatal Diagnosis and PGD to Prevent Mitochondrial Disorders" (2008) 14(1) *Human Reproduction Update* 83, 90; T. Krahn, "Where Are We Going with Preimplantation Genetic Diagnosis?" (2007) 176 (10) *Canadian Medical Association Journal* 1445, 1445.

[122] G. Quinn, "Conflict between Values and Technology: Perception of PGD among Women at Increased Risk for Hereditary Breast and Ovarian Cancer" (2009) 8 *Familial Cancer* 441, at 447; see also 445.

[123] R. Callaghan, "Don't Throw the Baby Out with the Bathwater" *West Australian*, 1 November 2006, 25.

not always be appropriate, depending on factors such as the severity of the disease, the probability of its occurrence, the age at onset, and the time of gestation at which selection would occur."[124] Robertson argues that the case for regarding Huntington's disease as a "serious condition" is "even stronger" than that for regarding hereditary cancers as being "serious" as the disease is "not preventable, as may be the case with susceptibility genes."[125] Some of those within families in which the gene is present believe that the condition should be considered serious despite its late onset. In a media account of a family in which the Huntington's disease has been transmitted, Bridget, who has the *HD* gene and chose to use PGD to select against the gene, is quoted as saying: "It's quite a difficult thing to process something horrible that hasn't happened yet but will definitely happen ... I move from grieving [for my mother] to thinking about the future of my first son, to grieving myself."[126]

In the United Kingdom, the HFEA held a public consultation on whether PGD should be available for serious, lower penetrance, later onset genetic conditions such as inherited breast, bowel, and ovarian cancer. In its decision, the HFEA stated:

> The Authority recognises that inherited forms of these diseases are rare (less than 10 per cent of cases of breast and bowel cancer are thought to be inherited). Carrying the faulty gene can cause significant anxiety which is not lessened by the fact that the condition is not fully penetrant. The Authority considers conditions of this type to be serious genetic conditions.[127]

[124] A. Brandt, M. Tschirgi, K. Ready, C. Sun, S, Darilek, J. Hecht, B. Arun, and K. Lu, "Knowledge, Attitudes and Clinical Experience of Physicians Regarding PGD for Hereditary Cancer Predisposition Syndromes" (2010) 9 *Familial Cancer* 479, 485.

[125] J. Robertson, "Extending Preimplantation genetic diagnosis: The Ethical Debate" (2003) 18(3) *Human Reproduction* 465, 468.

[126] T. Kirby, "Unwanted Gene That Runs in the Family: Huntington's Disease" *Australian*, 31 July 2010.

[127] Human Fertilisation and Embryology Authority, "Authority Decision on the Use of PGD for Lower Penetrance, Later Onset Inherited Conditions": see

Thus, in 2006, the HFEA agreed that PGD could be used for conditions such as inherited breast, ovarian, and bowel cancers because of the "aggressive nature of the cancers, the impact of treatment and the extreme anxiety that carriers of the gene can experience."[128]

In Australia, Victoria is the only jurisdiction where there has been specific guidance on late onset, low penetrance conditions, although policies operating in other jurisdictions are probably flexible enough to accommodate this indication.[129] The ITA PGD policy, which, of course, is no longer being applied, stated that:[130]

> In Victoria to date, PGD has been used for: ...
>
> – direct testing for single gene mutations which are known to increase the risk of certain cancers (for instance, the BRCA mutations, which increase the lifetime risk of breast and other cancers) ...

http://www.hfea.gov.uk/docs/The_Authority_decision_Choices_and_boundaries. pdf (accessed on 22 June 2011).

[128] Human Fertilisation and Embryology Authority, "Authority Decision on PGD: Statement on Use of Preimplantation Genetic Diagnosis (PGD) for Inherited Cancer Susceptibility" press release, 10 May 2006: see http://www.hfea.gov.uk/622. html (accessed on 21 June 2011).

[129] The NHMRC Guidelines do not prohibit PGD for such conditions. They merely provide that "people seeking testing should be encouraged to consider the following factors when deciding the appropriateness of PGD: information about the likelihood of false positive and false negative results; genetic and clinical information about the specific condition; their previous reproductive experience; the distinction between the genotypic and phenotypic expression of the condition, disease or abnormality; the variable range of effects of the condition, disease or abnormality, including the likely rate of degeneration in the case of progressive disorders; the experiences of families living with the condition; the likely availability of effective therapy or management now and in the future; and the extent of social support available": National Health and Medical Research Council, "Ethical Guidelines on the Use of Assisted Reproductive Technology in Clinical Practice" 2007, 12.5.1. There is also no prohibition in the WA Reproductive Technology Council's "Policy on Approval of Diagnostic Procedures Involving Embryos" (March 2008).

[130] Infertility Treatment Authority, "Genetic Testing and the Requirements of the *Infertility Treatment Act* 1995: Policy in relation to the use of pre-implantation genetic diagnosis (PGD)" (2009), 1.

– exclusion testing, which enables a person who is at risk of an autosomal dominant condition (such as Huntington's Disease), but who wishes to remain unaware of their own genetic status, to conceive an unaffected pregnancy.

Further on, the policy provided that[131]

it is the Authority's view that the use of PGD in the types of indications outlined in lists A and B of the schedule of Approved Genetic Testing is not precluded by the Act.

The *BRCA1* and *BRCA2* mutations and Huntington's disease all appeared in List B of the schedule.[132]

4.3 Late Onset or Low Penetrance Conditions and Parental Preferences

That there was any controversy surrounding the use of PGD for late onset conditions was disputed by C3:

In fact, it's not controversial here at all ... and I don't know whether it's a cultural difference but there's never been any controversy for PGD for adult onset disorders or even semi-manageable disorders in this country and, in fact, many people believe these are just the disorders that PGD works well for ... things like Huntington disease and early onset Alzheimer disease and then the familial cancer syndrome.

When we raised the point that treatments exist for some of these conditions, C3 responded:

It depends who you talk to about treatability. I mean we know that we don't have perfect screening for women with BRCA mutations,

---

[131] Infertility Treatment Authority, "Genetic Testing and the Requirements of the *Infertility Treatment Act* 1995: Policy in Relation to the Use of Pre-implantation Genetic Diagnosis (PGD)" (2009), 5.1.

[132] Infertility Treatment Authority, "Approved Genetic Testing" (October 2009), 2.

for example. We know that if she had her ovaries out and her breasts removed, she's very unlikely to get cancer and a surgeon would probably regard that as having perfectly treated the patient. But you ask the woman and she'd probably say, "I'd prefer not to have had this." And then there's the issue of passing it on to subsequent generations. So there's a line of thought, which you come across commonly, that these are the very disorders that PGD is effective for.

This again raises the issue of whether there is a distinction, between a "serious" or "severe" condition and a condition that one prefers not to have or to transmit. It seems that, as the age of forty is an age at which many people still have young, dependent children and are seen as being at the beginning of midlife, to develop a life-threatening or fatal illness at this time is an extremely serious matter. There are a number of anecdotal stories that have appeared in the media indicating that some regard the *BRCA1* gene to be sufficiently serious to justify the use of PGD. For example, Penny Quinn, who used PGD to avoid transmitting the *BRCA1* gene to her child, was reported as saying: "We just feel so proud that we were committed to the process. We wouldn't change any part of the journey .... I really believe that it was our purpose. We were meant to push the boundaries."[133]

In another article, Krystal Barter, who had intended to use PGD to avoid the *BRCA1* gene, states: "[o]ur family tree looks like a war zone ... The number increases every year. Nan gets calls all the time saying, 'Did you know this person has cancer?'"[134] Interestingly, however, although Ms. Barter lives with the risk of developing breast cancer and has direct experience of its impact, when she inadvertently became pregnant without PGD she did not choose to abort. This may be because when faced with the direct question of whether living with the risk of breast cancer was so significant that she would not want to

---

[133] J. Robotham, "How Genetic Magic Halted a Deadly Family Inheritance" *Sydney Morning Herald*, 23 October 2006.

[134] D. Teutsch, "Four Generations, One Aim: To Beat the Curse" *Sun Herald*, 4 July 2010, 5.

have a child in that situation, she found herself valuing her own life positively. Many people faced with PGD-type decisions will in fact have some experience of disability or illness that they can draw upon to make the calculus of what is in fact "serious" enough. However, the irony (which we explored in Chapter 4) is that while parental judgments about disability and risk have been integral to the processes of constructing the meaning of "serious" in the field of PGD, this process is not generally permitted to operate in reverse: Parents are not generally at liberty to select an affected embryo, although in the United Kingdom this may be possible if the only choice is between an affected embryo and none at all.[135] This in fact recognizes and allows some scope for parents to revise their assessment of "seriousness" in light of their new circumstances.

But this might lead us to ask: If parents do revise their opinions about seriousness when an unaffected embryo is not available, does this indicate that avoidance of the condition is a preference rather than an imperative? Does that mean that seriousness is already being interpreted as parental preference? There are those who believe that to allow late onset conditions to fall within the definition of "serious" conditions does signal a move away from the initial conceptualization of "serious," and a step in the direction of "perfecting." C4 stated, for example:

> Pre-implantation genetic diagnosis really ... has led to referrals for a large number of conditions where prenatal diagnosis would not be ... would very rarely be considered or used and a good example there is the cancer predispositions, many adult onset conditions.

If PGD clearly may be used to avoid conditions for which prenatal testing would not be used, then it seems arguable that social norms and clinical practice have begun to drift from the original anchor point of alignment between PGD and abortion for avoiding disability.

---

[135] Human Embryology and Fertilisation Act 2008, s 13(9).

5 CONCLUSION

The perceived seriousness of a condition is a major factor in termination decisions/attitudes about whether PGD should be used, but what is a "serious disability" is the subject of much disagreement. There is general agreement that it is impracticable and undesirable to draw up a list of serious conditions. This is partly because there is disagreement about which conditions are "serious," partly because a focus on the condition is not sufficiently adaptable to each family's unique circumstances and partly because a list would, in the view of some doctors, constrain their professional discretion (either to assist or to refuse to assist a woman seeking termination). Although lists have been resisted as a solution to the problem of definition in the context of both PGD and abortion, the approved lists of conditions for the former and available statistical data for the latter give us a sense of which conditions are being interpreted as being serious.[136]

There seems to be general agreement that early onset, life threatening conditions are serious disabilities. With other conditions, though, much will depend on the circumstances of the individual case; that is, it is for doctors and families to determine whether a disability is serious enough to justify abortion or, in the case of PGD, selection against it. Scott's contention that parents' views are important when deciding whether a condition is sufficiently serious is reflected throughout the literature. For instance, in "Choices and Boundaries," the HFEA states

---

[136] Although lists of conditions for which TOP is available have not been created, some jurisdictions (such as the United Kingdom and South Australia) have legal reporting requirements that insist that notification be provided where abortions for fetal abnormality have taken place and that the condition for which these abortions were performed be specified. For the United Kingdom, see Abortion Act 1967 (UK), s 2(1) and Abortion Regulations 1991 (UK), regs. 3(1)(a) and 4(1)(a), Schedule 1, Part 1, and Schedule 2. For South Australia, see Criminal Law Consolidation Act 1935 (SA), s 82A(4)(b) and Criminal Law Consolidation (Medical Termination of Pregnancy) Regulations 1996, reg. 4(1) and (3), and Schedule 1.

that "the perception of the seriousness of the condition by those seeking treatment is an important factor in the decision making process."[137] The RCOG Policy on Termination of Pregnancy, too, states that "the impact ... on the family into which the child would be born"[138] is relevant to whether the condition is or is not serious. Doctors' views are also very important.

Finally, the social and/or moral status of the fetus and the increased risk involved in late termination procedures seem to bear quite significantly on the determination of whether a disability is serious or serious enough. These factors operate as self-limiting constraints on the use of abortion to avoid disability, quite apart from any legal or other regulatory barriers. However, it is important, we think, to emphasize that these self-imposed constraints are absent or significantly reduced in the context of PGD, where the entities being deselected are not embodied. While we do not suggest that PGD is within every woman's reach or that there are not significant financial, psychological, and physical hurdles involved in using the technology, we suggest that PGD is not perceived as carrying the same degree of moral risk or taint as termination. We think this is significant both in terms of future uptake of the technology (and the new disability avoidance technologies that supersede it) and in terms of the way in which "serious disability" is interpreted in this and future contexts. From a regulatory perspective, it puts significant pressure on efforts to align the appropriate use of PGD with abortion law. Not surprisingly, we see evidence that this alignment has already weakened with the approval of testing for late onset, low penetrance conditions.

---

[137] Human Fertilisation and Embryology Authority, "Choices and Boundaries: Should People Be Able to Select Embryos Free from an Inherited Susceptibility to Cancer?" (November 2005), 4.1.

[138] Royal College of Obstetricians and Gynaecologists, "Termination of Pregnancy for Fetal Abnormality in England, Scotland and Wales: Report of a Working Party" (May 2010), 10.

6

Futures

In Australia the Department of Health and Aging[1] and in the United
Kingdom the HFEA[2] both have a special panel to undertake "Horizon
Scanning" to examine the legal, ethical, and scientific implications of
new scientific techniques that are in the process of development.[3] In this
chapter we too look to the future and examine four new disability avoidance technologies that are on the clinical horizon. Some of these technologies are already in use though still considered highly experimental,

---

[1] Australian Government Department of Health and Aging, Australian and New
Zealand Horizon Scanning Network (ANZHSN), available at http://www.health.gov.
au/internet/horizon/publishing.nsf/Content/58685F8B48CC9EE7CA2575AD0080
F340/$File/Final_MRI_fetal_HS_report.pdf (accessed on 28 June 2011)

[2] Human Fertilisation and Embryology Authority, Horizon Scanning Panel, available
at http://www.hfea.gov.uk/1132.html. (accessed on 28 June 2011)

[3] ANZHSN, *Horizon Scanning Technology Horizon Scanning Report: MRI for the
Detection of Foetal Abnormalities* (October 2007), available at http://www.health.gov.
au/internet/horizon/publishing.nsf/Content/58685F8B48CC9EE7CA2575AD00
80F340/$File/Final_MRI_fetal_HS_report.pdf, (accessed on 28 June 2011) and
ANZHSN, *Horizon Scanning Technology Prioritising Summary: Non-invasive Prenatal
Testing for Down's Syndrome*(August 2008), available at http://www.horizonscanning.
gov.au/internet/horizon/publishing.nsf/Content/BB580B674729F620CA2575AD0
080F351/$File/Volume_21_Aug_2008_No-invasive%20prenatal%20diagnostic%20
test%20for%20Down's%20Syndrome.pdf.(accessed on 28 June 2011) The HFEA
Horizon Scanning Panel has recently considered mitochondrial DNA: see http://
www.hfea.gov.uk/docs/Horizon_Scanning_Report_2009–10.pdf. (accessed on 28
June 2011).

some are the subject of research and development, and others exist only in the scientific imagination and may never eventuate.

In the first part of this chapter we will explore the legal and ethical implications of two very different prenatal testing technologies that are in the early stages of their development. The first is a noninvasive prenatal diagnostic (NIPD) test using free fetal deoxyribonucleic acid (DNA) or ribonucleic acid (RNA) from maternal blood. The test aims to offer women a noninvasive, early detection, reliable prenatal test for abnormalities such as Down syndrome.[4] The second, fetal magnetic resonance imaging (fetal MRI), can be used to detect conditions in the developing fetus, such as congenital defects and anomalies of the central nervous system, and to enable assessment of possible damage to the fetus. It is currently used in conjunction with ultrasound. We will consider how or whether these developments raise new questions regarding the way we currently regulate prenatal testing and how we might regulate it in the future.

In the second part we look at the emerging technology of inheritable genetic modification (IGM). Developments in this area differ markedly from prenatal testing and preimplantation genetic testing technologies because they do not require the deselection of the embryo or fetus. Instead they involve treatment of that embryo or fetus or the gametes that went into making it. This is done using gene manipulation techniques. Within this discussion we explore one form of IGM that has already been trialed – cell fusion to prevent mitochondrial disease.

We conclude with a brief examination of advances in preconception testing technology aimed at identifying carrier status in adults for severe childhood disorders. The expectation of these screening tests is that once people know of their carrier status and the risk of passing on a debilitating condition, they will take preventative or precautionary measures to avoid producing a child with the relevant disorder. We

---

[4] See the website of the Murdoch Children's Research Institute: http://www.mcri.edu.au/pages/research/research-group.asp?P=projects&G=41.(accessed 28 June 2011).

consider the implications of this kind of testing, which occurs prior to the existence of even a conceptus, and speculate on how it constitutes the ultimate demand for perfected pregnancy.

1 PRENATAL TESTING TECHNOLOGIES OF THE FUTURE

Part 1 is divided into two sections. In the first half we look at existing regulatory limits on the use of current and future prenatal testing technologies in our key comparator jurisdictions. In the second half we describe two new prenatal testing technologies and consider their implications in light of existing regulation and possible future regulatory limits.

1.1 The Law

Regulation limiting access to prenatal testing during pregnancy is uncommon. It is more common for legislatures to provide a limit on access to abortion. For instance, in Australia, the United Kingdom, Canada, and the United States there is no direct regulation limiting access to prenatal testing. Rather, access is determined by professional best practice guidelines,[5] laws and codes governing the doctor-patient relationship,[6] and laws governing the quality and production of the

---

[5] In Australia, see http://www.ranzcog.edu.au/publications/statements/C-obs4.pdf; in the UK, see http://www.nice.org.uk/nicemedia/live/11947/40115/40115.pdf; in Canada see http://www.sogc.org/guidelines/documents/187E-CPG-February2007.pdf; in the United States see http://www.acog.org/from_home/publications/press_releases/nr01-02-07-1.cfm. (accessed 28 June 2011).

[6] For example, in Australia the relevant Code of Conduct is issued by the Medical Board of Australia, which is empowered to provide such guidance under s 39 of the uniform legislation on registration of medical practitioners (collectively referred to as the Health Practitioner Regulation National Law Act[as in force in each state and territory]).

testing technologies themselves.[7] Recent developments in therapeutic goods regulation in Australia, for example, include in vitro devices (IVDs) such as prenatal tests in the purview of therapeutic goods management. The Therapeutic Goods Administration (TGA) approves and regulates products on the basis of an assessment of risks against benefits. IVDs such as prenatal tests that screen for congenital disorders in the fetus are classified as Class 3,[8] which is the class designated for devices that pose a "moderate public health risk or high personal risk."[9] *High personal risk* refers to "the risk posed to an individual by an erroneous result."[10] In the case of prenatal testing, the relevant risk occurs

In the United Kingdom, see the Medical Act 1983 (UK) and General Medical Council, Management for Doctors – guidance for doctors (February 2006): see http://www.gmc-uk.org/guidance/ethical_guidance/management_for_doctors.asp# confidentiality_and_access_to_information (accessed on 28 June 2011). In Canada, see the Canadian Medical Association, "CMA Code of Ethics" (2004): see http://policybase.cma.ca/PolicyPDF/PD04–06.pdf (accessed on 28 June 2011). In the United States, see American Medical Association, "AMA's Code of Ethics": see http://www.ama-assn.org/ama/pub/physician-resources/medical-ethics/code-medical-ethics.page (accessed on 28 June 2011).

[7] In Australia, see the Therapeutic Goods Act 1989 (Cth). In the United Kingdom, see the Consumer Protection Act 1987 (UK) and the Medical Devices Regulations 2002 (UK). In the United States, see the Code of Federal Regulations 21–1-862, 21–1-864, and 21–1-866. In Canada, see the Food and Drugs Act (R.S.C., 1985, c.F-27) and the Medical Devices Regulations (SOR/98–282).

[8] Therapeutic Goods (Medical Devices) Regulations 2002 (Cth), Schedule 2A, s 1.3(i)(j).

[9] Therapeutic Goods (Medical Devices) Regulations 2002 (Cth), s 3.3(2)(b)(iii). For further explanation of the classification system, see http://www.tga.gov.au/industry/ivd-framework-overview.htm#class3 and http://www.tga.gov.au/industry/ivd-classification.htm.(accessed on 28 June 2011). Of particular interest is the comment that "[s]oftware that is supplied as a 'stand-alone' IVD, for use in the interpretation of a series of results obtained as part of a first trimester screening assessment in order to determine foetal risk of trisomy 21 is a Class 3 IVD": see Classification Rule 1.3, at http://www.tga.gov.au/industry/ivd-classification.htm (accessed on 28 June 2011). This suggests that new ultrasound and fetal MRI technologies might also fall into this classification.

[10] See http://www.tga.gov.au/industry/ivd-framework-overview.htm#class3.(accessed on 28 June 2011).

when an erroneous result "would have a major impact on outcome (death, severe disability, possible follow up measures)" and "because of stress and anxiety resulting from the information and nature of the possible follow-up measures."[11] As we shall discuss later, advances in the technology of prenatal diagnostic and screening tests will require new assessments of risks and benefits as testing becomes simpler and the range of conditions tested becomes broader. In the context of the regulation of therapeutic devices described previously, one can imagine that as prenatal testing for less serious or less prevalent conditions becomes more widespread, there might be a shift in the balance of assessment by the TGA of risk versus benefits. This could occur, for instance, where the risk that the technology will provide a false positive result is moderate to high and the seriousness of the condition is moderate or low. But what of the situation where the risk of a false positive result is very low and the seriousness of the condition is also very low? Therapeutic goods regulation is limited in what it can achieve. In fact, current Australian therapeutic goods regulation only regulates those devices that claim to be therapeutic. IVDs that provide testing for nontherapeutic trait selection, including sex, would therefore not be covered by the TGA.[12]

Consequently, a question arises as to whether access to prenatal tests – performed and acted upon in the early stages of pregnancy – should, as with PGD, be subject to a seriousness threshold in

---

[11] See http://www.tga.gov.au/industry/devices-ivd-definitions.htm. (accessed on 28 June 2011).

[12] Further, it is unclear whether PGD is included within this framework. While s 1.3(1) (j) of Schedule 2A of the Therapeutic Goods (Medical Devices) Regulations 2002 (Cth) specifically refers to congenital disorders in the fetus, the TGA elsewhere notes that "Class 3 IVDs used for screening for congenital disorders include pre- and post-natal tests for trisomy 13, trisomy 18, trisomy 21 or Klinefelter's syndrome; tests for alpha-fetoprotein (AFP) when used in the detection of foetal open neural tube defects" (see http://www.tga.gov.au/industry/ivd-classification.htm under Classification Rule 1.3) (accessed on 28 June 2011). PGD can be considered a "pre-natal" test, suggesting that PGD tests would also be subject to Class 3 classification and TGA monitoring.

legislation or guidelines. So far it seems most of the jurisdictions we have examined have answered this question in the negative and have preferred instead to leave these determinations in the domain of the doctor-patient relationship. We have also seen that some of the stricter regulatory regimes around access to PGD have recently been relaxed, reflecting a general trend away from regulatory control of reproductive testing technologies except at the very outer limits – choosing disability or choosing sex.[13]

But what is the likely impact of new prenatal testing technologies that make testing simpler, faster, and less invasive? What is the impact of testing technologies that, although no less invasive, are more refined, detailed, and accurate?

It is possible that some kind of legislative limit on the use of prenatal tests for non-medical trait selection, sex selection, or testing for minor disabilities and abnormalities might be considered. While there is little doubt that most of the governments considered in this book will not intervene to prohibit a woman from undertaking an abortion in the first weeks of pregnancy, it is possible that they may see fit to limit access to prenatal testing technologies where they consider the conditions being tested to be either insufficiently serious or inappropriate.

We now turn to look at some of the developments in the field of prenatal testing technologies to illustrate this possibility.

1.2 The New Technologies

1.2.1. NIPDs – Diagnosing Cell-free Fetal Nucleic Acids in Maternal Blood

While the majority of DNA is contained within the nucleus or mitochondria of cells, low levels of short pieces of DNA have been found to exist

---

[13] For more on this regulatory trend in the context of PGD, see Chapter 4.

in blood serum.[14] It is thought that cells eject this DNA during cell death. It has been found that maternal blood, apart from containing maternal DNA, also contains low levels of "cell-free fetal nucleic acids."[15] In recent tests scientists have been able to detect fetal DNA from as early as four weeks gestation, but most reliably from seven weeks gestation. Scientists from the Chinese University of Hong Kong recently reported having scanned the entire DNA of an unborn child from the mother's blood sample to check safely for genetic disorders.[16] While these NIPD tests are still under development, if fetal DNA can be detected in maternal blood and subsequently tested, that would indicate the potential to replace invasive procedures, such as chorionic villus sampling (CVS) or amniocentesis, with a simple blood test. Most of the discussion that has occurred around these NIPDs has been in the context of testing for trisomy 21 (Down syndrome),[17] however, cell-free fetal nucleic testing has also been used to test for Huntington's disease,[18] achondroplasia (dwarfism),[19] and myotonic dystrophy (adult onset muscular dystrophy).[20]

[14] C. Wright and H. Burton, "The Use of Cell-free Fetal Nucleic Acids in Maternal Blood for Non-invasive Prenatal Diagnosis" (2009) 15(1) *Human Reproduction Update*, 139.

[15] Y.M.D. Lo et al., "Presence of Fetal DNA in Maternal Plasma and Serum" (2007) *Lancet* 350, 485.

[16] Y.M.D. Lo et al., "Maternal Plasma DNA Sequencing Reveals the Genome-Wide Genetic and Mutational Profile of the Fetus" (2010) 2(61) *Science Translational Medicine* 61ra91.

[17] ANZHSN Horizon Scanning Technology Prioritising Summary "Non-invasive Prenatal Diagnostic Test for Trisomy-21 (Down's Syndrome)" Update: November 2009, and R.W.K. Chiu et al., "Non-invasive Prenatal Assessment of Trisomy 21 by Multiplexed Maternal Plasma DNA Sequencing: Large Scale Validity Study" (2011) 342 *British Medical Journal* 7401, 217.

[18] M.C. González-González et al., "Huntington Disease–unaffected Fetus Diagnosed from Maternal Plasma Using QF-PCR" (2003) 23(3) *Prenatal Diagnosis*, 232–234.

[19] H. Saito et al., "Prenatal DNA Diagnosis of a Single-gene Disorder from Maternal Plasma" (2000) 356(9236) *Lancet* 1170; Y. Li et al., "Improved Prenatal Detection of a Fetal Point Mutation for Achondroplasia by the Use of Size-fractionated Circulatory DNA in Maternal Plasma – Case Report" (2004) 24(11) *Prenatal Diagnosis* 896.

[20] P. Amicucci et al., "Prenatal Diagnosis of Myotonic Dystrophy Using Fetal DNA Obtained from Maternal Plasma" (2000) 46(2) *Clinical Chemistry*, 301.

Carrier status for autosomal recessive diseases can also be tested. While these can be much harder to diagnose,[21] conditions that have been tested include cystic fibrosis,[22] hemoglobinopathies (including beta-thalassemia),[23] and congenital adrenal hyperplasia.[24] Further, scientists have been able to test accurately for male sex. A recent study accurately diagnosed male sex in thirty-four of thirty-six cases.[25] This means that the test also has important implications for screening for sex-linked disorders. It has also been suggested that the test might be used to diagnose paternally inherited single-gene disorders in high-risk families, to diagnose pregnancy-related disorders, and to diagnose aneuploidy.[26]

Many of the new technologies currently under development for prenatal testing would be used very early in the pregnancy and, as noted previously, would be far less invasive than existing technologies such as CVS and amniocentesis and would not carry the risk of miscarriage.

There are, however, significant ethical questions around this new technology. First, NIPDs are intended to replace more invasive tests, such as amniocentesis and CVS, that aim to diagnose the same conditions. However, it is likely they will also replace the initial screening test. The effect of this will be to capture a much larger group of women than were previously included in the diagnostic stage of testing. In

---

[21] This difficulty is due to the fact that there is currently no way to distinguish between identical maternal and paternal alleles.

[22] M.C. González-González et al., "Prenatal Detection of a Cystic Fibrosis Mutation in Fetal DNA from Maternal Plasma" (2002) 22(10) *Prenatal Diagnosis*, 946.

[23] R.W.K. Chiu et al., "Prenatal Exclusion of [beta] Thalassemia Major by Examination of Maternal Plasma" (2002) 360 (9338) *Lancet*, 998.

[24] R.W.K. Chiu et al., "Non-invasive Prenatal Exclusion of Congenital Adrenal Hyperplasia by Maternal Plasma Analysis: A Feasibility Study" (2002) 48(5) *Clinical Chemistry*, 778.

[25] T.V. Zolotukhina et al., "Analysis of Cell-free Fetal DNA in Plasma and Serum of Pregnant Women" (2005) 53(3) *Journal of Histochemistry and Cytochemistry*, 297.

[26] For example, it may be possible to test for a copy of the rhesus gene or for elevated levels of total cell-free fetal DNA (suggesting abnormal levels of fetal cells are dying).

other words, whereas currently most women will only undergo CVS or amniocentesis if they are found to be at high risk in the initial screening test or are of advanced maternal age, NIPD could be used to test all women whether they are at increased risk or not. De Jong argues that this would be likely to result in a degradation of the quality of informed consent achieved. She argues that since the sheer volume of women being tested would increase significantly, providing sufficient detailed information would be difficult.[27]

Second, prenatal testing technologies that allow identification of previously undiagnosable disorders or enable testing for a greater range of potential disorders raise complex questions regarding the need for the test in the first place. As noted in Chapter 2, Abby Lippman has suggested that "[w]ith respect to prenatal diagnosis, 'need' seems to have been conceptualized predominantly in terms of changes in capabilities for fetal diagnoses: women only come to 'need' prenatal diagnosis after the test for some disorder has been developed."[28] Here too we might ask: Does the need predate the test or does the test create the need? It seems clear that, insofar as NIPD is replacing invasive testing technologies, the need preceded the invention of the test. However, as noted, researchers are currently developing tests that can scan the entire DNA of a growing fetus. This development – overlaid with the larger question we have been asking about whether there ought to be a limit on the kinds of disabilities and diseases for which testing is allowed – raises important questions for those of us concerned with appropriate regulatory responses. We might, for instance, want to consider whether new technologies such as these NIPDs demand greater regulatory oversight just as PGD did in its infancy. Are we happy, given the kind of framework of interpretation and decision making that occurs in the clinician's rooms (described in detail in Chapter 5),

---

[27] A. de Jong et al., "Non-invasive Prenatal Testing: Ethical Issues Explored" (2010) 18(3) *European Journal of Human Genetics*, 272.

[28] A. Lippman, "Prenatal Genetic Testing and Screening: Constructing Needs and Reinforcing Inequities" (1991) 17 *American Journal of Law and Medicine* 15, 27.

to leave the management of access to these testing technologies to the doctors who administer them in consultation with the patients who use them?

A key difference from existing testing may be that low intervention broad spectrum testing technologies result in a greater uptake of what some might perceive as "unnecessary" testing. If risk-free testing becomes universally available, it is worth asking how it will affect women's ability to negotiate questions about the appropriateness of this testing. Will women be given the opportunity to appreciate fully the consequences of this practice and the incredible anxiety and uncertainty a negative result can cause throughout the early months of pregnancy? As discussed in Chapters 1, 2, and 5, we have already seen how the normalization of testing is reshaping women's decision making about their pregnancies. This trend will no doubt continue if screening and testing using NIPDs become a routine part of ordinary antenatal care for all women rather than just those at increased risk of having a child who has a serious abnormality.[29] Further, if NIPDs make it possible to test easily for a much larger range of rarer disorders, we face the possibility that the range of normal pregnancies will decrease. This is because, as suggested in Chapter 2, where the pool of potential harms is based on progressively minute statistical risk calculations, it becomes increasingly difficult to identify the range of tolerable deviations from the "norm."

Given the current state of the development of NIPDs it is unlikely that there will be widespread analysis of cell-free fetal DNA for some time, other than for sex-linked conditions. Nevertheless it is something to consider for the future. It is worth noting, for comparative purposes, that the early uses of PGD were initially limited to identification of sex and sex-linked disorders. Over the course of the last twenty years, however, PGD has become a boutique technology in

---

[29] A. de Jong et al., "Non-invasive Prenatal Testing: Ethical Issues Explored" (2010) 18(3) *European Journal of Human Genetics*, 272.

which tests for inherited genetic conditions are developed as and when requested and the list of available testable conditions continues to grow.

If a broader range of conditions does become easier to diagnose prenatally, women may feel pressured to undergo a termination for conditions that previously were not considered serious enough to warrant this kind of intervention. This is particularly so where the testing technology is applied at a very early stage in the pregnancy. De Jong notes that an interesting side effect of earlier detection of abnormalities might be that women go through a process of what she calls "unnecessary decisionmaking"[30] with respect to pregnancies that may otherwise have spontaneously miscarried. On the other hand, as miscarriage can be a devastating outcome for some women, being able to anticipate and control that process may well be viewed as a benefit.

While termination of a pregnancy of an undesired sex or unwanted paternity is, of course, already possible, there has, as yet, been no significant community or legislative pressure in the jurisdictions we have examined, where abortion is available, to intervene to limit this capacity, and it seems unlikely that new limits will be placed on access to abortion early in pregnancy. However, it is possible that legislatures might try to limit access to NIPD tests for non-medical sex selection, as has been done with PGD.

Finally, although beyond the scope of our book, it is worth noting that whenever whole DNA scanning is made possible, as appears to be the case with this new NIPD testing technology, the potential for genetic discrimination and invasion of privacy is raised as a worrying specter. If parents undertake an NIPD that allows a doctor to scan the entire DNA of their developing fetus and a range of conditions or genetic predispositions are identified, the child may be vulnerable to

---

[30] A. de Jong et al., "Non-invasive Prenatal Testing: Ethical Issues Explored" (2010) 18(3) *European Journal of Human Genetics*, 273.

exclusion from insurance and employment on the basis of the genetic profile.[31]

We now want to turn to a new and developing prenatal technology that exists at the other end of the testing spectrum.

1.2.2 Fetal Magnetic Resonance Imaging (Fetal MRI)

Fetal MRI requires a pregnant woman to lie on a table that slides into a large cylinder and submit to a scan using a magnetic field and radio waves to take pictures of the fetus. Magnetic resonance imaging provides highly detailed information about the contrast between soft tissues and so is useful in anatomically and pathologically based diagnosis (such as determining whether structures are normal or abnormal). Detailed images allow a clearer examination of the morphology of the fetus than can often be obtained with an ultrasound. Like the ultrasound it is safer than computed tomography (CT) and X-ray scans because it does not use ionizing radiation. It provides a larger field of view than ultrasound, enabling examination of larger abnormalities, and has very fast scanning capability. Nevertheless, despite being considered a noninvasive procedure, it is more likely to trigger anxiety than an ultrasound, as many people find confinement inside the cylinder uncomfortable or distressing.

Fetal MRI has been used since the early 1980s, but it has only recently started to be viewed as a proven technology. Currently, fetal MRI is used as an adjunct to ultrasound where an ultrasound has

---

[31] In Australia, for example, Federal and State privacy laws require record keepers to protect the privacy of health information including genetic information; however, these laws are limited and may not be adequate to protect the individual in all circumstances. Privacy Act 1988 (Cth), ss 95A and 95AA. For a detailed discussion of some of these issues, see the 2003 Australian Law Reform Commission Report *Essentially Yours: The Protection of Human Genetic Information in Australia (ALRC Report 96)*, available at http://www.alrc.gov.au/publications/report-96.(accessed on 28 June 2011).

identified something anomalous. In February 2007, the Australian and New Zealand Horizon Scanning Network classified the technology as "nearly established" in Australia;[32] by October of the same year, the network had recommended its use in conjunction with ultrasound for the diagnosis of "some foetal anomalies." The network's report noted that "[u]ltrasound remains the gold standard in the screening of pregnant women" and further provided that fetal MRI should only be "conducted in tertiary centres where parents may access the appropriate level of counselling."[33] Meanwhile, significant clinical studies are being undertaken on a number of aspects of the technology elsewhere in the world. For instance, the University of California, San Francisco, is currently undertaking a study on fetal MRI that aims to test "how accurately fetal MRI detects changes in the fetus' brain and spine during pregnancy compared to ultrasound" and to "learn how various congenital (inherited) abnormalities detected on fetal MRI correlate with childhood development." They note on their website that "[c]urrently it is very difficult to counsel parents who have a fetus with a brain abnormality, because outcomes can vary widely."[34] Thus it is clear that while fetal MRI might be offering greater diagnostic capacity, there is still a

---

[32] Australia and New Zealand Horizon Scanning Network, "National Scanning Unit Horizon Scanning Prioritising Summary: Magnetic Resonance Imaging for the Detection of Foetal Abnormalities" (February 2007) 15(6), 1: see http://www.health.gov.au/internet/horizon/publishing.nsf/Content/6B81AEB3E7EE0001CA2575AD0080F344/$File/Feb%20Vol%2015%20No%206%20-%20Magnetic%20resonance.pdf (accessed on 24 June 2011).

[33] Australia and New Zealand Horizon Scanning Network, "Horizon Scanning Technology Horizon Scanning Report: MRI for the Detection of Foetal Abnormalities" (October 2007): see http://www.horizonscanning.gov.au/internet/horizon/publishing.nsf/Content/58685F8B48CC9EE7CA2575AD0080F340/$File/Final_MRI_fetal_HS_report.pdf (accessed 24 June 2011).

[34] O. A. Glenn, Department of Radiology and Biomedical Imaging, University of California San Francisco "Fetal MRI" at http://www.radiology.ucsf.edu/research/labs/baby-brain/fetal-mri (accessed on 24 June 2011). See also O.A. Glenn, "MR Imaging of the Fetal Brain" (2010) 40(1) *Pediatric Radiology*, 68.

significant lack of understanding about what the information derived from the scans is telling the clinician. Recent news that researchers had been able to diagnose with 90 percent accuracy, using MRI brain scans, whether the brain they were looking at belonged to a person who had autism spectrum disorder has had a very mixed response.[35] Carl Heneghan, director of the Centre for Evidence Based Medicine at Oxford, for instance, challenged both the presentation of the statistics and the reliability of the information. First, he notes:

> But, the real worry ... is the numbers without the disease who test positive. This will be substantial: 1,980 of the 9,900 without the disease. This is what happens at very low prevalences, the numbers falsely misdiagnosed rockets. Alarmingly, of the 2,070 with a positive test, only 90 will have the disease, which is roughly 4.5%.[36]

Then he points out that clinical research that uses a population already diagnosed with a condition to test the device for diagnosing it runs into problems when the same diagnostic device is applied to patients who have a less advanced or less severe form of the disease.

Applying this analysis to fetal brain scans, one would have to be particularly concerned about its use to diagnose such conditions as autism. This is not unlikely given that autism is a condition for which PGD is already authorized in a number of jurisdictions. It is not difficult to imagine that, in the not very distant future, fetal MRI might be employed to assist with a diagnosis prenatally. A question that must be raised, then, is whether it is ever appropriate to use this kind of technology to diagnose these kinds of disorders, given both the nature of the disorder and the varying levels of severity.

[35] A. Jha, "Autism Can Be Diagnosed with Brain Scan Study" *Guardian*, 10 August 2010: see http://www.guardian.co.uk/science/2010/aug/10/autism-brain-scan (accessed on 28 June 2011).

[36] C. Heneghan, "Why Autism Can't Be Diagnosed with Brain Scans," *Guardian*, 12 August 2010: see http://www.guardian.co.uk/science/blog/2010/aug/12/autism-brain-scan-statistics?intcmp=239 (accessed on 28 June 2011).

Karen O'Connell argues, for instance, that "[v]iewing the autistic brain on a reductionist or individualistic model neglects the possibility of what a differently ordered brain might have to offer." She refers to the work of the neuroscientist Antonio Damasio, who has made the argument that the immense talents that autistic people possess in other areas will be lost if the primary focus is the alleged neurological defect.[37]

Nevertheless, fetal MRI has been successful in diagnosing some congenital conditions that had often been misdiagnosed in the past, and fetal MRI can also be used where a treatable condition has been identified and in utero procedures are recommended or a particular method of delivery is necessary. Most of the limitations in relation to fetal MRI relate to cost and restricted availability.[38]

In a study comparing fetal MRI and ultrasound, Levine et al. found that the use of fetal MRI changed the ultrasound-based diagnosis in twenty-six of sixty-six central nervous system abnormalities, and it affected patient counseling in thirty-three of those cases.[39] Simon et al. found that twenty-four of fifty-two central nervous system abnormalities were managed differently after fetal MRI.[40] In yet another study Whitby et al. found that fetal MRI changed the diagnosis in twenty-nine cases, and in eleven of those cases the MRI did not confirm abnormalities previously detected by ultrasound. The authors note that the

---

[37] Karen O'Connell, "From Black Box to 'Open Brain': Law Neuroimaging and Disability Discrimination" (2011) 20(3) *Griffith Law Review* 883 at 901; see also Antonio Damasio, "Neurodiversity Forever; The Disability Movement Turns to Brains," *New York Times*, 9 May 2004.

[38] Ultrafast fetal MRI uses short acquisition times (400 milliseconds per slice) during imaging, which eliminate the need for sedating the fetus see: T.A. Huisman et al., "Fetal Magnetic Resonance Imaging of the Central Nervous System: A Pictorial Essay" (2002) 12(8) *European Radiology*, 1952.

[39] D. Levine et al., "Central Nervous System Abnormalities Assessed with Prenatal Magnetic Resonance Imaging" (1999) 94(6) *Obstetrics & Gynecology*, 1011.

[40] E.M. Simon et al., "Fast MR Imaging of Fetal CNS Anomalies in Utero" (2000) 21(9) *American Journal of Neuroradiology*, 1688.

parents in two of these cases had decided to terminate if the MRI confirmed the ultrasound finding.[41]

While fetal MRI does not involve physical penetration of the body, it is nevertheless a fairly onerous procedure likely to cause some level of distress for the mother, who will be required to place her entire pregnant body in the MRI machine. In addition, with the ascertainment of more detailed information arises a likelihood of further interventions where the problem diagnosed is susceptible to some kind of in utero treatment. So it is again worth asking whether there is some role for the law or regulatory guidelines to ensure that, for instance, the scope of precautionary responses women are expected to have toward their pregnancies is limited. If fetal MRI can enhance the quality of information women receive from prenatal testing, then it is clearly a technology worth pursuing. However, as outlined in the Horizon Scanning Report, new technologies aimed at enhancing the efficacy of existing technologies can add to rather than limit the number of anomalies identified that may not be clinically relevant. The report describes this as an "obstetric technology cascade" and lists a number of ways in which this might occur. First, if the ultrasound findings in the first instance are equivocal, fetal MRI might be used as a backup or verification technology. They argue that "[o]nce clinicians are aware that there is a 'backup' technology that can confirm or rule out suspicious findings, there may be *much* wider use of the technology."[42] Second, they note that clinicians "will need to make decisions about whether to inform women of findings that may not be of major clinical

---

[41] E.H. Whitby et al., "Comparison of Ultrasound and Magnetic Resonance Imagining in 100 Singleton Pregnancies with Suspected Brain Abnormalities" (2004) 111(8) *British Journal of Obstetrics and Gynaecology*, 784.

[42] ANZHSN, *Horizon Scanning Technology Horizon Scanning Report: MRI for the Detection of Foetal Abnormalities* (October 2007), 29 [original emphasis]. The report is available at http://www.health.gov.au/internet/horizon/publishing.nsf/Content/58 685F8B48CC9EE7CA2575AD0080F340/$File/Final_MRI_fetal_HS_report.pdf (accessed on 24 June 2011).

significance but which could be assessed more precisely with foetal MRI screening," and, third, they note that there is no clear answer to the question whether "MRI screening ha[s] its own accuracy problems in identifying anomalies that may not be of clinical significance."[43]

The introduction of fetal MRI as a means of detecting physical abnormalities or more accurately diagnosing those already detected by ultrasound is perhaps most ethically justifiable where the information obtained is limited to clinically significant abnormalities that are already known to have a serious (however defined) impact on the future child. However, it is clear from the literature that fetal MRI is going to be an increasingly important tool for diagnosing neurological and developmental abnormalities associated with congenital disorders. At the moment, little information is known about the accuracy of predicted brain dysfunction on the basis of fetal MRIs, and studies are necessary to measure what is seen at the fetal stage against childhood developmental outcomes.[44]

Given the limitations of the technology it is worth asking whether there needs to be some kind of statutory guideline limiting PND using fetal MRI to only known "serious" conditions. One point that seems clear is that these technologies are constantly developing, and so any regulatory solution must be flexible enough to develop along with the technologies it regulates. Further, definitions of what is serious vary among clinicians and patients, and it may be that a regulatory limit is too blunt a tool to manage these variations. Professor Judy Illes, who is well known for her work in neuroethics, is currently conducting a study

[43] ANZHSN, *Horizon Scanning Technology Horizon Scanning Report: MRI for the Detection of Foetal Abnormalities* (October 2007), 29 [original emphasis]. The report is available at http://www.health.gov.au/internet/horizon/publishing.nsf/Content/58 685F8B48CC9EE7CA2575AD0080F340/$File/Final_MRI_fetal_HS_report.pdf (accessed on 24 June 2011).

[44] O.A. Glenn, "MR Imaging of the Fetal Brain" (2010) 40 *Pediatric Radiology* 1, 68; see also http://www.horizonscanning.gov.au/internet/horizon/publishing.nsf/Conten t/58685F8B48CC9EE7CA2575AD0080F340/$File/Final_MRI_fetal_HS_report. pdf (accessed 24 June 2011).

that explores patient expectations of fetal MRI and decision making. The project has been conceived precisely because "the increasing use of *in utero* MRI and the vast amount of new information that this imaging modality can provide about the status of the fetal CNS [central nervous system], but the paradoxically few guidelines that exist for utilizing that information and for counseling patients" make this kind of study a necessary next step.[45]

2 MODIFYING THE FUTURE GENOME

Arguably inheritable genetic modification (IGM) represents the next technological stage in disability avoidance. Instead of aborting affected fetuses or deciding not to implant those embryos identified as carrying a genetic mutation, it may be possible to alter the genome of an affected embryo/fetus in order to treat the condition. And yet in nearly all the jurisdictions we have examined in this book IGM is prohibited. As we have argued at various points, one of the ways in which prohibitions against new biotechnologies are overcome is via arguments about their capacity to ward off or eliminate debilitating forms of illness and disability. IGM is no different. Over the last decade we have seen significant shifts in the laws of both the United Kingdom and Australia toward a relaxing of prohibitions on techniques that involve IGM to avoid disability, and we will turn to these shortly. In the United States, however, regulation seems to have developed on a piecemeal basis with some states prohibiting any kind of research on an embryo and others providing no guidance.[46] Accordingly, we have divided this part into five sections. First, we provide a brief overview of IGM

---

[45] http://bioethics.stanford.edu/research/projects/illes_fetal_mri.html. (accessed 24th June 2011).

[46] For instance, the following laws prohibit nontherapeutic research on an embryo: SD Cod. Laws 34–14–17; Minn Stat Ann § 145.422 subd. 1, 2 (1989); ME Rev Stat Ann tit 22, § 1593 (1992); and LA Rev Stat Ann §§ 9:122 (1991).

therapies. Next, we provide a case study of one form of IGM – that which involves cell fusion to treat mitochondrial disorders – which has already been undertaken in the United States and has been the subject of a recent inquiry to consider its legalization in the United Kingdom.[47] Third, we examine existing regulatory limits on the use of IGM in our key comparator jurisdictions. Fourth, we canvass the arguments for and against allowing IGM. Finally, we explore the public attitudes to the use of IGM and consider what, if any, regulatory response we ought to have to its introduction as a disability avoidance technology.

2.1 What Is Gene Therapy?

Gene therapy involves the introduction of nucleic acid (DNA or RNA) into a human cell to modify gene expression in that cell. Somatic gene therapy involves the modification of cells that will not be passed onto future generations, whereas germ line gene therapy involves modifying the patient's egg/sperm cells such that the changes are inherited. Gene transfer to ,a developing embryo or fetus could also achieve germline gene therapy if the transfer occurred prior to cell differentiation. Given that most preimplantation embryos are transferred around about the eight-cell stage or at the blastocyst stage, gene therapy carried out on such an embryo has the potential to result in inheritable modification. Inadvertent germ line gene transfer (GLGT) is currently considered a

---

[47] In the United States, IGM involving ooplasmic transplantation to avoid mitochondrial disease was undertaken more than ten years ago at the Institute for Reproductive Medicine and Science of St. Barnabas in New Jersey. This produced a number of live births of children who had a small quantity of additional mitochondrial DNA not inherited from either parent. See J.A. Barritt et al., "Mitochondria in Human Offspring Derived from Ooplasmic Transplantation: Brief Communication" 16(3) *Human Reproduction*, 513. In the United Kingdom, the HFEA completed its report entitled *Scientific Review of the Safety and Efficacy of Methods to Avoid Mitochondrial Disease through Assisted Conception* on 18 April 2011; see http://www.hfea.gov.uk/6372.html (accessed on 24 June 2011).

risk in all gene therapy including somatic cell therapy – though the risk is considered to be very small. Gene therapy has a number of potential applications that might allow it to take the place of prenatal and pre-implantation testing. These include treatment of single-gene inherited disorders.[48] Trials of gene therapy for diseases where the target cell population is large have not yet produced any success (e.g., the lungs for cystic fibrosis and muscle cells for muscular dystrophy).[49] This limitation could theoretically be overcome by germline gene therapy

[48] An example of a single-gene disorder that has been treated by gene therapy is severe combined immunodeficiency caused by adenosine deaminase deficiency, Leber's congenital amaurosis (an inherited blindness), and X-linked adrenoleukodystrophy: see A. Aiuti et al., "Gene Therapy for Immunodeficiency Due to Adenosine Deaminase Deficiency" (2009) 360(5) *New England Journal of Medicine* 447; A. Aiuti et al., "Correction of ADA-SCID by Stem Cell Gene Therapy Combined with Nonmyeloablative Conditioning" (28 June 2002) 296(5577) *Science* 2410; A.M. Maguire et al., "Safety and Efficacy of Gene Transfer for Leber's Congenital Amaurosis" (22 May 2008) 358(21) *New England Journal of Medicine* 2240; A.V. Cideciyan et al., "Human *RPE65* Gene Therapy for Leber Congenital Amaurosis: Persistence of Early Visual Improvements and Safety at 1 Year" (September, 2009) 20(9) *Human Gene Therapy* 999; A.M. Maguire et al., "Age-dependent Effects of *RPE65* Gene Therapy for Leber's Congenital Amaurosis: A Phase 1 Dose-escalation Trial" (7 November 2009) 374(9701) *Lancet* 1597; F. Simonelli et al., "Gene Therapy for Leber's Congenital Amaurosis Is Safe and Effective through 1.5 Years after Vector Administration" (March 2010) 18(3) *Molecular Therapy* 643; N. Cartier et al., "Hematopoietic Stem Cell Gene Therapy with a Lentiviral Vector in X-linked Adrenoleukodystrophy" (6 November 2009) 326(5954) *Science* 818.

[49] A low amount of gene expression was detected in this trial of gene therapy for Duchenne muscular dystrophy: M. Kinali et al., "Local Restoration of Dystrophin Expression with the Morpholino Oligomer AVI-4658 in Duchenne Muscular Dystrophy: A Single-blind, Placebo-controlled, Dose-escalation, Proof-of-concept Study" (2009) 8 *Lancet Neurology* 918. For a review of the challenges facing gene therapy for cystic fibrosis see U. Griesenbach et al., "Cystic Fibrosis Gene Therapy: Successes, Failures and Hopes for the Future" (2009) 3(4) *Expert Review of Respiratory Medicine* 363; see also U. Griesenbach et al., "Gene Transfer to the Lung: Lessons Learned from More than 2 Decades of CF Gene Therapy" (2009) 61 *Advanced Drug Delivery Reviews* 128.

because this involves the manipulation of a small cell population that expands to become a whole organism (e.g., gametes, an embryo). However, as we shall see, germline (inheritable) genetic modification is not allowed in most jurisdictions we have examined.

2.2 IGM A Case Study: Cell Fusion to Treat Mitochondrial Disorders

In addition to the genes contained within chromosomes in the nucleus of a cell, thirty-seven genes are contained within a cell's mitochondria. Mitochondrial disorders are generally caused by mutations to these mitochondrial genes. In a fertilized egg, the mitochondria are derived from the egg, not the sperm. Mitochondrial DNA is always inherited maternally.

Ooplasmic transfer is one treatment that is currently used for mitochondrial disease.[50] This involves injecting mitochondria from a donor cell into the egg of a woman who has a mitochondrial disorder. The result is a "cybrid embryo," or cytoplasmic hybrid embryo, created by taking the nucleus containing the genetic material from one cell and inserting it into a donor egg cell from which the genetic material has been removed. The resulting embryo has the original donor's DNA but also a small amount of mitochondrial DNA from the cytoplasm donor. It enables a woman who has a mitochondrial disorder to have a genetically related child because the child's nuclear DNA is still derived from that woman and her partner, while the child's mitochondrial DNA is derived from a donor cell. This modification is heritable, in that if the child is female, those mitochondria from the donor oocyte will be passed on. As of 2001, ooplasmic

---

[50] J. Cohen, R. Scott, M. Alikani, T. Schimmel, S. Munné, J. Levron, L. Wu, C. Brenner, C. Warner, and S. Willadsen, "Ooplasmic Transfer in Mature Human Oocytes" (1998) 4(3) *Molecular Human Reproduction* 269.

transfer had been performed successfully to result in the births of thirty children worldwide.[51] Thus, ooplasmic transfer is a possible precedent for IGM.

In the United Kingdom, the Horizon panel presented an assessment of "the three techniques that have the potential to prevent the transmission of mitochondrial disease."[52] These are:

- PGD;
- Maternal spindle transfer (MST) involving the transfer of a woman's nuclear DNA from her oocyte into an enucleated oocyte from a woman with normal mitochondrial DNA, which is then fertilized using sperm from the woman's partner;[53] and
- Pronuclear transfer (PNT), using a nuclear transfer technique similar to somatic cell nuclear transfer (SCNT)to transfer pronuclei into a donor oocyte.[54]

Both maternal spindle transfer and pronuclear transfer are not currently permitted under the HFE Act 1990 and are still considered experimental (see Part 2.3).

The panel concluded that PGD can "reduce, but not eliminate" the risk of transmitting mutations in mitochondrial DNA because

[51] J. A. Barritt, C. A. Brenner, H. E. Malter, and J. Cohen, "Mitochondria in Human Offspring Derived from Ooplasmic Transplantation: Brief Communication" (2001) 16(3) *Human Reproduction* 513.

[52] Human Fertilisation and Embryology Authority, "Scientific Review of the Safety and Efficacy of Methods to Avoid Mitochondrial Disease through Assisted Conception" (April2011):seehttp://www.hfea.gov.uk/docs/2011–04–18_Mitochondria_review_-_final_report.PDF (accessed on 23 June 2011).

[53] Human Fertilisation and Embryology Authority, "Scientific Review of the Safety and Efficacy of Methods to Avoid Mitochondrial Disease through Assisted Conception" (April 2011), para. 4.1.2: see http://www.hfea.gov.uk/docs/2011–04–18_Mitochondria_review_-_final_report.PDF (accessed on 23 June 2011).

[54] L. Craven, H. A. Tuppen, G. D. Greggains, S. J. Harbottle, J. L. Murphy, L. M. Cree, A. P. Murdoch, P. F. Chinnery, R. W. Taylor, R. N. Lightowlers, M. Herbert, and D. M. Turnbull, "Pronuclear Transfer in Human Embryos to Prevent Transfer of Mitochondrial DNA Disease" (2010) 465(7294) *Nature* 82.

unaffected girls born after PGD may still be carriers of mitochondrial disease.[55] While MST and PNT have the potential to eliminate mitochondrial disease and might therefore be useful technologies for parents at risk of transmitting "severe or lethal genetic disease," their relative novelty, as well as uncertainty about mitochondrial biology, necessitates further research into their safety and efficacy.[56]

The report focuses exclusively on the safety and efficacy of PGD, MST, and PNT and does not consider the ethical and legal issues that may be raised. Nevertheless, it is clear that those who argue in favor of allowing the technology are inspired to do so by its capacity to alleviate or eliminate disease. In other words, the reason why this technology is being considered is because of its potential to prevent the transmission of serious disease. For instance, it is noted in the report that

> although relatively rare, the seriousness of these diseases and the unusual inheritance pattern of mtDNA [mitochondrial DNA] mutations have made them a focus for research into preimplantation methods to reduce or avoid a disease in offspring.[57]

Mutations in any of the fifteen hundred nuclear genes required for mitochondrial function can lead to severe disease. The prevalence of mutations in mitochondrial DNA is 1 in 5,000 births and probably a

---

[55] Human Fertilisation and Embryology Authority, "Scientific Review of the Safety and Efficacy of Methods to Avoid Mitochondrial Disease through Assisted Conception" (April 2011), para. 1.1.2: see http://www.hfea.gov.uk/docs/2011–04–18_Mitochondria_review_-_final_report.PDF (accessed on 23 June 2011).

[56] Human Fertilisation and Embryology Authority, "Scientific Review of the Safety and Efficacy of Methods to Avoid Mitochondrial Disease through Assisted Conception" (April 2011), 4: see http://www.hfea.gov.uk/docs/2011–04–18_Mitochondria_review_-_final_report.PDF (accessed on 23 June 2011).

[57] Human Fertilisation and Embryology Authority, "Scientific Review of the Safety and Efficacy of Methods to Avoid Mitochondrial Disease through Assisted Conception " (April 2011), para. 1.1.1: see http://www.hfea.gov.uk/docs/2011–04–18_Mitochondria_review_-_final_report.PDF (accessed on 23 June 2011).

higher proportion of fetuses (which may be nonviable and spontaneously abort).[58]

The end of "preventing the transmission of serious disease" appears
to be so worthwhile that the HFEA panel made sure to distinguish
both MST and PNT from reproductive cloning:

> Although similar methodology is employed, it is important to stress
> that neither MST nor PNT is equivalent to reproductive cloning
> (somatic cell nuclear transfer, or SCNT). Any children resulting
> from MST or PNT would have arisen from fertilisation and be
> genetically unique. They would be the genetic child of the woman
> receiving treatment and her partner. MST and PNT do not involve
> reprogramming cells or nuclei as SCNT does, which is a relatively
> inefficient process and associated with significant risks of abnormal
> development.[59]

2.3 The Law

Currently in Australia, the United Kingdom, North America, and
Europe there are significant legislative limits on intentionally causing an inheritable genetic modification. However, legal limitations on
noninheritable gene therapy or gene transfer are not as widespread.
Because the cells of an embryo prior to implantation are pluripotent
until differentiation occurs, any kind of gene therapy intervention on an
embryo may result in changes to a cell that subsequently differentiates

[58] Human Fertilisation and Embryology Authority, "Scientific Review of the Safety
and Efficacy of Methods to Avoid Mitochondrial Disease through Assisted
Conception" (April 2011), para. 2.2: see http://www.hfea.gov.uk/docs/2011–04–18_
Mitochondria_review_-_final_report.PDF (accessed on 23 June 2011).

[59] Human Fertilisation and Embryology Authority, "Scientific Review of the Safety
and Efficacy of Methods to Avoid Mitochondrial Disease through Assisted
Conception" (April 2011), para. 4.1.3: see http://www.hfea.gov.uk/docs/2011–
04–18_Mitochondria_review_-_final_report.PDF (accessed on 23 June 2011).

into a germ cell. The effect of such an intervention would therefore be an inheritable genetic modification and prohibited in most of the jurisdictions we are examining. Thus it is safe to say that gene therapy on an embryo would automatically be considered to be a potentially inheritable alteration.[60]

2.3.1 Australia

In Australia, the Prohibition of Human Cloning for Reproduction Act 2002 (Cth) (PHCR Act) together with the Research Involving Embryos Act 2002 (Cth) (RIHE Act) prohibits the creation of certain kinds of embryos unless permitted under license. Before the Acts were amended in 2006 it was not possible to create a cloned embryo using somatic cell nuclear transfer (SCNT) either for research or for reproduction. Other kinds of inheritable genetic modification of embryos were also prohibited. After the Acts were amended, however, section 22 of the RIHE Act made it possible to apply for a license to create embryos other than by fertilization, and this was intended to allow the development of cloned or SCNT embryos for research purposes. By virtue of section 9 of the PHCR Act, however, such an embryo was prohibited from being used for the purposes of reproduction. Thus as a consequence of these amendments it is now possible to create a genetically modified embryo in the form of a cloned embryo, but there is no question of its heritability since it may not be used for reproduction. With respect to other forms of IGM the PHRC Act was more restrictive. Section 13 of PHRC Act prohibits

---

[60] See J.L. Roybal et al., "Stem Cell and Genetic Therapies for the Fetus" (2010) 15(1) *Seminars in Fetal & Neonatal Medicine* 46–51. Roybal et al. argue that if treatment occurs after germ cells have been compartmentalized and the treatment is targeted to the tissue of interest, then the risks are low and cite a study that found low levels of gene transfer in germ cells. Nevertheless, given that there was still some gene transfer in the germ cells, it seems, at this stage, that such treatment would be precluded under laws prohibiting IGM.

the creation of a human embryo by fertilization of an egg by sperm, where that human embryo contains genetic material from more than two persons. This means that techniques such as cell fusion to treat mitochondrial disease (see section 2.2) would be illegal because the resulting child would have three genetic progenitors. In the Issues Paper of the Lockhart Committee seeking submissions for its review of both the PHC Act and the RIHE Act one reason given for this legislative ban was that "it avoids confusion of genetic identity for the person born."[61]

While the Act would not limit the creation of a human embryo containing genetic material from more than two persons by SCNT if permitted under a license, use of such an embryo for reproductive purposes would not be possible, and therefore sufferers of mitochondrial disease do not have this technology as an available treatment option in Australia. Section 15 of the PHRC Act also prohibits intentional heritable alterations to the genome of a human cell. The maximum penalty for all prohibited practices listed in Division 1 is fifteen years imprisonment.

2.3.2. The United Kingdom

Prior to 2008 the Human Fertilisation and Embryology Act 1990 (HFE Act) prohibited the creation of transgenic embryos, which extended to both treatment and research purposes.[62] In 2008 substantial changes were made to the HFE Act to allow for the possibility that the technology might advance to a stage where it was appropriate to permit genetic modification of embryos.

---

[61] Lockhart Committee, Legislation Review: Prohibition of Human Cloning Act 2002 and Research Involving Human Embryos Act 2002, Issues Paper: Outline of Existing Legislation and Issues for Public Consultation (August 2005) at 14. Note that this statement is not supported by any evidence presented in the paper itself.

[62] See the former Schedule 2 of the Human Fertilisation and Embryology Act 1990 (UK).

Schedule 2, paragraph 3, of the HFE Act as amended deals with licenses for the purpose of research, and para 3(4) states, "A licence under this paragraph cannot authorise altering the genetic structure of any cell while it forms part of an embryo, except in such circumstances (if any) as may be specified in or determined in pursuance of regulations."

Schedule 2, paragraph 2(4), of the HFE Act 1990 states that

> a licence under this paragraph cannot authorise altering the nuclear or mitochondrial DNA of a cell while it forms part of an embryo, except for the purpose of creating something that will by virtue of regulations under section 3ZA(5) be a permitted embryo.

Section 3ZA(5) then states:

> Regulations may provide that – (a) an egg can be a permitted egg, or (b) an embryo can be a permitted embryo, even though the egg or embryo has had applied to it in prescribed circumstances a prescribed process designed to prevent the transmission of *serious mitochondrial disease*. [emphasis added]

The effect of these new provisions is to foreshadow the possibility that cell fusion to treat mitochondrial disease may be allowed once the technology is proved safe. As noted in Part 2.2 of this chapter, the HFEA Horizon Scanning Panel has recently completed a study examining these procedures and has concluded that further research into their safety and efficacy needs to be undertaken before the procedure can be approved for use in the population.[63]

2.3.3. The United States

Legislation in the United States regarding inheritable genetic modification is piecemeal and inconsistent. Some states probably prohibit

---

[63] Scientific and Clinical Advances Advisory Group of the HFEA, *Horizon Scanning Briefing: Genetic Modification of Embryos*, 7 November 2008, para 5.2 6.1–7.2.

IGM by virtue of laws that prohibit research on live fetuses, although this is by no means clear.[64] States such as South Dakota,[65] Minnesota,[66] Maine,[67] and Louisiana[68] prohibit nontherapeutic research or experimentation on an embryo, but it is unclear whether this would extend to prohibiting procedures such as cell fusion to treat mitochondrial disease, which have a therapeutic goal but are still highly experimental. As noted, such procedures have already been undertaken successfully in the U.S. state of New Jersey, resulting in a number of live births.[69]

2.3.4 Canada

IGM is banned in Canada under s 5(1)(f) of the AHR Act 2004, which states, "No person shall knowingly ... alter the genome of a cell of a human being or *in vitro* embryo such that the alteration is capable of being transmitted to descendants." Again this would make the use of IGM for treatment of an affected embryo difficult, since, as noted earlier, it is likely that any gene modification of an embryo will lead to inheritable alterations.

2.3.5. European Law

First, it is worth noting that Article 13 of the European Convention for the Protection of Human Rights and Dignity of the Human Being with regard to the Application of Biology and Medicine 1997 (the "Oviedo Convention") prohibits inheritable genetic modification. Article 13

[64] See Mass Gen Laws Ch 112, § 12J(a)(I) (1996); Mich Comp Laws Ann § 333.2685 and 333.2692 (1996); ND Cent Code § 14–02.2–01(1) (1991); RI Gen Laws § 11–54–1 (1994); PA Cons Stat Ann §§ 3216 (1995).
[65] SD Cod. Laws 34–14–17.
[66] Minn Stat Ann § 145.422 subd. 1, 2 (1989).
[67] ME Rev Stat Ann tit 22, § 1593 (1992).
[68] LA Rev Stat Ann §§ 9:122 (1991).
[69] J.A. Barritt et al., "Mitochondria in Human Offspring Derived from Ooplasmic Transplantation: Brief Communication" 16(3) *Human Reproduction*, 513.

states: "An intervention seeking to modify the human genome may only be undertaken for preventive, diagnostic or therapeutic purposes and only if its aim is not to introduce any modification in the genome of any descendants." However, as noted in Chapter 4, the Oviedo Convention has received a very mixed response within Europe, and several notable countries (including the United Kingdom, France, Belgium, Sweden, Germany, and Russia) have decided not to ratify it. Interestingly, despite their unwillingness to ratify this convention, most of these jurisdictions have implemented domestic legislation that prohibits IGM. For example, Swedish law provides that "[e]xperiments for the purposes of research or treatment that entail genetic changes that can be inherited in humans may not be carried out" and that "[t]reatment methods that are intended to bring about genetic changes that can be inherited in humans may not be used."[70] Similarly, German law prohibits the "artificial ... alter[ation]" of "the genetic information of a human germ line cell" or the use of such a germ cell line "for fertilization."[71]

2.4 Arguments for and against IGM

As noted at the beginning of this section, some argue that the next stage in disability avoidance technology using assisted reproduction is gene therapy and inheritable genetic modification in particular.

One of the key advantages IGM has over PND followed by termination of pregnancy or PGD followed by selection of unaffected embryos is that it allows the affected embryo or fetus to continue to develop after the particular abnormality or defect has been treated. Thus, this kind of technology would answer concerns raised in some of the parliamentary debates discussed in Chapters 3 and 4 that prenatal

---

[70] The Swedish Genetic Integrity Act (2006:351) of 18 May 2006, Chapter 2 ss 3 and 4.
[71] The German Act for the Protection of Human Embryos (1990), s 5(1) and (2).

and preimplantation testing technologies are focused on people prevention rather than the treatment of conditions. It does not, however, resolve entirely concerns about eugenic impulses. Genetic modification inevitably involves a preference for some traits and the rejection of others. LeRoy Walters and Julie Palmer[72] argue that IGM is a potentially efficient and effective means of treating diseases that affect many different organs and cell types (including those for which prenatal and preimplantation testing are currently used, such as cystic fibrosis). In this way, they argue that IGM protects rather than penalizes people who have disabilities. They state:

> In our view, a strategy of attempting to prevent or treat potential disease or disability in the particular biological individual accords more closely with the mission of the health sciences and shows greater respect for children and adults who are afflicted with disease or disability.[73]

Further, they suggest that IGM could reverse the negative message that is sent to people living with the disabilities tested, where selective abortion and selective discard are utilized.[74]

However, a number of prominent disability researchers dispute these claims that IGM is a preferable technology from a disability rights perspective. For instance, Jackie Leach Scully notes that those from the deaf community who consider deafness to be a cultural attribute would view the intergenerational eradication of this trait as being highly problematic.[75] Further, the assumption that it is better to take

[72] L. Walters and J. Gage Palmer, *The Ethics of Human Gene Therapy* (New York: Oxford University Press, 1997), 80–2.

[73] L. Walters and J. Gage Palmer, *The Ethics of Human Gene Therapy* (New York: Oxford University Press, 1997), 85.

[74] L. Walters and J. Gage Palmer, *The Ethics of Human Gene Therapy* (New York: Oxford University Press, 1997), 82.

[75] J. Leach Scully, "IGM and Disability: Normality and Identity" in J. Rasko, G. O'Sullivan, and R. Ankeny (eds.), *The Ethics of Inheritable Genetic Modification: A Dividing Line?* (Cambridge: Cambridge University Press, 2006), 179.

the risks attendant on being born with an altered genome than to be born with a disability is highly questionable.[76] Obviously, such a determination can only be made after considering the level of risk involved and the nature of the condition to be avoided. However, as soon as we require the application of a risk calculus, we are taken back to the driving questions of this book – how serious must the condition be, and who decides that the condition is serious enough?

These questions can be answered in several ways. Jackie Leach Scully, for instance, reminds us of the importance of a disability perspective[77] when making these determinations about appropriate future therapies. She notes that IGM is most likely to be used as therapy and therefore is of central relevance to people living with illness or impairment. She proceeds to observe that disabled and chronically ill people have experiences that give them different perspectives on "normality," "disability," and "health," which are cornerstones of the IGM debate. This accords with the kind of arguments we developed in Chapter 1. There we noted a study by Albrecht and Devlieger where it was found that there was an array of different responses to the question of whether the person had a good quality of life that depended heavily on the kind of disability that person was managing. Scully argues that terms like "healthy" and "abnormality" are poorly characterized, particularly as phenotypic variation is the norm for any living population. She says:

> At some point, phenotypic diversity crosses a line into impairment or illness – but exactly where this happens will often depend on the environmental circumstances, and in human communities on the social and medical means available to support people who function anomalously, and on cultural understandings of deviance. Labeling

[76] M. Salvi, "Shaping Individuality: Human Inheritable Germ Line Gene Modification" (2001) 22 *Theoretical Medicine* 527.

[77] J. Leach Scully, "IGM and Disability: Normality and Identity" in J. Rasko, G. O'Sullivan, and R. Ankeny (eds.), *The Ethics of Inheritable Genetic Modification: A Dividing Line?* (Cambridge: Cambridge University Press, 2006), 179.

a deviation from a genetic norm as a problem, before the degree of disadvantage (if any) has been established, is a judgment that may be more strongly influenced by cultural habitude than the reality of the embodied experience.[78]

She goes on to suggest that making changes at the genetic level – particularly changes that will have an intergenerational impact – fails to recognize that in the social context in which we operate "there is so little genuine accommodation to variant embodiment" that "we cannot rule out the possibility that there may be aspects of impairment which people or communities might wish not to lose" and, finally, that "we are still too ignorant about the meaning of most genetic impairments to push enthusiastically for their germ-line eradication."[79]

Given Leach Scully's claims about societal and clinical attitudes to disability, it is useful to consider some of the empirical research that has been conducted on public attitudes to IGM.

2.5 Public Attitudes to IGM

Attitudes toward the acceptability of altering genes vary, depending on the circumstances. People tend to distinguish between nonmedical and medical applications, and among somatic, germ line, and in utero applications.

In a recent study undertaken by the Wellcome Trust,[80] respondents were asked whether they support gene therapy to treat heart disease.

---

[78] J. Leach Scully, "IGM and Disability: Normality and Identity" in J. Rasko, G. O'Sullivan, and R. Ankeny (eds.), *The Ethics of Inheritable Genetic Modification: A Dividing Line?* (Cambridge: Cambridge University Press, 2006), 178–9.

[79] J. Leach Scully, "IGM and Disability: Normality and Identity" in J. Rasko, G. O'Sullivan, and R. Ankeny (eds.), *The Ethics of Inheritable Genetic Modification: A Dividing Line?* (Cambridge: Cambridge University Press, 2006), 185.

[80] Wellcome Trust, "What Do People Think about Gene Therapy? A Report Published by the Wellcome Trust," 9 August 2005.

While 82 percent said they would support somatic gene therapy to treat heart disease, a smaller number, 64 percent, would have supported germline gene therapy for the same disorder. Even fewer, 49 percent, supported in utero gene therapy to treat heart disease. The Wellcome study also found that participants were more supportive of the use of gene therapy for more serious conditions. Of the participants, 92 percent said they would support somatic gene therapy to treat cystic fibrosis, while 63 percent said they would support somatic gene therapy to treat baldness. Although the fact that fewer participants supported the use of somatic gene therapy for baldness than for cystic fibrosis suggests that the seriousness of the condition does affect the level of support, it is nevertheless interesting to note that such a large proportion of participants in the study, more than 50 percent, would have supported the use of the technology for what many would view as a cosmetic enhancement. This contrasts with the figure of 34 percent who said they would support somatic gene therapy to improve memory.[81] One would have to think that improved memory has greater social utility than lower rates of baldness, but the figures tell a different story. The figures drop in the case of germ line and in utero therapy, but the approval rates for use with each of the conditions retain the same relationship: cystic fibrosis with the highest approval for somatic, germ line, and in utero gene modification, followed by heart disease, baldness, and memory.

It seems safe to surmise from the results of this study that, for the majority of people, serious, life-threatening medical conditions justify the risks of gene therapy and can even justify the risks of germ line gene therapy as well as in utero gene therapy. The study states:[82]

> Participants rationalised that the risks of gene therapy were worth taking in circumstances where they judged the condition to be serious, potentially life threatening, or where the quality of life was

[81] Wellcome Trust, "What Do People Think about Gene Therapy? A Report Published by the Wellcome Trust," August 2005, 8–9.
[82] Wellcome Trust, "What Do People Think about Gene Therapy? A Report Published by the Wellcome Trust," August 2005, 11.

felt to be very poor. In these cases, panel members sometimes even overcame their opposition to germline and *in utero* gene therapy, arguing that the associated risks were worth taking if it would prevent serious medical conditions being passed on, or developing.

In another study, Evans et al. found that the seriousness of the condition that the germ line gene therapy (GLGT) was used to avoid significantly influenced people's willingness to embrace the technology. The researchers "took care to provide" participants with a balanced introduction to GLGT, which was neither "unduly favourable" nor "unduly hostile" to it.[83] When participants were asked whether they would support the use of GLGT to avoid a serious genetic defect – described as a defect leading to death within a couple of years – the authors noted "a slight tilt" in favor of gene therapy.[84] However, interestingly, GLGT was still viewed as less acceptable than abortion. When asked whether they supported GLGT for a minor physical defect (the example given to participants was cleft palate or an extra toe), participants said that they considered GLGT to be more acceptable than abortion, although support for GLGT's use for these defects was weaker than it was for serious genetic defects.[85] Finally, when asked whether they supported GLGT to achieve a good-looking child, study participants generally answered that they approved of neither GLGT nor abortion for this purpose, although abortion was significantly less popular than germ line gene therapy.[86] The authors note:

> The findings reported here suggest differentiated moral views on GLGT depending on the particular issue under consideration.

[83] M.D.R. Evans, J. Kelley, and E. D. Zanjani, "The Ethics of Gene Therapy and Abortion: Public Opinion" (2005) 20(3) *Fetal Diagnosis and Therapy* 223, 225.

[84] M.D.R. Evans, J. Kelley, and E. D. Zanjani, "The Ethics of Gene Therapy and Abortion: Public Opinion" (2005) 20(3) *Fetal Diagnosis and Therapy* 223, 226.

[85] M.D.R. Evans, J. Kelley, and E. D. Zanjani, "The Ethics of Gene Therapy and Abortion: Public Opinion" (2005) 20(3) *Fetal Diagnosis and Therapy* 223, 227–8.

[86] M.D.R. Evans, J. Kelley, and E. D. Zanjani, "The Ethics of Gene Therapy and Abortion: Public Opinion" (2005) 20(3) *Fetal Diagnosis and Therapy* 223, 228.

Opinion is quite divided about the use of GLGT to remedy a "death sentence" genetic defect, with the average opinion being near the neutral point. Many more people find abortion morally acceptable under these circumstances. In the less dire circumstances, there is less support for both GLGT and abortion. But here there is a bit of a twist: on the minor remediation and enhancement issues, GLGT is about as acceptable as abortion, or even more so. People's moral reservations about changing the human race are in some instances greater, and in some instances less, than the reservations they have about abortion.[87]

Here we see again, as we saw in Chapter 5, that there are differential approaches to the meaning and function of disability (or indeed enhancement) depending on the social and moral status of the embryo/fetus. In Chapter 5 we saw how perceptions of what is a serious disability in the context of decisions to undergo a late termination were influenced by the moral status of the viable fetus. The absence of a viable entity in the context of PGD (as we saw in Chapter 4) and in the early stages of pregnancy has allowed for a broader range of conditions to be tested and selected against. A similar analysis can be applied here. In this case, the public seems willing to allow both abortion and GLGT where the condition is very serious, but uncertainty about GLGT leads to a favoring of abortion in this context. However, the reverse is the case when minor conditions are in issue. Although neither abortion not GLGT is popular, in fact, GLGT is slightly more favored than abortion for minor and non-serious conditions. This suggests that the population at large will be more tolerant of perfecting technologies (as opposed to serious disability avoidance technologies) if the intervention occurs earlier in the pregnancy or prior to a pregnancy. This is why, as we will see in a moment, the

---

[87] M.D.R. Evans, J. Kelley, and E. D. Zanjani, "The Ethics of Gene Therapy and Abortion: Public Opinion" (2005) 20(3) *Fetal Diagnosis and Therapy* 223, 232.

developing technology of preconception screening raises so many important questions.[88]

While ordinary citizens seem to have some tolerance for genetic modification technologies, researchers offer a different perspective. A study conducted by Isaac Rabino found that biomedical researchers strongly support using somatic gene therapy to cure life-threatening diseases but reject germ line gene therapy for that purpose.[89]

The authors compared acceptability of current practices of prenatal diagnosis followed by abortion and in vitro preimplantation testing followed by selection/discard, on one hand, with gene therapy to treat such diseases or disorders, on the other. They found that the larger proportion (46 percent and 42 percent, respectively) of those surveyed considered it appropriate to continue "with present methods, which are less risky and less costly."[90] They noted, however, that "nearly 30% of each group of respondents agrees more with 'moving toward gene therapy in order to move away from termination.'"[91]

While the lack of proven safety was a significant factor motivating researchers' reluctance to support GLGT, there were some other rather interesting reasons given for opposing the use of the technology. Some of the most interesting arguments against GLGT that the authors described included the view that it was the "duty of the present generation to protect ... the genetic quality of the next," a concern about the reduction in diversity of the human genome, and a belief

---

[88] see Part 3 of this chapter.

[89] I. Rabino, "Research Scientists Surveyed on Ethical Issues in Genetic Medicine: A Comparison of Attitudes of US and European Researchers" (2006) 25(3) *New Genetics and Society* 325–334.

[90] I. Rabino, "Research Scientists Surveyed on Ethical Issues in Genetic Medicine: A Comparison of Attitudes of US and European Researchers" (2006) 25(3) *New Genetics and Society* 325, 335.

[91] I. Rabino, "Research Scientists Surveyed on Ethical Issues in Genetic Medicine: A Comparison of Attitudes of US and European Researchers" (2006) 25(3) *New Genetics and Society* 325, 335.

that a child has the right to have a genome that has not been tampered with.[92] The authors also note that:[93]

> On the subject of gene therapy, European researchers join the Americans in strong support for its potential use to cure life-threatening genetic diseases or to remedy mental retardation. But, as with genetic testing, as soon as it is proposed that such therapies be used for less severe conditions, ethical concerns arise and support drops – but much more precipitously among Europeans than among Americans, e.g., from 96% to cure a life-threatening disease to 49% to correct a learning disorder, compared to a drop among U.S. respondents from 96% to 70%. European respondents are also consistently much less in favor of germline gene therapy and less supportive of all the reasons posed to justify it.

A study conducted by Condit comparing prenatal testing, preimplantation genetic diagnosis, and germ line gene therapy[94] provides further evidence that public approval of new technologies depends partly upon how serious is the disorder or condition that the technology is used to avoid. In that study, it was found that "the purpose for which a technology is used is as important as the nature of the technology itself in determining attitudes about it."[95]

All of these studies lend support to the argument we have been making throughout this book that a desire to avoid disability is a key factor in regulatory support for technologies that might otherwise be construed as frightening and transgressive. At the same time, we have

---

[92] I. Rabino, "Research Scientists Surveyed on Ethical Issues in Genetic Medicine: A Comparison of Attitudes of US and European Researchers" (2006) 25(3) *New Genetics and Society* 325, 337.

[93] I. Rabino, "Research Scientists Surveyed on Ethical Issues in Genetic Medicine: A Comparison of Attitudes of US and European Researchers" (2006) 25(3) *New Genetics and Society* 325, 339.

[94] C.M. Condit, "Public Attitudes and Beliefs about Genetics" (2010) 11 *Annual Review of Genomics and Human Genetics* 339.

[95] C.M. Condit, "Public Attitudes and Beliefs about Genetics" (2010) 11 *Annual Review of Genomics and Human Genetics* 339 at 348.

noted that embryonic and fetal development also have an impact on technological uptake. As we have seen, testing for less serious conditions at the preimplantation and prefertilization stage (i.e., testing gametes and using IGM) is considered to be more acceptable than is the use of abortion to avoid these disabilities, although in neither case was the support overwhelming.

But we have also noted the diversity of views about these technologies (and about their uptake and use with assisted reproduction) among those actively engaged in the disability community. It is important, therefore, to examine some of the empirical research that Jackie Leach Scully has undertaken concerning patients' perceptions regarding ethical issues surrounding gene therapy.[96] Scully's study found that patients had very different opinions from one another and that this reflected their different experiences of disability or chronic illness. For example, multiple sclerosis (MS) patients were the most positive toward gene therapy, and deaf and achrondroplasic participants were the most negative. Further, Scully found that while medical professionals considered the "therapeutic imperative" to be the overriding positive value in their ethical evaluation, potential patients had more variable responses. They tended to note the value of diversity and expressed skepticism toward "blanket" use of the therapeutic imperative. MS and cystic fibrosis (CF) patients considered that "risk" referred not only to physical side effects, but also to disruption of their daily lives, and they also considered social and economic aspects of risk – for example, the "cultural risk" of "estrangement from their community."

These differences are important. They recall the argument that we made in Chapter 1 that, while we may think that regulation should limit/enable access to "disability avoidance technologies," how to

---

[96] J. Leach Scully, "IGM and Disability: Normality and Identity" in J. Rasko, G. O'Sullivan, and R. Ankeny (eds.), *The Ethics of Inheritable Genetic Modification: A Dividing Line?* (Cambridge: Cambridge University Press, 2006), 181.

ensure that that regulation is crafted in such a way as to take account of varying and contextual concerns is an extremely fraught question. We return, then, to the questions with which we began, but here applied to potential new technologies such as inheritable genetic modification. In other words, should regulatory limits be imposed on access to these technologies, or should the grant of access to them be matter for the clinician to determine in consultation with the patient?

There are some who would argue that when it comes to IGM, an individual, patient-based approach is inappropriate. For instance, George Annas and those who support a UN Convention on the Preservation of the Human Species seek to strictly limit "species-altering" research. Annas argues that because "it is the meaning of humanness (our distinctness from other animals) that has given birth to our concepts of both human dignity and human rights, altering our nature necessarily threatens to undermine both human dignity and human rights."[97]

On the other hand, Morris Fiddler and Eugene Pergament argue that IGM has the benefit of reducing the incidence of disease in subsequent generations (unlike somatic gene therapy, which treats future generations) and that, because of this, we have a duty to embrace it. By using IGM, they argue,

> medicine would not only be fulfilling its social and scientific mandate but would also be providing parents at high reproductive risk for genetic disease an option for the birth of an infant with markedly improved prospects for a healthy life. It is, therefore, in the interests of all of us to support germline gene therapy through whatever means is suitable and acceptable to, and for, the common good.[98]

Eric Juengst argues, alternatively, that it is not "genism" that is the problem: "It is the social perception of genetic difference, not the

[97] G. Annas, "The Man on the Moon, Immortality and Other Millennial Myths: The Prospects and Perils of Human Genetic Engineering" (2000) 49 *Emory Law Journal* 753, 772.

[98] M. Fiddler and E. Pergament, "Germline Gene Therapy: Its Time Is Near" (1966) 2(2) *Molecular Human Reproduction* 75, 76.

actual biologic differences, which fuel human rights abuses. These perceptions, the prejudices they bolster, and the abuses they feed, will be coming for the foreseeable future not from the lunatic fringes of genetic research, but from its brightest hopes: from the new work in human genetic variation research, 'public health genetics', and pharmacogenomics."[99]

In the end, it is necessary to ask: What are the advantages of IGM over *existing technology?* Many genetic diseases can be addressed through less risky means, such as preimplantation screening, prenatal diagnosis followed by abortion, and even somatic gene therapy. If the advantage of IGM is that it allows for treatment of distinct biologic entities, rather than their prevention, then larger debates about the way in which value is accorded to these entities that are not yet persons must be engaged. Is there sufficient justification in this claim, for instance, to warrant the redirection of resources both financial and physical toward research in this area? Given these concerns, we will conclude this final chapter with an examination of the burgeoning field of preconception screening. This technology raises yet more questions about the way in which we prevent disability and the kinds of limits we think are appropriately imposed on autonomous individual decisionmakers.

3 CONCLUSION: SIMPLE UNIVERSAL PRECONCEPTION TESTING AND THE END OF IMPERFECTION?

Recent technological advances have resulted in the development of a single *preconception carrier-screening* test for more than 448 "severe

---

[99] E. T. Juengst, "'Alter-ing' the Human Species' Identity" in J. Rasko, G. O'Sullivan, and R. Ankeny (eds.), *The Ethics of Inheritable Genetic Modification: A Dividing Line?* (Cambridge: Cambridge University Press, 2006), 149–58, 155.

recessive childhood diseases."[100] This test has been described in the press as being able to test for "almost 600 catastrophic conditions"[101] and "genetic mutations that could cause up to 600 'life threatening disorders.'"[102] The *Australian* also reports the views of Christine Patch, a consultant genetic counselor at Guy's and St Thomas' Hospital in London, who notes, "As most people will carry some mutations, everybody is going to need genetic counselling, yet for most couples the risk will be very low."[103]

These developments in preconception screening and testing have led to a movement among some clinical geneticists toward encouraging universal carrier screening tests. Further, the simplicity and accessibility of the testing technology have made preconception screening much easier to undergo. Even individuals with no family history of disease or disability are being encouraged to have preconception screening. Unlike preimplantation testing of embryos and late term abortion – which may only be accessed where this is necessary to avoid transmitting a serious disability – or IGM – which is generally prohibited – there are almost no limits on access to preconception screening in the jurisdictions that we have examined. Indeed, far from limiting access, the UK government's advisory body on genetics, the Human Genetics Commission, recommended, in its 6 April 2011

[100] C. J. Bell et al., "Carrier Testing for Severe Childhood Recessive Diseases by Next-Generation Sequencing" (2011) 3 *Science Translational Medicine* 65ra4; National Health Service, "Gene Test 'predicts 448 Child Diseases'": see http://www.nhs.uk/news/2011/01January/Pages/dna-gentic-test-for-parents-before-pregnancy.aspx (accessed on 28 June 2011); see R. Alleyne, "New Genetic Test for Severe Childhood Diseases" *Daily Telegraph*, 12 January 2011: see http://www.telegraph.co.uk/health/healthnews/8255685/New-genetic-test-for-severe-childhood-diseases.html (accessed on 28 June 2011).
[101] "Testing Time before Conception" *Advertiser* (14 January 2011), 27.
[102] M. Henderson, "Gene Test to Reduce Diseases" *Australian* (14 January 2011), 9.
[103] M. Henderson, "New Test for Genetic Mutations to Be Offered to Parents," *Australian* (13 January 2011).

report, that preconception genetic screening should be made more widely available.[104]

Preconception testing uses a model of tandem (couple) testing to establish accurately the risk that a couple has of having a child with either common serious genetic disorders or rarer but readily identifiable disorders. The literature on the Counsyl website (Counsyl is the main U.S. corporation that offers such testing) suggests that the tests are necessary for everyone contemplating pregnancy. Among other statements of this nature, the website states that "every adult of reproductive age needs the Counsyl test" and that "universal genetic testing can drastically reduce the incidence of genetic diseases, and may very well eliminate many of them."[105] While preconception testing is not mandatory, it is sometimes supported by government funded health insurance rebates and by a burgeoning profession of clinical geneticists and genetic counselors who provide testing and support to individuals seeking to ascertain their carrier status before having a child.

We suggest that these interventions create an expectation of "responsible" reproduction. In other words, it is assumed that once these tests are universally available, people will use them before deciding to have a child, to ensure that they are not at risk of passing on a genetically inherited condition.

The avoidance of "serious disability" is recognized as a justification for a range of prenatal testing and screening practices (including preimplantation screening). However, in the context of preconception screening there has been little or no discussion about when its use is

---

[104] Human Genetics Commission, "Increasing Options, Informing Choice: A Report on Preconception Genetic Testing and Screening" (April 2011): see http://www.hgc. gov.uk/UploadDocs/DocPub/Document/Increasing%20options,%20informing%20 choice%20-%20final.pdf (accessed on 23 June 2011). They did also spend a considerable amount of time considering the issue of potential stigma for people who did not wish to undergo testing.

[105] See https://www.counsyl.com/ (accessed on 23 June 2011).

appropriate. Concerns might be raised that such screening will have unwanted consequences of a eugenic nature. As the testing technology improves, allowing for the identification of ever more recessive and hereditary conditions, oversight of this technology may become a more pressing concern. However, the difference between this technology and IGM, for example, is that it is already in use. As a result, regulating now could be resisted as an unwieldy attempt to close the gate once the horse has bolted. By the time the legislative process begins, it may well be argued (as it was with PGD) that there is a "moral obligation"[106] to use the technology. Indeed, it is possible that a legislative decision to prohibit certain uses of the technology would be judged to be socially irresponsible.[107] This interpretation seems to be supported by the fact that those jurisdictions that were early developers of PGD technology were almost always the most liberal in terms of its regulation. As this issue suggests, one of the main challenges we face is how to respond to the inevitable march of medical technology. On one hand, legislators are hesitant about legalizing new technologies because of fears about the way they may be put to use in the future. On the other hand, in the abortion context legislators were concerned proactively to insulate medical professionals from future uncertainty about liability should they use new PND technology to diagnose (and subsequently terminate) affected pregnancies. Attempts by governments such as those of the United Kingdom and Australia to set up horizon scanning panels to stay one step ahead of medical science seem to have had a limited impact in terms of preconception screening. Once it becomes routine any new legislative limits imposed on individuals in relation to preconception screening will seem to be a removal of choice – the

---

[106] S. Franklin and C. Roberts, *Born and Made: An Ethnography of Preimplantation Genetic Diagnosis* (Princeton, NJ: Princeton University Press, 2006), 59.

[107] There is also indirect pressure on legislatures in the form of economic considerations. Biotechnical innovation is unlikely to thrive in a jurisdiction where the legislature suggests the technology is morally or socially wrong.

kind of informed choice that is touted in the context of prenatal and preimplantation testing.

However, as we saw in Chapters 1 and 2, the assertion that prenatal testing has the purpose of conveying information to prospective parents to facilitate an "informed choice" ignores the fact that it provokes anxiety and uncertainty based on a sometimes statistically remote risk. Furthermore, the absence of an entity such as a fetus or an embryo in the context of preconception screening may give people a false sense of the simplicity of the process. The fact that a test exists for a particular condition has the effect of perpetuating its characterization by society as a disability. Once people have undergone testing and know they are at risk of passing on a particular hereditary condition, they may feel, not surprisingly, that they are under an obligation to reproduce responsibly no matter how low the risk. In the same way that prenatal testing generates nonnormative identities, preconception screening will lead to a situation where it is increasingly difficult to identify which disabilities are in fact tolerable and which are not.

Further, as we noted in Chapter 1, the choice *not* to make an informed choice is often construed as irresponsible. Thus, if preconception screening is available and both relatively noninvasive and inexpensive, one can foresee tremendous pressure being applied to individuals to undergo testing. Indeed, the fact that the Human Genetics Commission in the United Kingdom recommended that preconception screening be made more widely available suggests this is already presumed.

A significant question arises then as to whether we can identify more and less serious preconception harms and whether it is appropriate to limit access to preconception screening.

Conclusion

Never before has the prenatal and preimplantation phase of human reproduction been so transparent. This transparency has given us unprecedented access to information about the genetic and congenital makeup of our prospective progeny. This has, in turn, made it possible to make choices about whether to continue with a pregnancy where there is the chance of giving birth to a child with a potential disability or abnormality. At the same time, it has increased the burden on women, and to a lesser extent men, to become informed about available testing technologies, to evaluate their own as well as their future progeny's projected health status, and to undertake subsequent testing to avoid having a child who has a disability.

We do not dispute that there are significant advantages to these technologies, but nor do we embrace these technologies with uncritical acceptance. The wide-scale deployment of prenatal and pre-implantation genetic technologies raises some thorny legal and regulatory challenges, which we have sought to identify and explore throughout this book. There are, of course, still other technologies that need to be considered and, as we saw in Chapter 6, some of these lie just over the horizon, targeting both the prenatal and the preconception period. These technologies throw up profound challenges for how we regulate our reproductive futures. Given that regulators and legislators will likely turn to their existing toolkit in developing frameworks for these future technologies, a sound understanding of the existing

Conclusion

frameworks, their capacities and limitations, is a critically important undertaking.

One of our primary aims in writing this book was to explore the way in which we place limits on reproductive choice, legally, politically, and socially while at the same time making demands on women and their families to arrive at particular kinds of "choices." The availability of the choice not to implant a particular embryo or continue a pregnancy on the basis of genetic or other information has been embraced by many in the health professions, and by the community, in the name of reproductive freedom, familial well-being, and common humanity. There is a strong and understandable social preference prospectively to avoid the potential for pain and suffering in future children through the use of these reproductive technologies. However, we need to be cautious in our deployment of such technologies because their very existence changes or informs the manner in which we think about what constitutes disability, and sometimes transforms what we imagine to be choices into burdens. This is in part because we as "future" parents feel the weight of moral responsibility to act in the projected interests of our "future" children since they are beings we expect and desire to nurture, to love, and to care for. But it is also because there are externally imposed social expectations placed upon women to strive for the birth of only those children who meet certain standards, that testing may be used to ensure so-called responsible reproduction.

In light of these social complexities, it is perhaps not surprising that legal and regulatory frameworks have been developed to structure our engagements with these technologies and to place some limits on their use. As lawyers, we have been motivated to examine and better understand these frameworks and to assess their strengths and weaknesses within the social and historical contexts in which they have arisen. The regulatory responses to these technologies have been framed by the concepts of "disability" (in particular "serious" disability) and "risk," and for this reason we began our analysis with an exploration of the critical disability and feminist literature around these two concepts in

Chapters 1 and 2. Our starting point was the observation that although there seems to be general social agreement that the pursuit of selection practices in cases of "serious disability" is ethically sound and should be lawful, our understandings of what constitutes serious disability are diverse and varied. As we saw in Chapter 1, for example, there is evidence that the seriousness of disabilities is often overestimated by the nondisabled, and that many of those who would be regarded as seriously disabled nonetheless rate their quality of life as high. This has led many in the disability studies movement to raise concerns about the premises of prenatal and preimplantation testing and their broader impact on our capacity to foster a society that welcomes and accommodates human diversity. These are concerns that we argue should be given serious consideration.

An important dimension to the widespread and growing availability of testing technologies is the effect on our understanding of what constitutes a disabling condition. If the availability of testing for a particular condition has the effect of perpetuating its social characterization as a disability, it becomes important to think about the category of disability as something of a moving feast, with its openness to definition and redefinition difficult to separate from the technologies that we may deploy for its detection.

The cognate concept of risk introduces a further layer of complexity, for, as we saw in Chapter 2, it is through the concept of risk that anxieties about imagined futures are mediated. As we noted, there has been a push toward "informed reproduction" with the routinization of screening and testing for an increasing list of conditions. This push is embedded in the larger structures of "risk culture" – that is, a culture in which the concept of risk is a pervasive conceptual tool driving regulatory and policy responses. One effect of risk aversion strategies is to render the *possibility* of disability even more potent than its material effects. Thus, the very act of offering a test for a particular condition carries with it the implicit claim that the test is necessary and desirable and that the information gleaned from that test will be acted upon. We suggest, therefore, that routine screening and testing create an environment in which women who choose not to undergo testing are sometimes presented as irresponsible and where women who continue with a pregnancy where there is a risk of an abnormality are viewed as culpable. The concept of risk plays a crucial role in the idea that these women have been the "authors of their own misery" by "taking the risk." As a consequence, there is a danger that women and men who challenge dominant attitudes about risk and disability will be increasingly viewed as transgressive and marginalized. We have argued, accordingly, that while this unprecedented prenatal transparency has opened up new horizons of reproductive choice, it has also entailed new burdens, particularly for women, who have been encouraged to embrace prenatal testing in order to become "responsible" reproducers, viewing their pregnancies as processes that can be perfected.

Formulating frameworks for the regulation of these technologies too has been fraught by the conflicting social responses to disability avoidance strategies mentioned previously. Testing technologies have been aimed at reducing the burden of human suffering thought to be entailed by disability and, at the same time, enhancing reproductive freedom and autonomy. These aims may be aligned, for example, when there is a diagnosis of anencephaly, and the woman does not wish to proceed with the pregnancy or when PGD detects an embryo with Tay Sachs disease and the parents do not wish for this embryo to be transferred. However, these aims may not be aligned, for example, where a woman or couple wish to have an embryo transferred despite PGD of a disability or, at the other end of the spectrum, where a women or couple wish to terminate a pregnancy at a late stage for an abnormality that may not seem very serious to health care providers. These instances of misalignment have tended to provoke intense public interest; for example, we have seen media furors in both the United Kingdom and Australia around the termination of pregnancy at a late stage for conditions such as cleft lip and palate and achondroplasia and in the United States around attempts to use PGD to select in favor of deafness and achondroplasia. The reporting of these stories seems to have captured an underlying ambivalence about the uses to which prenatal testing might be put. It would seem, then, that the social approval of these technologies is not without limits. Instead there are a group of contentious disability avoidance strategies that it is argued should be confined to "seriously" disabling conditions or at least "not trivial" conditions.

As a result, legislators and regulators are faced with determining which reproductive wishes will be sanctioned and which will not. One strategy for achieving this is to limit the use of PGD and late term abortion to the avoidance of "serious" disabilities. In Chapters 3 and 4 we have carefully detailed the historical development of these legal frameworks, paying particular attention to the instantiation of the category "serious disability" as a legal or regulatory limit and its impact on women's reproductive decision making. It is worth noting again that the task of tracing the development and deployment of serious disability as a regulatory limit is complicated by a number of factors. First of all, abortion is not only or even primarily used as a disability avoidance strategy. In many of the jurisdictions considered in this book, in practice medical abortion is available on request in the first trimester. However, in general, law and/or policy does become more restrictive later in pregnancy, which is precisely when abortions for fetal abnormality may be requested. Second, generalizing about the regulation of abortion is complicated by the fact that many jurisdictions have undertaken reforms to loosen the nature and scope of criminal prohibition. In Australia, for example, some (but not all) Australian legislatures have enacted such reforms at different points in time (ranging from 1969 through to 2008), and these legislative reforms have varied in detail. Although generalization about legislative approaches across Australia is difficult, it is reasonable to claim that, in general, either law or policy in every Australian jurisdiction accommodates the use of abortion to avoid the birth of a child with a "serious" disability to some extent. This is true of other jurisdictions as well, including the United Kingdom.

Conclusion

Bearing these considerations in mind, we closely examined the legislative debates that preceded significant abortion law reform in the United Kingdom, South Australia, and Western Australia on the basis that these debates constitute key examples of legislative engagement with the question of how to craft a law that expressly permits later abortion as a disability avoidance strategy. As such, these debates wrestle with many of the competing tensions already described and which continue to plague the regulation of these fields in practice elsewhere. These legislative histories are also, of course, important in understanding the development of regulatory frameworks for PGD in Australia and the United Kingdom and we have closely examined the legislative debates that preceded significant law reform in this area too. In many instances these frameworks initially sought alignment with the abortion provisions relating to fetal abnormality and serious "handicap."

Our analysis of the legislative debates across both fields indicates that three questions emerged as central: First, is it possible to draw a line between serious and trivial disabilities? Second, assuming that it is possible, how precisely should this be done (this may encompass who is given the authority to do so), and, finally, what does drawing this line say to those whose condition/disability falls on the "wrong" side of the line? While these are important questions, we want to argue for a shift in focus to questions about which there was, in fact, insufficient discussion in the parliamentary debates, namely, how the law as finally crafted impacts on the rights and freedoms of women to make decisions about their reproductive futures. In the case of abortion, or more particularly late abortion for fetal abnormality, this discussion was somewhat constrained by overarching legal structures that did not conceptualize abortion as an unconditional right, and, in the case of PGD, this issue was dwarfed by the dominant concern to constrain the imagined specter of designer babies.

Almost all of the debates that we considered concluded that drawing a line was possible and necessary. To reach this point, the language of "risk" and fear of disability featured as powerful rhetorical maneuvers. Those legislatures that did not – most noticeably the early WA approach to PGD (subsequently reversed) – instead concluded that no line should be drawn and that prohibition was a better solution. For those legislatures that chose to draw a line, however, it became quickly apparent that this line could not be defined with any precision. In many ways, this made the decision to deploy "serious disability" a remarkable legal and regulatory strategy. To put the point bluntly, legislators were. willing to enact a limit on the use of late abortion or PGD, but the limit was itself uncertain, perhaps even undefinable. In other words, the frameworks were built on unstable ground, and this instability is in a sense perpetually fueled by the expansion of testing technologies that themselves construct the condition to be tested as problematic. Interestingly, various ways in which the limit could have been more precisely articulated, such as legislative lists of conditions or a legislative definition of "serious disability," have not, to date, been taken up. This of course leaves the law open to allegations of uncertainty and lack of clarity, and in a sense these criticisms are quite valid.

On the other hand, the reticence to particularize further the meaning of the legislative limit signaled the recognition that disability's meaning is complex and contextual and, above all, amounts to more than a particular clinical diagnosis. In light of this, legislatures have drawn upon nonlegislative resources to build a more flexible regulatory framework, including regulatory bodies with broad disciplinary and community input, the ethics and professional standards of doctors, and even hospitals ethics committees. This focus on how, rather than where, the line should be drawn is not of course free from difficulty. For a start, a focus on process requires the identification of a person or class of people who are best qualified to make decisions about where the lines will be drawn. In each jurisdiction that we considered, this role was conferred by legislatures on the medical community, certain representatives of the medical community, and/or regulatory bodies with powers to apply legislative or regulatory criteria for determining which conditions are serious and after such assessments issuing (or not) licenses or guidance. In Chapters 4 and 5, we have carefully detailed these quasi-regulatory approaches.

These measures alone do not establish whom the line-drawing process is meant to benefit. Is it the woman/couple, the child to be born, or society at large? In the context of PGD in particular, different answers to this question complicated attempts to mediate between the desire to help avoid disability-related suffering and the desire to prevent "designer babies." Notably, there was fairly limited discussion about why the medical community was best placed to be the line drawers. In initial attempts at regulation or reform, this was clearly assumed to be the case. In more recent reforms, the debate has shifted toward an acknowledgment that the women/families involved also have important knowledge to add to this process and coextensively that any disability avoidance strategy would have to be enacted on and through the bodies of the women who were intended to have the child. In our interviews with regulators and clinicians, we have gained some insights that provide a starting point for understanding how the complexities of decisions about avoiding disability are negotiated within the clinical encounter.

This then takes us to the fraught question of what drawing this line says to those whose condition/disability falls on the wrong side of the line. In one sense, this question puts us on the horns of a dilemma. We accept the argument that the availability of testing technologies, together with strong social imperatives to avoid disability, are all part of the context within which certain conditions come to be known, negatively, as disabilities. We also remain committed to women's rights to reproductive autonomy. We suggest that if we are going to use the idea of seriousness as a threshold for when certain disability avoidance strategies may be deployed, we need to move the debate away from the idea that objective judgment of serious disability is the determinative pivot for regulation. Since it is not possible to reach objective determinations of "serious disability," that term should instead carry the meaning that it is given by the woman/couple affected by the pregnancy or prospective pregnancy. Ideally this meaning will emerge from a careful consideration of a range of important sources of information, including information from people living with the disability in question if the parents do not already have this knowledge (they may). Furthermore, the focus should be clearly kept on the parents' capacity to cope with what they imagine is ahead of them, rather than the perceived welfare of the future child. A focus on the perceived welfare of the future child is problematic for two reasons. First, it potentially constrains women's reproductive choices whatever they may be (to continue or not with a pregnancy or embryonic transfer) and, second, it tethers the reproductive decision to the idea that an objective statement about the undesirability of certain traits is being made. By insisting that these assessments are the subjective assessments of the individuals closely concerned, rather than assessments upon which we must all agree or a majority of us must agree, the negative social effects of the choice to avoid a particular outcome that might be classed as disability are lessened. Indeed, it then becomes open to the community to challenge the individual's imaginary account of that outcome, since it is not enshrined in any kind of legal or policy doctrine. Of course, this is not a perfect solution. Throughout this book we have shown that there are multiple complexities, ambiguities, and pressures that together create the conditions under which women might feel that they have to make certain decisions about the trajectory of their pregnancies. These forces operate at the level of the social, the legal, and the clinical, and they intersect in uncertain ways. We need to take full account of how these forces impact on women so that we can work toward legal and regulatory frameworks that minimize the negative and distorting effects that they can produce. We believe that finding ways to unburden women from the responsibility of having perfect pregnancies is essential if we are to support women's reproductive freedom while mitigating the eugenic and discriminatory effects of prenatal and preimplantation testing technologies.

Bibliography

ARTICLES/BOOKS

Aarden, E. et al., "Providing preimplantation genetic diagnosis in the United Kingdom, The Netherlands and Germany: a comparative in-depth analysis of health-care access" (2009) 1(1) *Human Reproduction* 1

Aiuti, A. et al., "Correction of ADA-SCID by stem cell gene therapy combined with nonmyeloablative conditioning" (28 June 2002) 296(5577) *Science* 2410

"Gene therapy for immunodeficiency due to adenosine deaminase deficiency" (2009) 360(5) *The New England Journal of Medicine* 447

Albrecht, G.L. and Devlieger, P.J. "The disability paradox: high quality of life against all odds" (1999) 48 *Social Science and Medicine* 977

American College of Obstetricians and Gynaecologists Committee on Ethics, "Committee opinion on sex selection" (February 2007), available at http://www.acog.org/from_home/publications/ethics/co360.pdf (accessed on 18 June 2011)

American College of Obstetricians and Gynaecologists Committee on Ethics, "Sex selection" (February 2007) vol. 360, available at http://www.acog.org/from_home/publications/ethics/co360.pdf (accessed on 10 June 2011)

American Medical Association, "Health and ethics policy of the AMA House of Delegates: H-5.982 late pregnancy termination techniques," available at http://www.ama-assn.org/ad-com/polfind/Hlth-Ethics.pdf

American Society of Reproductive Medicine, "Preimplantation genetic testing: a practice committee opinion," available at http://www.asrm.org/uploadedFiles/ASRM_Content/News_and_Publications/Practice_Guidelines/Committee_Opinions/Preimplantation_genetic_testing(1).pdf (accessed on 18 June 2011)

Amicucci, P. et al., "Prenatal diagnosis of myotonic dystrophy using fetal DNA obtained from maternal plasma" (2000) 46 *Clinical Chemistry* 2

Bibliography

Amundson R. and Tresky, S. "On a bioethical challenge to disability rights" (2007) 32 *Journal of Medicine and Philosophy* 541

Amundson, R. "Against normal function" (2000) 31(1) *Studies in History and Philosophy of Biological and Biomedical Sciences* 33

Amundson, R. and Tresky, S. "Bioethics and disability rights: conflicting values and perspectives" (2008) 5 *Bioethical Inquiry* 111

Andre, J., Fleck, L.M., and Tomlinson, T. "On being genetically 'irresponsible'" (2000) 10(2) *Kennedy Institute of Ethics Journal* 129

Annas, G. "The man on the moon, immortality and other millennial myths: the prospects and perils of human genetic engineering," (2000) 49 *Emory Law Journal* 753

Asch, A. "Disability equality and prenatal testing: contradictory or compatible?" (2003) 30 *Florida State University Law Review* 315

"Prenatal diagnosis and selective abortion: a challenge to practice and policy" (1999) 89 *American Journal of Public Health* 1649

Assisted Conception Unit, "FAQ," available at http://www.ivfdirect.com/information/faqpage.aspx

Australia and New Zealand Horizon Scanning Network, "Horizon scanning technology prioritising summary: non-invasive prenatal diagnostic test for trisomy-21 (Down's sydrome) Update" (November 2009), available at http://www.horizonscanning.gov.au/internet/horizon/publishing.nsf/Content/68B1 F63984E68993CA2575AD0080F3E2/$File/PS%20Update%20NIPD%20 for%20Down%27s%20syndrome.pdf

"Horizon scanning technology horizon scanning report: MRI for the detection of foetal abnormalities" (October 2007), available at http://www.health.gov. au/internet/horizon/publishing.nsf/Content/58685F8B48CC9EE7CA2575A D0080F340/$File/Final_MRI_fetal_HS_report.pdf

"Horizon scanning technology prioritising summary: non-invasive pre-natal testing for Down's syndrome," (August 2008) available at http:// www.horizonscanning.gov.au/internet/horizon/publishing.nsf/Content/B B580B674729F620CA2575AD0080F351/$File/Volume_21_Aug_2008_ No-invasive%20prenatal%20diagnostic%20test%20for%20Down's%20 Syndrome.pdf

"National scanning unit horizon scanning prioritising summary: magnetic resonance imaging for the detection of foetal abnormalities" (February 2007) 15(6), available at http://www.health.gov.au/internet/horizon/publishing.nsf/Conten t/6B81AEB3E7EE0001CA2575AD0080F344/$File/Feb%20Vol%2015%20 No%206%20-%20Magnetic%20resonance.pdf (accessed on 24 June 2011)

Australian Capital Territory Health, "Maternity shared care guidelines" (May 2008), available at http://health.act.gov.au/c/health?a=dlpol&policy=115085 6562

Bibliography

Australian Institute of Health and Welfare, "Congenital anomalies in Australia 2002–2003" (2008), available at http://www.preru.unsw.edu.au/PRERUWeb.nsf/resources/CA+2/$file/ca3a.pdf

"Neural tube defects in australia: an epidemiological report" (2008), available at http://www.aihw.gov.au/publications-catalogue/?taxonomy_id=6442451339, 6442451130)

"Recommendations for development of a new Australian Birth Anomalies System" (2004), available at http://www.aihw.gov.au/publications-catalogue/?taxonomy_id=6442451339,6442451130)

"Use of routinely collected national data sets for reporting on induced abortion in Australia" (2005), available at http://www.aihw.gov.au/publications-catalogue/?taxonomy_id=6442451339,6442451130)

Australian Law Reform Commission Report, "Essentially yours: the protection of human genetic information in Australia" (ALRC Report 96), available at http://www.alrc.gov.au/publications/report-96.

Barritt, J.A., Brenner, C.A., Malter, H.E. and Cohen, J. "Mitochondria in human offspring derived from ooplasmic transplantation: brief communication" (2001) 16(3) *Human Reproduction* 513

Baruch, S., Kaufman, D., and Hudson, K. "Genetic testing of embryos: practices and perspectives of US in vitro fertilization clinics" (2008) 89(5) *Fertility and Sterility* 1053, available at http://www.dnapolicy.org/resources/GeneticTestingofEmbryos.pdf

Baruch, S. "PGD: genetic testing of embryos in the United States" (presentation, 15 February 2009), available at http://ec.europa.eu/dgs/jrc/downloads/jrc_aaas_2009_03_baruch_pgd.pdf

Bauer, P. "The abortion debate no one wants to have: prenatal testing is making your right to abort a disabled child more like 'your duty' to abort a disabled child," The Washington Post (18 October 2005), available online at http://www.washingtonpost.com/wp-dyn/content/article/2005/10/17/AR2005101701311.html

Bauman, Z. *Modernity and Ambivalence* (Cambridge: Polity Press, 1991)

Postmodernism and Its Discontents (Cambridge: Polity Press, 1997)

Beck, U. "Risk society revisited: theory, politics and research programmes" in B. Adam, U. Beck and J. Van Loon (eds.), *The Risk Society and Beyond: Critical Issues for Social Theory* (London: Sage, 2000)

Beck, U. and Beck-Gernsheim, E. *Individualization: Institutionalized Individualism and Its Social and Political Consequences* (London: Sage, 2002)

Bell, C.J. et al., "Carrier testing for severe childhood recessive diseases by next-generation sequencing" (2011) 3 *Science Translational Medicine* 1

"Reactions to prenatal testing: reflections of religiosity and attitudes toward abortion and people with disabilities" (2000) 105(1) *American Journal on Mental Retardation* 1

Bibliography

Bennett, B. *Health Law's Kaleidoscope: Health Law Rights in a Global Age* (Ashgate: Aldershot, 2008)

"Prenatal diagnosis, genetics and reproductive decision-making" (2001) 9 *Journal of Law and Medicine* 28

Boyd, P.A. et al., "Survey of prenatal screening policies in Europe for structural malformations and chromosome anomalies, and their impact on detection and termination rates for neural tube defects and Down's syndrome" (2008) *Fetal Medicine* 689

Brandt, A. "Knowledge, attitudes and clinical experience of physicians regarding PGD for hereditary cancer predisposition syndromes" (2010) 9 *Familial Cancer* 479

Bredenoord, A.L. et al., "Dealing with uncertainties: ethics of prenatal diagnosis and PGD to prevent mitochondrial disorders" (2008) 14(1) *Human Reproduction Update* 83

Breslau, N. et al., "Abortion of defective foetuses: attitudes of mothers of congenitally impaired children" 49(4) (1987) *Journal of Marriage and the Family* 839

Bryant, J., Sullivan, E., and Dean, J., *Assisted Reproductive Technology in Australia and New Zealand 2002: Supplement* (Sydney: Australian Institute of Health and Welfare, 2004)

Buchanan, A. et al., *From Chance to Choice: Genetics and Justice* (Cambridge: Cambridge University Press, 2000)

"Choosing who will be disabled: Genetic Intervention and the morality of inclusion" (1996) 13 *Social Philosophy and Policy* 18

Campbell, F.K. *Contours of Ableism: The Production of Disability and Ableness* (New York: Palgrave Macmillan, 2009)

Carlson, L. *The Faces of Intellectual Disability: Philosophical Reflections* (Bloomington: Indiana University Press, 2010)

Cartier, N. et al., "Hematopoietic stem cell gene therapy with a lentiviral vector in X-linked adrenoleukodystrophy" (6 November 2009) 326(5954) *Science*, 818

Centre for Genetics Education, "Preimplantation genetic diagnosis" (Fact sheet 18, June 2007), available at http://www.genetics.com.au/pdf/factsheets/fs18.pdf

Chapman, A.R. and Frankel, M.S. *Designing Our Descendants: The Promises and Perils of Genetic Modifications* (Baltimore: Johns Hopkins University Press, 2003)

Cheffins, T. et al., "The impact of maternal serum screening on the birth prevalence of Down's syndrome and the use of amniocentesis and chorionic villus sampling in South Australia" (2000) 107 *British Journal of Obstetrics and Gynaecology* 1453

Bibliography

Chen, E.A. and Schiffman, J.E. "Attitudes toward genetic counseling and prenatal diagnosis among a group of individuals with physical disabilities," (2000) 9(2) *Journal of Genetic Counseling* 137

Chiu, R.W.K. et al., "Non-invasive prenatal assessment of trisomy 21 by multiplexed maternal plasma DNA sequencing: large scale validity study" (2011) 342 *British Medical Journal* c7401

"Non-invasive prenatal exclusion of congenital adrenal hyperplasia by maternal plasma analysis: a feasibility study" (2002) 48 *Clinical Chemistry* 5

"Prenatal exclusion of [beta] thalassemia major by examination of maternal plasma" (2002) 360 *Lancet* 9338

Cideciyan, A.V. et al., "Human RPE65 gene therapy for Leber congenital amaurosis: persistence of early visual improvements and safety at 1 year" (September 2009) 20(9) *Human Gene Therapy* 999

Cohen, J., Scott, R., Alikani, M., Schimmel, T., Munné, S., Levron, J., Wu, L., Brenner, C., Warner, C., and Willadsen, S. "Ooplasmic transfer in mature human oocytes" (1998) 4(3) *Molecular Human Reproduction* 269

Condit, C.M. "Public attitudes and beliefs about genetics" (2010) 11 *Annual Review of Genomics and Human Genetics* 339

Cotterell, L. "Preconception health care" (18 June 2004) *Australian Doctor*, 35, www.australiandoctor.com.au/htt/pdf/AD_HTT_035_042___JUN18_04.pdf

Council of Europe, "Explanatory report to The European Convention for the Protection of Human Rights and Dignity of the Human Being with regard to the application of biology and medicine 1997," available at http://conventions.coe.int/treaty/en/Reports/Html/164.htm (accessed on 12 December 2011)

Craven, H.A., Tuppen, G.D., Greggains, S.J., Harbottle, J.L., Murphy, L.M., Cree, A.P., Murdoch, P.F., Chinnery, R.W., Taylor, R.N., Lightowlers, M.H., and Douglass M.T. "Pronuclear transfer in human embryos to prevent transfer of mitochondrial DNA disease" (2010) 465(7294) Nature 82

Croyle, R.T. and Lerman, C. "Risk communication in genetic testing for cancer susceptibility" (1999) 25 *Journal of the National Cancer Institute, Monographs* 59

Damasio, A. "Neurodiversity forever; the disability movement turns to brains," *New York Times*, May 9 2004

Davis, L. (ed), *The Disability Studies Reader* (New York: Routledge, 2006 (2nd edition))

de Crespigny, L. and Savulescu, J. "Pregnant women with fetal abnormalities: the forgotten people in the abortion debate" (2008) 188 *The Medical Journal of Australia* 100

de Jong, A. et al., "Non-invasive prenatal testing: ethical issues explored" (2010) 18 *European Journal of Human Genetics* 3

Bibliography

de Lago, M. "Spain allows abortion on demand up to 14 weeks" (2010) 340 *British Medical Journal* 559

Department of Health and Social Security, *Human Fertilisation and Embryology: A Framework for Legislation*, Cm 259 (London: HMSO, 1987)

Legislation on Human Infertility Services and Embryo Research: A Consultation Paper, Cm 46 (London: HMSO, 1986)

Report of the Committee of Inquiry into Human Fertilisation and Embryology, Cmnd 9314 (London: HMSO, 1984)

Dery, A.M. et al., "Attitudes towards the acceptability of reasons for pregnancy termination due to fetal abnormalities among prenatal care providers and consumers in Israel" (2008) 28 *Prenatal Diagnosis* 518

Disability Rights Commission, "Statement on s1(1)(d) of the Abortion Act," (5 July 2003), available at http://www.drc-gb.org/library/policy/health_and_independent_living/drc_statement_on_section_11.aspx accessed on 5 May 2007

Dixon, D. "Informed consent or institutionalized eugenics? How the medical profession encourages abortion of fetuses with Down syndrome" (2008) 24(1) *Issues in Law and Medicine* 3

Douglas, M. *Risk Acceptability According to the Social Sciences* (New York: Russell Sage Foundation, 1985)

Drake, H.M. et al., "Attitudes towards termination for fetal abnormality: comparisons in three European countries" (1996) 49 *Clinical Genetics* 134

Edwards, S.D. "Book review: disability rights and wrongs" (2008) 34(3) *Journal of Medical Ethics* 222

"Disability, identity and the 'expressivist objection'" (2004) 30 *Journal of Medical Ethics* 418

"The impairment/disability distinction: a response to Shakespeare" (2008) 34 *Journal of Medical Ethics* 26

Ehrich, K. and Williams, C. "'A healthy baby': The double imperative of preimplantation genetic diagnosis" (2010) 14 (1)*Health* 41

Ehrich, K., Williams, C., and Farsides, B. "The embryo as moral work object: PGD/IVF staff views and experiences" (2008) 30(5) *Sociology of Health & Illness* 772

Ellwood, D. "Late termination of pregnancy – an obstetrician's perspective" (2005) 29(2) *Australian Health Review* 139

The Ethics Committee of the American Society of Reproductive Medicine, "Sex selection and preimplantation genetic diagnosis" (1999) 72(4) *Fertility and Society* 595

Ettorre, E. *Reproductive Genetics: Gender and the Body* (London: Routledge, 2002)

"Reproductive genetics, gender and the body: 'Please doctor, may I have a normal baby?'" (2000) 34 *Sociology* 403

Evans, M.D.R., Kelley, J. and Zanjani, E.D. "The ethics of gene therapy and abortion: public opinion" (2005) 20(3) *Fetal Diagnosis and Therapy* 223

Fiddler, M. and Pergament, E. "Germline gene therapy: its time is near" 2(2) *Molecular Human Reproduction* 75–76

Fineman, M. "The vulnerable subject: anchoring equality in the human condition" (2008) 20 *Yale Journal of Law and Feminism* 1

Fisher, J. "Termination of pregnancy for fetal abnormality: the perspective of a parent support organisation" (2008) 16 (31-Supplement) *Reproductive Health Matters* 57

Fox, M. "The Human Fertilisation and Embryology Act 2008: tinkering at the margins" (2009) 17 *Feminist Legal Studies* 333

Franklin, S. and Roberts, C. *Born and Made: An Ethnography of Preimplantation Genetic Diagnosis* (Princeton, NJ: Princeton University Press, 2006)

Garland-Thomson, R. "Integrating disability, transforming feminist theory" (Fall 2002) 14(3) *NWSA Journal* 1–32

Genetics and Public Policy Center John Hopkins University, "Reproductive genetic testing: a regulatory patchwork," available at http://www.dnapolicy. org/policy.international.php?action=detail&laws_id=63

Genetics and Public Policy Center, "Oversight of PGD" (July 2007), available at http://www.dnapolicy.org/images/issuebriefpdfs/Oversight_of_PGD_Issue_ Brief.pdf (accessed on 18 June 2011)

Giddens, A. *Modernity and Self-identity: Self and Society in the Late Modern Age* (Stanford, CA: Stanford University Press, 1991)

Gidiri, M. et al., "Maternal screening for Down syndrome: are women's perceptions changing?" (2007) 114 *British Journal of Obstetrics and Gynaecology* 458

Gillon, R. "Is there a 'new ethics of abortion'?" (2001) 27 *Journal of Medical Ethics* 5

Gillott, J. "Screening for disability: a eugenic pursuit" (2001) 27 *Journal of Medical Ethics*, Supplement II, ii21

Glenn, O. "Fetal MRI" at http://www.radiology.ucsf.edu/research/labs/baby-brain/ fetal-mri (accessed on 24 June 2011)

"MR imaging of the fetal brain" (2010) 40 *Pediatric Radiology* 1

Glover, J. *Choosing Children: Genes, Disability and Design* (Oxford: Clarendon Press, 2007)

Goering, S. "'You say you're happy, but…': contested quality of life judgments in bioethics and disability studies" (2008) 5 *Bioethical Inquiry* 125

González-González, M.C. et al., "Huntington disease-unaffected fetus diagnosed from maternal plasma using QF-PCR" (2003) 23 *Prenatal Diagnosis* 3

"Prenatal detection of a cystic fibrosis mutation in fetal DNA from maternal plasma" (2002) 22 *Prenatal Diagnosis* 10

Government of Canada, "A brave new world: where biotechnology and human rights intersect" (July 2005), available at http://biostrategy.gc.ca/humanrights/ humanrightse/Biotech_CH1_E.pdf (accessed on 19 June 2011)

"Family-centred maternity and newborn care: national guidelines" (2000), available at http://www.pentafolio.com/portefolio/images/FCMC.pdf

Green, J. "Obstetricians' views on prenatal diagnosis and termination of pregnancy: 1980 compared with 1993" (1995) 102 *British Journal of Obstetrics and Gynaecology* 228

Green, R. "Letter to a genetic counselor" (1992) 1(1) *Journal of Genetic Counseling* 55

Green, R.M. *Babies by Design: The Ethics of Genetic Choice* (New Haven, CT: Yale University Press, 2008)

Griesenbach, U. et al., "Cystic fibrosis gene therapy: successes, failures and hopes for the future" (2009) 3(4) *Expert Rev. Resp. Med.* 363

"Gene transfer to the lung: lessons learned from more than 2 decades of CF gene therapy" (2009) 61 *Advanced Drug Delivery Reviews* 128

Guttmacher Institute, "State policies in brief: state funding of abortion under medicaid as of November 1, 2011," available at http://www.guttmacher.org/statecenter/spibs/spib_SFAM.pdf

Guttmacher Institute, "State policies in brief: state policies on later-term abortions as of November 1, 2011," available at http://www.guttmacher.org/statecenter/spibs/spib_PLTA.pdf

Habiba, M. et al., "Late termination of pregnancy: a comparison of obstetricians' experience in eight European countries" (2009) 116 *British Journal of Obstetrics and Gynaecology* 1340

Handyside, A.H. et al., "Pregnancies from biopsied human preimplantation embryos sexed by Y-specific DNA amplification" (1990) 344 *Nature* 768

Hannah-Moffat, K. and O'Malley, P. "The gendered risks: an introduction" in Hannah-Moffat, K. and O'Malley, P., *Gendered risks* (New York: Routledge-Cavendish, 2007)

Harris, J. "Is there a coherent social conception of disability?" (2000) 26(2) *Journal of Medical Ethics* 95

Health Canada, "Issues related to the regulation of pre-implantation genetic diagnosis under the Assisted Human Reproduction Act" (2005), available at http://www.cdph.ca.gov/programs/pns/pages/default.aspx

Health Council of the Netherlands, "Preconception care: a good beginning (2007)," available at http://www.gezondheidsraad.nl/en/publications/preconception-care-good-beginning

Holm, S. "The expressivist objection to prenatal diagnosis: can it be laid to rest?" (2008) 34 *Journal of Medical Ethics* 24

Hopwood, P. "Breast cancer risk perception: What do we know and understand" (2000) 2(6) *Breast Cancer Research* 387

House of Commons Science and Technology Committee, "Scientific developments relating to the Abortion Act 1967: Twelfth Report of Session

Bibliography

2006–07 (Volume 1)," available at http://www.publications.parliament.uk/pa/cm200607/cmselect/cmsctech/1045/1045i.pdf (accessed on 21 June 2011)

Hudson, K.L. "Preimplantation genetic diagnosis: public policy and public attitudes" (2006) 85(6) *Fertility and Sterility* 1638

Hughes, B. and Paterson, K. "The social model of disability and the disappearing body: towards a sociology of impairment" (1997) 12(3) *Disability and Society* 325

Huisman, T.A. et al., "Fetal magnetic resonance imaging of the central nervous system: a pictorial essay" (2002) 12 *European Radiology* 8

Human Fertilisation and Embryology Authority, "Consultation document on preimplantation genetic diagnosis" (1999), available at http://www.hfea.gov.uk/cps/rde/xbcr/hfea/PGD_document.pdf

Human Fertilisation and Embryology Authority and Advisory Committee on Genetic Testing, "Consultation document on preimplantation genetic diagnosis" (1999), available at http://www.hfea.gov.uk/cps/rde/xbcr/hfea/PGD_document.pdf (accessed on 12 December 2011)

Human Fertilisation and Embryology Authority and Human Genetics Committee, "Outcome of the public consultation on preimplantation genetic diagnosis" (2001), available at http://www.hfea.gov.uk/cps/rde/xbcr/hfea/PGD_outcome.pdf (accessed on 12 December 2011)

Human Fertilisation and Embryology Authority, "Embryo testing and sex selection," available at http://www.hfea.gov.uk/496.html

"Authority decision on PGD: statement on use of Preimplantation Genetic Diagnosis (PGD) for inherited cancer susceptibility," Press release, 10 May 2006, available at http://www.hfea.gov.uk/622.html

"Authority decision on the use of PGD for lower penetrance, later onset inherited conditions," available at http://www.hfea.gov.uk/docs/The_Authority_decision_Choices_and_boundaries.pdf

"Choices and boundaries: should people be able to select embryos free from an inherited susceptibility to cancer?" (November 2005)

"Clinical guidance letter" (13 August 1999), available at http://www.hfea.gov.uk/3219.html (accessed on 24 June 2011)

"Code of practice" (6th Edition, 2003), available at http://www.hfea.gov.uk/docs/Code_of_Practice_Sixth_Edition.pdf (accessed on 12 December 2011)

"Code of practice" (8th edition), available at http://www.hfea.gov.uk/70.html

"Guidance on preimplantation testing" (15 May 2003), available at http://www.hfea.gov.uk/2686.html (accessed on 21 July 2011)

"Horizon scanning panel," available at http://www.hfea.gov.uk/1132.html

"Interim policy on preimplantation tissue typing" (November, 2001), [no longer available electronically, on file with the authors]

"PGD conditions listed by the HFEA," available at http://www.hfea.gov.uk/cps/hfea/gen/pgd-screening.htm (accessed on 27 June 2011)

"Pre-implantation diagnostic testing ('PGD') explanatory note for licence committee" (2010), available at http://www.hfea.gov.uk/docs/2010-10-28_Licence_Committee_PGD_Explanatory_note.PDF

"Report: preimplantation tissue typing" (2004), available at http://www.hfea.gov.uk/docs/PolicyReview_PreimplantationTissueReport.pdf (accessed on 24 June 2011)

"Scientific review of the safety and efficacy of methods to avoid mitochondrial disease through assisted conception" (April 2011), available at http://www.hfea.gov.uk/docs/2011-04-18_Mitochondria_review_-_final_report.PDF (accessed on 23 June 2011)

Human Fertilisation and Embryology Authority, "Sex selection public consultation document" (1993), available at http://www.hfea.gov.uk/docs/Sex_Selection_Consultation_1993.pdf (accessed on 12 December 2011)

Human Genetic Commission, Advisory Committee on Genetic Testing, "Prenatal genetic testing, report for consultation," (February 2000), available at http://www.dh.gov.uk/prod_consum_dh/groups/dh_digitalassets/@dh/@en/documents/digitalasset/dh_4014675.pdf (accessed on 12 December 2011)

"Increasing options, informing choice: a report on preconception genetic testing and screening" (April 2011), available at http://www.hgc.gov.uk/UploadDocs/DocPub/Document/Increasing%20options,%20informing%20choice%20-%20final.pdf

Human Genetics Commission, "Making babies: reproductive decisions and genetic technologies" (January 2006), available at http://www.hgc.gov.uk/UploadDocs/DocPub/Document/Making%20Babies%20Report%20-%20final%20pdf.pdf (accessed on 12 December 2011)

Human Genetics Society of Australasia, "Guidance: clinical geneticist's role", Document Number GD01 (August 2010), available at https://www.hgsa.org.au/website/wp-content/uploads/2009/12/s-Role-2010GD01.pdf (accessed on 12 December 2011)

"Guidelines for training and certification in genetic counseling" Document Number 2010 GL01, available at https://www.hgsa.org.au/website/wp-content/uploads/2010/03/2010GL01-Guidelines-for-Training-and-Certification-in-Genetic-Counselling.pdf (accessed on 12 December 2011)

Hunt, L.M. et al., "Do notions of risk inform patient choice? Lessons from a study of prenatal genetic counseling" (2006) 25 *Medical Anthropology* 193

Hyder, N. "German parliament to debate PGD bills," *Bio News*, 23 May 2011, available at http://www.bionews.org.uk/page_94555.asp (accessed on 10 June 2011)

Bibliography

Infertility Treatment Authority, "Genetic testing and the Requirements of the Infertility Treatment Act 1995: policy in relation to the use of preimplantation genetic diagnosis" (2003) reviewed 2009. [no longer available electronically, on file with the authors]

"Annual report 2009," available at http://varta.org.au/annual reports/w1/ i1003573/

"Approved genetic testing" (October 2009), [no longer available electronically, on file with the authors]

"Genetic testing and the requirements of the Infertility Treatment Act 1995: Policy in relation to the use of pre-implantation genetic diagnosis (PGD)" (2009), [no longer available electronically, on file with the authors]

"Tissue typing in conjunction with preimplantation genetic diagnosis" (January 2007, rev. ed.), [no longer available electronically, on file with the authors]

Jackson, E. "Abortion, autonomy and prenatal diagnosis" (2000) 9(4) *Social and Legal Studies* 467

Regulating Reproduction: Law, Technology and Autonomy (Oxford–Portland, Or: Hart Publishing, 2001)

Joint Human Genetics Society of Australasia/Royal Australian and New Zealand College of Obstetricians and Gynaecologists Prenatal Diagnosis Screening Committee, "Joint HGSA/RANZCOG prenatal diagnosis policy" (College Statement no. C-Obs 5, November 2006), available at http://www.ranzcog. edu.au/component/content/article/503-c-obs/287-prenatal-diagnosis-policy-c-obs-5.html (accessed on 12 December 2011)

Joint Research Centre of the European Commission, "JRC scientific and technical reports: preimplantation genetic diagnosis in Europe" (2007), available at ftp://ftp.jrc.es/pub/EURdoc/eur22764en.pdf (accessed on 19 June 2011)

Juengst, E.T. "'Alter-ing' the human species' identity" in John Rasko, Gabrielle O'Sullivan and Rachel Ankeny (eds.), *The Ethics of Inheritable Genetic Modification: A Dividing Line?* (Cambridge: Cambridge University Press, 2006), 149–158

Kalfoglou, A.L. et al., "Opinions about new reproductive genetic technologies: hopes and fears for our genetic future" (2005) 83(6) *Fertility and Sterility* 1612

Karatas, J.C. et al., "Women's experience of pre-implantation genetic diagnosis: a qualitative study," (2010) 30(8) *Prenatal Diagnosis* 771

Karpin, I. "Choosing disability: preimplantation genetic diagnosis and negative enhancement" (2007) 15 *Journal of Law and Medicine* 89

"The uncanny embryos: legal limits to the human and reproduction without women" (2006) 28(4) *Sydney Law Review* 599

Karpin, I. and Mykitiuk, R. "Feminist legal theory as embodied justice" in M. Fineman (ed.), *Transcending the Boundaries of the Law: Generations of Feminism and Legal Theory* (Abingdon: Routledge, 2011)

Bibliography

Katz Rothman, B. "The products of conception: the social context of reproductive choices" (1985) 11 *Journal of Medical Ethics* 188

The Tentative Pregnancy: Prenatal Diagnosis and the Future of Motherhood (New York: Viking, 1986)

Kerr, A. and Cunningham-Burley, S. "On ambivalence and risk: reflexive modernity and the new human genetics," (2000) 34(2) *Sociology* 283

Kinali, M. et al., "Local restoration of dystrophin expression with the morpholino oligomer AVI-4658 in Duchenne muscular dystrophy: a single-blind, placebo-controlled, dose-escalation, proof-of-concept study" (2009) 8 *The Lancet Neurology* 918

Klitzman, R. et al., "Decision-making about reproductive choice among individuals at-risk for Huntington's disease" (2007) 16 *Journal of Genetic Counselling* 347

Koch, T. "Disability and difference: balancing social and physical constructions" (2001) 27 *Journal of Medical Ethics* 370

"Is Tom Shakespeare disabled?" (2008) 34 *Journal of Medical Ethics* 18

"One principle and three fallacies of disability studies" (2002) 28 *Journal of Medical Ethics* 203

"The Difference that difference makes: bioethics and the challenge of 'disability'" (2004) 29(6) *Journal of Medicine and Philosophy* 697

Kondrashov, A.S. "Contamination of the genome by very slightly deleterious mutations: why have we not died 100 times over?" (1995) 175 *Journal of Theoretical Biology*, 583–594

Koshland, D. "Sequences and consequences of the human genome" (1989) 246 *Science* 189

Krahn, T. "Where are we going with preimplantation genetic diagnosis?" (2007) 176(10) *Canadian Medical Association Journal* 1445

Leach Scully, J. "Disability and the thinking body" in K. Kristiansen, S. Vehmas. and T. Shakespeare (eds.), *Arguing About Disability – Philosophical Perspectives* (Oxford: Routledge, 2010)

Lee, E. "Who's Afraid of Choice?" (2003), http://www.prochoiceforum.org.uk/ocrabortdis3.asp (accessed on 8 June 2011)

Legislative Assembly of Western Australia, "Select Committee on the Human Reproductive Technology Act 1991 Report" (1999), available at http://parliament.wa.gov.au/parliament%5Ccommit.nsf/%28Report+Lookup+by+Com+ID%29/F2564DBF28FD970348257831003E9515/$file/rp1-pt1.pdf (accessed on 12 December 2011)

Levine, D. et al., "Central nervous system abnormalities assessed with prenatal magnetic resonance imaging" (1999) 94 *Obstetrics & Gynecology* 6

Li, Y. et al., "Improved prenatal detection of a fetal point mutation for achondroplasia by the use of size-fractionated circulatory DNA in maternal plasma – case report" (2004) 24 *Prenatal Diagnosis* 11

Bibliography

Lippman, A. "Choice as a risk to women's health" (1999) 1 *Health, Risk and Society* 281

"Embodied knowledge and making sense of prenatal diagnosis" (1999) 8(5) *Journal of Genetic Counseling* 255

"Letter: eugenics and public health" (2003) 93(1) *American Journal of Public Health* 11

"Prenatal genetic testing and screening: constructing needs and reinforcing inequities" (1991) 17 *American Journal of Law and Medicine* 15

"The genetic construction of prenatal testing: choice, consent or conformity for women?" in K.H. Rothenberg and E.J. Thomson (eds.), *Women and Prenatal Testing: Facing the Challenges of Genetic Technology* (Columbus: Ohio State University Press, 1994)

The Inclusion of Women in Clinical Trials: Are We Asking the Right Questions? (Toronto: Women and Health Protection, 2006), 18

Lo, Y.M.D. et al., "Maternal plasma DNA sequencing reveals the genome-wide genetic and mutational profile of the foetus" (2010) 2 *Science Translational Medicine* 61

"Presence of fetal DNA in maternal plasma and serum" (2007) *Lancet* 350

Lofland, J. and Lofland, L.H. *Analyzing Social Settings: A guide to qualitative observation and analysis* (Belmont, CA: Wadsworth Publishing Company, 1984)

Lohmueller, K.E. "Proportionally more deleterious genetic variation in European than in African populations" (21 February 2008) 451 *Nature* 994

Lupton, D. "Risk and the ontology of pregnant embodiment" in D. Lupton (ed.), *Risk and Sociocultural Theory: New Directions and Perspectives* (Cambridge: Cambridge University Press, 1999)

Maguire, A.M. et al., "Age-dependent effects of RPE65 gene therapy for Leber's congenital amaurosis: a phase 1 dose-escalation trial" (November 7, 2009) 374(9701) *Lancet* 1597

"Safety and efficacy of gene transfer for Leber's congenital amaurosis" (May 22, 2008) 358(21) *The New England Journal of Medicine* 2240

Mandel, P. and Metais, P. "Les acides nucleiques du plasma sanguin chez l'homme" (1948) *Comptes Rendus de l'Académie des Sciences de Paris* 142

Maron, J.L. and Bianchi, D.W. "Prenatal diagnosis using cell-free nucleic acids in maternal body fluids: a decade of progress" (2007) 145C *American Journal of Medical Genetics* 1

Medical Practitioners Board of Victoria, "Report on late terminations of pregnancy in Victoria" (April 1998), [no longer available electronically, on file with the authors]

Melbourne IVF, "Advanced Embryo Selection™," available at http://www.mivf.com.au/ivf-fertility-treatments/genetic-testing-pgd/advanced-embryo-selection.aspx (accessed on 19 June 2011)

Bibliography

"Genetic Testing (PGD)," available at http://www.mivf.com.au/ivf-fertility-treatments/genetic-testing-pgd.aspx

"New IVF technique: testing of every chromosome embryos" (25th October, 2010), available at http://www.mivf.com.au/ivf-latest-news/new-ivf-technique-testing-of-every-chromosome-embryos.aspx

Monash IVF, "fact sheet: confirmatory prenatal diagnosis following preimplantation genetic diagnosis (PGD)" (November 2006), available at http://www.monashivf.com/site/DefaultSite/filesystem/documents/confirmatory-Prenatal-Diagnosis-following-PGD.pdf

"fact sheet: preimplantation genetic diagnosis with chromosome screening" (May 2009), available at http://www.monashivf.com/site/DefaultSite/filesystem/documents/PGD-for-chromosome-screening.pdf

"Fact sheet: preimplantation genetic diagnosis with sex selection for X-linked genetic disorders," (May 2009), available at http://www.monashivf.com/site/DefaultSite/filesystem/documents/PGD-with-sex-selection.pdf

"Pre-implantation genetic diagnosis," available at http://www.monashivf.com/Services/Pre-implantation_Genetic_Diagnosis__PGD_.aspx

Morgan, K.P. "Contested bodies, contested knowledge: women, health, and the politics of medicalization" in S. Sherwin (Coord.), *The Politics of Women's Health: Exploring Agency and Autonomy* (Philadelphia: Temple University Press, 1998), pp. 64–82

Morton, N.E., Crow, J.F. and Muller, H.J. "An estimate of the mutations damage in man from data on consanguineous marriages" (1956) 42 *Proceedings of the National Academy of the Sciences of the United States of America* 855

Murdoch Children's Research Institute, "Public health genetics: project one: evaluation of prenatal screening and diagnosis," available at http://www.mcri.edu.au/pages/research/research-group.asp?P=projects&G=41

"Your choice: screening and diagnostic tests in pregnancy" (2004), available at http://www.mcri.edu.au/Downloads/PrenatalTestingDecisionAid.pdf.

Murphy, T. "When choosing the traits of children is hurtful to others" (2011) 37 *Journal of Medical Ethics* 105

Mykitiuk, R. and Scott, D.N. "Risky pregnancy: liability, blame and insurance in the governance of prenatal harm" (2011) 43 (2) *University of British Columbia Law Review* 311

National Ethics Committee on Assisted Human Reproduction, "Guidelines on preimplantation genetic diagnosis" (March 2005), available at http://www.ecart.health.govt.nz/moh.nsf/pagescm/30/$File/pgd.pdf (accessed on 12 December 2011)

National Health and Medical Research Council and the Australian Research Council Australian Vice-Chancellors' Committee, "National statement on ethical conduct in human research" (2007), available at http://www.nhmrc.gov.

au/_files_nhmrc/publications/attachments/e72.pdf (accessed on 12 December 2011)

National Health and Medical Research Centre, "Statement on human experimentation and supplementary notes 1982: supplementary note 4 – in vitro fertilisation and embryo transfer" (February 1984) XXVIII(1) *Australasian Radiology* 65

National Health and Medical Research Council, "Ethical guidelines on the use of assisted reproductive technology in clinical practice and research" (2007), available at http://www.nhmrc.gov.au/_files_nhmrc/publications/attachments/e78.pdf (accessed on 12 December 2011)

National Health Service Fetal Anomaly Screening Programme, "Review of the model of best practice 2008: Down's syndrome screening for England," available at http://fetalanomaly.screening.nhs.uk/getdata.php?id=11297

"Screening for Down's Syndrome: UK NSC policy recommendations 2007–2010: model of best practice," available at http://fetalanomaly.screening.nhs.uk/getdata.php?id=10938

"Screening tests for you and your baby," available at http://fetalanomaly.screening.nhs.uk/getdata.php?id=11279, pp. 17–41

National Health Service, "Gene test 'predicts 448 child diseases,'" available at http://www.nhs.uk/news/2011/01January/Pages/dna-gentic-test-for-parents-before-pregnancy.aspx (accessed on 27 June 2011)

NSW Health, "Diagnosis of abnormality in an unborn baby: the impact, options and afterwards" (August 2006), available at http://www.genetics.edu.au/pdf/birthabnormbooklet.pdf (accessed on 12 December 2011)

"Policy directive: pregnancy – framework for terminations in New South Wales Public Health organisations" (2005), available at http://www.health.nsw.gov.au/policies/pd/2005/pdf/PD2005_587.pdf (accessed on 12 December 2011)

"Prenatal testing/screening for down syndrome and other chromosomal abnormalities" (8 August 2007), available at http://www.health.nsw.gov.au/policies/pd/2007/pdf/PD2007_067.pdf

"Prenatal testing: special tests for your baby during pregnancy" (8 August 2007)

"When your unborn baby has a problem: how to manage the weeks ahead (a book for families)" (March 2006), available at http://www.genetics.edu.au/pdf/whenunbornbaby.pdf (accessed on 12 December 2011)

"When your unborn baby has a problem: how to manage the weeks ahead (a book for families)" (March 2006)

Nussbaum, R. et al., "A qualitative description of receiving a diagnosis of clefting in the prenatal or postnatal period" (2008) 17 *Journal of Genetic Counselling* 336

Bibliography

O'Connell, K. "From black box to open brain: law neuroimaging and disability discrimination" (2011) 20(3) *Griffith Law Review*, 883

O'Leary, P. et al., "Regional variations in prenatal screening across Australia: stepping towards a national policy framework" (2006) 46 *Australian and New Zealand Journal of Obstetrics and Gynaecology* 427

Oliver, T. *The Politics of Disablement* (London: MacMillan Education, 1990)

O'Malley, P. "The Government of Risks" in A. Sarat (ed.), *The Blackwell Companion to Law and Society* (Oxford: Blackwell, 2004)

Parens, E. and Asch, A. "Disability rights critique of prenatal genetic testing: reflections and recommendations," (2003) 9 *Mental Retardations and Developmental Disabilities Research Reviews* 40

"The disability rights critique of prenatal genetic testing: reflections and recommendations" (1999) 29(5) Special Supplement *Hastings Center Report* S1

The Practice Committee of the Society for Assisted Reproductive Technology and the Practice Committee of the American Society for Reproductive Medicine, "Preimplantation genetic testing: a practice committee opinion" (November 2008) vol. 90, Supp. 3 *Fertility and Sterility* 136, available at http://www.asrm.org/uploadedFiles/ASRM_Content/News_and_Publications/Practice_Guidelines/Committee_Opinions/Preimplantation_genetic_testing(1).pdf (accessed on 10 June 2011)

The President's Council on Bioethics, "Reproduction and Responsibility: The Regulation of New Biotechnologies" (March 2004)

Queen Elizabeth Hospital press release, "IVF Researchers Win Awards at International IVF Congress," May 1999, available at www.tqeh.sa.gov.au/repositories/files/IVF%20Researchers%20win.doc (accessed on 16 June 2011)

Queensland Government, "Topic: preconception," available at http://access.health.qld.gov.au/hid/WomensHealth/PregnancyandChildbirth/preconception_ap.asp.

Queensland Health, "Screening for Down syndrome in pregnancy," available at http://www.health.qld.gov.au/rbwh/docs/ds-screening.pdf (accessed on 12 December 2011)

Quinn, G. "Conflict between values and technology: perception of PGD among women at increased risk for hereditary breast and ovarian cancer" (2009) 8 *Familial Cancer* 441

Rabino, I. "Research scientists surveyed on ethical issues in genetic medicine: a comparison of attitudes of US and European researchers" (2006) 25(3) *New Genetics and Society* 325

RANZCOG College Statement, "Prenatal screening tests for trisomy 21 (Down Syndrome), trisomy 18 (Edwards syndrome) and neural tube defects" C-Obs 4, July 2007, available at http://www.ranzcog.edu.au/publications/statements/C-obs4.pdf

Bibliography

Royal Australian and New Zealand College of Obstetricians and Gynaecologists, "Prenatal screening for fetal abnormalities" (College Statement no. C-Obs 35, March 2010), available at http://www.ranzcog.edu.au/the-ranzcog/policies-and-guidelines/college-statements/286-prenatal-screening-for-fetal-abnormalities-c-obs-35.html (accessed on 12 December 2011)

Royal Australian and New Zealand College of Obstetricians and Gynaecologists, "Prenatal screening tests for trisomy 21 (Down syndrome), trisomy 18 (Edwards syndrome) and neural tube defects" (College Statement no. C-Obs 4, July 2007), available at http://www.ranzcog.edu.au/the-ranzcog/policies-and-guidelines/college-statements/412--prenatal-screening-tests-for-trisomy-21-down-syndrome-trisomy-18-edwards-syndrome-and-neural-tube-defects-c-obs4.html

Rapp, R. "Refusing prenatal diagnosis: the multiple meanings of biotechnology in a multicultural world," (1998) 23 *Science, Technology & Human Values* 45
Testing Women, Testing the Fetus: The Social Impact of Amniocentesis in America (New York: Routledge, 2000)
"Women's responses to prenatal diagnosis: a sociocultural perspective on diversity" in K. Rothenberg and E. Thomson (eds.), *Women and Prenatal Testing: Facing the Challenges of Genetic Technology* (Columbus: University of Ohio Press, 1994), 219–233

Reindal, S.M. "Disability, gene therapy and eugenics – a challenge to John Harris" (2000) 26 *Journal of Medical Ethics* 89

Reproductive Technology Council, "Policy on approval of diagnostic procedures involving embryos," (March 2008)

Roberts, C. et al., "The role of genetic counselling in the elective termination of pregnancies involving fetuses with disabilities" (2002) 36(1) *The Journal of Special Education* 48

Robertson, J.J. "Extending PGD: the ethical debate" (2003) 18(3) *Human Reproduction* 465

Rose, N. "In search of certainty: risk management in a biological age" (2005) 4(3) *Journal of Public Mental Health* 14
"Beyond medicalization" (2007) 369 *The Lancet* 700
"The politics of life itself" (2001) 18 *Theory, Culture & Society* 1

Royal Australian and New Zealand College of Obstetricians and Gynaecologists, "Termination of pregnancy" (College Statement no. C-Gyn 17, March 2009), available at http://www.ranzcog.edu.au/the-ranzcog/policies-and-guidelines/college-statements/467-termination-of-pregnancy-c-gyn-17.html (accessed on 12 December 2011)

Royal College of Obstetricians and Gynaecologists, "Termination of pregnancy for foetal abnormality in England, Wales and Scotland" (January 1996), [no longer available electronically, on file with the authors]

Bibliography

"Briefing on HFEA Bill: RCOG parliamentary briefing on the Human Fertilisation and Embryology Bill (HL) 2007–08," available at http://www.rcog.org.uk/what-we-do/campaigning-and-opinions/briefings-and-qas-/human-fertilisation-and-embryology-bill/brief

Royal College of Obstetricians and Gynaecologists, "Termination of pregnancy for fetal abnormality in England, Scotland and Wales: Report of a Working Party" (May 2010), available at http://www.rcog.org.uk/files/rcog-corp/TerminationPregnancyReport18May2010.pdf (accessed on 12 December 2011)

"Understanding how risk is discussed in childcare," available at http://www.rcog.org.uk/understanding-how-risk-is-discussed-healthcare (last reviewed 19 January 2011)

Roybal, J.L. et al., "Stem cell and genetic therapies for the fetus" (2010) *Seminars in Fetal & Neonatal Medicine* 15

Sagi, M. et al., "Application of the health belief model in a study on parents' intentions to utilize prenatal diagnosis of cleft lip and/or palate" (1992) 44 *American Journal of Medical Genetics* 326

Saito, H. et al., "Prenatal DNA diagnosis of a single-gene disorder from maternal plasma" (2000) 356 *Lancet* 9236

Salvi, M. "Shaping individuality: human inheritable germ line gene modification" (2001) 22 *Theoretical Medicine,* 527

Samerski, S. "The 'decision trap': how genetic counselling transforms pregnant women into managers of foetal risk profiles'" in Hannah-Moffat, K. and O'Malley, P., *Gendered Risks* (New York: Routledge-Cavendish, 2007)

"The unleashing of genetic terminology: how genetic counselling mobilizes for risk management" (August 2006) 25(2) *New Genetics and Society* 197

Sandel, M. *The Case Against Perfection: Ethics in the Age of Genetic Engineering* (Cambridge, Ma: Harvard University Press, 2009)

Savell, K. "Turning mothers into bioethicists: late abortion and disability" in B. Bennett, T. Carney and I. Karpin (eds.) *Brave New World of Health* (Sydney: The Federation Press, 2008)

Savulescu, J. "Is current practice around the termination of pregnancy eugenic and discriminatory?" (2001) 27 *Journal of Medical Ethics* 165

Savulescu, J. "Deaf lesbians, 'designer disability' and the future of medicine" (2002) 325 *BMJ* 771

Savulescu, J. and de Crespigny, L.J. "Pregnant women with fetal abnormalities: the forgotten people in the abortion debate" (2008) 188 *The Medical Journal of Australia* 100

Savulescu, J. and Kahane, G. "The moral obligation to create children with the best chance of the best life" (2009) 23(5) *Bioethics* 274

Bibliography

Scientific and Clinical Advances Advisory Group of the HFEA, "Horizon scanning briefing: genetic modification of embryos," (7 November 2008), available at http://www.hfea.gov.uk/docs/SCAG_Genetic_Modification_of_EmbryosNov08.pdf (accessed on 12 December 2011)

Scott, R. "Prenatal testing, reproductive autonomy and disability interests" (2005) 14 *Cambridge Quarterly of Healthcare Ethics* 65

Choosing Between Possible Lives: Law and Ethics of Prenatal and Preimplantation Genetic Diagnosis (Oxford: Hart Publishing, 2007)

"Prenatal screening, autonomy and reasons: the relationship between the law of abortion and wrongful birth" (2003) 11 *Medical Law Review* 265

"The appropriate extent of pre-implantation genetic diagnosis: health professionals' and scientists' views on the requirement for a 'significant risk of a serious genetic condition'" (2007) 15 *Medical Law Review* 320

Shakespeare, T. "Choices and rights: eugenics, genetics and disability equality" (1998) 13(5) *Disability and Society* 665

"Debating disability" (2008) 34 *Journal of Medical Ethics* 11

Disability Rights and Wrongs (London: Routledge, 2006)

The Shared Maternity Care Collective, "Guidelines for shared maternity care affiliates (2010)," available at http://www.health.vic.gov.au/maternitycare/smcaguidelines-2010.pdf

Sharp, S. and Earle, S. "Feminism, abortion and disability: irreconcilable differences?" (2002) 17 *Disability and Society* 137

Sheldon, S. and Wilkinson, S. "Should selecting saviour siblings be banned?" (2004) 30 *Journal of Medical Ethics* 533

Sheldon, S., and Wilkinson, S. "Termination of pregnancy for reason of fetal disability: are there grounds for a special exception in law?" (2001) 9 *Medical Law Review* 85

Shildrick, M. "The disabled body, genealogy and undecidability" (2005) 19 *Cultural Studies* 755

Silvers, A. "On the possibility and desirability of constructing a neutral conception of disability" (2003) 24 *Theoretical Medicine* 471

Simon, E.M. et al., "Fast MR imaging of fetal CNS anomalies in utero" (2000) 21 *American Journal of Neuroradiology* 9

Simonelli, F. et al., "Gene therapy for Leber's congenital amaurosis is safe and effective through 1.5 years after vector administration" (March 2010) 18(3) *Molecular Therapy* 643

Sivell, S. et al., "How risk is perceived, constructed and interpreted by clients in clinical genetics, and the effects on decision making: systematic review" (2008) 17 *Journal of Genetic Counseling* 30

Skene, L. and Thompson, J. (eds.), *The sorting society: the ethics of genetic screening and therapy* (New York: Cambridge University Press, 2008)

Society of Obstetricians and Gynaecologists of Canada (SOGC), "Practice guideline on prenatal screening for fetal aneuploidy" (February 2007), available at http://www.sogc.org/guidelines/documents/187E-CPG-February2007.pdf

Society of Ostetricians and Gynaecologists of Canada, "SOGC technical update: preimplantation genetic diagnosis" (August 2009) 232 JOGC 761, available at http://www.sogc.org/guidelines/documents/gui232TU0908.pdf (accessed on 10 June 2011)

South Australian Council for Reproductive Technology [SARCT], "Memorandum 12 to reproductive medicine units re. preimplantation genetic diagnosis (PGD) – definition of 'a genetic defect' for the purpose of determining eligibility for treatment" (reproduced in the SARCT Annual Report 2004, p 39)

South Australian Department of Health, "Perinatal practice guidelines," available at http://www.health.sa.gov.au/PPG/Default.aspx?tabid=222

Sparrow, R. "A not-so-new eugenics: Harris and Savulescu on human enhancement" (January–February 2001) 41(1) *Hastings Centre Report* 32

Statham, H. et al., "Late termination of pregnancy: law, policy and decision-making in four English fetal medicine units" (2006) 113 *British Journal of Obstetrics and Gynaecology* 1402

Steinbock, B. *Disability, Prenatal Testing and Selective Abortion* (Washington, DC: Georgetown University Press, 2002)

Sydney IVF, "PGD fees," available at http://www.sydneyivf.com/GeneticDisorders/PGDfees/tabid/129/Default.aspx,
    "PGD for inherited disease," available at http://www.sydneyivf.com.au/GeneticDisorders/PGDforinheriteddisease/tabid/368/Default.aspx
    "PGD overview," available at http://www.sydneyivf.com/GeneticDisorders/PGDoverview/tabid/125/Default.aspx

Tremain, S. "On the government of disability: foucault, power and the subject of impairment" in L. Davis (ed.), *The Disability Studies Reader* (New York: Routledge, 2006 (2nd edition))

U.S. Department of Health and Human Services, Centers for Disease Control and Prevention, "Recommendations to improve preconception health and health care" (April 21, 2006, Vol. 55, No. PR-6:7)

Victorian Assisted Reproductive Treatment Authority, "Information for registered ART providers" (December 2009), available at www.varta.org.au/secure/downloadfile.asp?fileid=1003795 (accessed on 12 December 2011)

Victorian Law Reform Commission, "Law of abortion: final report" (March 2008), available at http://www.lawreform.vic.gov.au/resources/2/0/2022d5 80404a0cac9718fff5f2791d4a/vlrc_abortion_report.pdf (accessed on 12 December 2011)

Bibliography

Victorian Perinatal Data Collection Unit, "Summary of ten most frequently reported birth defects in Victoria 2003 -2004," available at http://www.health. vic.gov.au/ccopmm/downloads/summary04.pdf (accessed on 12 December 2011)

Victorian Shared Maternity Care Collective, "Guidelines for shared maternity care affiliates" (2010), available at http://www.health.vic.gov.au/maternity-care/smcaguidelines-2010.pdf

Walters, L. and Palmer, J.G. *The Ethics of Human Gene Therapy* (New York: Oxford University Press, 1997)

Wang, Y., Chambers, G., Sullivan, E. and Dieng, M. "Assisted reproductive technology in Australia and New Zealand 2007 supplement tables" (Sydney: Australian Institute of Health and Welfare, National Perinatal Statistics Unit, 2009)

"Assisted reproductive technology in Australia and New Zealand 2008" AIHW (Sydney: Australian Institute of Health and Welfare, National Perinatal Statistics Unit, 2010)

Wang, Y., Dean, J. and Sullivan, E. "Assisted reproductive technology in Australia and New Zealand 2005" (Sydney: Australian Institute of Health and Welfare, National Perinatal Statistics Unit, 2007)

Wang, Y., Dean, J., Badgery-Parker, T. and Sullivan, E. "Assisted reproductive technology in Australia and New Zealand 2006" (Sydney: Australian Institute of Health and Welfare, National Perinatal Statistics Unit, 2008)

Wang, Y., Dean, J., Grayson, N. and Sullivan, E. "Assisted reproductive technology in Australia and New Zealand, 2004," (Sydney: Australian Institute of Health and Welfare, National Perinatal Statistics Unit, 2006)

Ward, L.M. "Whose right to choose? The 'new' genetics, prenatal testing and people with learning difficulties" (2002) 12(2) *Critical Public Health* 187

Wates, A., Dean, J. and Sullivan, E. "Supplement to assisted reproductive technology in Australia and New Zealand 2003" (Sydney: Australian Institute of Health and Welfare, National Perinatal Statistics Unit, 2006)

Wellcome Trust, "What do people think about gene therapy? A report published by the Wellcome Trust" (August 2005), available at http://www.wellcome. ac.uk/stellent/groups/corporatesite/@msh_peda/documents/web_document/ wtx026421.pdf (accessed on 12 December 2011)

Wertz, D. and Fletcher, J. "A critique of some feminist challenges to prenatal diagnosis" (1993) 2 *Journal of Women's Health* 173

Wertz, D. and Knoppers, B., "Serious genetic disorders: can or should they be defined?" (2002) 108 *American Journal of Medical Genetics* 29

Wesley Monash IVF, "Genetic screening and diagnosis: preimplantation genetic screening and preimplantation genetic diagnosis," (October 2009), available at http://wesley.monashivf.edu.au/WESLEY%20NEWSLETTER_Oct%2009.

pdf; Monash IVF, "Pre-implantation genetic diagnosis," http://www.monashivf.com/Services/Pre-implantation_Genetic_Diagnosis__PGD_.aspx

Western Australia Department of Health, "Planning to get pregnant," available at http://www.health.wa.gov.au/havingababy/before/planning.cfm.

Western Australian Reproductive Technology Council, "Policy on approval of diagnostic procedures involving embryos" (March 2008)

Wheeler, D.A. et al., "The complete genome of an individual by massively parallel DNA sequencing" (2008) 452 *Nature* 872

Whitby, E.H. et al., "Comparison of ultrasound and magnetic resonance imagining in 100 singleton pregnancies with suspected brain abnormalities" (2004) 111 *British Journal of Obstetrics and Gynaecology* 8

Wilkinson, S. *Choosing Tomorrow's Children: The Ethics of Selective Reproduction* (Oxford: Oxford University Press, 2010)

Williams, C. et al., "'Drawing the line' in prenatal screening and testing: health practitioners' discussions" (2002) 4(1) *Health, Risk and Society* 61

Woodrow, N.L. "Termination review committees: are they necessary?" (2003) 179 *Medical Journal of Australia* 92

World Health Organisation, "International classification of functioning, disability and health," available at http://www.who.int/classifications/icf/en/ (accessed on 17 June 2011)

"International statistical classification of diseases and related health problems 10th revision version for 2007," available at http://apps.who.int/classifications/apps/icd/icd10online/ (accessed on 21 June 2011)

Wright, C. and Burton, H. "The use of cell-free fetal nucleic acids in maternal blood for non-invasive prenatal diagnosis" (2009) 15 *Human Reproduction Update* 1

Young, I.M. "Foreword" in M. Corker and T. Shakespeare (eds.), *Disability/Postmodernity: Embodying Disability Theory* (London: Continuum, 2002)

Zolotukhina, T.V. et al., "Analysis of cell-free fetal DNA in plasma and serum of pregnant women" (2005) 53 *Journal of Histochemistry and Cytochemistry* 3

LEGISLATION

Abortion Act 1967 (UK)

Abortion Law Reform Act 2008 (Vic)

Abortion Regulations 1991 (UK)

Act for Protection of Embryos of 13 December 1990 (Germany)

Assisted Human Reproduction Act 2004 (Canada)

Assisted Reproductive Treatment Act 2008 (Vic)

Assisted Reproductive Treatment Act 2008 (SA)

Assisted Reproductive Treatment Regulations 2010 (SA)

Bibliography

Crimes Act 1900 (ACT)

Crimes Act 1900 (NSW)

Criminal Code 1899 (Qld)

Criminal Code Act 1913 (WA)

Criminal Code Act 1924 (Tas)

Criminal Code Act 1983 (NT)

Criminal Law Consolidation (Medical Termination of Pregnancy) Regulations 1996 (SA)

Criminal Law Consolidation Act 1935 (SA)

Health Act 1911 (WA)

Health Act 1993 (ACT)

Human Cloning and Embryo Research Act 2004 (ACT)

Human Reproductive Technology Act 1991 (WA)

Human Cloning and Other Prohibited Practices Act 2003 (NSW)

Human Cloning and Other Prohibited Practices Act 2003 (TAS)

Human Embryonic Research Regulation Act 2003 (TAS)

Human Fertilisation and Embryology Act 1990 (UK)

Human Reproductive Technology Act 1991 (WA)

Infertility (Medical Procedures) Act 1984 (Vic)

Infertility Treatment Act (1995) (Victoria)

Iowa Administrative Code

Irish Constitution (1937)

Louisiana Revised Statutes Annotated, Civil Code (1991)

Law No. 14 of 26 May 2006 on human reproduction procedures (Spain)

Law No. 40 of 19 February 2004, Regulating Medically Assisted Reproduction (Italy)

Law Number 50 of 13 June 1975 on the termination of pregnancy (as amended by Law Number 66 of 16 June 1978) (Norway)

Law No. 66 of 20 October 1986 of the Czech People's Council concerning the artificial termination of pregnancy

Law No 79 of 17 December 1992 on the protection of the life of the foetus (Hungary)

Law No. 94–654 of 29 July 1994 governing the donation and use of elements and products of the human body, medically assisted reproduction and prenatal diagnosis (France)

Law No. 460 of 10 June 1997 on artificial fertilisation in connection with medical treatment, diagnosis and research (Research on embryonic stem cells)

Law on IVF embryo research of 11 March 2003 (Belgium)

Legalization of Abortion: Law 194 of the Italian Republic (1978)

Maryland Code Annotated, Health-General

Massachusetts General Laws (1996)

Bibliography

Maine Revised Statutes Annotated (1992)

Medical Services Act (NT)

Michigan Compiled Laws Annotated (1996)

Minnesota Statutes Annotated (1989)

Mississippi Code of 1972

North Dakota Century Code (1991)

New Hampshire Revised Statutes Annotated (1994)

New Mexico Statutes Annotated (1994)

Order No. 286 of 23 April 2004 on the use of pre-implantation diagnosis in specific cases

Pennsylvania Consolidated Statutes Annotated (1995)

Penal Code (as amended by Law No. 1609 of 28 June 1986 on voluntary termination of pregnancy, protection of women's health and other provisions) (Greece)

Privacy Act 1988 (Cth)

Prohibition of Human Cloning Act 2002 (Cth)

Prohibition of Human Cloning for Reproduction and the Regulation of Human Embryo Research Amendment Act 2006 (Cth)

Reproductive Technology (Clinical Practices) Act 1988 (SA)

Research Involving Human Embryos (New South Wales) Act 2003 (NSW)

Research Involving Human Embryos Act 2002 (Cth)

Research Involving Human Embryos Act 2003 (SA)

Research Involving Human Embryos and Prohibition of Human Cloning Act 2003 (QLD)

Rhode Island General Laws 1994)

South Dakota Code

Swiss Law on Reproductive Medicine of 18 December 1998

Texas Health and Safety Code

The Act of 7th January 1993 on Family-Planning, Human Embryo Protection and Conditions of Legal Pregnancy Termination (Poland)

The Artificial Conception Act 1984 (NSW)

The Choice on Termination of Pregnancy Act 1996 (South Africa)

The European Convention for the Protection of Human Rights and Dignity of the Human Being with regard to the Application of Biology and Medicine 1997 (the "Ovideo Convention")

The Genetic Integrity Act (2006:351) (Sweden)

The Human Reproductive Technology Act 1991 (WA)

The Medical Termination of Pregnancy Act 1971 (India)

The Prohibition of Human Cloning Act 2002 (Cth)

The Prohibition of Human Cloning for Reproduction Act 2002 (Cth)

Therapeutic Goods (Medical Devices) Regulations 2002 (Cth)

Therapeutic Goods Act 1989 (Cth)

Bibliography

Utah Code Annotated
Virginia Code Annotated

CASES

CES v Superclinics (Australia) Pty Ltd (1995) 38 NSWLR 47
Jepson v The Chief Constable of West Mercia Police Constabulary [2003] EWHC 3318 (Admin)
Planned Parenthood v Casey 505 U.S 833 (1992)
R v Bayliss and Cullen (1986) 9 Qld Lawyer Reps 8
R v Bourne [1939] 1 KB 687
R v Davidson [1969] VR 667
R v Wald (1971) 3 DCR (NSW) 25
Reference re the Assisted Human Reproduction Act [2010] 3 S.C.R. 457
Roe v Wade 410 U.S 113 (1973)

Index

Index

Index

Index

Index

Index

Index

criteria-based approach to defining, 249,
   259–266
defined differently depending on which
   reproductive technology used,
   283–287, 295, 330
difficulty in defining, 57, 104, 131–135,
   143–156, 183–191, 218–222,
   229–230, 241–247, 345–346
disabilities incompatible with life, 109,
   117–118, 141, 145–147, 155, 172,
   266, 270
gestational limits, 136–143, 182
list of conditions, defining by, 144,
   155, 172, 216–217, 220–221, 241,
   248–259, 294, 346
parliamentary discussion of meaning
   of, 131–135, 143–155, 183–186,
   218–220
role of medical profession in defining,
   134, 148–151, 156, 295
Sex selection. *See* Preimplantation genetic
   diagnosis (PGD)
Shakespeare, Tom, 19, 45–46, 274
Sheldon, Sally, 37, 183–186, 202–203
Shildrick, Margrit, 15, 34
Sickle cell disease, 177
Significant/substantial risk
  abortion law, United Kingdom,
   128–131
  preimplantation genetic diagnosis,
   Western Australia, 217–218,
   220–221
Silvers, Anita, 16, 22–23, 30–34, 45, 56
Skene, Loane, 2

Society of Obstetricians and Gynaecologists
   of Canada (SOGC), 67, 73
South Australian Council on Reproductive
   Technology, 205–208, 211,
   223–225, 249
Sparrow, Robert, 92
Spina bifida, 138, 153, 242–243, 257–258,
   278, 281

Tay-Sachs, 166, 219, 262, 274, 343
Thalassaemia, 177
Thalidomide, 8, 122, 132–133, 241
Tremain, Shelly, 19–21
Tresky, Shari, 19
Turner's Syndrome, 242, 278

Universal Declaration of Human
   Rights, 182

Victorian Assisted Reproductive Treatment
   Authority (VARTA), 223–224
Victorian Law Reform Commission, 270

Warnock Report, 165
Western Australian Select Committee
   on the Human Reproductive
   Technology Act 1991, 194, 216
Williams, Clare, 6, 73, 254
Winston, Robert, 165
World Health Organisation's
   International Classification of
   Diseases, 257

Young, Iris Marion, 18